John Suchet is an award-winning television journalist and newscaster in England. As an ITN foreign correspondent he has reported from every country in Western Europe, as well as America, Africa, the Middle East and the Far East. He is now the regular presenter of the *Early Evening News* and frequently presents *News at Ten*.

Also by John Suchet

THE LAST MASTER: Passion & Anger, *Volume One*

THE LAST MASTER

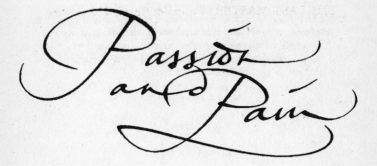

Passion and Pain

Volume two of a fictional biography of
LUDWIG VAN BEETHOVEN

by

John Suchet

LITTLE, BROWN AND COMPANY
Boston New York London

ISBN 1-316-68898-3

10 9 8 7 6 5 4 3 2 1

Printed in Great Britain

For Bonnie again

Contents

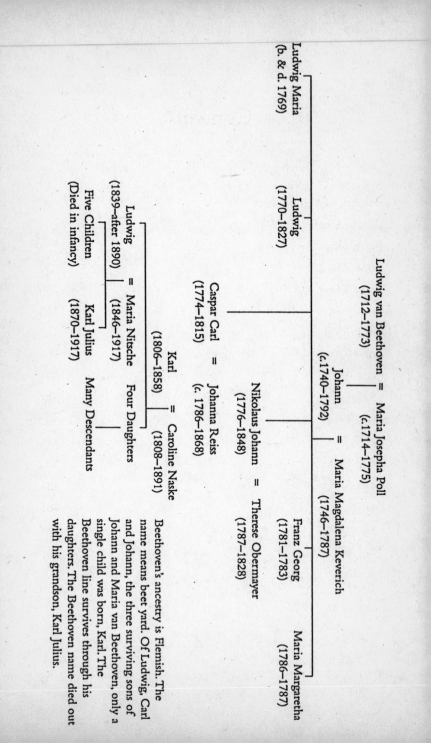

Ludwig van Beethoven
(1712–1773)
=
Maria Josepha Poll
(c.1714–1775)

Johann
(c.1740–1792)
=
Maria Magdalena Keverich
(1746–1787)

Ludwig Maria
(b. & d. 1769)

Ludwig
(1770–1827)

Caspar Carl
(1774–1815)
=
Johanna Reiss
(c. 1786–1868)

Nikolaus Johann
(1776–1848)
=
Therese Obermayer
(1787–1828)

Franz Georg
(1781–1783)

Maria Margaretha
(1786–1787)

Karl
(1806–1858)
=
Caroline Naske
(1808–1891)

Ludwig
(1839–after 1890)
=
Maria Nitsche
(1846–1917)

Four Daughters

Five Children
(Died in infancy)

Karl Julius
(1870–1917)

Many Descendants

Beethoven's ancestry is Flemish. The name means beet yard. Of Ludwig, Carl and Johann, the three surviving sons of Johann and Maria van Beethoven, only a single child was born, Karl. The Beethoven line survives through his daughters. The Beethoven name died out with his grandson, Karl Julius.

Cast of Characters

Continued from Volume One

Beethoven, Johanna van, *née* Reiss (1784–1868). Wife of Carl van Beethoven and mother of Karl. Daughter of an upholsterer, she married Carl in May 1806. Their only child was born less than four months later. Beethoven's belief that she was a wicked and immoral woman was reinforced by her conviction for stealing from her husband.

Bonaparte, Jerome (1784–1860). Youngest brother of Napoleon, who appointed him King of Westphalia. In 1808 he invited Beethoven to become *Kapellmeister* in the capital Kassel.

Bonaparte, Napoleon (1769–1821). French First Consul and later Emperor. Beethoven's initial admiration for Bonaparte's rise from humble origins and belief in equality for all led to his dedication of the *Eroica* Symphony to him. But when Napoleon crowned himself Emperor Beethoven angrily withdrew the dedication.

Braun, Baron Peter von (1758–1819). Director of the Imperial Court Theatres. In 1804 he purchased the Theater an der Wien, ending Beethoven's contract there, but making the theatre available for his opera *Leonore* in 1806. Baron von Hartl became Director in 1807 and angered Beethoven by repeatedly postponing his promised benefit concert.

Brentano, Antonie, *née* Birkenstock (1780–1869). The great love of Beethoven's life. Born in Vienna she married Franz Brentano in 1798 and reluctantly moved with him to Frankfurt. The relationship with Beethoven developed when she returned to her native city in 1809 on learning that her father was dying.

She stayed for three years, selling her father's huge collection of antiquities and in 1812 travelling with her husband and youngest daughter to Prague and Bohemia.

Brentano, Bettina (1785–1859). Half-sister of Franz Brentano, she had met Goethe several times. She sent Beethoven's score of *Egmont* to him and set up a meeting between the two in Bohemia in 1812.

Bridgetower, George Augustus Polgreen (1779–1860). Mulatto violinist, son of an African father and Polish mother who settled in London. His virtuosity brought him to the attention of the Prince of Wales, who retained him. He came to Vienna in 1803 and Beethoven composed the famous Sonata op. 47 for him and gave its first performance with him.

Clement, Franz (1780–1842). Violinist and orchestra leader at the Theater an der Wien. Beethoven wrote the Violin Concerto for him, though he did not receive its dedication.

Deym, Countess Josephine, *née* Brunsvik (1779–1821). A member of the Hungarian Brunsvik family. Beethoven fell in love with her, composing the song *An die Hoffnung* for her, but she rejected him. Widowed in 1804, she married her children's tutor, Count von Stackelberg, in 1810.

Erdödy, Countess Anna Marie, *née* Niczky (1779–1837). An excellent pianist who befriended Beethoven and was instrumental in efforts to prevent him leaving Vienna and taking up the appointment in Kassel.

Gleichenstein, Ignaz von (1778–1828). A native of Freiburg on the upper Rhine, he took over the handling of Beethoven's financial affairs after Ferdinand Ries (*q.v.*) left Vienna. In 1811 he married Anna Malfatti, younger sister of Therese (*q.v.*).

Grillparzer, Franz (1791–1872). As a boy he met Beethoven in Heiligenstadt in the summer of 1808, and was destined to become Austria's greatest playwright.

Klein, Franz (1779–after 1836). Viennese sculptor. In 1812 the Streichers commissioned him to sculpt a bust of Beethoven.

The life mask he took to work from is the most accurate representation of Beethoven's physiognomy that exists. The original is in the Beethovenhaus, Bonn.

Mähler, Willibrord Joseph (1778–1860). Portrait painter from Ehrenbreitstein in the Rhineland, who settled in Vienna. In 1804/5 he painted a famous portrait of Beethoven.

Malfatti, Dr Giovanni (1775–1859). Italian physician who settled in Vienna in 1795 and became Beethoven's doctor after the sudden death of Doktor Schmidt in 1809.

Malfatti, Therese (1792–1851). Beethoven fell in love with her and intended proposing marriage to her, but she became engaged to Baron Drosdick. He composed the famous Bagatelle WoO 59 for her.

Milder, Anna (1785–1838). Fine soprano admired by both Haydn and Beethoven. She took the title role in the first performances of *Leonore*.

Oppersdorff, Count Franz von (1778–1818). He had a private orchestra at his estate in Upper Silesia, which Beethoven visited with Prince Lichnowsky in 1806. The Count commissioned the Fourth and Fifth Symphonies, receiving the dedication of the Fourth.

Pasqualati, Baron Johann (1777–1830). Property owner in Vienna. Beethoven lived in the top-floor apartment of the building the Baron owned on the Mölkerbastei for longer than he lived anywhere else.

Razumovsky, Count Andreas Kirillovich (1752–1836). Russian ambassador in Vienna. He supported a permanent string quartet led by Schuppanzigh in which he often played second violin. He commissioned the set of quartets which came to be known as the Razumovsky quartets to commemorate the opening of the sumptuous new palace he built in the Landstrasse suburb.

Ries, Ferdinand (1784–1838). Worked tirelessly as Beethoven's assistant in Vienna, until he was forced to go back to Bonn to be conscripted into the French army. On his return to Vienna he resumed his attachment to Beethoven, before leaving the city for good in 1809.

Röckel, Joseph August (1783–1870). Fine tenor, he took over the role of Florestan in *Leonore*, after the first disastrous performances.

Schikaneder, Emanuel Johann (1751–1812). Manager of the Theater an der Wien, best known as librettist of Mozart's *The Magic Flute*. He appointed Beethoven as composer-in-residence at the Wien in 1803 and wrote a libretto, *Vestas Feuer*, for him.

Schlemmer, Wenzel (1760–1823). Senior copyist who was exceptionally good at deciphering Beethoven's difficult scores. He had a team of copyists working under him.

Seyfried, Ignaz Xavier (1776–1841). Kapellmeister at the Theater an der Wien. He turned pages for Beethoven at the premiere of the Third Piano Concerto and on a number of occasions conducted performances of Beethoven's music.

Sonnleithner, Joseph Ferdinand (1766–1835). Co-founder of the publishing house, Kunst-und-Industrie Comptoir, and librettist of the first version of *Leonore*.

Treitschke, Georg Friedrich (1776–1842). Playwright and poet engaged by the Kärntnertor theatre. Beethoven was to ask him to write the third and definitive version of *Leonore*.

BOOK ONE

Chapter 1

1803

Ludwig van Beethoven stood in front of the portrait, looking up at it. He wanted to reach out and touch it. He wanted to stroke the old man's cheeks, feel the roughness of the grey stubble, take the strands of grey hair and rub them between his fingers.

The face – fleshy, calm, dignified – was not the face he remembered. How could a painting capture the old man's vitality and strength, or the sparkle that had danced in his eyes? But the portrait was all he had to remind him of his grandfather, and to look at it was enough to bring into his mind the deep resonant voice and the scent of Turkish tobacco that his clothes gave off.

Kapellmeister Beethoven. In his fur turban and robes of office, a score open on his lap. How many long hours had Ludwig stood in front of the portrait as a boy, willing his grandfather to come back to life so he could talk to him? Tell him of his development as a musician and ask him for his advice.

He wanted to ask his advice now. 'Tell me, Grandfather,' he said aloud to the portrait. 'Tell me, what shall I do if my hearing grows worse? What shall I do if I become deaf?'

'You did what?' Ludwig asked incredulously, staring at his brother Carl.

Carl's smile was strained. 'I wrote to your publisher and told him you no longer trouble yourself with musical trifles and that you only compose oratorios and operas. It's what you told me yourself, so why are you so angry?'

Ludwig took a step towards his brother and was gratified to see him recoil slightly. 'I told you no such thing. I said I had stopped work on a piano concerto to start work on an oratorio.'

'Amounts to the same thing. Anyway, it doesn't matter. He's

still going to pay nine hundred florins for three sonatas. You should be pleased.'

Ludwig sat down and looked at his brother. What was he to do with the man? How could he stop him meddling in his affairs? Had the row between them in Heiligenstadt not been enough? The words that had passed between them should have left him in no doubt. 'Carl. I am saying this to you again. I have said it before, but it seems to have made no difference. I do not want you to concern yourself in my affairs. Do you understand?'

Carl was silent. Then he said, 'How's your hearing, Ludwig?'

There was a ringing sound in his ears, too loud for him to ignore. If it stopped there might be a buzzing instead, or the whoosh of waves crashing onto sand. And with the noise would come pain, and words would hurtle towards him like cannon shells, exploding against his ears.

'I can hear what you are saying. What I had will go. The doctors have told me.'

'You can only hear what I am saying because I am speaking loudly and clearly, to make sure you can hear. If I lower my voice . . . like this . . . can you still hear me?'

Anger surged through Ludwig, justifiably because he could hear his brother. 'I can hear you, do you understand? Every word. I wish I could not because all you ever say to me is drivel. Now leave me alone. I need to work.'

'Then if you can hear me, let me tell you something that you will not dismiss as drivel. That might even make you change your mind about me. I have secured you a full-time musical appointment. With free lodgings. And a commission as well. To compose an opera.'

Ludwig looked at his brother incredulously. 'How? But –'

'I thought that would surprise you. And that might not be all. But I cannot promise.'

Vienna was awash with rumours that Britain was about to declare war on France. In the taverns and coffee houses there was satisfaction that the new First Consul, who had decreed that henceforth he was to be known only by his first name, Napoleon, would soon be taught a lesson. Those pessimistic voices who said that declaring himself First Consul – albeit for life – was merely a prelude to crowning himself Emperor were roundly mocked.

Such a conversation was taking place on the first floor of the newly constructed Theater an der Wien, which sat alongside the narrow Wien river just south of the Bastion, the massive wall that encircled the city of Vienna.

'If he is not stopped,' said Bartholomäus Zitterbarth, 'he will declare war on the Empire again. His aim is simple. To be the sole Emperor in Europe. And then we will all be ruined.'

Emanuel Schikaneder mopped his brow with a lace-edged handkerchief. He held it under his nose. The air in the room was heavy and the fruit market on the opposite bank of the river gave it a pungency that hindered his breathing. He was relieved when Zitterbarth walked to the window and closed it, with a firm downward push.

'And then we will all be ruined,' Zitterbarth repeated, staring at the man he had appointed as director of the theatre whose reconstruction Zitterbarth himself had financed.

'If he does, I have no doubt he will be defeated. I am an artist, Herr Zitterbarth. I am more concerned to put on a programme here that will please the people of Vienna and thereby reward your generosity.'

'You have not begun well, Schikaneder. Losing Cherubini to Baron Braun was rather careless, do you not think?'

'Sir, with respect, even with your benevolence I can hardly compete with the court theatres. And Baron Braun travelled to Paris to secure the contract. You would not have taken it kindly if I had absented myself while –'

'What alternative are you offering?'

Schikaneder cleared his throat. He was listening for the tread on the stairs that would relieve the pressure on him and which was already overdue. 'There is a young German composer in the city. Maybe you have heard his name. Beethoven. Unusual name. Flemish, I think.'

Zitterbarth shook his head.

'He is an excellent pianist. He has played in the most important salons. Prince Lichnowsky, Baron Swieten, Prince Lobkowitz. I could name more. You surely heard of the improvisation contest against Herr Steibelt. He –'

'No, no,' said Zitterbarth impatiently. 'What of him? You are not going to commission him, are you? I do not want any risks. I cannot afford –'

At last Schikaneder heard the footsteps he had been waiting for, followed by a sharp knock on the door. It opened immediately and Carl van Beethoven entered the room, clutching a folder under his arm. 'Gentlemen. I apologize for my lateness. I was at Artaria's. My brother's reputation continues to flourish. You are fortunate to have his services. Now . . .' He opened the folder. 'I have the contract here. Prepared for signature. My brother is to be appointed composer in residence at the Theater an der Wien. He will write an opera for which you, Schikaneder, will provide the text. And he will have free lodgings here, which I will share with him.'

Schikaneder saw the shock on Zitterbarth's face, but to his relief the financier said nothing.

'The terms are agreed, as we discussed earlier, Schikaneder. So we have an agreement. Almost.'

'Almost?' said two voices, practically in unison.

'There is one other matter. Regrettably my brother is not satisfied. He wants a benefit concert. Here, at the Wien. The receipts will be split between him and the house. Eighty-twenty. It is agreed. Yes?'

Schikaneder spluttered and mopped his brow again. He tried to find the right response, but it was Zitterbarth who spoke first.

'You are very demanding, you Bethoffens, if that is what your name is. Too demanding. My generosity has limits.'

'Very well,' said Carl, shuffling papers. He made a show of crossing out some words with a pencil and scribbling above them. 'Seventy-thirty. That is settled, then. You will not be disappointed. You have the services of the finest composer in Europe.'

Ludwig called in Ferdinand Ries to help him with the oratorio. He was composing quickly, and Ries was useful for playing passages on the piano while Ludwig notated the score. He worked from a text written by the poet Franz Huber, which called for three soloists – Jesus, tenor, Peter, bass and a Seraph, soprano – and chorus. Ries found himself singing the roles of all three, as well as reproducing full orchestra on the piano.

The young man, who had been taught by Beethoven when he was just a small boy in Bonn, had grown particularly fond of his master. Certainly Beethoven treated him in a less kindly manner than he deserved, but Ries easily forgave it: he knew Beethoven was possessed of an extraordinary genius that seemed almost to control him. If his mood was difficult or irrational, then others should acquiesce and not fight it.

And if he had needed proof of the strain the older man was under, that fateful afternoon under the blazing sun on the hillside in Heiligenstadt had been enough to settle it. He had known that Beethoven's hearing troubled him and that he had seen doctors about it, but Ries had assumed it was a temporary affliction. Certainly, until that afternoon, Beethoven had never given him cause to think otherwise.

On his return to the city Ries had spoken to Beethoven's close friends, and had been surprised by what he heard. Nanette Streicher, who ran the piano factory with her husband Andreas in the Landstrasse suburb, told him that Beethoven feared he was losing his hearing. She had been distraught to hear Ries's account of how Beethoven had failed to hear the shepherd's pipe, and vowed she would keep a watchful eye on him.

Stephan von Breuning, whom Beethoven had known since childhood, nodded gravely. 'I suspected it,' he said. 'But surely there's something the doctors can do. People don't just start going deaf in adulthood. It must be a blockage that needs removing.'

Nikolaus Zmeskall, the short-sighted amateur cellist who worked at the Hungarian Chancellery, was equally optimistic: 'I noticed he sometimes couldn't hear. But it can't be permanent. He'll wake up one morning to find it is better. Have you spoken to Johann? He might be able to recommend something.'

Ries was reluctant to consult Beethoven's youngest brother; he knew of the antipathy between them although he did not fully understand what lay behind it – something about Johann changing his name when he came to Vienna. He had been christened Nikolaus Johann and had grown up known as Nikola. In Vienna he insisted on being called Johann, in memory of his late father. His elder brother found that intolerable and there had been furious rows. But Johann van Beethoven was an apothecary and his knowledge might be useful.

Ries did not like Johann. There was a smugness about him, accentuated by his wide mouth, which gave his face the appearance of a permanent sneer, and the drooping right eyelid made him seem sinister.

His opinion did not change when Johann shrugged his shoulders and said, 'Change his doctor. He obviously needs more than oil. I can't help. It's up to his doctor.'

*   *   *

Ludwig had decided on an ambitious programme for the benefit concert. His first two symphonies would be performed, as well as his third piano concerto and the new oratorio, *Christus am Ölberge*, Christ on the Mount of Olives. Apart from the first symphony, none had been performed in public before. Ignaz Seyfried, *Kapellmeister* at the Theater an der Wien, would direct; Franz Clement would lead the orchestra.

Ries soon found himself acting as intermediary between his master and Seyfried. While Ludwig, in his new rooms on the first floor of the theatre, composed the oratorio, Seyfried rehearsed the orchestra, section by section, in a small room at the back.

There was a difficulty, though, that Ries could see no way to resolve. The concert was set for 4 April, a matter of weeks away, and the current production did not end until the third, which meant that the full orchestra could not be rehearsed on stage until the day of the concert.

Ries tried to persuade his master to drop the piano concerto, since composition of the oratorio was taking all his time and a full rehearsal would be impossible. But Beethoven refused. To make matters worse, rehearsals were not going well. Several of the musicians – usually wind players, Ries noted – complained that the music was unplayable, and even loyal Seyfried pointed out that the opening of the symphony in D – a demi-semiquaver followed by a sustained crotchet – was almost impossible to play in unison.

There was something else, too, of which Ries was unaware but which concerned Schikaneder greatly. Tickets for the concert were not selling. He summoned Carl van Beethoven.

'We will be lucky to cover our costs, Herr Beethoven. That means no money for your brother and a loss for us. It is a disaster.'

'There is a simple solution, Schikaneder,' said Carl, his voice calm but with an icy edge. 'Increase the price of the seats.'

'Herr Beethoven, forgive me, but I fear you understand little about business. If the public fail to show an interest in an item, the way to stimulate their interest is to reduce the price of it, not increase it.'

'And that, Schikaneder, is where you demonstrate your own ignorance of business matters. If you lower the price people know immediately there is something wrong with what you are selling. Increase it, and they all want a share.'

'Very clever, Herr Beethoven. But it will not work. I have succeeded so far in selling only half the tickets in the theatre, and that means failure.'

'Here is what you do, Schikaneder. Show me that sheet of paper, the one with the prices on. Right.' He took a quill, dipped it in ink and crossed out as he read, adding new figures. 'Front stalls, price now doubled. Rear stalls, price now doubled. Boxes, reserved for the nobility, price doubled to twelve ducats. To satisfy demand.'

'I will not do it, Herr Beethoven.'

'Yes, you will, Schikaneder. Otherwise my brother withdraws his works. There will be no concert. That will mean an empty concert hall, and that is something you can afford least of all.'

Schikaneder sat back and sighed. He pulled the handkerchief from his sleeve and dabbed at his brow. He did not like Carl van Beethoven. He found him shifty. And – he knew it was uncharitable – ugly. He had a darting face, like an animal sniffing for its prey. His hair was a dusty red, matt and devoid of any sheen. And the man had no natural charm.

'Herr Beethoven, you may not be aware of this, but the rehearsals of your brother's music have been a disaster. Seyfried, my friend Ignaz, has had a potential mutiny on his hands several times. He and Franz Clement have barely been able to contain the musicians.'

'From what I hear, that is because the rehearsal room is too small for the whole orchestra, so Seyfried is rehearsing them in sections. That is hardly my brother's fault.'

'I concede that that is a problem. But there is another matter. The music your brother has written is . . . is . . . I know he is a fine composer – otherwise I would not have retained him to set my own text to music. But sometimes musicians think he writes music they cannot play for no other reason than to humiliate them.'

Carl shrugged.

'We have a problem, Herr Beethoven. Perhaps I should cancel the concert and admit to Herr Zitterbarth that my confidence in your brother was misplaced.'

Chapter 2

Ludwig sat at the small table in the dark room, a faint glow of moonlight barely penetrating the window which gave out on to the courtyard. He grasped the carafe and refilled his glass with red wine. He watched the bubbles dance in the light of the single flickering candle.

The score of the oratorio was spread in front of him – musical fragments, crossings out, blotches of ink. No matter, Wenzel Schlemmer the copyist would make sense of it. He looked at the notes. The work was almost finished. He had composed it rapidly, relishing the challenges Huber's text had set him.

The one that had beset him from the beginning was how to put words into the mouth of Jesus. Huber had said he would have three soloists and his intention had been to give Jesus by far the most dominant role, which would have been a mistake: the oratorio would have been unbalanced and made Ludwig's task much more difficult.

In the end he was satisfied with Huber's text, which stressed the suffering of Christ rather than his divinity. That, he knew, would be less hard to set to music. But had he been wrong to insist on a duet between Jesus and the Seraph? Huber had demurred, but Ludwig had prevailed. In the end he was pleased with it. He liked the interplay of the two voices. But it was certain to arouse criticism: a duet between Jesus and the Seraph – almost blasphemous, they might say.

He was aware of another weak element in the music. It came in the second number, a recitative from the Seraph, leading into an aria from the Seraph and the Chorus of Angels. He wanted the music to build to a fearful climax on the words 'Damnation is their lot'. He had done as much as he could but something was missing and he did not know what.

He crossed to the piano that stood in the darkest corner of the room and played some fragments, singing tunelessly to them.

He knew Carl would wake up and be angry, but he had not asked his brother to come to live with him.

He stopped and rested his hands on his thighs. The music continued in his head, but as it faded it became harsh and he braced himself for the dreadful noises that would replace it. Screwing up his eyes he walked back to the table, sat heavily in the chair and drank more wine, willing it to deaden his senses.

He looked towards his grandfather's portrait, unable to see more than a dark rectangle. Carl had not wanted him to hang the picture: 'After all, I never knew him,' he had said. Ludwig's response had been to put it on the wall directly opposite the window and to tell his brother that if he attempted to take it down he would have him ejected from the building.

The noises in his head began to subside. What was happening to his hearing? Doktor Schmidt had held a tuning fork to his ears, then placed it on the back of his head. He had heard it more clearly when it was against his head than when it was close to his ear. He had seen the anxious look flit across the doctor's face and the slight shrug of his shoulders. 'Still no cause for worry,' Schmidt had said. 'It has to correct itself. Drink less wine for a start. Go to bed at a decent time.'

Ludwig half smiled as he looked through the window at the darkness of the night and took another mouthful of wine. He put down the glass and clenched his fist. I am composing. I have composed a new work. And I can still play the piano. I will show them when I play my concerto at the concert. He brought his fist down sharply on the table.

Another sudden noise assaulted his ears. He knew what it was without looking up. He did not want to hear Carl's voice. He did not want to hear anything but the sounds of his music. He did not glance at the figure that stood in front of him, the candle throwing shadows across his nightshirt, and was relieved when he turned and went out.

My brothers, thought Ludwig, and shuddered. He reached for the carafe and cursed when he saw it was empty. Carl had secured a position in the Financial Office at the Hofburg on a small salary. Why, then, does he keep interfering in my affairs? And how can I stop him?

Then he thought of Nikolaus. Johann. Caspar and Nikolaus were the two brothers with whom he had grown up. Now they were Carl and Johann. He had finally agreed to call Caspar by the name he wanted, but had not been able to do the same for Nikolaus – even to the extent of leaving a blank for where his name should be on the last will and testament he had written in Heiligenstadt. It was irrational, he knew that. But they did not understand how Ludwig had suffered through their father's drunkenness. The man who had beaten him across the fingers as a child to make him practise, who had woken him in the middle of the night and made him stand at the piano till dawn, who had tried to thwart his trip to Vienna . . .

'Johann,' he said softly to himself. At least he stays away from me. An apothecary. More worthwhile than Carl. I will call him by the name he wishes – when I am ready.

His head was now pleasantly dull from the wine. He looked again at the score of the oratorio. Something missing.

Ferdinand Ries found Schikaneder in an unexpectedly receptive mood. 'That man, your master's brother, clever chap, eh?'

Ries fumbled with his eye patch, the legacy of his childhood smallpox. It was an involuntary gesture he had developed when someone said something to him that he did not immediately grasp, a way of securing a moment or two to digest the words. Now, though, it was more a defensive movement, since any news involving Carl van Beethoven was likely to be grim. He was pleasantly surprised by what he heard next.

'Tickets selling well, I'm pleased to say. At an increased price.'

Ries reminded him about the rehearsal difficulty.

'*Graf Armand*. Good opera. Good audiences. Must run as scheduled,' Schikaneder replied. 'But I'll put the concert back a day to the fifth of April. By the way, tell your master I'm working on the text for him. For his opera. *Vestas Feuer*, it's called. Ancient Rome. He'll like that.'

Ries left hurriedly when Schikaneder began to regale him with the story of how he had written the text for Wolfgang Mozart's opera *The Magic Flute*, and how he had played Papageno on the opening night.

The day's delay in the concert was a step forward, but Ries knew it was not enough. He decided to speak to one of Beethoven's patrons: perhaps he could intervene.

There were really only three he could approach: Baron Swieten, Prince Lobkowitz and Prince Lichnowsky. The fourth, Prince Ferdinand Kinsky, Ries discounted. Although a fervent admirer of Ludwig's music, he was still just twenty-two and trying to establish his military career while running his estate after the sudden death of his father.

Baron Swieten, Ries had heard, was unwell, perhaps seriously so. He was seventy and had not made an appearance in public for several months. He had been Ludwig's first patron in Vienna and had established the young musician's reputation early on by setting up an improvisation contest between him and Abbé Gelinek, which Ludwig had comprehensively won. Ludwig had dedicated his First Symphony to him. As his reputation had grown, Swieten had had less to do with him, principally because he was fully occupied in writing the texts for Joseph Haydn's great oratorios, *The Creation* and *The Seasons*.

Prince Lobkowitz, though, was becoming increasingly interested in Ludwig, particularly since he had received the dedication of the Opus 18 Quartets, Ludwig's first published set. But discreet inquiries revealed that the Prince was at present at his estate at Eisenberg in Bohemia, where he had gone to receive treatment from his doctors. His malformed hip, which had forced him to walk with a crutch since childhood, gave him more and more pain and the waters in Bohemia afforded him at least temporary relief.

With Baron Swieten ill and Prince Lobkowitz away, that left only Prince Lichnowsky, and Ries knew that he not only admired Ludwig's music but was also very fond of him. He and his wife, Princess Christiane, had taken the young composer into their own sumptuous apartment in the Alstergasse beyond the Schottentor when he had first come to Vienna. They had given him a fine set of rooms, and Ludwig had told Ries that they had been 'Like a mother and father to me. Too much like a mother and father. I was so stifled I could barely breathe.' They had understood why, and harboured no resentment, when he moved out into lodgings of his own. Even so, Ries hesitated. Prince Lichnowsky was his master's most senior patron. Ries had met him but only formally at the occasional soirée and only by virtue of his association with Ludwig. But what choice did he have?

'I know,' said Prince Lichnowsky sympathetically. 'I had heard. What can we do?'

'I am not sure, sir. The problem is that the orchestra has only rehearsed section by section. I wondered if . . . if maybe you could use your influence to . . . if the concert were postponed for a week, say?'

Lichnowsky shook his head. 'No. Schikaneder has a new show due to start on the sixth of April for a month's run. We must make it possible for the orchestra to rehearse on the day of the concert. The theatre will be clear.'

Ries nodded. 'But the musicians . . . It's very unlikely they'll – musicians never like to rehearse on the day of a performance.'

'Well, we'll see what we can do. There may be a way. Tell me, young man, how is your master? I know that his hearing . . . but he is composing, isn't he?'

'Yes. He's working on his new oratorio as if his hearing were normal. Yet I know his ears are not right. I have spoken to Doktor Schmidt . . .'

'He's a good doctor. What did he say?'

'He's established that Herr Beethoven's hearing is still deficient. Quite seriously so. He's concerned that it did not improve after last summer's holiday. But Herr Beethoven has been back for five months or more, and it hasn't worsened. And he *does* seem able to compose, thank the Lord.'

'Yes. I could not bear to think what would happen if he could not. Young man, I am pleased to make your acquaintance properly. I understand you are doing much to help your master.'

'I try to be of assistance to him, sir,' Ries said, modestly. 'My father knew him well when he was a boy in Bonn and Herr Beethoven taught me the piano when I was so young I had barely learned to speak.'

'And from what I hear you are a fine pianist.'

'No, no, sir. An exaggeration. Forgive me for contradicting you. But if I am of use to Herr Beethoven that makes me happy.'

At that moment there was a bustle in the doorway and Princess Lichnowsky swept into the room. One hand held a folded fan, the other lifted her dress almost clear of the floor. 'Oh, too dreadful, the poor dear man.' She saw Ries sitting opposite her husband. 'Good day to you. We have met in our salon.'

Ries stood up and bowed. 'Your Highness. Madame.' He took Princess Christiane's proffered hand and held it briefly below his bowed head. 'I will not detain you any longer, sir.'

'Not at all, Ries. Stay and have a glass of wine.'

Princess Christiane pulled her voluminous dress aside and sat down, fanning herself vigorously. 'Such sad news, Karl. Dear Baron Swieten has passed away. This very afternoon. I have just come from his residence. The servants are already filling the windows with black crêpe.'

Prince Lichnowsky's face fell and he let out a sigh. 'Poor Gottfried. Such a fine fellow. I hope he did not suffer unduly.'

'By all accounts not. The end, when it came, was sudden. He had already lost consciousness.'

'I must go round and pay my respects.'

Ries got up quickly. 'Forgive my intrusion, sir. I must –'

'Not at all, my boy. Not at all. As I said, I am glad to make your acquaintance. And do not worry. I will not forget our discussion. I will see what I can do. Give my regards to your master. Best not to tell him about Baron Swieten.' He thought for a moment. 'Or maybe you should. He will hear, anyway.'

Chapter 3

Ludwig sat in the front row of the parterre watching Seyfried rehearse the full orchestra. He wished he was standing in the other man's place, but there was no persuading Schikaneder: the Wien's *Kapellmeister* was to conduct. He leaned forward to hear better.

The opening bar of the symphony in D. Demi-semiquaver, sustained crotchet. Louder, he thought. *Fortissimo*. Slowly, from a ragged beginning, the players approached a unison. Ludwig expected the small figure of Seyfried to turn to him at any moment and plead with him to change the demi-semiquaver to a quaver. If the note was longer it would be so much simpler to achieve a unison.

He heard Seyfried say something to the players but could not distinguish his words. Seyfried raised his arms. The opening notes again: this time the orchestra played on – the four bars for wind only, which he had marked *piano*, linking to the next *fortissimo*. Ludwig's stomach tightened. Why were the wind – oboes and horns – not playing? But they were – he could see it from Seyfried gestures.

The *fortissimo* chords again, followed this time by *piano* strings. He could hear them. Could he? He was not sure. He leaned further forward. He could hear something but the sounds were not clear – and why was the damned piccolo playing above everything? Yet it was not. He had not even scored for piccolo.

Letting out a long sigh he got to his feet and walked to the back of the auditorium. Where was Ries? Damned boy. He's never here when I need him. Even as he thought it he knew it was unfair, but what did it matter? Ries was young, a capable musician, with a lifetime of music-making ahead of him. What future is there for me? he wondered, as he entered a small room off the main entrance and flopped heavily into a chair.

With a feeling of dullness in his head he thought of Baron Swieten. He had known his patron was unwell, but it had never occurred to him that it might be a mortal illness.

He was aware of movement and looked up. Ries had come in, and now threw a coat over a chair. He wore a broad smile.

'At last, Ries. Here. Go to the Weingartel and get me some wine. And ham.' He threw some coins on to the table.

'Of course, Herr Ludwig. In just a minute,' said Ries, dabbing under his eye-patch with a handkerchief.

Ludwig heard the words. There was a harsh edge to them, but he heard them.

'Speak clearly, Ries. My damned ears.'

'How is the rehearsal, sir?' The young man's face was eager, his forehead still shiny from the exertion of his walk, his black curly hair exaggerating each tiny movement of his head. Only the eye-patch marred what would otherwise have been a perfect picture of expectant youth.

Ludwig said, 'Ries, you look as if you have just personally defeated the entire French army.'

'Hah! Much better news than that, Herr Ludwig. I have come from Prince Lichnowsky's. He is to pay each member of the orchestra and all the singers a day's wages for rehearsing tomorrow. He will also provide a sumptuous lunch for them, here at the theatre. So we can now rehearse tomorrow morning and afternoon, before the concert in the evening. That way, with the symphonies rehearsed this morning and the piano concerto this afternoon, we can devote tomorrow to the oratorio. I have spoken to Schlemmer. The parts will be ready.'

Ludwig pursed his lips. 'You rehearse the concerto for me, Ferdi. You know it as well as I do. I want to work a little more on Christus.'

Consternation flitted across Ries's face. 'Sir. Herr Ludwig. Respectfully . . . Herr Schlemmer . . . I think it is too late for any changes. The parts would not be –'

Ludwig pulled himself out of the chair. 'Bring the wine up to my room, will you? And, Ferdi, you rehearse the concerto. I need time to think.'

Ludwig lay in bed unable to sleep. Old Baron Swieten's face came into his mind and a wave of sadness swept over him. The baron had been so kind to him when he first came to Vienna. It had been in Baron Swieten's salon that he had first played before an audience, and Baron Swieten who had first spread the word about the remarkable new musician from the Rhineland. I repaid him, Ludwig thought. I dedicated my symphony in C to him. My first symphony. So his name will live on with my music. He smiled at the immodest thought.

Wide awake now, Ludwig swung his legs out of the bed and pulled a gown over his nightshirt. He lit the candle by the bed and walked out into the small living room. He looked through the window down into the courtyard and up into the night sky. Pitch black. No shapes of buildings, no stars to break the darkness.

He put the candle down on the table and looked towards Carl's door. No light underneath it. He wondered what time it was. After midnight, certainly. He sat at the table and leaned back in the chair, stretching out his legs. The candle flame danced in front of him, the glare hurting his eyes. He leaned forward and pushed it away from him.

Joseph Haydn. He'll be at the concert, he thought, I know he will. What will he think? What will it matter? It will matter because he is the most venerated composer in Europe. But I doubt he will dare criticise my music too much. Ludwig smiled at the memory of the infamous disagreement between them over the third piano trio. *Do not publish it, my boy, it is not ready yet.* Ludwig had known Haydn was wrong and had not hesitated to tell him so. To be fair to him Haydn had apologised since – several times – and always with the plea that Ludwig put the words 'Pupil of Haydn' at the top of his next published piece.

Ludwig snorted at the thought. Could Haydn not see that what mattered was posterity? Future generations, down the years, down the centuries. I do not ever – *ever* – want to be known as the pupil of Haydn. I am Beethoven.

Ludwig drummed his fingers on the table. Haydn's reputation was secure, he knew that. And it was those two great oratorios that had made it so. Ludwig had to confess himself surprised at Haydn's unexpected late flowering: he had considered the old composer past his best, the main body of his work written. And it was good, as Mozart had once told him. Who could argue with over a hundred symphonies, each one distinctive in its own curious way? But it was *The Creation* and *The Seasons* that had sealed his fame for all time.

Suddenly Ludwig slammed the palm of his hand on the table. Trombones! That was what was missing in the oratorio. That worthy and neglected instrument. And it was in the second number, the recitative and aria for Seraph and Chorus of Angels, the first major moment of drama, where the music builds slowly until the chorus proclaims damnation for those who dishonour the blood of Christ, that they were needed. The weight, the gravitas, the drama of trombones.

He looked up, almost knocking over the chair. Carrying the candle and shielding it with his free hand, he went to a pile of papers on the floor by the wall. He leafed through them until he found what he wanted: several sheets of clean unmarked manuscript.

He threw them on the table, put down the candle beside them, went to Carl's door and pounded on it. 'Carl! Wake up. I need you to do something for me. Get up. Do you hear me?' He returned to the table.

He was already scribbling notes when Carl appeared before him, fists on the table. 'Have you completely lost your senses?' he demanded. Ludwig looked up at the pale face, shadows darting across it in the candlelight.

'Good. There you are. Get dressed. Go and get Ries. I need Ries. Do you understand? Go on. Hurry.'

He heard Carl say something, but Ludwig's head was full of other sounds. He sang as he scrawled on the paper and when he was not writing he gestured with his arms.

Later, suddenly overwhelmed with fatigue, Ludwig yawned, gathered up the papers and went into his bedroom. Sitting up in bed now, the pages strewn around him, he continued to compose the trombone parts.

He did not know how long it was before he looked up and saw the figure of Ferdinand Ries standing in the doorway. 'Good. There you are, Ferdi. Come in. Come in.' He heard a door slam – Must be Carl, he thought. 'Here. Here. The trombone parts. I've added them to the Seraph's aria, "Tremble Earth". After the Chorus of Angels comes in, at the second *accelerando*. It gives weight. Exactly what is needed.' He saw the horror on Ries's face. 'What is it, boy? What's the matter?'

'Sir, Herr Ludwig. Forgive me, it is too late now for changes. There isn't time to . . . Herr Schlemmer will not be able –'

'What? Come in, for heaven's sake. Don't stand in the doorway. Come nearer. Now, what is it? What time is it? Have I kept you up too late?'

Ries smiled. 'Herr Ludwig, it is five o'clock in the morning.

That is not the problem. I do not mind. But Herr Schlemmer and his team have completed the first half of the oratorio, the first three numbers, for rehearsal in the morning. They will work all morning to have the other parts ready for the afternoon and the performance in the evening. They cannot go back and add anything.'

Ludwig laughed. 'Old Schlemmer. He is only a few years older than I yet he behaves as if he were a hundred. Take him these sheets, Ferdi, and tell him they must be ready. He will do them, mark my words. Anyhow, I have not finished yet. Come. We will go to the piano downstairs.'

'That will not be possible, Herr Ludwig. Everything is locked up. All the rooms are shut.'

'All right, all right. Go and sit at the table. I will finish this shortly. Then take them to Schlemmer first thing. First thing, d'you understand?'

At eight o'clock on the morning of 5 April, twenty musicians, twenty choral singers and three soloists shuffled ill-humouredly on to the stage of the Theater an der Wien. True, they were being given an extra day's wages; true, lunch would be provided. But with a public performance due to begin at six o'clock that evening, there was not a person there who would not rather have been at home.

Ludwig leaned on the rail, in front of the players and to the side. He was watching Seyfried rehearse the orchestra and chorus.

He could hear the notes clearly – his notes, the music he had created – but the orchestra was mangling them. He looked at the three trombonists, chatting to each other. What did they think this was? A picnic?

He shouted something, he did not know what. Seyfried did not turn to look at him, nor did any of the musicians. He waved his arm in contempt, turned and took the two steps down into the parterre. 'Damned trombonists,' he muttered under his breath. 'Amateurs.'

He spotted Stephan Breuning coming towards him. 'Ludwig, Ferdi Ries has asked me to come and make sure everything is going well. He has had to give a piano lesson.'

Ludwig screwed up his eyes. His friend's voice was muffled. The orchestra was playing and the sound collided with it. 'Speak more clearly, Steffen, for God's sake. Come into the anteroom.'

They walked through to the small room at the front of the auditorium.

'Now, what's the matter?'

'Nothing's the matter, Ludwig. I came here because Ferdi had to go to the Alsergrund to give a lesson.'

'Damned boy. He'd better be here soon. I need him.'

'Don't be so hard on him, Ludwig. He's a young man trying to earn a living. And you know he sends much of what he earns back to his father. Old man Ries lost much of his income when the Electoral Orchestra was disbanded so Ferdi has to work as hard as he can. You're fortunate he's able to give you as much time as he does.'

'Bah! I wouldn't need him as much as I do if it wasn't for my wretched ears. When they get better, I'll send him on his way. He fawns. Always there like a puppy. Yes, Herr Ludwig, no, Herr Ludwig. Sometimes I feel like boxing his ears just to see the surprise on his face.'

'That's not fair,' Stephan remonstrated.

'Not fair? Life is not fair, or I would not be deaf.' He stopped abruptly, shocked by his own words. 'I'm hungry, Steffen, and thirsty. Can we go to the Weingartel for lunch?'

'Better than that, Ludwig. Come.'

Ludwig followed his friend back into the auditorium, thinking of Ries. Why did the boy irritate him so? Is it, he wondered, because he is the symbol of my disability, testimony to my need to rely on someone?

Stephan led Ludwig off the stage and through to a large room at the back. Two trestle tables covered in starched white linen ran nearly the length of the room. Each was covered with baskets of food. There was a profusion of cold meats, ham, chicken, sausage and beef. Fresh fruit — apples looking as if they had been polished — was piled high. Several carafes stood among the baskets, those containing white wine moist with condensation.

Musicians and singers were filing into the room, the despair of a thoroughly unsuccessful rehearsal etched on their faces. The sight of the sumptuous fare laid out before them did little to improve their mood but they looked longingly at the tables. 'Not for us,' grumbled one. 'We'll get a sausage each in the back room, if we're lucky.' There was a murmur of agreement.

Ludwig saw Prince Lichnowsky making final adjustments to

one of the dishes, before hurrying across. 'Ah, Ludwig. What do you think, eh? You may know how to feed the players' minds, but I know how to feed their stomachs.' He coughed loudly and waited until the room was silent. Then he said, 'Ladies and gentlemen, permit me just a few words before we eat. May I say what an honour it is to be among such a fine group of musicians? Professionals, each and every one of you. And may I say also that I have known our friend here,' he looked directly at Ludwig, 'for the best part of ten years. His music is devilish difficult to master, but once mastered it is of a quality which ranks him with the greatest musicians of our time, by which I mean Mozart, Haydn, Cherubini. His name will one day rank not just with theirs but with those of Bach and Handel too.'

Ludwig heard someone give a tentative clap, which two or three others took up. But the Prince held up his hand for quiet and continued, 'Tonight you are privileged to bring his music to the public. I am aware of the special difficulties you face. The oratorio . . . the ink on the music sheets is barely dry. But you will, I know, do honour to this great music. I also do honour to you, with this token of my esteem and gratitude.' He swept his arm towards the tables. 'This humble fare is for you. Eat and drink to your hearts' content, and allow yourselves to relax.'

There was more applause, but again the Prince gestured for silence. 'Let us reconvene in an hour from now – no, an hour and a half – for one final run-through of the Oratorio.' He ignored a single groan from the back of the room. 'Not a rehearsal, a complete run-through without stopping, and then come back in here where you will find more food laid out. This evening we will give the audience a concert to remember.'

The players moved like a wave towards the tables.

Lichnowsky came towards him and Ludwig saw him exchange a glance with Stephan, who said, 'Come into the side room, Ludwig. Something to tell you. Something exciting.'

The quiet of the small room brought a feeling of heaviness to Ludwig's ears. He held up his hands as he sat down. 'A moment. Wait a moment, or I won't be able to hear you.' He closed his eyes, praying that the dreadful noises would not begin. Mercifully the dullness slowly subsided. He looked up at the two men.

Stephan nodded deferentially to the Prince, who pulled a chair nearer to Ludwig.

'Ludwig, you are highly privileged. Most fortunate. The guest of honour at your concert this evening will be none other than His Imperial Highness Archduke Rudolph.'

Chapter 4

Ludwig stood in the first row of boxes at the back of the theatre, watching the audience file to their seats. He knew he should feel nervous, but curiously he did not. He knew the concert would not be a complete success – no concert of his ever had been. But by now he did not expect his music to be understood and liked at a single hearing and, with the exception of the First Symphony, no piece being played tonight had been heard before.

He felt a tug on his arm and turned to see the shock of prematurely white hair that denoted his friend from the Hungarian Chancellery, Nikolaus Zmeskall, eyes blinking behind the familiar thick spectacles. His arm was round young Carl Czerny's shoulders.

'Nikola. Zmeskallovich. I did not expect . . . And you have brought the boy with you.'

Ludwig looked at the tousle-haired lad who could not have been more than twelve or thirteen. Carl Czerny, whom he had agreed to take on as a pupil after hearing him play the *Grande Sonate Pathétique*. 'You must come for a lesson soon, young man. We must make progress.'

'I want to, sir, very much. Unfortunately my father will not let me cross the river and come into town on my own.'

Ludwig found the soft rather high-pitched voice difficult to hear. He bent his head. 'What are you saying, boy?'

Czerny stepped back a pace. Zmeskall intervened, speaking clearly into Ludwig's ear. Ludwig felt his friend's thick glasses against his head. 'His father, Ludwig. Says he is too young to come into the city alone.'

'Then how is he here tonight?' asked Ludwig, and laughed.

'I know the family. I offered to bring him and return him safely tonight.'

'Safely tonight? Are you aware my music is not safe, my boy?

You are in more danger here in the theatre than you are on the street!' And he laughed again.

Then he froze as he saw his two brothers approaching. How incongruous they looked, he thought. Carl, short and stocky like himself, but his trunk always leaning forward and his head darting this way and that – like a hyena looking for its prey, someone had once said. Nikola, tall and good-looking, square-jawed. Mother's looks, he thought to himself. A Keverich, not a Beethoven. But that eye, slipping to the side, spoiled his strong-boned face. Tall, unlike either Carl or me. And stupid. The set smile – making the broad mouth even broader – which sat constantly on his face to make up for his lack of comprehension.

'Ludwig,' Carl said sharply, 'glad to see you're looking tired. You deserve to be. Well, you have something else to be grateful to me for. See? Down there? Look at them coming in. It'll be full. You'll make money.'

'Make money, Ludwig. Make money,' said Johann.

'Yes. Like Johann,' said Carl, provocatively.

Ludwig felt the blood rise to his cheeks. He looked from one brother to the other. He wanted to say something, a few words to hurt them both, make them shrink away from him but he felt a pull on his sleeve.

Stephan Breuning led him gently away. 'Your guest of honour has arrived,' he said.

Ludwig's stomach lurched. Angrily he dismissed it. He had no need to feel nervous. Archduke Rudolph was a mere boy. Besides that, he had a fine musical sense. Hadn't he alone recognised the extraordinary nature of the opening chords of the First Symphony – and been so impressed he had asked Ludwig to give him lessons? But his voice had the softness of youth, making it difficult to hear. Where, in God's name, was Ries? He should be here to help me. He can tell instinctively if I have not heard something.

He saw Prince Lichnowsky bow low, one arm across his chest, the other held out in a grand sweep of homage. 'Your Imperial Highness. We are honoured by your gracious presence here tonight.'

Ludwig looked at the boy, courtiers on either side of him. He remembered now the long, sensitive face, which had acquired a certain fleshiness in the mid-teenage years. His eyes were deep set and his heavy Habsburg lower lip was unmistakable. Yet overall his appearance expressed frailty.

Ludwig felt a certain revulsion as he looked at the courtiers. How bound up in ridiculous protocol this city was, he thought. I like the boy because he appreciates music. But I feel no less than him even though he is a Habsburg. They will expect me to bow to him, as Lichnowsky has, as everyone has. But I will not.

'Herr Beethoven,' said Archduke Rudolph suddenly, walking forward, his hand extended.

Ludwig took his hand and looked straight into his eyes. 'Thank you for coming to my concert, sir. I am honoured.'

'No more than I am, Herr Beethoven, I assure you. What will we hear tonight? The dominant seventh symphony, I hope.'

As he had with young Czerny, Ludwig found his voice difficult to hear. But the Archduke seemed to understand. He repeated what he had said, louder and more distinctly.

Ludwig smiled. 'My First Symphony will begin the concert. Followed by my new symphony. It is in D. After the interval I will play a new piano concerto, and to close, an oratorio I have composed.'

'Will we hear you improvise?

'No. Tonight is for orchestral works.'

The Archduke leaned close to Beethoven. The courtiers who still stood either side of him bent forward too. 'I still want you to teach me to compose, Herr Beethoven. I am soon to have my own chambers in the Hofburg Palace. Will you come to me there?'

Ludwig smiled. 'Maybe. We shall see.'

'I wish you luck tonight, Herr Beethoven.' The Archduke moved away.

Stephan Breuning said, 'I am told it is time now, Ludwig. Now that His Imperial Highness is here. We should take our seats. Come.'

'I will sit in the wings, off stage. I want to be nearer the orchestra so I can hear all the instruments, and I want to be able to watch Seyfried direct.'

With the orchestra in place, Seyfried came up to Ludwig, shook his hand and walked out on to the stage. He bowed to the audience's applause and motioned the orchestra to rise.

Ludwig looked at the faces of these men who were to play his music. Players, like so many hundreds more in Vienna and Europe. Musicians, players – but not composers. Creators. That was what mattered. To create.

The dominant seventh opening chords of the symphony in C. The shock they had caused in the Burgtheater. He wondered what the faces of the audience said this time. He watched the players, appreciating the concentration on their faces. He looked across at the double-basses. For so long just the anchors of the orchestra, playing little more than the tonic, dominant, tonic. But they had not met Domenico Dragonetti. Ludwig thought of the little Italian with the extra long arms and the oversized double bass he had had made especially for him. He has played one of my cello sonatas on his double-bass! Such skill, such virtuosity. Ludwig had vowed to give a new importance to the role of the double-bass. And the studied looks of the double-bass players confirmed that he had kept his promise.

Ah, the Minuet. So close to a *scherzo*, but not quite there yet. That comes in the next symphony.

Ludwig realised with joy that he was hearing the orchestra clearly. It was true that he was sitting only a short distance from it but he could hear it clearly.

He looked up and saw with a start that Seyfried was walking towards him, arm outstretched. The symphony had finished and there was warm applause in the auditorium.

Ludwig walked out on to the stage with him. A sea of faces looked up at him, most of them smiling. At the back of the auditorium he saw the Archduke stand up and all those around him do likewise. He nodded at the audience briefly – it was too early for much applause – and returned quickly to his chair. Seyfried turned once more to the orchestra, waited for silence, and brought down his baton for the crucial demi-semiquaver and sustained crotchet opening of the symphony in D.

Yes, it was good, Ludwig thought to himself. The orchestra was playing well. *Forte, piano, forte, piano.* Not too fast, Seyfried. Not too fast. *Legato.* Gently. Now you can increase the speed. The symphony is under way.

Am I ready to compose another symphony? Will I follow Mozart and Haydn and write symphony after symphony? He knew the answer was no. I will write a symphony only if I can develop it from where I am now. I cannot do what Mozart and Haydn did: their music was right for their time but this is a new century, a new era. There will be new music for it, and I will compose it.

Seyfried was taking the *scherzo* fast. That was good. No more minuets. They have had their day. They belong to the seventeenth century. Rules and regulations. 'You must write a minuet as the third movement of a symphony,' Haydn had told him. That was now all in the past.

He heard the applause again, but this time he did not want to go out on to the stage. He had heard his second symphony and it had pleased him. The first and second symphonies. My call to attention. Listen to my music, I am saying, and this is just the start. Am I ready for a third?

The applause faded from his head as he walked into the room behind the stage. The musicians would be in soon and he needed a few moments alone. The music still revolved in his head.

He saw a figure approaching him fast.

'Herr Ludwig,' Ries said breathlessly, 'I am so sorry. I was detained – I couldn't – I heard the applause.'

'Ries, where have you been? I needed you, d'you hear? *I needed you.*'

Ries's face fell. 'A pupil. I had to give a lesson unexpectedly. In Döbling. There was no way I could warn you. I am so sorry. I –'

'Damn it, Ries. I shan't rely on you again.'

Ries recovered his composure. 'Sir, Herr Ludwig. I have heard Herr Haydn is here. Shall I find him and take you to him?'

'What? Come nearer, man. You know I have trouble. What did you say?'

'Herr Haydn, sir. He is here. Shall I . . . ?'

'No. Not now. Later, maybe.'

Seyfried came over. 'Congratulations, Beethoven. Splendid compositions. Went down very well. Were you happy with our performance?'

'Happy? Yes. You did well, Seyfried. The speeds were good. The *scherzo* especially.'

'Good. Are you prepared for the concerto? They are taking the piano out on to the stage now.'

Ries said, 'I have your part here, sir. Although . . .'

Ludwig took it from him. 'You may not be able to play from it, Ries, but I can. The music is in my head.' As he spoke, he flicked through the pages. There were no staves, no long sequences of notes. Just musical jottings, promptings.

'Seyfried, you will need to turn the pages for me.'

Seyfried's jaw dropped. 'Turn, sir? Should I not direct the orchestra?'

'No. Let Clement do that. He is leader, is he not? Let him lead. You are the only other one who knows the music well enough. You must turn the pages for me.'

Ries interjected. 'Sir, Herr Ludwig, if you would like –'

'No!' Ludwig said sharply. 'You follow the score from offstage, where I was sitting. Seyfried, you turn the pages and the orchestra will take its lead from Clement.'

Ludwig saw Ries walk slowly away. He knew he had been cruel, but the young man had to be taught a lesson. I needed him, he thought, and he was not here.

'Now, let us find Clement and explain things to him.'

Clement was a tall, striking man with a sensitive face. His hair hung long and curly on his collar.

'Franz,' said Seyfried, 'the esteemed composer Herr Beethoven wishes to talk with you.'

Clement bowed low, passing his bow into his left hand, which already held his violin. 'Sir, I am greatly honoured.'

'Clement, you will lead the orchestra for the piano concerto. Seyfried will turn the pages for me.'

Clement shot an inquiring look at Seyfried, who nodded. 'Of course, sir. It will be my privilege. And I wish you luck for the performance, sir.'

'What? Thank you. Come, Seyfried, let us test the keys of this so-called piano of theirs.'

'Sir, before we go out on to the stage, may I see the music? Your part, sir. I should familiarize myself with it if I am to turn the pages for you.'

Ludwig handed Seyfried the bundle of papers, tied together with two pieces of cord. He watched with amusement as Seyfried leafed through the pages, panic growing on his face.

'Sir. It is not music, sir. In the conventional sense. I – I will not . . .'

Ludwig felt laughter begin to shake him. Seyfried's discomfort was so acute that his hands were trembling, and soon his body began to do likewise. The strands of hair he had combed forward so carefully on to his forehead quivered. Ludwig could not resist making the most of the moment. He began to sing, hopping from one foot to the other.

> 'Sey-fried! Sey-fried! Covered-in-fright, Sey-fried.
> Turn the pages and what do you see
> Swimming before your eyes?
> Black dots, just black dots,
> Oh, Lord, do you sympathise?
> Sey-fried, oh, Sey-fried . . .'

When Ludwig finally stood still, panting and grinning, Seyfried showed his colleagues two open pages and said, 'Here. See? The music of Herr Beethoven. Looks like Egyptian hieroglyphics but sounds like the heavens and angels above!' They guffawed at his neat turn of phrase – and in appreciation of his skilful manipulation of an awkward situation.

Ludwig put his arm round Seyfried and said close to his ear, 'Do not worry, Seyfried. I will give you a sign each time you have to turn.'

A few minutes later the orchestra began to file back on to the stage, then Seyfried guided Ludwig towards the piano, clapping as he went, the notorious folder under his arm.

Ludwig looked again at all the faces smiling at him. Why? he wondered. Did they understand my music? Or are they laughing at me, mocking me, as I was so often mocked when I was young? Do they know they are applauding the Spaniard? The Spaniard with the pockmarks on his face?

He turned quickly to the piano, his friend, who never said an unkind word to him, who made him the equal of anyone: emperors, princes, archdukes, electors, generals. He caressed it with one hand, then sat down and gazed at the keys. All lined up. Regular, not one out of place. And I will make them sing, sing, sing. Like no one else can. There was only one other. And I played for him. Just once. Now he is gone, and I am his successor. The successor to Wolfgang Mozart.

Ludwig looked over to Clement, who was waiting for his signal. He nodded and the opening *tutti* began. The whole orchestra, but just the orchestra, to state the theme, and then a second theme, and begin to develop them, but stop short of it because that was for the piano to do. A long *tutti*, but complete in itself. A small symphony, almost, but bursting with opportunities for the piano.

He waited for the *fortissimo* C crotchets followed by a sustained C minim. The slightest pause, and his fingers ran across the keys in the ascending scales that opened the solo part. Now he was happy. He was playing his music, the piano singing under his fingers, the orchestra singing behind him. And he could hear it all, every precious note of it.

He nodded to Seyfried, who turned the page. On he played. This time he knocked Seyfried's leg with his own. Seyfried glanced at him to try to establish if that was a signal. Ludwig ignored him. Then between notes he jabbed the hapless Seyfried with his left elbow. Seyfried turned the page.

I do not need the music, Ludwig thought, as he played on. He nodded again and felt Seyfried's sharp intake of breath: the two pages he had revealed bore barely a note. Ludwig smiled to himself. Poor Seyfried. He nodded immediately. Seyfried hesitated. Ludwig jabbed him again with his leg. He sang the melody as he played, not too loudly. How beautifully the orchestra was accompanying him. The dynamics were perfect. So important in my music, he thought. Future conductors must always obey my dynamics. If I write *forte* or *piano*, I write it because I mean it.

I shall let the *largo* sing, he thought, as he began the second movement. But *pianissimo*, always *pianissimo*. A hymn. And as the orchestra came in, he found himself conducting with his right hand in time to the flute's soaring melody above the muted strings. And now semiquavers from me. And demi-semiquavers, and semi-demi-semiquavers. And, yes, demi-semi-demi-semiquavers. Runs, furious runs, that will make them marvel. How can he move his fingers so fast and so accurately? they will ask.

But will they hear the music behind the skill? Will they? Will they?

They will be more comfortable with the *rondo*, the final movement, which skips along. But they will not be able to relax because of the key changes, the unexpected key changes, and the different tempos. And as the speed increases, and quavers become semiquavers, and the accent is off the beat, they will not know what to expect next, and when the final *fortissimo* chords sound . . . only then will they know they can breathe again.

He sensed rather than heard the applause. The music was still reverberating in his head. He knew he should stand and turn to the audience. Instead he looked at Seyfried. Sweat stood out on the other man's brow and his face was a mask of pain.

Suddenly Ludwig realised that since the middle of the first movement he had forgotten to signal page turns. Seyfried must have given up, unable to decipher his scribblings and fearing that at any moment Ludwig might forget the notes and blame him. As Ludwig looked at him and smiled, Seyfried began to smile too, relief oozing from every pore of his face. Ludwig put his hand on Seyfried's shoulder to steady himself, but instead of turning to the audience he walked across to Clement, grasped him by the hand, then held up his arms to acknowledge the whole orchestra. Several players put down their instruments and began to applaud.

Finally Ludwig walked to the front of the stage. The audience, in small sections at first, rose to their feet as they clapped. The sounds hurt his ears, but it did not matter. Slowly the echo of the notes dissipated as the roar of ovation took its place. He nodded at the audience, his arms at his sides. He did not bow. He saw that the Archduke was clapping. Lichnowsky was clapping. Everyone was clapping. But they are not clapping the music, he thought. I know that. They are clapping my virtuosity. How can I make them clap the music? I *will* write a symphony, he decided. A third symphony.

He left the stage and Ries came up to him. Ah, poor boy, thought Ludwig. I was unkind to him. He put his arm round Ries's shoulders. 'Did I perform it as well as you rehearsed it, Ferdi?' He saw that Ries had a handkerchief in his hand.

The young man turned away as he dabbed his eye. He turned back, adjusting his eye-patch in the hope that it would disguise his emotion. 'Sir. Herr Ludwig. That was masterful. There is no one who can play the piano like you. I despair.'

'No, Ferdi. You must not envy my playing. Envy my music. That is what is important. Now come, bring me a chair and let us sit and listen to the oratorio. What do you think? Will the trombonists have learned their parts by now?'

Ries relaxed at the change in his master's mood. 'I must say, Herr Ludwig, the way the orchestra is playing tonight, I believe they will do full justice to *Christus am Ölberge.*'

But Ludwig sighed as he sat down with Ries in the wings, a little further away from the stage this time. 'It doesn't matter. It is not right yet. I will do more work on it. I composed it in too short a time. If I am to publish it, it will need more work. But that will come later.'

Ries protested, but Ludwig flapped a hand at him to silence him just as the orchestra began its portentous introduction. He knew the audience would accept the oratorio: it would appeal to their piety – so Catholic, these Viennese, he thought as the first solo voice, that of the tenor Jesus, came in. Soon it was the Seraph's turn, with the Chorus of Angels. Ludwig smiled, his eyes shut, as the trombones lent their essential gravitas to the piece. Yes, it was worth it. I upset Carl; I upset Ries; I upset the musicians. But it was worth it, and they will all know that now.

Occasionally he glanced at Seyfried. He was directing well, better than Ludwig had expected. Well, it was his orchestra. Like the Burgtheater orchestra was Wranitzky's. Musicians must respect their director. I will compliment him afterwards.

He heard Ries's voice in his ear. 'They are calling for you, sir. They want you to come out on stage. The piece was a great success. My congratulations, sir.'

Suddenly Ludwig was enormously weary. 'No. It is enough for tonight. I'm tired. Is there food?'

'Yes, sir. I believe Prince Lichnowsky has arranged a dinner. Come, let me lead you to it.'

'Thank you, Ferdi. Thank you.'

Minutes later, in an upholstered chair, Ludwig gulped the red wine Ries had given him. He could already feel the effect it was having and he was grateful. He knew the concert had been a success.

He saw Archduke Rudolph walking towards him, his two chamberlains on either side and slightly behind him. The boy motioned at him not to stand. 'The piano concerto, Herr Beethoven. A masterpiece. The introduction, like a small symphony. Two main themes, I believe. Or was it three? But none developed. You left that to the solo piano. Ah, what an advance over Herr Mozart. And the *largo*. I will send for the score immediately. My congratulations, sir.'

There was a flurry of movement behind the Archduke and Ludwig sipped his wine. He was calm. There were no dreadful noises in his head, just the remnants of his own music. When he looked up it was to see a small wiry figure, a wig pulled down tightly over the ears, the face so familiar from his early years in Vienna. 'Herr Haydn,' he said, with genuine pleasure, 'I am glad to see you.'

'Stay seated, my boy. I may be considerably older than you, but I believe it is you who needs the chair beneath him.'

'Herr Haydn, it is too long since I last saw you. Is it too late to congratulate you on *The Creation* and *The Seasons*? I have studied the scores. They are masterpieces.'

'You are very kind. But I fear you will one day surpass me in oratorios as you have already in so many other fields.'

'No, sir. At least, not yet. Not with my *Christus am Ölberge*.'

'I shall not dispute that with you, Ludwig, but there will be more to come. I am most proud of my pupil. Most proud.'

Ludwig was a little annoyed at the word pupil, but he let it pass. His mood was buoyant and he was enjoying himself.

From somewhere in the room Prince Lichnowsky called loudly, 'Ladies and gentlemen, dinner awaits you all. Your Imperial Highness, I –'

'Very kind, Lichnowsky. I promised Mama I would return forthwith. Herr Beethoven, I hope to see you soon. I would like to talk to you. Herr Haydn, a pleasure as always.'

Archduke Rudolph left, accompanied by his courtiers and passing through an aisle immediately made for him by figures who bowed as he passed.

'My dear Lichnowsky,' said Haydn, 'a man of my years must respect the time. I shall retire, with many thanks to you for your generosity. Ludwig, I shall follow your progress.'

Ludwig drained his glass and motioned to Ries to refill it. 'Where is Seyfried?' he called out.

Seyfried, now fully recovered from his earlier ordeal, stepped forward, a glass of wine in his hand.

'Seyfried, I propose a toast to you. Not just for your fine conducting, but your extraordinary ability to read Egyptian hieroglyphics!'

Some time later an excited Ferdinand Ries came to Ludwig's lodgings in the Theater an der Wien. 'Herr Schikaneder is overjoyed. There was barely a seat empty for your concert, Herr Ludwig. Here is a draft for your earnings. Eighteen hundred florins – and that is after your brother has taken his percentage. And listen to this.' He pulled a piece of paper out of his case. 'It's the *Musikalische Zeitung*. I'll just read you the last part. "The whole concert was met with extraordinary approval, the longest applause being reserved for the new sacred work, *Christus am Ölberge*. It confirms my long-held opinion that Beethoven can in time effect a revolution in music like Mozart's. He is hastening towards this goal with great strides."'

Ludwig looked up at Ries. 'He has mentioned me in the same breath as Mozart?'

'He has, Herr Ludwig. He has. And now I have to tell you Herr Schikaneder is more keen than ever that you should collaborate with him on an opera.'

'Schikaneder, Schikaneder . . .' Ludwig sang.

'Schik–Schik–Schikaneder
Will–have–to–bide–his–time.
Will–have–to–bide–his–time.'

BOOK TWO

Chapter 1

'*Damn* it, Beethoven,' said Prince Lobkowitz, banging the floor with his crutch. 'Wish I could have been there. Would love to have heard the new pieces. Business matters in Bohemia, though. Had to go. No choice.'

The Prince's voice bounced off the walls of the pillared landing and jarred Ludwig's ears.

'Made money, I hope?' Lobkowitz asked, eyebrows raised, head poised in anticipation of a positive response.

'Enough. My brother had to have some, and Schikaneder took costs. But it will keep me for a while.'

'What now, Beethoven, eh?'

'An opera. For Schikaneder. He's supplying me with a libretto later in the year.'

'Bah!' Lobkowitz expostulated dismissively. 'Schikaneder's an ass. In Zitterbarth's pocket. He's the money-man behind the Theater an der Wien. Desperate to make a profit, which he won't do. Cost too much to build, see? I warned him.'

'It's a good theatre. I like it. The sound is good. I can hear –'

Lobkowitz jerked his head forward. 'Problem with your hearing, mmh? I heard. Someone told me.' Without thinking he spoke a little louder. 'Damned pity for a musician. At least it's not as bad as me, though.' He banged his crutch on the floor again. 'Useless cripple. Bad leg. Can't hide it, that's the trouble. People always pitying me. You're fortunate. People don't stare at you. Just ask them to talk louder.'

Ludwig felt a twinge of exasperation. Lobkowitz should not have known about his deafness, and if he did he should not have said anything. But everyone knew. It was obvious. He was the city's best-known musician. How could it possibly be kept secret? Anyway he liked Prince Lobkowitz, for whom music was an avowed passion. He was a competent violinist who, had it not been for his handicap, might have become a formidable one. He was one of the wealthiest and most influential musical patrons in Vienna, second only to Prince Lichnowsky in seniority. His palace in Vienna was regularly the scene of musical soirées, and it was in his concert room that Ludwig had defeated the arrogant Daniel Steibelt in the improvisation contest a few years before.

Lobkowitz had none of the usual stiff formality of the Viennese aristocracy: Fries, Schwarzenberg, the old Prince Kinsky, as well as his son and successor, and even Prince Lichnowsky behaved as if in accordance with some unwritten protocol. But Lobkowitz was a Bohemian and had the relaxed attitude to life for which Bohemians were renowned. He had inherited enormous wealth – as well as a seat in the Bohemian countryside, a palace in Prague and another in Vienna – and was content to spend it without a second thought. It was said that his wife, Princess Karolina, had tried to restrain him, but to no avail.

'Come. Let me show you the concert room while we are waiting for my esteemed guests to arrive. You haven't seen it since I improved it, have you? In fact, you haven't seen it since your demolition of Daniel Steibelt. Still talked about, y'know.'

Lobkowitz led Ludwig to the ornately carved double doors at the end of the landing and threw them open.

The extravagance for which he was most renowned was the concert room on the first floor of his Vienna palace and the orchestra he kept in residence. In the last year he had brought his grandiose plans to fruition: twelve banks of seats now ran the length of the wide back wall; six banks ran along the two narrower side walls. All the seats and their backs were covered with red linen and in front a low railing divided the audience from the orchestra. A thick carpet covered the entire floor and the Prince had carried out elaborate experiments with his musicians to place tapestries along the walls in the most efficacious positions to prevent the sounds echoing. 'Come in. Come in. There! What do you think, eh?'

Ludwig was amazed. How it had all changed since he had played here against Steibelt! It was now the most perfect concert room. He had seen the small and large Redoutensäale in the Hofburg Palace. They were more elaborate than this and somehow more impersonal. The Burgtheater and Theater an der Wien were, of course, large theatres used for plays and pageants, as well as concerts. This, though, had been created solely for music. And the audience were so close to the players! It was what Ludwig had always imagined. Not serried rows of seats retreating from the orchestra, all heads facing in the same direction, but seats around the musicians, so the listeners could be part of the music too. The beauty of the arrangement, Ludwig saw immediately, was that it suited all forms of musical performance, from a soloist to two musicians playing a sonata, to a quartet, quintet or octet, to full orchestra. He remembered how impressed he had been when he had first seen the room. Now it was a hundred times better.

'It must be the best in Vienna.'

'Certainly is, Ludwig. Best of its kind. Can't say my wife's too pleased. Cost a small fortune. But I'd rather spend my money on this than . . . Oh, I don't know, another palace, like some of the aristocrats of Vienna. The Lobkowitz concert room. Takes a Bohemian to get it right, eh?' he said, tapping Ludwig's arm gently with his crutch. 'And you know why, Ludwig? Because here in Vienna everything has to be grand. Grandiose. Seat of empire, mmh? But music is a dialogue. A conversation. Between the composer and the listener, through the player. Doesn't matter what sort of music. Loud or soft. Chamber piece or symphony. It's the same.'

Ludwig turned to Lobkowitz, a smile spreading across his face. 'You're right, sir. It's a language, and you should not have to shout.'

'Exactly. Now, tell me what comes next. You said an opera for Schikaneder. Pfft. What else?' Before Ludwig could answer, Lobkowitz slapped his forehead. 'I have it! Compose something for this hall, this concert room. And you shall give its first performance here.'

Ludwig let his eyes wander around the room again, its tall arched windows on the opposite wall, which allowed the light to flood in; the painted ceiling with its richly coloured frescoes depicting the pursuit of music; the music stands in position in the centre of the room; the piano, its sides decorated in woven filigree; the rich tapestries, the plush carpet . . . He could see the musicians sitting at their stands, hear them playing his music.

'A symphony,' he said.

'Splendid. Excellent.' Lobkowitz leaned forward. 'Can't

commission it, my friend. Wife would never allow it. But, by God, you shall have use of this room for it. Agreed?'

Ludwig nodded.

'Come now, let us go back downstairs. Our guests must be here by now.'

Ludwig watched Lobkowitz stand, wincing in sympathy as the Prince stretched out his leg and rubbed the muscles at the top. It was at least three years since they had first met and there was no doubt that Lobkowitz's deformity had worsened. His leg appeared to have become shorter, he clearly found it more difficult to walk, and the pain, particularly after he had been sitting for a while, was evidently worse.

'Good of you to come, Ludwig. Glad you could spare the time. Don't think you'll regret it. Do you know the Countess Erdödy?'

Ludwig thought for a moment as they descended the stairs. 'Yes. We met at a soirée, I think. At Prince Lichnowsky's. She's a pianist, isn't she?' He moved to the side of the staircase to give the Prince room to swing his bad leg without bending it.

'Yes. Rather fine one, actually. Lives in the same building as Lichnowsky in the Krugerstrasse so that's probably where you met her. Three small children. Husband's Hungarian. They've got an estate at Jedlesee, just across the river.'

'She's . . . doesn't she . . . her feet?'

'Hah! Damned cripples, all of us!' Lobkowitz said, in a piercing whisper. 'They don't know what the problem is, but they know what caused it. First baby. Three or four years ago. Her feet swelled up. Two more babies since. Never gone down. Trouble walking. Would help if she didn't insist on wearing small shoes. Latest fashion from Paris.'

Ludwig remembered her now. He *had* met her at the Lichnowskys' new apartment in the Krugerstrasse, to which they had moved from the Alsergrund suburb. It was very close to the Wasserkunstbastei and the Seilerstätte, where Ludwig had had rooms before his neighbours had forced him to leave. He remembered her seemingly boundless enthusiasm for his music.

'And Bridgetower, do you know him?'

Ludwig shook his head.

'Mulatto. Father dark-skinned, calls himself a prince. Mother from Poland, I think. Plays the violin like a devil. He's here as Schuppanzigh's guest.' He steadied himself on the banister. 'Think he might be asking you a favour. I'll say no more.

Come on, then.' He stepped off the last step with an audible sigh of relief and walked across the entrance lobby towards the drawing-room doors.

Ludwig followed, now regretting that he had come. He was increasingly reluctant to be in company, especially if he did not know the other people well. But he knew, too, that he could not hide away. However much he might wish for complete artistic freedom – which he had coveted ever since he had learned of the servitude under which Mozart and Haydn had laboured – he knew he could not have it. But at least his patrons, Lobkowitz, Lichnowsky, Kinsky, even the young Archduke, treated him with respect. And Prince Lobkowitz had offered him the use of that magnificent concert room.

A surge of pleasure swept over Ludwig at the sight of his old friend Ignaz Schuppanzigh, the violinist he had first met at the pavilion in the Augarten public park, where he arranged the weekly summer concerts at the pavilion. They began at eight o'clock in the morning, earlier in midsummer, and coffee and cakes were served to the audience. Ludwig noted that Schuppanzigh, whom he had not seen since his return from Heiligenstadt, had lost not an ounce in weight. He sat now in a chair that was clearly too small to contain his bulk.

'Ludwig!' he said, rising with some difficulty, and the two men clasped each other by the shoulder.

'Schuppi, old friend. Fat as ever!'

Schuppanzigh threw back his head and laughed. 'And with a piece of music by Beethoven to prove it.' He turned to the other guests. '"In Praise of the Fat One", composed by Ludwig van Beethoven, for full chorus and male solo voices. Dedicated with enormous respect to Ignaz Schuppanzigh. Mind you, it's less than a minute long, for which I am grateful, and the publishers are in no hurry to publish it!'

There was polite laughter. Lobkowitz directed Ludwig towards his two other guests. 'Ludwig, the Countess Erdödy, whom I know you have already met. A very good friend of mine.'

Ludwig took the gloved hand the Countess extended and bent his head low over it. Countess Erdödy was a small, dark-haired woman, with lively darting brown eyes. Her dress, longer than the prevailing fashion, hid her swollen feet.

'And may I present a stranger to our city, but a very welcome guest, Mr George Polgreen Bridgetower. I hope I have your name correctly, sir.'

Bridgetower bowed. He was tall and thin, with a mass of tightly curled black hair with a high sheen, almost as if it had been polished. His skin was exotically dark. A large nose with a prominent curve dominated his face; his forehead sloped away above it. His lips were curved and sensuous, and his eyes were huge, the pupils like two perfectly round black coals.

'Mr Bridgetower has played before His Majesty King George at . . . Where was it, sir?'

'Windsor castle, sir,' said Bridgetower, in a dark mellifluous voice.

'And is in the service of his son, the Prince of Wales. Am I right, sir?'

'Indeed, His Royal Highness has had the grace to give me a position of some seniority. I lead his private orchestra, which is in residence at the new Pavilion in Brighton. A fine ensemble of musicians. I also perform solos.'

Ludwig was thankful that he could hear Bridgetower's voice clearly. The man's accent, though, made it difficult to understand him. He did not know what Bridgetower's mother tongue was but his German was that of a foreigner: his accent suggested that his own language might have been one from the African continent that had been his father's birthplace.

Ludwig bowed to Bridgetower, wondering what to say to him. Schuppanzigh stepped into the breach. 'Ludwig, you shall hear Mr Bridgetower play. Such skill he possesses. Makes my own humble efforts seem wanting. Better even than Kreutzer, I assure you.'

'Hah, Kreutzer,' said Bridgetower dismissively. 'Only in Paris is he thought of so highly. In London we are not so impressed.'

'Not worth two kreuzer!' said Ludwig, laughing at his own humour. 'I learned the violin as a youth, Brischdauer. I appreciate its difficulties.'

'You have written for my instrument, sir?'

'Sonatas.'

Countess Erdödy clapped her hands. 'Ah, the Spring Sonata. So beautiful. I could hear it again and again. Especially with Herr Schuppanzigh playing the violin part. I pride myself that I can do justice to the piano part. My dear Ludwig, we have had such successes with your piece at soirées.'

'We have, Madame, we have,' said Schuppanzigh. 'Ludwig, it is hardly surprising the Spring has become so popular. It is playable – in the main – by most dilettantes, who can thus say they are able to play Beethoven's music.'

'So gentle, so amiable, so ... *cantabile*,' said the Countess, with an expressive wave.

Ludwig could hear her with no difficulty: her voice had a sharp, rather shrill edge. 'It was not my intention to write like that. Nor to give it the name. "Spring" is the invention of Mollo the publisher, I believe.'

'He denies it. He says – I have even heard that the name came from me,' said Schuppanzigh, in mock horror.

'Damn it, the piece is good, at any rate,' said Lobkowitz, with an emphatic thrust of his crutch. 'Will we hear you play it, Mr Bridgetower?'

Bridgetower bowed. 'I am at your disposal.'

Schuppanzigh said, 'I am fortunate, Your Excellency, to have secured Mr Bridgetower's promise to perform at one of my breakfast concerts at the Augarten pavilion. Is that not so, Mr Bridgetower?'

Bridgetower made him a theatrical bow with the top half of his body, sweeping his right hand across his body and up to his left shoulder.

Ludwig looked at Bridgetower, bemused. He felt himself drawn to the man, despite his rather obvious self-assurance, arrogance almost. Perhaps it was that he was a mulatto, a half-caste who could never expect to rise high in society; he would always be something of a curiosity. He, too, felt like an outsider in Viennese society. He realised that Bridgetower was speaking to him.

'Herr Beethoven, your name is known to us in London. Through Herr Salomon we have heard some of your works. I only await the publication in London of your sonata for my instrument to make myself acquainted personally with your works.'

'Ah, the Spring, the Spring,' said Countess Erdödy again. 'Will we hear you play it at the Augarten pavilion, sir? That would be such a treat.'

'I was going to ask, Herr Beethoven, if you would do me the honour of creating a work for me?'

Lobkowitz banged his crutch on the floor twice. 'Splendid idea! What d'you say, Ludwig?'

Countess Erdödy clasped her hands together. 'Oh, Herr Beethoven, how wonderful that would be. A new work, a violin sonata, that is what you will write, isn't it?'

Schuppanzigh glanced apprehensively at Ludwig, knowing his dislike of composing to order.

Ludwig was aware that all eyes in the room were on him, awaiting his decision. He had decided that his next work would be the new symphony. That would be his summer task. The offer from Lobkowitz of his concert hall – and, of course, his orchestra – was a crucial factor. There should be no need to book the date weeks or even months ahead, as he would have to if he used any of the Imperial theatres; no fretting from Schikaneder over ticket sales if he used the Theater an der Wien. And after the symphony, he had to compose the opera for Schikaneder.

'You shall have your sonata, Brischdauer,' he said. 'When is the Augarten recital, Schuppi?'

'The twenty-second of May. A month from now.'

'Ries will help me. We will test your virtuosity, Brischdauer.'

Bridgetower again bowed low. 'Monsieur Kreutzer will shed tears of pain as he plays before his audience in Paris.'

'Splendid outcome, Ludwig, Bridgetower,' said Lobkowitz. 'We shall have some wine to celebrate.' He hobbled to the wall and pulled the long tasselled cord that hung from the ceiling. 'Sit down, sirs. I want to hear more of London. Bridgetower, what of that Italian composer who lives in London? Giovanni Viotti? I heard –'

'Viotti. Signor Viotti,' said Bridgetower. 'A fine composer.'

Schuppanzigh interjected, 'Indeed. I have played several of his concertos for violin and they have met with great approval. I thought he was in Germany.'

Bridgetower nodded. 'He was. He had to leave London after involving himself a little too closely in political matters. There was much joy in London at the victory against the French in the Nile – the British are proud of their navy. But our friend has retained too great an affection for the French. He was asked to leave. He went to Hamburg but returned to London two years ago.'

'Brave man.'

'He was well received. The English have forgiven him. But he has given up music.'

'Given up music?' exclaimed Schuppanzigh. 'Impossible. What can there be of more pleasure to him than music?'

Bridgetower made sure he had the attention of everyone in the room. 'Wine!' he said. 'He has given up music for the wine trade!'

Ludwig laughed. 'Hah! Maybe this Italian is not such a stupid man. Shall we do the same, Schuppi? Maybe you should give up music for the food trade!'

The laughter that followed Ludwig's joke assaulted his ears and he wished he had not made it.

'And the war? Have you defeated this arrogant Corsican yet?' Lobkowitz asked.

Ludwig leaned forward. He wanted to hear more about the Frenchman, whose name was on everyone's lips.

Bridgetower shrugged. 'I am an artist. What do I know of such things? But since Mr Pitt resigned we have been at war again with the French. There are rumours Bonaparte is planning an invasion. At Court they talk of nothing else. And do you know what else they say?'

Ludwig leaned forward a little more.

'That he will one day proclaim himself Emperor of France. To rival our king and *your* emperor.'

Lobkowitz banged his crutch. 'Impudent puppy! Impossible!'

Ludwig clenched his teeth. 'No. You are misjudging him, Brischdauer. You and the English. He is a common man. A peasant who has risen to lead his country. All he seeks is the welfare of his people. He does not want personal gain.'

'Not an admirer, are you, Beethoven?' Lobkowitz looked at him quizzically.

Again Ludwig wished he had not spoken. But the truth was that despite the French invasion and occupation of his own homeland, the Rhineland, he had come to admire the French First Consul. The man knew exactly what he wanted.

'He does not make war for war's sake,' he said. 'Only to preserve the freedom the French people secured with their revolution.'

'Must say, Beethoven, glad you're a musician and not a diplomat. Hah!'

Ludwig was relieved that Lobkowitz' humour had lightened the moment.

Chapter 2

Ludwig walked out of the Theater an der Wien, crossed the narrow Wien river and made his way round the bustling fruit market opposite. Hands thrust deep into his pockets, he walked along the river bank. He was on his way to see some old friends: he had an idea to put to them.

He did not look up at the ornate garden of Prince Schwarzenberg's palace, or pay attention to the cries of the sellers in the hay market, although his nose wrinkled at the smell of the horses which stood contentedly in the spring sun. He crossed the Neustädter canal and turned into the Ungargasse, the quiet street that ran parallel to the main road of the Landstrasse suburb, and walked into the courtyard of the house named the Red Rose. He smiled contentedly as he heard clearly the sound of a single piano key being struck – the sound he would always associate with the piano builder Andreas Streicher and his wife Nanette.

What dear friends they were, he thought. He remembered how kind Nanette had been to him, all those years ago, when he had met her at her father's house in Augsburg. He had been on his way home from Vienna to Bonn, forced to leave before he could begin lessons with Mozart because of his mother's dire illness. Nanette and her husband had moved to Vienna to open a piano factory a few years after he had come here, and Nanette had kept a watchful, motherly eye on him since.

He did not need to ring the bell that hung down beside the outside door. He went into the front room and sat in an easy chair. He closed his eyes and – for at least the thousandth time – ran through the notes in his head. He knew they were right. He knew what he wanted to do with them.

He looked up as Nanette brought a tray of coffee into the room and set a cup in front of him. There was no need for questions or polite greetings.

'Dear Ludwig. Here we are, both living outside the Bastion. In the country, almost. The air is so much purer.'

Ludwig smiled. 'I walked along the Wien river. Through the markets. The smells are so strong. Fruit, hay, horses.'

'I know. Andreas and I love it so much in Landstrasse. He can bang away on his piano with no fear of complaint. How are your lodgings in the Wien?'

Ludwig could hardly hear her voice. It was naturally gentle, without the edge that would have allowed it to pierce the dullness in his ears, and the irregular sound of Andreas testing his pianos made it more difficult. At least there was no pain in his head which, given the walk he had just completed, surprised him.

'Dark and small. One little window on to the courtyard. And I have Carl to contend with.'

Nanette said benevolently, 'I'm sure he's a great help to you. Especially with . . . since . . .' She leaned forward and touched his hand. 'What about your hearing, Ludwig?'

He sighed, reached for the coffee and drank a mouthful, although it was still too hot. He looked at Nanette's kindly face. 'It is not improving. I do not know if it is getting worse. I can hear most of the time. I can hear you now. But it is more difficult than it used to be. And if I have pain in my head, too, then I find it most difficult. Especially after music it is difficult. The notes are still in my head, voices sound harsh and I cannot make out the sounds.'

'What about Doktor Schmidt? What does he say?'

Ludwig shrugged. 'He is confident. He says it has not worsened, but it has not improved either.'

'Well, if he is not concerned –'

'I am, Nanette. I am concerned. Whatever any doctor says, I know what is happening. I am going deaf. One day I will be completely deaf.' He reached forward again and drank more coffee, enjoying the strong bitter taste. When he put down the cup, he saw that Andreas had entered the room. Nanette was talking to him quietly. Ludwig did not need to ask what she was saying – it was obvious from the anxious look on Andreas's face.

'Ludwig, my old friend. No need for pessimism. I agree with Nanette. If the doctors say it will improve, I'm sure it will.'

Ludwig did not want to talk about it any more. 'Maybe. I

hope so. How is my new piano coming along? You are building me one, aren't you?'

'I am, Ludwig. And you are forcing me to build a better, stronger piano than I ever have before. Sturdier legs. Thicker wire. To cope with your unique demands,' he added, laughingly.

Ludwig guffawed with him. 'I will pound it all the more mercilessly, in the hope it will drive Carl out of my lodgings.'

Nanette was about to say something conciliatory, but Ludwig held out his hands. 'I am not serious. But one day he will have to move out – it is not satisfactory, living together.'

Andreas sat on the arm of Nanette's chair. 'Congratulations on the success of your benefit concert, Ludwig,' he said, and before Ludwig could reply, he continued, 'word reaches me that you have agreed to compose a new piece for the English violinist who is in the city.'

Ludwig reached for his coffee cup, which Nanette had refilled. 'How did you hear?'

'Schuppi,' said Andreas. 'He was rather surprised you agreed to take it on. But he's delighted you're going to perform it with Mr . . . I don't recall his name, at an Augarten concert.'

'Brischdauer,' said Ludwig. 'The final movement is already written. I wrote it for an earlier sonata but it was not right. I will use it for this one. The other two . . .' He paused. 'I have a week or so.' He put down his cup and a brightness came into his eyes. 'But that is not why I have come to see you. There is something else. Something I want to play to you.' He stood up and walked to the piano in the corner. Nanette and Andreas exchanged looks. This was how they had first heard the Grande Sonate Pathétique. Ludwig had sat at the piano in the workshop and played it for them.

Now he played just four notes. E flat, B flat above, B flat an octave lower, E flat. He repeated them and turned to his friends.

Nanette and Andreas looked at each other, puzzled. Andreas said, 'I know there is more to it than that, Ludwig. What comes next?'

Ludwig smiled and played the theme that grew out of the four notes. Da-daaa-da-daaa, da-daaa-da-daaa, da-daa-daa-daaa, da-da-da-da, da-da-da, daaa-daa.

Nanette let out a sigh of relief. 'Oh, yes, of course. Isn't that from your *Prometheus* music? The ballet you set to music for Signor Vigano?'

'Yes,' said Andreas, 'it's the theme for the Finale. You used it in the Finale.'

'Yes. Now listen.' Ludwig played the four notes, followed by the theme. Then he played one of the fifteen variations he had composed on it in Heiligenstadt.

'A variation,' said Andreas. 'It has potential, I can see that.'

Ludwig leaped up. 'Yes. Potential. In Heiligenstadt I wrote a set of fifteen variations on the theme. Just the four notes and the theme above them. Fifteen variations.'

'And you are to publish them?'

'Yes. Later this year. Breitkopf, I think.'

'Congratulations,' said Nanette. 'And you have come to tell us about it. Ludwig, how thoughtful of you. You are such a dear, sweet man.'

Ludwig left the piano and returned to his chair. He could still hear the notes in his head, mingled with Nanette's words. But her voice was gentle and there was no harshness in his head. 'No, no,' he said, shaking his head but smiling, 'that's not what I meant. What I am trying to say is that I have not yet finished with that theme. There is more I can do with it. I want to explore it until it has yielded everything to me. Everything it has.'

'I think I understand,' said Andreas, and went on, to his wife, 'Ludwig is going to use the theme for the new sonata he is composing for the English violinist. That is how he will be able to complete it in time for the concert. Isn't that right, Ludwig?'

Ludwig smiled wearily. 'No. It will be the theme for my new symphony.'

'Ferdi. Find me the violin sonata in A. I composed it a year ago, maybe more.'

'I remember, Herr Ludwig. You said you would dedicate it to the Tsar of Russia.'

'Yes. The final movement. The Allegro. That is what I want.'

'Herr Ludwig, I believe the work is already with the publisher. It is due to be published later this year.'

'Which publisher?'

'The Kunst-und-Industrie, I think.'

'Get it back. If they refuse, threaten to withdraw it. Tell them you'll give it to Hoffmeister. I want the final movement.'

'Sir, may I ask what you are planning to do?'

'The concert is in three weeks. I will not have a new sonata ready. If the final movement is already written, it will save time. It has already been copied by Schlemmer, so Brischdauer can read it. He may have to play the first two movements from my manuscript.'

Ries could not suppress a smile. 'But the earlier work, sir. If it is finished –'

Ludwig interrupted, 'The Allegro is not right for it. I knew it at the time, but decided to leave it. Now I will change it. It is too . . . bright. But it will suit Brischdauer.'

'Very well, sir. I will retrieve it for you from the Kunst-und-Industrie. Sir, Herr Ludwig, forgive my impertinence, but should you take on such a commission? Why not let Mr Bridgetower play one of your earlier pieces?'

Ludwig looked at the young man on whom he was relying now so much. He knew Ries was right. The same thought had occurred to him. It would be simple. Bridgetower would understand the time constraint. He would still be flattered to play a piece by Beethoven with the composer at the piano.

'No, Ferdi. I will give this Mr Brischdauer his sonata, and it will be a big work. Nothing small. I have decided. And then, the symphony.'

After Ries had left Ludwig sat at the table staring out of the window. It was a bright day outside, yet all that came into the room was a dull greyness from the internal courtyard. He wanted to be outside, not in the streets of the city but in the countryside, striding across the fields, breathing the sweet air, smelling the fragrance of nature.

He was bursting to compose. He felt it within himself, a burning need to put the notes down on paper. That was why he had accepted Bridgetower's request, and that was why he intended to work on the symphony next. Another big work. And he would get out of the city to compose it. Away from the pressures. Away from people asking him to play the piano for them. Away from people asking him about . . . about . . .

He felt the walls of the small dark room close in on him. He wanted to reach out and push them back. There was a heaviness in his head, the dullness that presaged the dreadful noises. Worse, surely, than Ries's lost eye, Lobkowitz's deformed leg, or Countess Erdödy's swollen feet.

Is that why I feel this compelling need to compose? To prove that I still can? And what if I can't? *What if I can't?*

Chapter 3

Stephan von Breuning allowed his housekeeper to clear away the dinner plates and refilled the wine glasses. He sat at the top of the table, with Ferdinand Ries to his left and a new arrival in Vienna, Ignaz Gleichenstein, to his right.

'So how is it in Freiburg, Ignaz? As dreadful as it is further north?'

Gleichenstein shook back the wave of hair that lay over his forehead. He had a youthful face, with keen eyes. 'No. More peaceful. The French are less interested in us, I am pleased to say. At least so far. But my parents wrote to me saying there are rumours the French will soon introduce conscription. They have told me to stay in Vienna as long as I can.'

Ries fiddled with his napkin. 'It's already happening in the Rhineland. My father wrote to me. All my friends are now wearing French uniforms. He fears I might have to go back.'

'But they can't force you, can they?'

'They can put pressure on my father. Make his life miserable. And I could not allow that.'

Stephan gestured to his friends' glasses. 'Drink up, gentlemen. Let us at least enjoy the civilised life in this civilised city. In fact, let us drink to our homeland, in the hope that it will soon be free of French soldiers.'

The three raised their glasses.

'What news on Beethoven?' said Stephan to Ries. 'I hear he's taken on a new commission.'

'It is for this English violinist, who asked him for a new sonata. Herr Ludwig agreed, but he's only got two weeks and I don't see how he can possibly have it ready. At least, not in time for Mr Bridgetower to rehearse it properly.'

'I am so looking forward to meeting Herr Beethoven – his fame has spread to Freiburg. People know his name. Since he is a Rhinelander, and we are Rhinelanders, we claim him as one of ours, even if we're from different ends of the river.'

Stephan and Ries laughed. 'That is allowed,' said Stephan. 'We will be generous with him. And you are a musician yourself, Ignaz, are you not?'

Gleichenstein held up his hands in mild protest. 'No, no. And certainly not compared to you, Ferdinand,' he said, turning to Ries. 'I play the cello, but not in public, I assure you. I am better at reading and writing documents than I am at playing notes. Stephan, I am really most grateful to you for securing me an appointment at the Hofburg.'

Stephan picked up his glass and drank. 'So what will happen if Ludwig does not complete the new piece? The concert is set, is it not?'

Ries nodded. 'I don't know. Mr Bridgetower will have to give a performance on his own. Works he is already familiar with. It will be a huge disappointment. You know Herr Ludwig has asked me to retrieve an earlier piece from the publisher?'

Stephan's eyes widened in astonishment. 'What do you mean? You can't, can you?'

'No, not really. He wants the last movement. For the new piece. The publisher, understandably, points out that he has paid for the work and says he is entitled to keep it. I don't know what to do. I really don't.' He mopped his brow, which had broken out in a light sweat.

'He puts you under a lot of pressure, Ferdi, doesn't he?'

Ries sipped the wine. His face was drawn. 'That's not my only problem. He wants to get away for the summer, to write a new symphony, and he wants me find somewhere for him to stay. He assumes I have the time to do that. But I have lessons to give. It is my sole source of income.'

'Let me know if I can help,' said Gleichenstein. 'I would gladly be of assistance.'

'That's kind of you, Ignaz. I sometimes wonder why I allow myself to take on so much for him. But, you know, there's a kind of . . . vulnerability about him. It's not just his deafness. There's something more. As if his head is always so full of music he needs someone to take care of everything else.'

'You're right, Ferdi. And he's always been like that. My mother used to say almost the same thing back in Bonn. She used a word for it. *Raptus*. She would say "Ludwig has his *raptus* again."'

'Yes. He will always need someone to help him but I doubt they will ever receive much gratitude.'

The noise of conversation, punctuated by the irregular staccato of laughter, bounced off the marble pillars of Taroni's coffee house in the Graben. The sounds hurt Ludwig's ears, but the taste of the strong bitter coffee went some way to alleviate the discomfort. He watched Bridgetower sip his tea, his little finger crooked. Earlier the Englishman had played the final movement of the sonata for him – Ries having at last persuaded the Kunst-und-Industrie to part with it – and Ludwig, accompanying him on the piano, had realised that despite his foppish ways, his exaggerated mannerisms, Bridgetower was a master musician.

'We must go, Brischdauer. Too much noise here.'

'We will be early if we leave now.'

But Ludwig was already moving towards the large double doors.

They walked out on to the wide Graben and turned past the monument to the plague and went towards St Stephansdom. Ludwig walked slightly ahead of Bridgetower to dissuade him from conversation. But the Englishman soon came level with him. 'I need the first two movements, Herr Beethoven. I need to rehearse. There is less than a week.'

Ludwig took a deep breath. He did not know what to say. He was having unusual trouble composing the opening of the sonata. He had written it once, but discarded it. He wanted to create something different, something to show the violinist's virtuosity and also to signal that this was to be a large and important work. It was there, in his mind, he knew it. But it had eluded him.

A carriage rattled by, the noise of the iron-rimmed wheels on the cobbles jarring Ludwig's ears. Without looking at Bridgetower he spoke to him as they turned into the Kärntnerstrasse. 'Too many people,' he said. 'Is London like this? Carriages everywhere. People shouting. It must be quieter in London.'

'Herr Beethoven,' said Bridgetower, in a firm, mellifluous voice, 'I am sorry to tell you that, compared to London, Vienna is like a country village.'

Ludwig shook his head in disbelief. 'And Paris? Have you been there?'

'Nearly as bad as London, and much worse than Vienna.

They say the city has changed for ever since the Revolution. Before there were rich and poor. Now everyone is the same. All poor. But you must not say so in public. Once only the rich rode in carriages. Now there are no carriages. Everyone goes on foot to prove they are ordinary, like everybody else.'

'Then Paris cannot be so bad. The acclaimed violinist Kreutzer is there.'

'Rudolphe Kreutzer. A charlatan. A string-scraper. Plays the violin as if he was sawing wood. They play differently in Paris. Very decorative. Trills, *glissandi*, double-stopping. Very impressive, but there is no substance. I play like that too. Especially double-stopping. But with weight. Substance. Importance.'

Ludwig suddenly stopped and looked at him. 'Double-stopping. Double-stopping. I remember how difficult it was when old Father Ries taught me the violin in Bonn. But you are right. It must have weight.'

Bridgetower nodded. 'Yes. Not just for show. It must encapsulate the drama of the piece.'

Ludwig looked at him. 'The drama, did you say? I completely agree with you, my dear Brischdauer. I agree. Now, we turn here. The Krugerstrasse. The Countess lives in the same building as Prince Lichnowsky and his wife.'

'They will be there for dinner too?'

Ludwig sighed. 'Regrettably. You will see why I say that. He is fawning and she is . . . emotional. Health problems always. They were kind to me, but . . . I could not be free of them. I was expected at dinner at the same time every day, clean-shaven and properly dressed. I felt like a servant.'

'I have heard he is a great lover of music.'

'Used to give matinées every Friday – Schuppanzigh led his quartet. I played as well, when they lived on the Alstergasse and I lived with them. But they moved here some time ago. There are rumours that his vast fortune has been depleted – the war, his wife's health.'

'So they live in the same building as Countess Erdödy. She is a good pianist, isn't she?'

'I believe so, but I do not know her well.'

The two men mounted a wide staircase and walked along a corridor hung with faded tapestries.

Ludwig looked around him as he walked. 'D'you see all this, Brischdauer?' he asked, gesturing around him. 'It belongs to a different class of people. You and I, are we not from humble stock? Yet because –'

Bridgetower stopped and turned to Ludwig, his face unsmiling. 'My father, sir, was an African prince.'

Ludwig hesitated a moment, hearing the words again in his mind to be sure he had understood them, then cackled loudly.

'Hah! My dear Brischdauer, forgive me! And I am the son of a prince from the Rhineland. We are princes among men.' He began walking again. 'I do not mean to insult you. Just that because we are musicians we gain entry to places other men will never enter.'

A servant in an elaborate braided tailcoat bowed to the two men and opened a set of double doors.

They entered a large room hung, like the corridor, with tapestries. These would absorb the sound of voices, preventing the harshness hurting his ears, Ludwig thought. But people would have to speak distinctly. He had, mercifully, no pain or sounds in his head, just the dullness. As long as it stays like that, he thought.

The Countess's voice reached him. It had a sharp edge, for which he was grateful. '. . . so delighted, so honoured, to have two such brilliant guests tonight. Dear Ludwig, come here. Let me greet you.'

Ludwig saw her arms stretched out towards him. He remembered her feet and that she would not stand until she had to. He walked towards her and allowed her to take his hands in hers. He felt her pull on them but he did not bend forward.

'And dear Mr Bridgetower,' she said. 'What wonderful reports I have heard of your playing. And you have brought your violin with you. I shall not allow you to leave before you have demonstrated your skills for us.'

Bridgetower took her proffered hand and bowed low over it, allowing his lips to brush the white cotton glove.

Embarrassment swept over Ludwig as he watched. It was so elaborate, so contrived . . . so transparent. And yet the Countess responded to it exactly as Bridgetower had intended. She raised her other hand to her cheek and patted it, as if to beat down the blush that had already begun to highlight it. He saw Bridgetower's satisfied smile. The distaste he felt for the Englishman's manners was, he knew, tinged with envy.

The Countess's arms were open wide again and she was

looking over Bridgetower's shoulder. 'Ah! How wonderful of you to come! My dear neighbours.'

Ludwig was struck at how Prince and Princess Lichnowsky had aged even since he had last seen them. The Prince seemed careworn, the heavy bags under his eyes seeming to drag his face down. The Princess was shrunken, her face sharper and more angular. And there had been rumours that her always unpredictable behaviour had become even more so, and that this had taken its toll on the Prince.

Ludwig recoiled as Princess Christiane came straight towards him. 'Dear Ludwig, oh, it has been so long, so long. Are you well? I hear disturbing reports of your health. Do tell me there is nothing wrong.'

The Prince came hurrying over, as if to rescue him. 'Ludwig is fine, my dear. Now come. Let us bid good evening to our hostess. Marie, how nice to see you and so good of you to think of us.' He acknowledged Ludwig and Bridgetower courteously and gently guided his wife towards the Countess.

Ludwig saw the Countess thrust her hands towards the Prince, but she gave the Princess a cursory nod, as if resenting the presence of another woman and one who was higher in rank than she was.

Over wine, Ludwig found to his relief that he could hear everyone: both Lichnowsky and Bridgetower had firm deep voices and the two women spoke animatedly and with emphasis. He began to enjoy the effect of the fine wine on his senses.

At dinner he said little. The focus of interest was the flamboyant George Polgreen Bridgetower, who exhibited an easy and charming manner, particularly when talking to either of the women. Very soon, albeit subtly, the Princess and the Countess were competing for his attention. More than once Prince Lichnowsky caught Ludwig's eye with a look that invited sympathy.

Ludwig was pleased that, for a time at least, no one drew him into the conversation. He was content to observe the interplay of relationships, the two women trying to outdo each other in their efforts to make an impression on Bridgetower and how expertly he strung both of them along, flattering them in equal measure.

Eventually, though, Countess Erdödy said, 'So, my dear Ludwig, what will you and Mr Bridgetower play for us? Will it be your Spring Sonata?'

Ludwig groped for a reply. He wanted to say no, but knew he could not. He was relieved when he heard Bridgetower's sonorous voice. 'My dear Countess, I rather hope Herr Beethoven will accompany me in the final movement of the sonata he is composing especially for me. You will, sir, will you not? I have the parts in my violin case. He has taken the movement from an earlier work for which he considered it inappropriate, so it is complete. Meanwhile he is working on the earlier movements. My performance is barely a week away, so he is working vigorously. Are you not, sir?'

Ludwig did not blame Bridgetower for raising the matter in this way, showing his anxiety in public. If only he knew the truth. But something Bridgetower had said earlier had given him an idea. 'You shall have your sonata, Brischdauer. I cannot promise you as much rehearsal as you would like, but you will have it.'

'You will play it with Mr Bridgetower for us, Ludwig, won't you?' asked Princess Lichnowsky eagerly.

A flash of irritation shot through Ludwig. That chirping cajoling voice that he had grown so tired of when he had lived with the Lichnowskys so many years before: he had forgotten how he had come to dread hearing it. Prince Lichnowsky had soon understood this and had always tried to ease the tention he knew it caused, as he did now. 'My dear, let us allow Ludwig to decide for himself.'

Ludwig did not want to hurt Countess Erdödy, or even disappoint her. But he knew that if he simply said yes, the demands would not stop. Princess Lichnowsky would tell her friends triumphantly how she had persuaded the great Beethoven to play for her, just for her, and he had to show her that he was no longer at her disposal.

He picked up his glass and took a long draught. Then he said, 'No, not tonight. Mr Brischdauer can entertain us alone.'

There was a chorus of disappointment from around the table, and Bridgetower's face flashed with anger, which Ludwig saw.

'Herr Beethoven. I shall be performing your new work in public with little rehearsal, as you yourself have already said. If we play the final movement now, it will be the first time we have played it together. It will be − if the distinguished company will allow me to say so − like a rehearsal. I ask you please to oblige.'

Ludwig felt all eyes on him. This was his moment. His music, his art, that made him the equal of anybody in the room. He signalled to the servant to replenish his glass, shook his head and looked up. Ah, the disappointment on their faces. The anger on Brischdauer's! I, Ludwig, can command their emotions, he thought. They have their wealth and their rank, but I have my music, and with it I can control them.

Suddenly, into the silence that had fallen, Countess Erdödy exclaimed, 'I know! I have it! I shall play it with you, Mr Bridgetower. You will permit me to, Ludwig, won't you?'

Ludwig looked at her, astonished. His immediate thought was to forbid it. But there was that smile, with the raised questioning eyebrows, the look of vulnerability. He could not disappoint her. 'Countess, I should be most greatly honoured if you were to direct your talents to my humble music,' he said, in a theatrical tone that stopped just short of mockery.

Delight shone in her eyes. 'Oh, Mr Bridgetower, come. We will play the piece you have talked about. I do hope it is not too difficult, Ludwig. Let us go through to the music room.'

The group stood and allowed the Countess to lead the way. Ludwig noticed how her billowing dress hid the awkwardness of her legs.

All except Ludwig arranged themselves in chairs. He wanted to stand. He saw Bridgetower's nervous expression. 'Do not worry, Brischdauer, I shall not interrupt your playing. But I need to hear both instruments properly.'

He watched as the Countess looked over the piano part. He waited for her reaction. When it came he was surprised at the calmness of her voice. And even over the sounds of Bridgetower tuning his instrument, he could hear her quite clearly. 'Have you written a sonata for violin accompanied by piano, or one for piano accompanied by violin?'

Bridgetower spoke before Ludwig could answer. 'From the foremost pianist in Vienna, one could not expect mere accompaniment from the piano. I have studied the movement. It calls for virtuoso playing from both instruments. It is a sonata for both violin and piano.'

Ludwig was flattered. From his earliest instrumental sonatas, whether for violin, cello, even French horn, the soloist had always complained to him that their part was unnecessarily difficult and that the piano accompaniment was a solo piece in itself. 'The audience are to be impressed by my playing, not yours,' one musician had said to him.

Ludwig went to the piano. 'Brischdauer is right,' he said to the Countess. 'For me, the piano can never be just an accompaniment. My sonatas are for two equal instruments.'

'This occasion may be an exception to that,' said the Countess, to polite but genuine laughter.

Ludwig was surprised at his own composure. 'Play it more slowly than I have written it,' he said to the Countess. 'Ignore the *presto* marking. And, Countess, I do not mind wrong notes. Too much attention is paid to wrong notes. What I mind is the markings. Where I have written *sforzando*, as here in the sixth bar,' he pointed to the manuscript, 'you must play *sforzando*. Where I have written *fortissimo*, or *pianissimo*, you must play it that way. And you, Brischdauer,' he said, turning to the violinist, 'do not play every note if you cannot. But obey my markings.'

Bridgetower bowed. 'Herr Beethoven, as a performer it is my duty to play what the composer has written. Every note you have written will sound from my violin.'

There was a squeal of delight from Princess Lichnowsky, and the Prince put out a restraining arm.

Ludwig stood off to the side, his hands linked behind his back, his head thrust forward. Although he had composed the movement a year or so before and had played it himself with Ignaz Schuppanzigh, he had put it to one side. He knew it transcended anything he had written for violin and piano. It demanded more virtuosity than any of his previous violin sonatas. And now I must compose a first movement to match it, balance it. And Brischdauer, unwittingly, has given me the solution to the opening.

The Countess played the sustained opening chord of A major. *Fortissimo*, just as he had written it. And Bridgetower, with a remarkable delicacy of touch, played the bouncing motif that was the driving force of the movement. *Piano*, again, exactly as he written it. And there were the *sforzandos*, from both instruments.

Ludwig put one hand under his chin, fist clenched, supporting the elbow with the other hand. Really, he thought, the Countess is an exceptionally good player. He knew the opening was difficult – how old Schuppi had complained! – the violin playing sets of triple quavers over the piano's crotchet-quaver rhythm. 'How can I possibly keep time?' Schuppi had asked. 'We will never reach the end together.'

There was the occasional wrong note from the piano. He noticed that the Countess simplified some chords, omitting the middle notes. That did not matter. He recalled the stream at Heiligenstadt, along which he had walked so often. That is how music should be, he thought. Constantly flowing. Incapable of being stopped.

The time signature changed. He knew the short passage so well. Two-four time. Minims. Calm. Lyrical. Gentle. The water flowing peacefully. Then the rocks again, forcing the water round in eddies. Staccato chords, a sustained trill, as if the water is deciding which path to take ... And away it flows again.

Ludwig looked at the Countess, her small lively face locked in concentration, her eyes fixed on the music before her, her mouth half open. How nimbly her small hands moved across the keys.

His hand still under his chin, he inclined his head towards Bridgetower. The violinist stood with one foot ahead of the other, his body swaying rhythmically, his large eyes half closed, the lids bulging. With every downward sweep of the bow he lowered the upper half of his body. Ludwig knew he was making the music seem more difficult to play than it actually was, but he did not mind that. Why should a musician not do all in his power to impress his audience?

As they played, they increased in confidence. Countess Erdödy, familiar now with the rhythm and pace of the music, became more adept at adapting the piano part, dropping notes, or even whole sequences, without halting the flow. Bridgetower, his fingers moving on the fingerboard as if driven by some force outside his control, was practically note-perfect. Clearly he had practised the piece several times; it was, after all, the sole movement of the new sonata available for him to work on.

Ludwig knew that the ending of a piece determined the audience response. He had written a rushing tumultuous conclusion. Again, that awkward rhythm of which Schuppanzigh had complained – triple quavers, though not triplets, in the piano; crotchet quaver, crotchet quaver in the violin.

Ludwig felt Bridgetower drive towards the end. Yes, yes, he thought, ever-flowing, like water. He looked at the small audience. The Lichnowskys, sitting as if they were not breathing, the Princess's hands raised, frozen, in the air.

The final A sounded. Just a single note on the G string

for the violin; two single As, both in the bass register, for the piano.

The Lichnowskys burst into applause, and Ludwig noticed that two servants and a number of the kitchen staff were standing and clapping in the doorway.

Bridgetower held his instrument and bow in one hand away from his body and bowed deeply. He stood upright, took a handkerchief from his sleeve, mopped his forehead and bowed again.

Countess Erdödy remained seated at the piano, looking at Ludwig and smiling admiringly. He walked towards her and took both her hands in his, brushed them with his lips and lowered them.

He looked at Bridgetower, expecting acknowledgement, but he was talking to the Lichnowskys.

Finally the violinist looked across and spoke to Ludwig in his deep, clear voice. 'A fine piece of writing, Herr Beethoven. But you will, of course, adjust the slow section, at the time change, will you not? You have written three minims, four crotchets, then the quaver run. So.' He played the short passage, calling out the notes as he played. 'G sharp, C sharp, B, A, A, A, A, la-la-la-la laa-laaa. You must surely mean four minims, thus.' He played again, singing the notes. 'G sharp, C sharp, B, A, and only then A, A, A, A, up to B-la-la-la laa-laaa. Yes? Surely? Do you not think so, Countess?'

Ludwig saw the Countess's small smile and shake of the head. 'No, Mr Bridgetower,' she said. 'I believe it is perfect as it is.'

Ludwig inclined his head towards her and returned to his chair. He expected Countess Erdödy to continue praising his work – he rather wanted her to – but Princess Lichnowsky's voice reached him instead. 'So wonderful, dear Ludwig. So utterly wonderful. How do you do it? You are a genius. I have always known it.'

'Come, my dear,' said the Prince, who had materialised by her side. 'We must not bother our young friend. Sit down and let me give you a glass of wine.'

As they moved away, Ludwig saw Bridgetower standing behind the Countess, his arms round her, still holding his instrument. He felt blood rush through him – and with it revulsion – at the spectacle. He glanced at the Lichnowskys, but they had moved to the sideboard where a servant was filling their glasses.

'You hold it so,' Bridgetower said. Ludwig saw that he was

pressing his body against the Countess and as his left hand brought up the violin to her chin, his right hand, swinging the bow, brushed blatantly against her breast.

She emitted a small squeal and her cheeks reddened but she made no attempt to move away.

'Do you see?' said Bridgetower, more as a statement than a question. 'You must involve your whole body in playing on this beautiful instrument, not just your hands. Your whole body.'

With the violin under the Countess's chin, he began to play, his own chin resting on the Countess's shoulder. As he played he whispered something in her ear. This time her squeal was louder and Ludwig caught the shocked look in her eye. He stood up. The Countess returned to her chair as swiftly as her swollen feet would allow, but Bridgetower came up to him. 'Sir,' he said, 'you are a genius, and I a mere humble practitioner. I bow before you.'

Ludwig found himself looking at the top of the man's head.

The Countess was still flushed, but smiling. 'Mr Bridgetower is right, Ludwig. He can only play what you have composed. And what you compose is the work of a genius.'

Chapter 4

Double-stopping. That was the clue Bridgetower had given him.

Ferdinand Ries came to see Ludwig and gave him the welcome news that Schuppanzigh had put back the concert by two days, to 24 May. That was five days from now. Bridgetower, Ries explained, was worried. He had sent Ries with a message. 'Sir. Herr Ludwig. Mr Bridgetower says that if you have no objection, he asks most humbly if, as you complete each page, you might give it to me so that I can pass it on for him to begin work on. If that is all right, sir.'

Ludwig sighed. 'Ferdi, tell Mr Brischdauer he will have to wait. I cannot work like that. A page at a time. Ridiculous. He will have time to rehearse. Tell him I guarantee it.' He looked up at Ries and his smile had a touch of mischief is it. 'Look, Ferdi. Come to the piano. Now listen.' He played a chord of A major. Four notes, two in the left hand, two in the right. 'Now. Still A major.' With his right hand alone, he played a sequence of descending chords, ending with three three-note chords, tailing off in a quaver. 'There. The four-bar opening to the sonata.'

'And then the violin enters?' asked Ries.

'No, Ries, damn you. Can you not see what I am getting at? Listen.'

Ludwig played the sequence again and gazed up at Ries, who looked mystified. He evidently hoped his master would speak first.

Ludwig's face relaxed. 'That, Ferdi, is the violin introduction. Solo. No piano.'

'But, Herr Ludwig, how can the violin play . . . ? There are so many notes. I don't —'

'Double-stopping, Ferdi. Double-stopping.' He played the opening A major chord. 'Double-stopping on all four strings.

Two and then two. But no pause. Together. A full chord crossing all four strings.'

'To – to open the piece?'

'To open it, Ferdi. The first notes.'

'Sir. Herr Ludwig. With your permission, may I give just those four bars to Mr Bridgetower. I am sure he will want to practise them.'

Ludwig laughed. 'Yes, Ferdi. Here. Take them. Tell him to practise. And tell him to observe my markings. *Forte* for the first chord. Then immediately *piano*. Immediately, d'you hear?'

Ries nodded unhappily.

Unlike his earlier attempt at writing the sonata, Ludwig found that this time the music flowed. He knew what he was trying to achieve. The key to it, he realised, was that the final movement was already written. He had even heard it played. He knew now where the first movements were heading.

Yet despite his concentration on the sonata, his mind kept straying to the symphony he would write next. It was as if he was preparing himself for the massive task that lay ahead. But why such huge undertakings now? His largest sonata for violin and piano, to be followed by a symphony that he knew already would bear no resemblance to the two earlier ones. Why? He could not answer his own question.

The last movement of the sonata was written. That is why I am able to compose the first two, he thought. It will be the same with my symphony. I will compose the final movement first so that the other movements will lead to it. And I know already how I will begin it, he thought. He remembered the bemused faces of Andreas and Nanette Streicher. Everyone will be bemused, he thought. Let them be!

A weak sun rose to the east, beyond the Hungarian plain, as the two men crossed the Augarten bridge over the Danube Arm, the canal that had been diverted from the main river to run across the northern side of the city. Ries carried a bundle of manuscript papers under his right arm, his left hand clutching them for added protection.

'I came here, to the Augarten, soon after I first came to Vienna, Ferdi. I had heard in Bonn about the morning concerts, but I did not believe it. Mozart himself played here. Gluck. Christoph Gluck. That was the music I heard as I crossed this bridge all those years ago. From his opera *Alceste*.'

They continued towards the ornamental gate, the entrance to the park, with its round embossed shield bearing the late Emperor Joseph's message to his people: 'To All Men This Place Is Dedicated By Their Protector.'

Down the Lindenallee they walked, under the arch of the trees that had been trained to meet high above the path. The smell of spring, soon to yield to summer, was in the air.

'I am going to get away again this summer, Ferdi. I need to. I cannot stay in the city. The heat and dust and noise . . .'

'Where to, Herr Ludwig? Heiligenstadt again? But you stayed in Mödling one year, didn't you?'

'I composed the symphony in C there. No, somewhere different this time. Döbling, maybe. It's nearer than Heiligenstadt, but still well away from the city. Will you look into it for me?'

'Of course, sir,' said Ries.

'The new symphony, Ferdi. I'm ready to begin it.'

'Good, sir. First, though, if I might be bold, there is the little matter of this concert. Look at the people!'

Ludwig felt a twist in his gut. He was grateful for the cool of the morning air against his face, which was suddenly hot. He laid a restraining hand on Ries's arm and stood still for a moment. 'Stay close to me. In case I can't hear what people are saying.'

They approached the Augarten pavilion, the low, wide building that had taken the place of the old Imperial summer palace destroyed by Turkish invaders a century before. There must have been a hundred or more people milling around, most standing, but others sitting at round tables covered in starched linen cloths. Steaming cups of coffee sat on the tables or were held in gloved hands. The men were dressed formally, in city suits or military uniforms. The women wore the latest summer fashions from Paris: the warm weather had provided their first chance to show them off.

Ries and Ludwig walked into the pavilion, where there was only one topic of conversation: exactly a week before, Britain had declared war on France, seizing all French ships in British ports. In retaliation Napoleon ordered the arrest of all British residents in France. There was a strong rumour that he was considering invading England.

Ludwig felt Ries's arm on his. The young man directed his attention to a group standing near the front of the room, engaged in earnest talk. He saw Prince Lichnowsky, Prince Lobkowitz and George Bridgetower with them. There were two others, one whom Ludwig recognised but whose name he could not recall. 'Who are the two tall men?' he asked Ries.

'The one on the left is the Russian ambassador, Count Razumovsky. I don't know who the other is.'

'Ah, yes.' Razumovsky had been at Ludwig's first public performance in Vienna, at the Burgtheater at least eight years ago. Ludwig remembered his wavy hair, parted in the middle in the Russian style, and the two jewel-encrusted stars he wore on his left breast as symbols of his ambassadorship.

'He was recalled for a short while in the late nineties,' Ries whispered directly into Ludwig's ear, 'probably because he was spending too much of the Tsar's money, but he's been reappointed.'

Lichnowsky caught Ludwig's eye and beckoned him and Ries over. 'My dear Ludwig,' said the Prince, 'what a splendid gathering.'

Lobkowitz struck the floor a couple of times with his crutch and nodded conspiratorially at Ludwig. It was evident that he had not forgotten their agreement that the new symphony would be performed in his new concert room.

Razumovsky bowed low, sweeping his hand across his body. 'My dear sir,' he said to Ludwig, 'if you remember me I shall consider myself honoured for life. I was one of those fortunate individuals who witnessed your concert at the Burgtheater many years ago. The impression your divine music made upon me lives with me still.'

'Your Excellency,' said Ludwig, with a nod. 'I do remember you, sir. Thank you for your kind words.'

'And also,' Lichnowsky continued, 'may I present His Excellency the Honourable Arthur Paget, British ambassador, representative of His Majesty King George?'

'Sir,' said a tall man, with straight silver hair, in an abrupt, clipped voice, 'Mr Bridgetower has told me about you. Most honoured. Mr Bridgetower is in the employ of His Royal Highness the Prince of Wales, son of His Majesty King George, and has asked me to express his pleasure to you all, for the welcome he has received in the Imperial capital.'

'Damned rotten business, this war, eh?' said Lobkowitz.

'His Majesty's government had no choice,' the ambassador

replied. 'Bonaparte has violated the terms of Amiens, leaving us no alternative.'

Ludwig looked at Bridgetower, who had been trying to catch his eye. Bridgetower motioned him aside and Ludwig moved away from the group. 'So, Brischdauer, are you prepared?'

He understood the look on Bridgetower's face even before he heard the words. 'Herr Beethoven, it is not going to be easy. I have rehearsed only the final movement, and the ink is barely dry on the other two. That would not matter if you had written an ordinary piece, but you have called for extraordinary virtuosity. Also, your writing is not the easiest to read.'

'Hah! Egyptian hieroglyphics, eh, Brischdauer? We will see what you make of them.'

Ignaz Schuppanzigh came hurrying over. 'Ludwig, George. Are you ready?'

Bridgetower said, with a pained look, 'Schuppanzigh, my country has just declared war on France. I would rather be in the front line with the Household Cavalry than here in the Augarten pavilion this morning.'

'You will be wonderful, George. Just open those huge eyes of yours and the ladies will all faint before you have played a note.'

'Come on,' said Ludwig, with an edge of irritation. 'What is first?'

'I am playing a Mozart quartet,' said Schuppanzigh, 'followed by a Haydn quartet. Then, after the interval, is your new sonata from Mr Bridgetower.'

'Come, Brischdauer. Let them begin. You and I will go outside and I will take you through the first two movements.'

'Excellent.'

Schuppanzigh nodded approval. 'I will not expect to see you until the interval.'

Ludwig and Bridgetower went outside, followed by Ries. The tables were empty now as the audience was taking its seats; servants were clearing away cups and plates and shaking the linen cloths. They sat down and Ries spread the folder he had been carrying on the table. 'The variations, Mr Bridgetower. The violin part,' he said. 'I . . . I've . . .' he shot a look at Ludwig, 'I've clarified a number of points. Where Herr Beethoven's . . . his writing . . . See here. The accidentals . . .'

Ludwig sat back and let the spring air bathe his face. He was in a better mood than he had expected. He had heard conversations satisfactorily. He was about to perform a new composition. He did not doubt that Bridgetower would be up to it. He watched as the Englishman played an imaginary fingerboard with his left hand, humming as he did so. Really, thought Ludwig, he is an arrogant man, with an insolence towards women that should not be tolerated. But he is a fine musician, and I have given him a piece that will stretch his talents to the full.

'Yes, I see. And the piano? What does it play here, while the violin rests?'

Ludwig leaned forward. 'Even I do not know the answer to that,' he said, and laughed.

'My part contains even more Egyptian hieroglyphics than yours.'

Ries gestured politely to his master not to make any noise. The sound of the Mozart quartet was wafting out of the pavilion on the still, warm morning air. He said timorously to Bridgetower, 'Herr Beethoven will be playing just from sketches. He has no manuscript.'

Bridgetower looked expressionlessly at Beethoven. Ludwig suppressed laughter. 'Hah! Brischdauer. We will test your virtuosity this morning. The double-stopping. Have you practised it?'

The violinist raised his eyebrows. 'Not double-stopping, Herr Beethoven. Double double-stopping. Alone, and right at the start. Was that necessary, sir?'

Ludwig felt a little guilty but was enjoying Bridgetower's discomfiture. The man was so at ease in all other situations that it was good to see him nonplussed for once.

'It was. And I expect you to carry it off to my satisfaction, and the audience's.'

'Herr Beethoven, I am used to performing before royalty. I have performed at the Assembly Rooms in the city of Bath, at Westminster Abbey and at the Drury Lane Theatre. The reception accorded to me has never been less than rapturous. It will be the same this morning.' He and Ries returned to the manuscript.

Ludwig leaned back in his chair and let his eyes wander up to the leaves of the linden trees high above the path. The sun was beginning to filter through them and with it the promise of summer. Away from Vienna, I will compose my new symphony. He could hear the sounds in his head. The four notes and the theme, that soaring theme.

He was startled out of his reverie by the sound of feet crunching on the gravel. Ries was talking to him. 'Sir, Herr Ludwig . . . The quartets are finished. There is an interval now. Half an hour, I think. Perhaps you and Mr Bridgetower . . .'

He felt a hand on his shoulder. It was Nikolaus Zmeskall.

'Hah, Nikola! Famed cellist. Renowned Muckcart Driver!' Then spotted the boy standing at Zmeskall's side and his conscience pricked. 'Czerny. Yes, we must have lessons. Ries will arrange it. I'm busy. Going away for the summer. Ferdi, will you give this boy lessons? Of course you will.'

'Mr Bridgetower.' Zmeskall bowed to the violinist.

'Come now, Herr Beethoven,' Bridgetower said, 'let us go inside. It is time for us to confront the enemy.'

Ludwig stood up and Ries gathered up the manuscripts.

As they entered the pavilion Ludwig caught sight of Stephan von Breuning, wiping his brow. Ignaz Gleichenstein was with him. 'Ludwig. I was afraid we would be too late. Our carriage let us down. You have not played the sonata yet?'

Ludwig shook his head. 'I'm glad to see you, Steffen. You have not brought my brother with you, I hope?'

Stephan smiled. 'No. He sends his apologies. He was required in the Exchequer Office. But may I introduce a new friend. Ignaz Gleichenstein. From Freiburg. A Rhinelander, like us.'

Ludwig looked at the young man. He was clean cut, with an open, ready smile that Ludwig liked immediately.

'A cellist,' said Stephan, 'like our friend Zmeskall.'

'Good,' said Ludwig, and added to the newcomer, 'We must play together.'

'No, no, sir. Herr Breuning does me too much credit. I am a civil servant by profession. My skills as a musician are sadly wanting, though not my enthusiasm. But may I say, sir, your fame has spread to the Upper Rhineland. I cannot tell you how privileged I am to meet you.'

Stephan's eyes flickered round the room. 'Quite a gathering. I hear the British and Russian ambassadors are here. The British, no doubt, are trying to persuade the Russians to join them in the fight against the French. They will be trying to persuade us too. But there is no stomach here for more war.'

'The war, sir,' Bridgetower said, 'is about to take place in this very room. Your friend the composer has not made my task simple.'

Ludwig's eye was caught by a wave from the front row of

seats: Countess Erdödy. He watched Bridgetower walk towards her and bring her hand to his lips. Once again, revulsion swept over him. At that moment, the Countess saw him, pulled her hand away from Bridgetower and held out her arms to him.

Ludwig went to her. 'Countess, I'm pleased to see you.' He could almost feel the resentment smouldering in Bridgetower.

'Dear Ludwig. Oh, dear Ludwig, how I am looking forward to hearing your new piece. You will forgive me for not coming to seek you out earlier, won't you? My poor feet.'

Ludwig inclined his head and felt Bridgetower's tug on his sleeve. 'Countess, if you'll forgive me.'

Ludwig saw Ries arranging the violin part on the stand. He crossed to the piano and sat down. Ries hurried over and put the piano part – which consisted of jottings and reminders – before him.

'Sir,' said Ries, tremulously, 'should I turn for you?'

Ludwig waved him away. 'No. Go, Ries. I do not need help.' He spoke more sharply than he had intended, but he did not want Ries's over-zealous attention.

Ludwig looked up at Bridgetower, who had, in effect, begun his performance. He brought out a red silk handkerchief from his top pocket, flapped it ostentatiously in the air and laid it on his left shoulder. With a wide sweep of the arm he placed the violin under his chin, nestling it until it was comfortable. Then he removed it again, took a step forward and bowed low to the audience.

Ludwig knew this charade should annoy him. Music was not about making the audience fall in love with you. But he envied the ease with which Bridgetower was manipulating the audience. He was marshalling their support before he had played a note. Was there anything wrong with that? No, Ludwig thought. As long as your performance measures up to expectations.

Ludwig saw Bridgetower take a step towards him, motioning him to stand. He could see the audience applauding enthusiastically. Reluctantly he got up. Bridgetower clasped his shoulders. He waited for the audience to be silent, then said, 'Your Excellencies, my lords, ladies and gentlemen, I am fortunate to enjoy two distinct privileges today. The first is to display my humble talents before such an illustrious gathering. The second is to perform with the great Herr Beethoven, whose fame is firmly established in the great city of London.'

More applause. Ludwig felt Bridgetower turn towards him and could see that the audience's eyes were on him. He bowed his head and the applause intensified. Bridgetower had laid down his violin and bow and was clapping too.

The emotion welled in Ludwig. He had not expected this. The audience and the soloist were acknowledging him as the composer of the music they were about to hear. Not as pianist or performer, but as composer. And they had been encouraged to do this by the man whom he had expected to take all the adulation, all the glory.

He took Bridgetower's outstretched hand and shook it warmly. Then he sat down again at the piano and nodded to Bridgetower that he was ready. He watched Bridgetower perform the elaborate ceremony of placing his violin under his chin, then raise his bow in a wide arc, as if commanding the audience to be still.

In that moment of quiet, Ludwig braced himself to hear those opening four bars of double-stopping. Double double-stopping.

There they were, as Ludwig had never heard them. The opening chord across all four strings. All the drama, the urgency, yet ending in a question, a tailing-off almost. Bridgetower played to perfection, dropping immediately from the *forte* opening to *piano*, as Ludwig had written.

Ludwig played the piano response, a four-bar answer to the question; then the piano and violin dialogue, before the sudden and unexpected shift to the minor key and the beginning of the central section, the Presto. In the eighteenth bar, Bridgetower paused to allow Ludwig to play the huge piano flourish – no fewer than thirty-six notes in the space of a single bar – ending on a sustained low C. Almost a tiny *cadenza* for piano.

The two instruments played on to the end of the first part of the Presto, where Ludwig had written two dots, signifying a repeat. Looking at each other to co-ordinate their entry, he and Bridgetower began the Presto again. In the eighteenth bar Bridgetower again paused to allow Ludwig to play the piano flourish. This time, though, instead of continuing to the passage marked *A tempo*, Bridgetower shot Ludwig a mischievous look – and imitated the semiquaver flourish across all four strings, up to high E and ending on low C, just as Ludwig had. A *cadenza*, this time, for violin – which Ludwig had not written.

Ludwig jumped up from the piano, his arms held out wide.

There was a collective intake of breath from the audience, who were unaware that Bridgetower had departed from the music. On Bridgetower's face the smile of achievement froze.

'Brischdauer! Brischdauer!' Ludwig said excitedly. 'Excellent! Again! Again!' He sat down again, looked at Bridgetower, brought down his head and they began the Presto again. At the eighteenth bar, Ludwig played the piano flourish. After the sustained C, he played a full chord of C major, holding the pedal open. Bridgetower again imitated the flourish, this time adding four additional notes high up on the E string, taking him a whole octave higher than on the first run, so that his fingers were pressed together, almost off the fingerboard and on the bare string. With a flourish he crossed all four strings and ended on the sustained C on the G string.

Again Ludwig leaped from his stool and applauded. The audience took their cue from him. Bridgetower, his face suffused with excitement, made a courtly bow to the audience, and another to Ludwig.

Ludwig sat again and looked at Bridgetower, who played the crotchet E to dotted minim F which began the A tempo. They continued the huge first movement, playing faultlessly, as if they had rehearsed together for weeks past.

The second movement, the Theme and Variations – four variations, as Ludwig had intended – was the perfect contrast to the lively first movement. Bridgetower, reading from the manuscript in Ludwig's own hand, seemed to have an instinctive grasp of the composer's ideas. The trill passages of the first variation he played with a lightness of touch that astounded Ludwig. Again, it was lightness that characterised the *perpetuum mobile* demi-semiquavers of the second variation, Bridgetower obeying every slur and staccato point. Ludwig's shoulders swayed with the *legato* of the third. And in the final variation, Bridgetower allowed the piano to dominate, just as Ludwig had wanted, ending not with a *forte* flourish to impress the audience, but a *piano decrescendo* as Ludwig had written.

Ludwig was unprepared, in the stillness that followed the final F, low down in the bass of the piano and high up on the violin's E string, for the eruption. At first the noise startled him. Then he saw their hands. They were applauding the Theme and Variations, with its quiet ending! And what was that extra sound that made him half close his eyes to ease the pain in his ears?

'Encore! Encore!'

He turned to Bridgetower, whose eyes were on him, brows raised questioningly. He nodded. They waited a few moments for the audience to subside, then Ludwig played again the solo piano opening, the eight-bar statement of the theme.

As he played, he closed his eyes and let it revolve in his mind as he played the variations. Such a simple theme, a melody really. Nothing more. Just as Mozart had told him. Simple themes, always simple themes. He heard Bridgetower's notes coming pure and clean from his violin, almost like a nightingale singing, every note perfectly pitched. Can my music ever be as pure as the music of nature? he wondered. I can try. I can only try.

This time Ludwig winced as the harsh sound of the renewed applause swept over him. Could they really be demanding a second *encore*, a third performance of the Theme and Variations?

He looked at Bridgetower again and saw his expectant smile. He was tempted to vary the opening, the first statement of the theme but he decided not to. This was not the time for improvisation: the audience wanted to hear the movement again and enjoy Bridgetower's virtuosity. He played the opening again, this time giving the second beat of the first two bars just a touch more emphasis – *sforzando* off the beat.

He could hear Bridgetower's violin so clearly, that pure tone which became even purer as he moved higher and higher up the E string. When he composed the movement Ludwig had wondered whether to end the second variation so high – F, two octaves above the E of the E string. He could easily have ended it an octave lower, but now, as he saw Bridgetower's little finger moving nearer and nearer to the instrument's bridge and heard the sheer purity of the sound, he was pleased with his decision.

At the end of the fourth variation, Ludwig barely paused before sounding the sustained chord of A major which ushered in the final movement.

Bridgetower, to Ludwig's delight, set a swift pace with the staccato crotchets and quavers, which Ludwig matched at his entry a bar later.

Ludwig swayed with the music and his shoulders hunched over the keys. On the music ran, the two instruments seeming at times to be chasing each other with the crotchet-quaver rhythm. When it reached the final note, a single A crotchet on the G string from the violin, a single A in the treble and bass for the piano, the audience exploded.

Ludwig looked at Bridgetower, who was already bowing low. After a few moments the violinist turned to him, his arms outstretched. Ludwig stood up and moved towards him. He heard the applause increase and the shouts that accompanied it. His head began to throb. It was the effect of standing, and the sweet sound of the music being replaced by the applause and the shouting. Even so, he could not suppress a smile. Bridgetower was smiling too, and it seemed that so was every face in the audience. The performance was a triumph.

Ludwig felt a surge of joy. The violin sonata was the major work he had intended it to be. He had composed it – the final movement excepted – so swiftly and he knew why: he had been preparing himself for the new symphony. Now he was ready.

He braced himself as he saw familiar faces moving towards him.

Prince Razumovsky gave a celebratory dinner that evening at his embassy on the Johannesgasse. Ludwig was in ebullient mood, enjoying the excellent French wine the Russian ambassador received regularly from Bordeaux.

Razumovsky informed the gathering that he was about to begin negotiating with the Hofburg to purchase a piece of land in the Landstrasse suburb to build a new Russian embassy. 'A palace in honour of our new young tsar, God bless His Majesty,' he said. 'And, Herr Beethoven, you may rest assured I shall ask you to compose a piece of music to mark the occasion.' There was a chorus of approval.

With a glance at his master, Ries put in helpfully, 'Herr Schikaneder has commissioned an opera, Your Excellency. And I know Herr Beethoven is soon to begin work on a new symphony. He will not be able to start yet.'

'Of course,' said the Prince. 'I understand perfectly. But don't forget.'

Ludwig inclined his head in agreement, losing the frown that the mention of Schikaneder's opera had brought to his face. He took a sip of wine and called for silence.

'Brischdauer, do you have the sonata with you? The manuscript?'

'In my violin case, Herr Beethoven.'

'Bring me the top sheet.'

Bridgetower went to his violin case, which was resting on a small sofa, and opened the lid, which bulged inside with papers and documents, some of which fell on to the violin. He found the top sheet of the sonata and handed it to Ludwig, who asked Ries for a quill, which Ries provided, first dipping it in ink.

Ludwig wrote across the opening bars – the violin introduction with its double double-stopping:

Mulattick Sonata. Composed for Brischdauer, great mulattick and lunatick composer.

Chapter 5

In the days following the Augarten concert Ludwig's mood changed. He tried to fight off the depression that weighed him down, but could not. Sensing the change, Countess Erdödy invited him to spend a few days at her estate at Jedlesee, on the far bank of the Danube. He did not want to go, but felt unable to refuse. He was pleased at least to be outside the city, and enjoyed sitting in the arbour in the garden with its fine view of the river.

On the afternoon before he was due to return to the city he saw the Countess approaching along the path that ran round the garden. Pity rose in Ludwig at the sight of her stiff, ungainly walk, and he could see that although her face was taut she seemed filled with a nervous energy.

'I must not distract you, Ludwig. I know how you concentrate on your music.'

'I am grateful to you, Countess. It has been restful for me here. I am ready to return.'

'Are you feeling better?'

'It is as if everything is too much. I want to start work on my new symphony, but I feel overwhelmed. So many ideas.'

'And your hearing? May I ask?'

Ludwig shrugged. 'Here it is fine. In the calm and quiet. But I am worried about what will happen when I return to the city.'

'You should see Doktor Schmidt again. Let him advise you.'

Ludwig said nothing. He looked at the Countess and saw pain in her face. 'What is the matter, Countess? Are you unwell?'

'No, no. It is nothing. Really nothing.' She wrung her hands and tears welled in her eyes. She looked away quickly.

Ludwig did not know what to do. He wanted to reach over and put his hand on hers, but it might embarrass her. He was fond of the Countess, and he knew she admired him, but their relationship was formal and he was determined – as he was sure she was – that it should not move beyond that.

'What has happened?'

Countess Erdödy dabbed at her nose with a small handkerchief. 'Really it is nothing,' she said, forcing a smile. 'I am behaving like an immature girl.'

'Will you tell me?'

'Oh, it is only that silly man, Mr Bridgetower. He did not behave properly. I was at my apartment in the city yesterday. He knows my husband is at our estate in Hungary. He tried . . . he wanted . . . I had to push him away. He became angry and insulted me.'

Ludwig caught his breath. 'Brischdauer? The Englishman? He did that? Damned scoundrel. He will hear some words from me.'

'No, no,' she said. Her hand flew to his arm but she withdrew it quickly. 'I should not have said anything. It was really nothing. He leaves soon anyway.'

On his return to the city Ludwig went to see Doktor Schmidt.

'Do not worry, Ludwig. Such a mood is to be expected. After the great triumph of your performance at the Augarten, it is natural for you to feel a little low.'

'Why?'

Schmidt smiled. 'Often if a person experiences a sudden extreme success, it is followed by the reverse. That is all that is happening to you. It will pass. Now tell me about the hearing. Any change?'

Ludwig shook his head. 'Worse, maybe. I can't tell.'

'Forgive me for stating the obvious, Ludwig, but you have no difficulty in hearing me now.'

Ludwig said, wearily, 'That is because we are alone in a room and you are talking directly to me. I've said that to you before. But if I am in company, or if I have been playing music . . .'

Schmidt crossed to a table on which various instruments lay. 'Let's see, then.' He picked up two tuning forks, one larger than the other, and walked back to Ludwig. 'Now. As I did before. First this larger one, with the lower note.'

Schmidt rapped the fork against his knee and held it to Ludwig's right ear. 'Better here . . . or here?' He pressed it against the back of Ludwig's head, behind his ear. 'Here . . . or here,' he said, repeating the procedure.

'I don't know. It's different. The second time it's in my head. Not louder, but clearer, somehow.'

Schmidt said nothing. He picked up the smaller instrument, rapped it and held it close to Ludwig's ear. Ludwig winced. Schmidt pressed it to the back of his head. 'Better there,' said Ludwig. 'Much better. It hurts outside my ear. But in my head . . .'

Schmidt repeated the procedure with Ludwig's left ear. His reactions were the same.

Ludwig watched Schmidt lay down the turning forks and return to his chair. He looked keenly at the doctor's face but it remained impassive. Finally Schmidt spoke. Ludwig noted immediately that he enunciated his words a fraction more carefully, just as his friends did. 'It appears you hear as well in your head as through your ears,' Schmidt said.

'I could have told you that without all your nonsense with the forks,' Ludwig growled. 'When I play the piano I hear the music in my head, feel it in my body, more than through my ears. What does it mean?'

'That the nerves that allow you to hear are more highly developed than in most people. That would be normal for a musician. But . . .' The doctor's voice trailed away.

'But what does it mean for my hearing?'

'That there has been a loss.'

'I know that.'

'Yes,' retorted Schmidt sharply. 'But medically . . . Have you stopped using the almond oil?'

'Yes. All it did was make a mess of my clothes. Or my pillow. And it looked so unpleasant that it made people treat me like – like –'

Schmidt leaned forward. 'Ludwig,' he said earnestly, 'have you ever noticed any discharge from your ears? I mean, have you ever woken up in the morning and found, say, wax on your pillow? Or have you ever felt any trickle from your ear during the day?'

Ludwig said he had not. Schmidt went on, 'I am beginning to believe your deafness – your hearing problem, rather, it is not as bad as deafness and never will be – may not be due to earwax.'

'I've always known it wasn't,' Ludwig said irritably. 'So what is it? And can you cure it?'

'Ludwig, the worst thing a doctor can say to a patient is that he doesn't know the cause of their illness. A diagnosis is what a patient always wants to hear. I have colleagues who will always give a diagnosis, even when they do not believe it themselves. Anything, rather than admit they do not know.'

'You do not know, do you?'

'No, my friend, I do not.'

'I told Ries to find me somewhere in Döbling. Why has he not done it yet? Damned boy! Sometimes I wonder if his brain is fully formed.'

Zmeskall took off his spectacles and polished them with a handkerchief. Ludwig gazed at the deep groove the heavy lenses had left across the bridge of his friend's nose.

'Harsh words, my friend. And not entirely fair. He –'

Ludwig knew he was allowing his dark mood to get the better of him, but he did not want to control it and knew, anyway, that he could not. He needed an outlet for his tension. 'Look at this place, Zmeskall. It is a prison. Fine view – straight into the courtyard. I cannot bear it, even with Carl gone. He did not leave a moment too soon. If he had not left, I would have had to throw him out.'

'Ludwig, my friend. You live rent-free, in a theatre. A place of art. You should be pleased.'

'Bah!' Ludwig went over to the table and filled two glasses with wine from the carafe that stood there. He handed one to Zmeskall, and took a gulp from his own. 'Nikola, Schmidt says he can do nothing for my hearing. And he is a fine doctor. I respect him. When he does not know, he says so.'

'But what does he say will happen to it? Will it get worse? Or better?'

'He does not know. But he has told me not to expect any improvement.'

Zmeskall said, reassuringly, 'Ludwig, I'm sure you don't need –'

'No!' Ludwig snapped. 'Always people tell me not to worry. It will be all right. You. Nanette Streicher. Friends. Schuppanzigh. But I have always known. Since that day in Heiligenstadt.' He walked to the window. 'Where is Brischdauer?' he said suddenly. 'I need to speak to him.'

'He is at the Blumenstock,' said Zmeskall. 'He leaves the city tomorrow.'

'Come on. We are going there.' Ludwig was already at the door. His head had begun to pound and there was a whistling in his ears. He would teach this so-called virtuoso a lesson for his behaviour towards Countess Erdödy. He would punish him in the one way he knew would hurt. More than a blow, more than words.

The two friends strode up the Kärntnerstrasse and into the Himmelpfortgasse. Ludwig walked slightly ahead of Zmeskall who, he knew, was hurrying to keep up. They turned into the narrow Ballgasse, and the darkness enveloped them.

The light outside the Zum Alten Blumenstock glowed, warm and welcoming. Ludwig stepped aside and allowed Zmeskall to go in first, then he followed. They went into the small back room.

Candles flickered on the table. At first Ludwig could not make out the faces, but he heard the unmistakable voice of Ignaz Schuppanzigh. 'Ludwig. Nikola. What splendid fortune. Come. More wine! And shall we not order more girls too?'

'So, Herr Beethoven,' said a deeper, more resonant voice, 'the genius of Vienna, at whose feet the noble ladies of the city fall but who brushes them away with a flick of the hand. Thus.'

Ludwig saw a hand move out, take some bouncing ringlets, appearing to weigh them, then contemptuously toss them to the side. A girl giggled.

Ludwig felt anger bubble inside him. He had had enough of this man, this so-called virtuoso, this – this – mulatto showman who insulted women. 'Brischdauer, you are a fool and I have nothing but contempt for you. I am going to repay you for your behaviour.'

To his surprise Bridgetower laughed good-naturedly. 'Come now, Beethoven, do not be so serious. So stern. Life is to be enjoyed. Look. See how I enjoy myself. See what my talents allow me to enjoy.'

His eyes now accustomed to the candlelight, Ludwig saw that Bridgetower, sitting with his back to the side wall, had each arm around a girl. He could make out their faces clearly now. They were young and pretty, with tumbling hair and heavily rouged lips. Both wore loose-fitting, low-cut dresses. As he spoke, Bridgetower turned to one and kissed her full on the lips, his hand reaching down into her dress for her breast.

Ludwig felt heat flow through him, but with it came a wave of rage.

Zmeskall pressed a glass of wine into his hand and he drank it quickly. 'Relax, Ludwig. No anger tonight.'

'Brischdauer, you have insulted a lady. That is not to be forgiven.'

'Hah! A lady. You are not a lady, my dear, are you?' Bridgetower said to one of the girls, who tittered.

'Brischdauer, you behaved badly to Countess Erdödy. You insulted her.' He was pleased to see a sudden change in the man's expression.

'What did you say? How did you –'

Zmeskall's hand was on Ludwig's arm and he heard Schuppanzigh say something. Both were trying to calm him, he knew that.

'Erdödy,' said Bridgetower, contempt in his voice. 'Let me show you the Countess Erdödy. Go, both of you, let me out.' The two girls scurried away and Bridgetower manoeuvred himself from behind the table. He stood in the middle of the small room. 'The Countess Erdödy,' he said, and waved both arms in the air. He turned to Ludwig and walked the four or five steps towards him, his ankles stiff and his knees unbending. Just before reaching Ludwig, he half fell, saving himself by clasping the edge of the table. Laughing uproariously he returned to his seat and quaffed more wine.

Ludwig felt calm. He drank his wine too. If before he had had the slightest shred of doubt at the Countess's story he now knew that it was true. The man was beneath contempt and deserved to be punished.

Schuppanzigh spoke in a cheery voice, attempting to lighten the atmosphere. 'Do you leave tomorrow, Mr Bridgetower? We shall miss you.'

'Yes. Tomorrow. With my violin and my bags packed, and in my bag a certain piece of music. A sonata for violin composed exclusively for me and dedicated to me by our friend who now sits opposite. The Bridgetower Sonata. Eh, Beethoven?'

Ludwig paused. All three men were looking at him, waiting for his response.

'You will return the manuscript to Ries tomorrow. Do you hear?'

Bridgetower's mouth fell open. 'Why?'

'I am going to send it to a real violinist, a true virtuoso. Rudolphe Kreutzer in Paris.'

BOOK THREE

Chapter 1

Ludwig climbed the stone steps to the top of the Bastion. As he emerged into the sunlight from the chill shadow thrown by the great wall a perfectly formed idea came into his mind.

The evening air was warm and sweet with the scents of early summer. Couples strolled arm in arm and children ran about, kicking balls across the broad walkway. Jugglers lined the side walls, magicians beckoned to the children to watch their tricks and puppeteers acted out preposterous plots in small, covered booths.

Tradesmen mingled with the crowd, calling out the price of their wares. On their trays lay freshly baked cakes, marzipan rabbits, toffee apples. Elaborately decorated urns stood on tables along the wall, drops of thick black coffee clinging to their taps.

Occasionally, despite the profusion of sweet aromas that mingled in the air, a slight change in the direction of the evening breeze would bring other city odours – horses' sweating flanks, manure, unwashed clothes.

Ludwig stood by the outer side wall, sipping strong black coffee from a small china cup with no handle, passing it from one hand to the other so as not to burn himself. He looked out across the roof tops towards the Vienna Woods. So many roofs, all sloping the same way, all neatly arranged, as if they had come from a child's toy box and been laid out according to a set of instructions. He drained the cup, tossed a couple of coins on the table, and walked on. He unbuttoned his coat and untied the top of his shirt, enjoying the coolness of the air on his skin. He caught the occasional disapproving glance: the Bastion promenade was the province of the city's upper class and a certain decorum was expected among its users.

He untied his shirt a little more, opened it and scratched his chest. What an absurd city this was! So many rules and customs

to be obeyed, so many classes and divisions of human beings.
And it was so wrong, so unnatural, so against the order of things.
He thought again of Paris and the man who recognised that a
new century had begun, and with it a new era. A man who
knew that the conventions and formalities which elevated some
people above others belonged to a past age.

A small crowd was gathering to watch a side show and Ludwig
joined it. There was the man – the great man – portrayed as
an absurd puppet with a revolutionary beret on his head, the
circular tricolour pinned to its side. 'Napoleon! Napoleon!'
the crowd cried, then booed and hissed. Laughter went up
as a second puppet – a voluptuous dark-skinned woman, her
breasts exposed, the nipples rouged – moved seductively towards
the first.

'Josephine! Josephine!' The cries mingled with more laughter
as both puppets began to speak in strangulated voices.

Ludwig could not make out the words: it was as if the
puppeteer had a device in his mouth to distort them. On top of
that he was speaking in a Viennese dialect with a French accent.
I hear the words yet I do not understand them, he thought. I do
not dress like these people; I do not follow their conventions.
And I admire the man you are so cruelly misrepresenting.

Briefly he considered arguing with them. Should I shout out
and tell them they are wrong? That this man belongs to the new
century, and they are all living in the past?

He knew he would not. His accent would mark him straight
away as an outsider. He would be one against many, and what
if someone became abusive towards him? And he knew that if
he became agitated the noises would start: he would not be able
to hear properly.

With disgust he watched the Napoleon puppet turn to the
audience, say something that caused yet more laughter, then
reach up, take off his beret and hurl it away. There were cries
of delight as the puppeteer misjudged the movement and the
tiny hat fell over the front of the small stage to the ground. A
young man lunged forward and picked it up.

Now Napoleon bounded towards his wife, shot a quick look
at the audience then, in a flash, disappeared under her dress.
The shrieks of mirth hurt Ludwig's ears and he put his hands
to them. Josephine staggered to maintain her balance, falling
this way, then that. At last she stood stock still. There was no
movement under her dress. The audience was silent. Slowly

Napoleon emerged from under her skirt, first his dangling legs, then his body, and finally his head.

The puppeteer whipped his hand upright and the crowd jeered as Napoleon stood, a crown on his head.

No, Ludwig, wanted to say. You are wrong. Do you not see? This is a man of the people. A son of the Revolution. You believe he will crown himself emperor. But you are wrong.

A cheer went up as a new puppet stood where Josephine had been. It was an Austrian hussar, resplendent in his uniform and tall braided hat. He was broad-shouldered, with firm fine features. He turned to confront the French emperor. Napoleon cowered, retreated, then rushed at him. The soldier did not move. Napoleon bounced off him, flying high and landing on his back. A cheer went up. Napoleon charged again. The soldier stood impassively, his gaze turned on the audience. Again Napoleon bounced off and landed on his back. The crowd cheered again. Napoleon moved this way and that, unsure what to do next. The hussar moved across the little stage. Deftly he snatched the crown off Napoleon's head and flung it into the audience. There were cheers as another spectator dived forward and retrieved it. Then the hussar leaned back and, with an almighty kick, sent the humiliated emperor flying up in the air and off the stage. Now he stood alone and bowed at the rejoicing crowd.

Ludwig pushed his way clear of the throng. So stupid, he thought to himself. All these people are so stupid. What he had witnessed only reinforced the decision he had taken. The momentous decision.

He was pleased to find Ries waiting for him outside his rooms at the Theater an der Wien. 'Come in, Ries. Come in. Now, first, have you found somewhere for me for the summer?'

'Gleichenstein has, Herr Ludwig. He knows . . .'

Ludwig lowered his head. The dullness in his ears had become a pounding and with each beat of his heart a wave of pain crashed through his head. He should not have walked so quickly. It had made his skin perspire and his head hurt. But he was angry, angry at the ignorance of everyone in this city. This absurdly outdated city.

'What?' he snapped at Ries. 'Get me a glass of wine. Over there. Hurry, man.'

The wine soothed him slightly. He paused, drank again, then went to the table himself and poured more. He sat down and looked up at Ries's ever eager face. 'Now, start again, Ries. And speak clearly.'

'I'm sorry, Herr Ludwig. I was saying that Gleichenstein has found lodgings for you for the summer.'

'Gleichstein? I didn't ask him to find me lodgings.'

'Herr Ludwig, he is a good friend. I thought . . . I was busy . . . I asked . . .'

Ludwig was amused by the tinge of fear on Ries's face, though it made him feel a little guilty. Such an amenable young man, he thought. Always trying to do the right thing. Always trying so hard not to upset me. So much so that he upsets me *because* he is so amenable.

'I asked you to find me somewhere, Ries. I did not ask you to ask someone else to do it.'

He saw Ries force a smile. 'Gleichenstein knows somebody in Döbling. A vinegar maker. He lets rooms. You said Döbling would be suitable. Close to the city. Only an hour's carriage ride.'

Ludwig nodded. 'Did you send the sonata to Kreutzer?'

'I did. As you asked. Herr Ludwig, please do not think me presumptuous, but is that what you really wish? Should not Mr Bridgetower –'

'Brischdauer! Brischdauer! I do not want to hear the name again! You should hear soon from Kreutzer. Let me know when you do.'

'Yes, Herr Ludwig. I am sure he will –'

'Let me know, d'you hear?' Ludwig refilled his glass again. 'God, this place is dreadful. Dark, miserable. I must get out.'

'Döbling will refresh you, Herr Ludwig,' said Ries, brightly.

'No, Ries. You do not understand. You do not understand at all. I mean Vienna. This damned city, with its black wall making it into a prison. Vienna, Döbling, Heiligenstadt, Grinzing . . . It doesn't matter where. I have had enough of it all.'

Ries was bewildered.

'I have made a decision, Ries. I am leaving Vienna. I am going to live in Paris.'

Ries's face registered shock. 'Paris? *Paris*, Herr Ludwig? But –'

'I have made up my mind. France is leading Europe. It has had its revolution. Other countries – Austria, Britain, Russia – they still have theirs to come. France has an enlightened leader.'

'He is a despot, sir.'

'Bah! You do not know what you are talking about, Ries. He is a man of the people. A hero. A true hero. You are as ignorant as those fools on the Bastion. He is no emperor. He is an ordinary man who will lead his people to greatness.'

Ries's jaw tightened but he said nothing.

'That is why I have decided to dedicate my new symphony to him. A heroic symphony for a hero. Then he will welcome me to Paris. People will already know me through Kreutzer. It is where my future lies, Ries.'

Ludwig grimaced at the sharp smell that pervaded the room.

'Do not worry, sir,' said Herr Nusser. 'We do not boil every day, and I can assure you that if you open the windows on the front you will not smell anything.'

'I need a piano, Nusser. Do you have one?'

A sceptical look settled on Nusser's face. 'Sir, did I understand you correctly? You are asking me, a vinegar maker, if I possess a piano?'

'Can you get one? Just tell me. I do not –'

'No, sir, I cannot,' said Nusser firmly. 'And may I ask how long –'

But Ludwig had turned on his heels and did not hear the rest of the question.

Despite his irritation with Nusser, Ludwig was in buoyant mood. He went into the larger of the front rooms and threw open the window. The sweet fragrant smell of early summer wafted in from the vineyard that ran down to the Krottenbach, the stream whose waters Ludwig could see meandering gently through a natural gorge down towards Heiligenstadt. He wondered if it was the same stream he had walked along so often during his stay in Heiligenstadt the previous summer. That fateful stay, during which he had written his last will and testament.

Before leaving for Döbling he had taken the document from the back of the drawer where it was hidden. He had not read it through – he remembered too well the pain of writing it – but he let his eyes drift over the words. *I am deaf.* There they were, those three small words, so insignificant on the page yet so portentous. And I confronted them and overcame them, he thought. *And I can still hear my music.* Only when I can no longer hear my music, only then . . .

This symphony will decide my life, he thought. Will I hear

the sounds I make on the piano? And, if not, will I hear them in my head? Will I be able to compose, even though I am deaf? If not . . . if not . . .

He strode out of his room into the inner courtyard and under the arch into the vineyard in front of the house. He stood for a moment and breathed in the air. Vinegar! But as he walked between the vines down to the Krottenbach the smell of the earth and leaves around him, wet with recent rain, filtered though his senses. The smells of the countryside. And the sounds. He stopped and listened, furrowing his brow in concentration. Yes. The birds were singing.

And there was the rushing sound in his ears, the sound he had learned to dread as the portent of worse to come. But he smiled as he walked on down the slope, heedless of the mud clinging heavily to his boots: the rushing sound was of water, the Krottenbach. He stood watching it, suddenly fierce and foam-flecked as the natural gorge forced it through the narrow passage, then further downstream, where the high rocks gave way to the sloping bank, resuming its peaceful passage to Heiligenstadt.

When he had taken his will out of the drawer, he had seen another document behind it. He had not noticed it when he had originally put the will there. He took it out and looked at it, puzzled at first. Then he remembered what it was. The _divertimenti_ for wind that Wolfgang Mozart had given him at their one and only meeting all those years before. 'Go back to your lodgings and study them,' the Master had said. He had done as he was told and had found the letter from his father. He had returned to his dying mother in Bonn and had never seen Mozart again.

But just by holding the manuscript in his hands and looking at the notes, Ludwig had felt the spirit of Mozart course through him. So neat. Every note written clearly and without hesitation, as if dictated by God and written by his servant Mozart.

Can I ever . . . ? Yes. He knew he was Mozart's worthy successor, deafness or no deafness. He knew it as surely as if God had appeared before him and told him.

He turned and walked back up to the house. Paris. That was the answer. And it was that fool Bridgetower who had given him the idea. His talk of Kreutzer and Paris had planted the first seeds in Ludwig's mind. A new city, a fresh start. With Kreutzer performing the violin sonata to admiring audiences.

And the First Consul, Napoleon Bonaparte, in gratitude for the dedication to him of the new symphony, would demand to see him and hear him play. And he would perform for him, improvise, demonstrate his virtuosity to the man who was leading his nation into a new era.

But first, he thought, I must compose my new symphony. And I am ready. Absolutely ready. He hummed his *Prometheus* theme, then sang it. So simple, so noble. So heroic.

He sat at the table, pulled a sheet of paper towards him and dashed off a note to Ries, telling him to arrange for a piano to be sent to him from Vienna.

E flat, B flat, B flat, E flat. E flat, B flat, B flat, E flat. Steibelt's upside-down notes. And the theme that soared above them, that had come to him unbidden. La-laaa-la-laaa, la-laaa-la-laaa, la-laa-laa-laaa, la-la-la-la, la-la-la, laaa-la. In the piano variations he had composed in Heiligenstadt he had used them both. The four notes, extended to form a small theme themselves. And then the *Prometheus* motif as the main theme.

Now he would do the same again. He had known that for a long time. They would question it, the musicians and the critics. Why have you used the same notes again? they would ask. Have you nothing new to say?

What did they know? Nothing. They are not the creators, he thought. I am the creator. And I will show them that with just these two themes there is more to be said, so much more. But there would be one major difference between the new symphony and the piano variations. The piano piece opened with the four notes and the *Prometheus* theme. The symphony would close with them. They would form the final movement. The fourth and final movement. And each of the three movements would form part of a natural progression towards them. I will show how even such simple themes as these can be invested with a power and passion no one would have believed possible. And in so doing, he thought, I will prove once again how right Mozart was. Simple themes.

He sat at the piano and played a rush of descending semiquavers covering two octaves. Then great octave chords. A rallying cry, a call to attention. And then what? What momentous statement was about to follow?

He smiled to himself. Nothing great. Nothing momentous. Just Steibelt's four upside-down notes! Only this time they will lead to the staccato quavers and the sustained crotchet, just as they did in the piano variations.

Ludwig scribbled notes on the manuscript paper that lay on the table alongside him. A second set of staccato quavers, repeated in the wind section, and another sustained crotchet.

Ludwig sat back and thought of Mozart. Mozart would now give the audience what it wanted – what he had prepared it for. And so would Haydn. Great composers both, he thought, but . . . predictable. Was that too cruel a word? Conformists, who obeyed the rules. No, I will not think badly of either of them. If they had not obeyed the rules, could Beethoven have broken them?

It was obvious what should follow the final sustained crotchet. He was composing a symphony, a grand symphony, and this was the opening to the last movement. He had created tension by bringing the orchestra to a halt with the sustained crotchet. The rules dictated that the tension should be released. A welter of strings and wind would do it, rushing forward, carrying the audience with it to the end, just as Mozart had in his great last symphony.

Smiling to himself, Ludwig stretched his hands over the keys, then wrote a short section in counterpoint and fugue, based on Steibelt's four notes. He marked them for strings only and to be played *piano*. At the end he scribbled the word 'Repeat'. And now – at last – my *Prometheus* theme, noble and heroic. How shall I introduce it? With a fanfare? A call from the horns? A dramatic pause? A quiver on the strings? A tremolo in the bass? A Steibelt tremolo?

Dolce, piano, he wrote. He did not need to play the theme on the piano. It was in his head, revolving as it had, unbidden, for so long now. Such a sweet theme, so simple, so deceptively simple, yet with such promise. La-laaa-la-laaa, la-laaa-la-laaa.

The strings will assume it is theirs; the wind will not want it because they will be too exposed. Ludwig wrote 'Oboe, clarinet, horn ONLY' at the side of the paper. Let them complain. Let them complain.

The sounds of his music reverberated in his head. He could hear them clearly – but not as he had played them on the piano: as they would sound coming from a full orchestra.

Chapter 2

Emanuel Schikaneder wiped his forehead with a handkerchief and willed himself to stop perspiring. It was the summer heat, made worse by the pungent smell of fruit and vegetables wafting across from the market alongside the Wien river. He felt his stomach straining against the tight fully buttoned waistcoat and wished he could exchange his thick black woollen jacket for something a little lighter. He put two fingers inside his cravat and loosened it, looking enviously at Ignaz Seyfried sitting across the desk from him.

'You have too suspicious a mind, my friend. His motive was straightforward. It was a business arrangement, that was all, and one that has left me, I might say, quite comfortably off.'

Kapellmeister Seyfried, music director of the Theater an der Wien, sat forward with his arms down and his hands clasped between his legs, a position that emphasised his slight build. He surveyed the rotund Schikaneder. 'You may be right. But I urge you to be a little bit cautious.'

Anger flashed through Schikaneder at the reasonableness in Seyfried's voice. 'What do you mean, cautious? How can I be cautious? I am running a theatre. You cannot be a successful manager, and artist as well, by being cautious.'

Seyfried smiled. 'My dear Schikaneder. My friend. Let us not exchange angry words. We both wish the theatre to succeed. There is much at stake for both of us. And I am in no doubt it will succeed. It is only –'

'Only what, Seyfried?'

'Herr Zitterbarth. Can you be absolutely sure? Remember, he is not an artist like you and me. He is a businessman.'

'And a very successful one. How else would he be able to buy all my rights in the theatre for a not inconsiderable sum of money?'

'Quite so. But instead of asking how, have you asked why?'

Schikaneder allowed a small smile to cross his face. He employed the handkerchief again, on his cheeks as well this time, hoping that this did not make him seem nervous. 'You underestimate me, Seyfried. Of course I have asked that question. Indeed, I asked it of Herr Zitterbarth himself. His reply was that, as a businessman, he considered it appropriate to have full control of the theatre. It is his money, after all, that allowed the theatre to be built. How could I argue that he was not entitled to own it entirely?'

'It means that if he wishes to sell it he can do so without so much as informing you, his director.'

'I know that too,' said Schikaneder. 'And I put that very point to him. I may be an artist, Seyfried, but I do understand a little about business matters. He assured me he had no intention of doing that. But that even if he did, he would retain me as director. And I can assure you, my friend, I would retain you as *Kapellmeister* and Franz Clement as orchestra leader. So there is really nothing to be concerned about.'

'Well, that is reassuring. I shall, if you will permit it, inform Clement. I understand from him that there has been anxiety among the musicians.'

'Of course, my dear Seyfried. The Theater an der Wien can look forward to a prosperous future, I can assure you.'

'May I ask how the project with Herr Beethoven is progressing? Your opera? You have finished the libretto, have you not?'

'Indeed I have. It only awaits Herr Beethoven's return from the country. I understand from one of his assistants that he is in Döbling working on a new symphony. It has been on his mind for some time. But as soon as he returns he will turn his attention to my opera. So you see, Seyfried, within a very short time we shall have a new opera, from Vienna's most respected young composer. His first, indeed. And poor Baron Braun at the Hoftheater will have to go far afield to find something to match that.'

'So,' said Stephan Breuning, warmth suffusing his face, 'our numbers swell again. Soon there will be enough Rhinelanders in this city to form a society. The Honourable Society of Rhinelanders in Exile. Seriously though, Mähler, I am delighted to make your acquaintance. Now sit down, my friends, and allow me to refresh you.'

He walked to the sideboard and poured wine into four glasses.

'I wish I could offer you a glass of Johannisberger. Something to remind us of our homeland. I fear it will be a long time before I am able to do that. What news of the Rhineland, Mähler?'

'Not good, I am afraid,' said a young man in his mid-twenties, with a shock of dark hair and a wide cravat tied in a flamboyant knot. 'French soldiers now swarm through our cities, from Cologne down to Mainz and beyond. They have achieved their dream. Our Rhine is now the frontier between the French Empire and Germany, and they treat its cities as their own. And you heard, no doubt, that they have wandered further afield. They sacked Hannover.'

'"To further the interests of peace",' said Stephan, 'according to the French ambassador here. We hoped that when the English declared war again, it would take their minds off Germany.'

Gleichenstein and Ries, the two other Rhinelanders present in Stephan's apartment in the Rothes Haus, looked grim.

'My own home town, Ehrenbreitstein,' Mähler continued, 'now has practically as many French soldiers in it as citizens. In the taverns along the river only French voices are heard.'

'But if the English cross the Channel and engage the French,' said Ries, injecting some enthusiasm into his voice, 'then surely . . .'

Mähler's voice held a touch of weariness. 'I am afraid the opposite is the case. The First Consul is preparing to invade England.'

'Invade England?' asked Gleichenstein incredulously. 'But that is impossible. You cannot invade England. Otherwise someone would have done it more recently than the Norman King William.'

'It is true,' said Stephan. 'We recently had confirmation of what you say, Mähler. From our agents in northern France. Napoleon has concentrated a huge force on the coast at Boulogne. We don't know how many, but possibly more than a hundred thousand men.'

'But how?'

'He's building a flotilla of boats. Hundreds. With flat keels, according to our agents, to transport the soldiers across.'

'But they will walk into a trap. The English must be aware of what is going on. They will mass their armies on the south coast and the French will never get ashore.'

'Actually,' said Stephan, 'we believe they are being cleverer than that. Our agents in London report that the English plan to blockade the French in their own ports. The French may have the stronger army, but there is no navy in Europe to rival that of the English. Their ships are smaller and lighter than the French. Easier to manoeuvre. They will position them outside the ports and the French will be unable to move. If they do come out, the English will happily fight them at sea.'

The friends fell silent, contemplating the unthinkable: the defeat of France once and for all, which would allow them to return to their families in the Rhineland.

'Now,' said Stephan, refilling the glasses, 'enough gloomy talk. What brings you to Vienna, Willi?'

Willibrord Mähler took a sip of wine. 'I have secured a position as Court Secretary, so I shall be working not far from you both,' he nodded to Breuning and Gleichenstein, 'but I really want to try to earn my living as a painter of portraits.'

'An artist,' said Stephan. 'Well, it is a pleasure to welcome you into our group. To broaden our interests somewhat. For, if I am not wrong, until now music is the single art that binds us.'

'Yes,' said Ries. 'I am a pianist and composer. Ignaz, as you know, is a cellist. And Herr Stephan here, though he will deny it, is a capable violinist.'

'How can I deny it when my esteemed teacher was none other than your father!' said Stephan, with a chuckle. 'But I fear he would chastise me if he knew how I had neglected my practice. In fact, I have not touched my violin for far longer than I dare admit.'

Mähler smiled. 'Let me ask some advice of you right away. I am seeking commissions to paint portraits. Who do you think I might approach? I thought a patron of the arts might be suitable.'

'Yes. Someone like Prince Lichnowsky, or even better Prince Lobkowitz. But most of them have already had their portraits painted.'

'I shall approach them anyway. And if they say no, then I shall look elsewhere.'

'I will give the matter some thought,' said Stephan. 'Now, Ferdi, since we are Rhinelanders together, tell us about one of our number who is not here today. Our friend Ludwig Beethoven. You have seen him recently, haven't you?'

Ries sipped his wine and nodded. His face was grave. 'I am afraid Herr Ludwig may not be one of our number for much longer.'

'What on earth do you mean?' asked Stephan, astonished. 'Is he ill?'

'No, no. You know he is in Döbling working on his new symphony? He told me that when he has finished it he will dedicate it to Napoleon. Then he will leave Vienna for good and go to live in Paris.'

'Paris!' Stephan could not contain his shock. 'But he would find it impossible. He has no friends there. He cannot speak the language, I'm sure.'

'It began with the episode over the violin sonata. You remember, the one he was to dedicate to Mr Bridgetower.'

'Poor unfortunate Mr Bridgetower,' responded Stephan. 'Yes, he asked you to send the sonata to Paris, didn't he?'

'To Monsieur Kreutzer. Which I have. Herr Ludwig is convinced that, with the sonata and the symphony, his fame will be established in Paris and he will be welcomed there by the First Consul.'

'Despicable Corsican.' Gleichenstein almost spat out the words.

'I'm afraid Herr Ludwig rather admires him. He called him a hero of the people. He said he was composing . . . Yes. A heroic symphony for a hero.'

Ludwig sat by the Krottenbach looking down at the water rushing by. Small pieces of foliage tossed around on its surface. He followed them with his eyes. Some were still dancing in the spray as the water re-emerged from the gorge. It was not deep and the rocks that formed it were not jagged. And the water did not rush by furiously. It was all rather tame and civilised; so like the Viennese, he thought, not for the first time. And so unlike me – and my music.

The new symphony was complete. At any rate, it was complete in his meaning of the word, but only the copyist Schlemmer would be able to understand the score. Some passages were written out, others were just fragments, and innumerable pages contained so many crossings out that only two or three bars remained intact. Even Schlemmer will have problems he thought. But to me the work is complete.

And what a work! Ludwig knew he had created a piece of music unlike anything he had ever composed. On the most obvious level it was the longest single work he had written. More importantly, it was considerably longer than any symphony any other composer had written, including Mozart and Haydn. And the length was not achieved by frequent repeats.

He had not striven to achieve the length: it had come naturally, from within the music itself. He had never doubted that the *Prometheus* theme would provide him with enough material for the symphony, but even he had been surprised at how much he had been able to draw from it. The piano variations he had written in Heiligenstadt had been, he now realised, the essential step in the process. Through them he had been able to see inside the theme, strip it bare, reassemble it in another way – and go on doing it.

In the symphony he had done something different. He had kept the theme intact but this time he had revealed the full extent of its power. He had shown that from just four notes and a simple theme great music could be created.

He thought of the criticisms his music had aroused. Always the complaints were the same – and they echoed the complaints his teachers had made. *You cannot do that. You are not allowed. The rules forbid you.*

The sudden descent in only the fifth bar to the totally alien C sharp? He picked up a stone and tossed it into the water. Because music is art and art is nature, and in nature the unexpected sometimes happens. So it must be in music.

He picked up six stones and threw them hard at the water. The six great *sforzando* chords he had written in the first movement. Discords. *Discords! E natural in the strings! But, Herr Beethoven, the key is E flat. You cannot do that!*

He heard the chords in his head. Crashing sounds like the noise of a stick coming down on the keys of a piano. Followed by the whimpering sounds of a child as the stick stung his wrists. As the chords are followed by a sighing motif in the strings, pleading. *Stop, Father. Please stop.*

He stood and walked a few paces along the bank. The funeral march had taken him by surprise. It really had. He had not intended writing a funeral march, but once he had begun composing it he had been in no doubt.

Who was it for? They would ask him that. Of course. We understand. It is for the Austrian soldiers who have fallen on the battlefield. Isn't it, Herr Beethoven?

He thrust his hands deep into his pockets and walked further along the bank until it began the long, gradual descent to

Heiligenstadt. He could see the rooftops in the distance, and there was the onion dome of St Michael's Church, shimmering above.

Oh, all you people who think and say that I am hostile to you . . . No, it is not for the Austrian soldiers. But I will never tell you who it is for. I will never tell you that it is really for me. And because you do not know that it is for me, you will not understand the nature of the Scherzo, the third movement. Joyful, full of light. Listen to the horn calls. My acceptance of my affliction. Let no one doubt that my musical powers remain undiminished. And should you doubt it, there is the final movement. The movement that belongs to the hero, he who has triumphed over adversity. It belongs to Prometheus. It belongs to Napoleon Bonaparte. It belongs to me.

Ludwig wheeled round and strode back up the slope towards the house. That is the point about my third symphony. It is the story of a hero who faces adversity, who is nearly brought down by it, who overcomes it and triumphs. It is a story in musical form. Nature and life as music. Like no one has ever composed before.

He entered his rooms, threw his jacket on to a chair and poured himself a glass of wine. He thought for a moment, then took a quill, dipped it in ink, and wrote on the cover page of the symphony:

Grand Symphony in E Flat Major

Written on Bonaparte

By Ludwig van Beethoven

He sat back and looked at it. Another face floated into his mind: the face of a man, as clear as if it were actually before him. A faint smile played round his lips. In his mind Ludwig heard the deep, resonant voice. 'You have done well, Ludwig. You have said what needed to be said. Now you must give it to the world. Not for this generation, for they will not understand it. But for generations, countless generations, as yet unborn. I am proud of you, Ludwig. Proud of you.'

The voice and the image were so clear that Ludwig felt he could almost reach out and touch his grandfather. His dear grandfather.

Chapter 3

Ludwig returned from Döbling with renewed resolve. The composition of the symphony had drained him emotionally, but it had also strengthened his morale. He knew just what an achievement it had been. It was as if the two great crashing E flat chords that opened the first movement had propelled him into the new era. From now on he was his own master, in control of his own destiny.

He wrote a letter to Prince Lobkowitz, aware that the tone was not appropriate but dispatching it nonetheless.

> Most Honoured and Highborn Prince
>
> You promised me the use of your grand concert room for my new symphony. The work is now complete and the parts with the copyist. All that is needed is for you to set a date for a month hence, to allow for rehearsal.
>
> I expect you to communicate such information to your aristocratic confreres, as well as Herr Haydn. Also you should inform His Imperial Highness the Archduke Rudolph.
>
> You should ensure only the most skilled orchestral players are put at my disposal, since the music will make great demands of them.
>
> It is my intention to dedicate the work to a hero of France, who I believe is much misunderstood, and I shall shortly be making my home in the city that he too calls his home.
>
> Yr servant
> L van Bthvn

He summoned Ries to his rooms at the Theater an der Wien and was surprised – to an extent relieved – that it was Ignaz Gleichenstein who came in his place. A few years older than Ries, he had a more engaging personality and would be less intimidated by what Ludwig wanted him to do.

'Tell Schikaneder the text he has given me for an opera is

worthless. *Vestas Feuer*. Vestas Spark would be a better title. Give it back to him. It is over there, on the table. The Archduke wants me to begin composition lessons with him. Tell him I am too busy. Prince Lobkowitz is to arrange a date for the performance of my new symphony. Make sure he does it. And finally I am planning to move to Paris. Has there been any word from Kreutzer?'

'I will check with Ferdinand, sir. But I don't believe so. I am sure he would have told you if there had.'

The next day, as he walked across the Glacis towards the Kärntnertor gate, Ludwig reflected on the letter he had received from Nikolaus – Nikolaus Johann. He knew why his brother wanted to see him. He sensed it. 'A matter of personal importance to me,' Nikolaus had written. If the letter had come before his stay in Döbling, he might not have responded. But he was ready now.'

How long had he spent in the vinegar maker's house? A month, maybe longer. He had lost track of time. Work on his third symphony had totally absorbed him, and with it, at the age of thirty-three, he had achieved maturity as a composer. And maturity as a human being.

Carl had moved out of the lodgings they shared in the Theater an der Wien, which had contributed to Ludwig's sense of a new start, a new phase of his life. He hoped that would be the end of his problems with Carl. Now there was just this matter to clear up with Nikolaus. Johann.

He walked under the high arched gate, shivering in the cold shadow it threw, and turned left. Ahead of him stood the Kärntnertor theatre, the smaller more decorative of the two court theatres after the Burgtheater. He wanted to walk on towards it, enter it, imagine an orchestra sitting on the stage, hear the two great E flat chords . . .

Instead he pushed open the small glass-topped door, wincing at the sudden jangling of bells. He stood still until the noise subsided. The interior of the shop was dark and there was a strange smell, which reminded Ludwig of doctors.

'Brother, I'm glad to see you. Come through to the back.' Nikolaus brushed past Ludwig, pulled down a blind over the glass door and led the way through the gap in the counter to the office behind the shop.

Ludwig saw an easy chair and sat in it gratefully. The effort of the walk had brought out a light film of sweat on his skin and his ears were ringing. If he sat still the likelihood was that the noise would soon stop and he would have nothing worse than a dull throbbing in his head.

'Have you any wine?'

Nikolaus shook his head. 'It is not allowed on the premises. In case I mix the wrong chemicals.' He turned to reach for a wooden chair.

Ludwig was struck by his brother's stature: he seemed even taller and more broad-shouldered than he remembered, so unlike either him or Carl. It was our father's physique, Ludwig thought, realising suddenly that the thought of his father no longer induced hatred, fear or panic inside him.

Nikolaus turned. Where *had* that eye defect come from, that lazy muscle? He remembered their mother saying once that, when the two younger brothers had been fighting, Caspar had banged Nikola's head and caused the pupil in his eye to slip. Ludwig had never believed it: he had noticed Nikola's eye soon after his birth.

'Thank you again for coming. I wanted to have a talk with you.'

Ludwig sat still, his hands clasped in front of him. His brother's voice was strong and deep, and in the small room Ludwig could hear him quite clearly.

'Did you know I have been appointed manager? I am now in charge of the day-to-day running of the shop. It's a big responsibility. I'm going to hire an assistant. I have to do the books as well as buy all the medicines. Do you know what my ambition is?'

Ludwig raised his eyebrows.

'I want to buy my own apothecary shop. I'm putting money aside. Maybe one day.'

Ludwig wished he would come to the point.

'Are you pleased Carl has moved out? I imagine you are,' his brother asked.

Ludwig cleared his throat. 'It was time. The lodgings are too small. Now he has a job at the Hofburg.'

'He is not earning as much money as I am, but more than he did teaching music.'

'He had to give that up. He is no musician. And he has nothing more to do with my affairs. He has a talent for upsetting publishers. Carl makes enemies very easily.'

'Ah yes. Carl. You said Carl, didn't you? Not Caspar. Yes,

you are right. Quite right. Ludwig, there is something I wish to ask you. I know it will make you angry but I have to ask you. It has been on my mind for some time. I know you may think it unimportant but it is important to me.'

Ludwig took a deep breath and sighed. 'I do not know why you want to do it, Nikola. You have a perfectly good name. But if you want me to call you Johann from now on . . .'

Vienna was rife with rumour. It was the talk of the coffee houses on the Graben and the Kohlmarkt. It was the talk of the taverns. At the round table at the back of the Zum Weissen Schwan the Rhinelanders-in-exile barely needed to lower their voices.

'I believe it is true,' said Stephan Breuning. Instinctively he looked around before he continued. 'Everyone knows it. The Corsican, the so-called First Consul of France, is to crown himself emperor of France.'

'But our own emperor is descended from a long and illustrious line,' said Mähler. 'The Habsburgs have ruled the empire for nearly a thousand years.'

'I suppose a dynasty has to begin somewhere,' said Ries. 'Is it true he is declaring the title hereditary?'

'Apparently,' said Stephan. 'First, of course, he must have an heir. Let us pray the good Lord has done us the favour of making him impotent.'

There was laughter around the table. Ludwig listened carefully to what was being said, the welcome taste of the rough red wine easing the pressure on his ears. Could it be true? Had he misjudged the man? Surely not. But if Napoleon crowned himself emperor, it would show he was in reality no better than anyone else. A power-seeker, that was all.

'I still do not believe it,' he said, gruffly. 'You are misjudging him. Worse, you are misjudging events. There is no need for him to become emperor. He has all the powers he needs as First Consul. It would be against the aims of the Revolution if he —'

Ignaz Gleichenstein said, 'I do not believe history will be kind to the Revolution. Too much blood was spilled unnecessarily.'

'I agree,' said Stephan. 'The guillotine became a spectacle, an entertainment almost. If Napoleon declares himself emperor, who is to say that there won't be another round of blood-letting?'

Ludwig took another gulp of wine. 'What word from Kreutzer, Ries? Has he written yet?'

'No, Herr Ludwig, I'm afraid not. Sir, are you still intending to leave Vienna? To move to Paris?'

Ludwig was aware that conversation had stopped. 'Yes,' he said quietly.

'Herr Beethoven,' said Mähler eagerly, 'will you permit me a favour? May I paint your portrait? To preserve your likeness for us to remember you by. And for the people of Vienna to remember you by. When you are gone from us. Something to replace the sadness and emptiness we will feel.'

Ludwig swallowed. His stomach churned. He gave an almost imperceptible nod.

Baron Braun, director of the Imperial Court theatres, struggled to keep his voice calm. 'Herr Zitterbarth, I am pleased we have reached an agreement for the purchase of the Wien, even if you have struck such a hard bargain that I doubt the Imperial budget will recover.'

'Baron Braun, I assure you the price is fair. As we agreed, I shall tell the employees of the new arrangements. Let me check them with you once more.' He looked down at a piece of paper in the folder he held. 'Schikaneder to be dismissed, with one month's salary. Seyfried and Clement to be retained, as *Kapellmeister* and orchestral leader respectively. All orchestral players to be placed on new short-term contracts.' He closed the folder.

'Precisely. And there is a musician in residence, is there not?'

'Yes. The German. Ludwig von Beethoven.'

'He pays rental?'

'I believe not. Schikaneder said –'

'Tell him the agreement is terminated. He must leave immediately.'

Chapter 4

Ludwig lifted the portrait carefully off the nail, lowered it and laid it against the wall, draping a blanket over the frame to protect it. He looked at the piles of papers and books Ries had stacked, ready for removal. Damn Braun, he thought, bringer of so many problems over the years, from cancelled benefit concerts to this latest domestic crisis. Yet again he was without a home.

The Baron had asked to see him in his office at the Burgtheater. The sole purpose, Ludwig knew, was to give him official notice to vacate his rooms. He did not want to go. Could he send Ries or Gleichenstein in his place? No, he would have to go. Braun controlled all the city's most important theatres: he could not afford to make an enemy of him – or more of one than he already was.

Head down, Ludwig walked through the Michaelerplatz, ignoring the ornate, massive Imperial palace to his right, towards the less imposing building ahead. Before entering it he stopped and raised his head – an unconscious movement that had a startling effect on him. He felt a catch in his throat. Suddenly he was a boy again, not yet seventeen, in the city of Mozart for the first time, standing outside this same building where *The Marriage of Figaro* was first presented to the public. He had known, with a sure conviction, even then that his own works would one day be heard in the same great theatre, and his faith in himself had not been misplaced.

He looked round the square and thought how little it had changed. A sweet aroma still pervaded the air from the stalls selling honeyed cakes. Carriages still kicked up dust from the cobbles and a sudden gust of wind carried a brief whiff of a horse's sweating flank under his nose. But something had changed. He stood watching the people moving this way and that and realised what it was. The men in military uniform had lost something of the swagger they had once had. People walked with a slightly more determined tread, their faces pinched. The sedan chairs carrying noblemen and women were faded, the decoration on them chipped. On the Bastion promenade and in the Augarten and Prater public parks it was different, but that was just for display. Here in the city there was no disguising the effect of years of war against the French. Ludwig felt a pang of sadness for the people of Vienna.

He entered the Burgtheater and went up the stairs to the large office on the first floor. He rapped on the glass panel and, without waiting for a reply, went in. His eyes swept the room, taking in the small bald-headed figure of Baron Braun sitting behind his desk and seeing, to his consternation, another figure standing by the window. The man's face was in the shadow, but Ludwig knew he did not recognise it. He hoped both men would speak clearly.

'Ah, Herr Beethoven. Good of you to come. Sit down.' Braun indicated the chair that stood ready.

Ludwig sat, wishing he had waited to steady his breath after the climb before entering the room. But fortunately Braun carried on talking, and in a firm clear voice.

'I would like you to meet the new secretary of the Imperial Court theatres. My right-hand man. Joseph Sonnleithner. Director of a music publisher too. The Kunst-und-Industrie.'

Ludwig flinched as the man bowed, then came towards him, hand outstretched. Then he saw that Sonnleithner's eyes were sparkling.

'Sir, it is a very great pleasure to make the acquaintance of such a distinguished musician.'

The flattery was not lost on Ludwig and, combined with the fact that Sonnleithner spoke distinctly, he found himself somewhat at ease. He nodded at the stranger and turned again to Braun.

Braun held up his hands. 'Herr Beethoven, I apologise if I have given you problems but I had no choice. The Wien is losing money in the same way that blood haemorrhages from a wounded soldier on the battlefield. To have free lodgings was no longer sustainable, and I have other uses for the rooms.'

Ludwig stiffened. 'It is of no concern to me, Braun. I leave soon for Paris. I . . . I am leaving this city.' He squared his shoulders, hoping to lend weight to his words, but he knew his voice had lacked conviction.

'So I have heard,' said Braun, resting his arms on the desk. 'I wonder if I might put a proposition to you that will perhaps give you cause for . . . reflection.' He glanced at Sonnleithner, who nodded eagerly. 'You agreed to compose an opera for Schikaneder, did you not?'

Ludwig shifted in his chair. 'The libretto was impossible. I could not continue. Ridiculous words, ridiculous plot, not worthy of my music.'

'But you would welcome a suitable libretto, I assume?'

Ludwig said nothing but looked at Braun, unable to disguise the expectancy on his face. It was true: he did want to compose an opera. How did Braun know that? Guesswork, surely. But what did he have in mind?

Braun glanced at Sonnleithner, signalling to him to take up the theme.

'Herr Beethoven,' he said, 'do you know of a French play by an author named Bouilly? Jean-Nicolas Bouilly? It is called *Léonore, ou l'Amour Conjugal.*'

Ludwig shook his head. Sonnleithner continued, 'It is set in Seville, where a nobleman has been unjustly imprisoned. His wife disguises herself as a boy to work at the prison to try to rescue him. When the governor comes to murder the man, she steps between them, reveals her true identity and saves him. Apparently it is based on a true incident that took place in France during the Terror. A nobleman was imprisoned in Tours, but his wife saved him from the guillotine. Bouilly changed the setting to Seville, so as not to upset the authorities.'

'The authorities!' exclaimed Ludwig. 'Criminals, that is all they are. Even this man Napoleon, if it is true what they say about his ambitions. All that bloodshed for high ideals, but if anyone so much as criticises it they are thrown into prison. Power. They achieve power and it corrupts them.'

Sonnleithner stepped closer to the desk. 'That is the underlying message of this play. I am translating it into German. I think it is a wonderful plot, and ideally suited for an opera.'

Braun interjected, as if resolved to regain the initiative, 'The Imperial Court theatres would like to commission it from you, Herr Beethoven. An opera, to be performed at the Theater an der Wien.'

'What is the name of it again?' Ludwig asked.

'*Léonore.* The wife is called Léonore. She changes her name when she disguises herself as a boy.'

'What to?'
'Fidelio.'

In the final days before he moved out of the Theater an der
Wien Ludwig finished work on a piano sonata he had begun
some time before. It was a lively piece, with a long expansive
middle movement which he had marked *andante grazioso*. He
wondered if it was too substantial to sit between the first and
third movements. He decided to leave it where it was.

Stephan von Breuning came to see him with some welcome
news. 'Ludwig, I have spoken to the landlord of my building.
There is an apartment available. It is small, but it would suit you
perfectly until you . . . until you leave. And the Rothes Haus is
beyond the Bastion, as you know. You can walk on the Glacis.
Very peaceful. I will take you to see the landlord.'

When he saw the apartment Ludwig's heart sank. It was small,
the main room not much bigger than the attic room he had
occupied when he had first come to Vienna. Like the rooms
in the Theater an der Wien, there was no window out on to
the street, just a small one overlooking the inner courtyard. And
there was a problem.

'I must have my piano.'

'No musical instruments. It says so in the lease. Clause eight.
Read it for yourself.'

Stephan intervened: 'I will have it in my apartment. I have
room. It is precious. It cannot be stored.'

The landlord looked suspiciously at both men. 'You must
pay an indemnity, one month's rent, On top of the deposit.
Two months in all. If the piano is played, if anyone complains,
you lose the indemnity and I will terminate the lease.'

'Where do I sign?'

'Here. And remember, each month's rent paid in advance,
on the first day of the month. If it's late, you incur a penalty.
Right now, I need three months' rent. A hundred and thirty-five
gulden. One month in advance, the deposit and the indemnity.'

'I cannot pay you now. I –'

'I'll give you twenty-four hours.'

Ludwig felt his temper rise, but Stephan's restraining hand
was on his arm.

'I will pay it,' said Stephan. 'On Herr Beethoven's behalf.'

The two friends went to Stephan's apartment where Ludwig
gratefully accepted a glass of wine.

'Do you remember Count Waldstein?' asked Stephan.

Ludwig gasped. 'I owe it to him that I am in Vienna. He persuaded the Elector. He gave me letters of reference. Why do you mention him? Has anything happened? I remember the Elector told me something about him. He had upset him in some way, but I cannot remember the details.'

'He went to England to raise a regiment to fight the French, against orders from the Hofburg. He spent all his money, borrowed huge sums and lost that too. There were rumours he has been to Vienna in disguise to try to borrow more money, but his creditors found out and he had to flee. No one knows where he is now.'

Ludwig's eyebrows drew together in a frown. 'Sad. He was so influential in Bonn. As I said, I owe him a lot. I wish there was something I could do.'

Stephan shook his head. 'There is nothing. He is the architect of his own misfortune.'

In a moment of inspiration Ludwig said, 'I have just completed a new sonata for piano. I will dedicate it to him.' He shrugged. 'Maybe he will never know, but I want to do it.'

'A generous thought. Tell me, Ludwig, forgive my intrusiveness, but do you still intend to leave this city and live in Paris?'

Ludwig finished his wine and held out his glass for Stephan to refill. 'I believe in this man Napoleon, Steffen. He is a man of the people. I do not believe the rumours about him. He does not desire to be emperor. It would be against the aims of the Revolution.'

Several days later Ludwig was installed in the new apartment. The portrait of his grandfather still lay propped against the wall, a blanket over its frame: he did not want to put it up in such a dark, dismal room. His mood was as black as his surroundings. His ears were heavier than he had ever known them, with an intermittent high-pitched whistle that gave him an almost constant headache.

Also he had begun rehearsals for the new symphony, and they had been disastrous. He found it increasingly difficult to hear the wind section. He would shout at them to play, when they were already playing – the clarinettist had given up and left.

The principal horn player accused Ludwig of making a mistake by giving the horn a solo entry before the main theme re-enters half-way through the first movement. 'It sounds as if

I have mistimed it,' he said. To Ludwig's annoyance, Ries took the player's side and urged him to delete it.

Why would they not simply play what he had written? he had shouted at Ries, in front of the whole orchestra. His less than fulsome apology later had been accepted, but the air between them was still tense.

Ludwig knew that this symphony was crucial to his musical development. It could not afford to fail. It was the turning point for him; the harbinger of all that was to come. It was his Heroic Symphony. The *Eroica*. He liked the Latin name.

Ries knocked on his door and entered carrying a folder.

'What is it, Ries? Have you come to criticise my work again?'

'I have brought the manuscript for the symphony, Herr Ludwig. There is something I want to check with you. But before I do have you heard the news, sir? From Paris?'

'Kreutzer? Has he written?'

'No, Herr Ludwig, I am afraid not. I do not believe he will. He would have by now.'

'Damn him. I should have given it to Bridgetower, after all.'

'But, sir, the news. Have you not heard? Everyone is talking about it.'

'What, Ries? What is it? Tell me, for God's sake. Tell me, then leave me alone.'

'Napoleon, sir. He has declared himself emperor of France. He is to be crowned in the cathedral of Notre Dame at the end of the year. The date is set. The second of December, 1804. An infamous date.'

All the pent-up anger and frustration bubbled to the surface and exploded. '*What?* So it is true, then. He is nothing more than an ordinary man, after all. He cares only about his own ambition. He places himself above everyone else and is nothing more than a tyrant!'

He snatched the folder from under Ries's arm, opened it, ripped out the title page of the symphony, tore it in two and threw it to the ground.

'Tyrant!'

Chapter 5

The silence of the tiny apartment was oppressive. Ludwig found it affected his ears as much as noise did – and as the date of the concert approached his old tormentor, the stomach colic, plagued him.

Ludwig had handed over rehearsals to Seyfried and sat at the back of the room, dictating observations to Ries. The players, hired by Prince Lobkowitz, were mostly from the Theater an der Wien, with some from the Burgtheater. Clement was leader. Slowly the orchestra was coming to terms with the music. The horn player, resentful that Ludwig had refused to remove his solo entry before the recapitulation, had christened the work 'The Symphony of Heroic Length', to the amusement of his colleagues.

Doktor Schmidt gave Ludwig powders to quell his stomach pain and explained that the marked worsening of his hearing was a nervous reaction caused by the tension of the forthcoming concert; it should improve when it was over. In the meantime, he asked, was there not a larger apartment available in the Rothes Haus? A little more space would ease the oppressiveness Ludwig felt.

Ludwig decided to talk to his old friend.

Stephan looked wearily at him. 'Of course, Ludwig. I would like it.'

'Thank you, Stephan. It is what Doktor Schmidt recommended. I cannot stay in that dingy cell a moment longer.'

'Your piano is already in the spare room so I am afraid there is not much space. And remember what the landlord said about not playing it. That applies to my apartment too. And, Ludwig, you must give a month's notice to the landlord, otherwise you will lose your deposit.'

Ludwig nodded. 'I will speak to him.'

★　　★　　★

There was a knot in Ludwig's stomach and a throb in his head. The dullness in his ears blunted the hum of conversation around him, but mercifully the only sounds he could hear clearly were those of his own music, which was to be played in public for the first time tonight.

Now Prince Lobkowitz was banging his crutch on the floor. 'Ready at last, eh, Beethoven? Damn fine concert room. You couldn't want for a better place to launch your great symphony.'

Ludwig forced a smile but he wanted more than anything to be alone, in a small room at the back, to collect his thoughts. Instead he was on display, to be passed from one honoured guest to the next. But he had no choice, he knew that. He knew, too, that he owed a debt of gratitude to Prince Lobkowitz.

'Hear you decided not to dedicate it to that wretched Frenchman, after all?'

Ludwig understood the implication of the Prince's question. 'You shall have the symphony, Prince. The Eroica symphony. I will have the publisher put your name on the title sheet.'

'Most kind. Most kind.' The Prince moved closer to him. 'Important night for me too. His Imperial Highness the Arch-duke is guest of honour. Lichnowsky will be here. Young Kinsky, too – great admirer of your music. Countess Erdödy and, of course, all your friends and colleagues. Food and wine afterwards.'

Ludwig glanced round the room. People were arranging themselves in the linen-covered seating that ran round three walls in rows that rose one behind the other so each seat afforded a clear view of the orchestra.

He saw Stephan Breuning talking animatedly to a woman, whose face was hidden. All he could see were her auburn curls. He wanted to find out who she was, but Lobkowitz gripped his arm. 'Come, Beethoven. Vienna's other great composer. Most senior composer. Come.'

Ludwig followed Lobkowitz's gaze and saw the distinguished-looking figure of his former teacher.

How Haydn had aged, Ludwig thought, his now stooped shoulders emphasising his lack of height. He was more than seventy. Lobkowitz crossed the room to speak to him and Haydn seemed embarrassed as Lobkowitz lavished praise on him, holding up his hands modestly as the Prince encouraged the audience to welcome him.

As Lobkowitz led the applause, Haydn caught Ludwig's eye.

He bowed and began to move, somewhat unsteadily, towards him. 'So, dear Ludwig, now it is I who come to pay homage to you. Word has reached me of your new symphony. I believe we are to hear something quite different from anything that has gone before.'

Ludwig was leaning forward, but still could not hear clearly. The conversation coming from the benches was quite loud and Haydn's voice had lost its strength. But he heard enough to understand the older man's message. 'I would greatly value your opinion, Herr Haydn, more than anyone else's. But, I beg you, do not close your ears to what you are about to hear.'

Haydn allowed Lobkowitz to guide him to a seat in the front row.

A voice boomed from the double doors, 'Rise from your seats and pay due homage to the guest of honour, His Imperial Highness the Archduke Rudolph.'

Everyone stood as the young man entered and implored the audience to take their seats. He strode over to Lobkowitz, who bowed low to him, stretching his stiff leg out awkwardly.

Ludwig wanted to begin the performance. The distorted sounds of the orchestra tuning their instruments still hung in the air, assaulting his ears, and he knew the Archduke would speak to him – complain, no doubt, that Ludwig had not fulfilled his promise to teach him composition. He feared he would not be able to hear him properly.

Then a voice said in his ear, 'I am here, Herr Ludwig. I will help if you have any problems.'

'Where have you been? Damn you, Ries. I needed you earlier.' Ludwig knew that yet again he was being unjust, but he needed an outlet for his frustration and Ries was the only target.

Ludwig watched the Archduke's eyes move swiftly round the room and settle on him. Hand outstretched, he walked over.

Ludwig took a deep breath. 'Your Imperial Highness.'

'Herr Beethoven. Such a pleasure.' There was a twinkle in his eyes and he leaned forward, speaking distinctly. 'I am not to become a soldier after all. I finally persuaded my brother. I am to enter the Church instead. Very proper. It gives me more time for my music.' He glanced at Ries.

'His Imperial Highness wishes you to instruct him, Herr Ludwig.'

'Yes, yes, I know. When I have time, Your Imperial Highness. Meanwhile, practise. Read Fux. Do exercises on counterpoint. Ask Herr Haydn.'

The Archduke smiled benevolently. 'I have heard so much about this new symphony, Herr Beethoven. I cannot tell you how I am looking forward to hearing it.' He moved away, to take his seat in the centre of the front row.

Ludwig looked at the orchestra. They were ready. Seyfried was having a few words with Clement. Ludwig wanted to begin. He heard a voice echo round the room. Ries turned him slightly to hear it.

'. . . this wonderful piece of music, which we are about to have the pleasure of hearing,' said Prince Lobkowitz, his body at a slight angle as he leaned on his crutch. 'I profess myself humbled by Herr Beethoven's kind decision to dedicate it to me, a fact of which he informed me only a few minutes ago. It will, I know, do far more credit to my reputation in the years to come than I will do for its own. After the performance, I beg you all to stay for refreshments. Your Imperial Highness, the honour you do me by gracing my humble salon is far more than you can know. Herr Haydn, to have it blessed with your genius is to answer my prayer. Now, my noble masters and good friends, I place the members of the Lobkowitz orchestra in the hands of Herr Beethoven for the performance of his new symphony.'

Ludwig felt a shaft of fear. The dullness in his ears, the heaviness in his head, the pain that accompanied every beat of his heart . . . *Will I be able to hear my music?* He glanced up and saw Seyfried standing off to the side. It would be so easy . . . so easy to . . . No, he thought. This is my music, my message, not to the people sitting in this concert room, but to generations to come.

He turned to the orchestra and raised his arms. He could hear the opening chord clearly in his head. Ringing out even before it had been played. Across the room, the city, across Europe and beyond . . .

The sound he heard a moment later was ragged. Brass players obviously hadn't warmed their instruments, he thought. *Or is it my ears?* Their blast a fraction later than the strings robbed the first chord of the unison it needed. But the second chord was good, with the attack he had demanded.

The first theme sounded in the cellos and basses and he crouched low at the unexpected C sharp in the fifth bar, rising slowly as he conducted to indicate the *crescendo*. More than anything it was the dynamics he was trying to indicate. He had set the pace, which was swift; the players knew the notes. But the dynamics had to be right. *Forte, piano, fortepiano, fortissimo, pianissimo, crescendo* . . . the all-important *crescendos*.

With his body he gave the players the sign: crouching low for the soft passages, leaping suddenly high to indicate the *forte*. He could hear the music. His music.

That difficult horn entry. So perfectly placed. How could it not be there? How could it be any other way?

Ludwig saw Clement's little finger extend almost to the highest point of the E string for the closing bars. How the first violins had cursed! From the top of the E string, down to the G string in the same bar, then across all the strings, D, G A, G, E, G – and all double bowed – before the final two chords, echoing the two opening chords, closing the massive movement in the home key of E flat.

He held his arms high in the air long after the final chord had sounded, not to maintain silence but because he could still hear it reverberating in his head and he did not know, with his eyes tightly shut, if it was the echo of the chord or if the players were still playing.

But what was the harsh sound that intruded on it, that rough grating clamour that seemed to banish the music from his head? He saw Clement's face smiling up at him, gesticulating to the benches behind. He turned round. The audience was on its feet in thunderous ovation.

He shook his head and turned back quickly. No no, he wanted to say to them. The Allegro is nothing without the other three movements. The Marcia Funèbre must follow immediately. Each movement is a development of the one before.

Voices pierced his ears. He wanted to shut them out, stop them erasing the music from his head. 'Encore! Encore!' When would it stop? He glanced down at Clement who was turning back the pages, indicating to the other players to do the same.

The voices gave way again to applause, and then silence. Ludwig heard the silence. Nothing in his head, no pain, no dullness, just the great E flat chords that he knew would echo down the centuries.

He did not know whether any applause greeted the end of the movement this time, but as soon as he had brought down his arms for the final chord, he raised them again. And he heard clearly the doleful sounds, the triplet grace notes in the double basses, that began the funeral march.

Triplet demi-semiquavers in the strings, the tramp of boots on gravel as the coffin is carried on the bier to its final resting place. He closed his eyes and saw the face he had seen so often as a child, the eyes he had gazed into, the head that nodded encouragement . . . *For you, Grandfather, my symphony is for you. You who have given me the will to fight on.*

As clearly as he could wish he heard the plangent oboe soaring above the orchestra, trying so hard to bring light to the darkness, like the soul of the dead coming alive again. And the triplets now played in rising measures. Hope. Optimism. *Fortissimo.* Yes, *sforzando.*

And now, sweet strings, piano. He crouched low. Sing. Sing of hope and redemption. But it cannot last, it cannot last. The triplets soon descending again and the march begins anew. The march of death. If there is life there must be death. And soon the instruments drop away, leaving just the first violins, a last gasp, anchored by the double basses. But they are not alone. All mankind must ultimately die, all living things. And so the wind instruments come back, *pianissimo*, *pianissimo*, as the violins fade. And at the end, those triplets, in the double basses alone, and a soft final minor chord. Soft, soft.

He was crouching as the last vestige of sound died away. Now he stood and his eyes were wide and sparkling. After darkness there must be light. It is the natural order of things. He barely gestured with his arms and the delicate, floating sounds of the Scherzo wafted towards him. *Pianissimo*, always *pianissimo*. He wanted the audience behind him to strain to hear, to search out the light, to long for it – the first filtering of it at dawn, as it slowly breaks through the gloom of night.

And when it does, oh, glorious dawn! He leaped high in the air and had to restrain himself from calling out '*Fortissimo! Fortissimo!*'

The Scherzo was taking flight. But stop everything. Stop your playing. His arms froze in the air and he looked at the three horn players. Three! Sound your call, horns. Announce the Trio. He looked over the heads of the players as the horns' call rang out, through the high windows to the sky beyond.

Ah, Grandfather, can you hear? Tears brimmed in his eyes. He held his arms still in front of him. Silence, perfect silence, before the final unequivocal statement. That death is nothing, that after death there has to be life, or what is the point of living? *That you, Grandfather, live on in me.*

The tiny grace notes and then the huge *fortissimo* run that opens the final movement . . . But softly now. Crouch low. Stealthily. Then the blazing *fortissimo* triplet – the answer to the doom-laden triplets of the funeral march – leading to . . . just plucked quavers.

E flat, B flat, B flat, E flat, just those four notes, from which all else flows. And that soaring theme, that glorious, soaring theme. The theme that he had finally developed to its full potential until there was nothing more for it to say. Yes, he thought, sing out, wind, and sing out, strings. Let me hear it. Make the sounds cut through my useless ears, dissipate the dreadful noise I am fated to live with, until only the pure sound of my music is there. No pain, no hurt, no anxiety, no grief, no sadness, no sorrow. Just my music.

He felt Ries's hands on his shoulders, pushing him gently down into a chair. He did not resist. The final chord slowly faded from his head, to be replaced again by that raucous applause. He turned in his chair. Archduke Rudolph and Prince Kinsky applauded vigorously. Haydn, he saw, was clapping politely. Everyone was clapping. At the end of the front row, furthest from him, two men with notepads on their knees were conferring.

Suddenly the applause intensified, and Ludwig realised that it was for Clement and the members of the orchestra, who had all got to their feet. Ludwig looked up at Clement, but the violinist's eyes were towards the audience, his right hand holding his instrument, the left held out to encompass the orchestra.

The noise began to cut into Ludwig's head. Why would it not go away and allow the sound of his music to fade slowly in his head? He gestured to Ries. 'Boy, fetch me a glass of wine. And be quick.'

Ludwig knew people would want to speak to him, that he would have to listen and reply. He closed his eyes tightly and willed the dullness not to worsen.

He stood up, holding the back of the chair for a moment to steady himself. He saw the diminutive figure of Haydn walking towards him. 'Ludwig, my boy. You have written a splendid work.'

Ludwig bent forward a little and Haydn repeated his words, clasping Ludwig's hands in his. 'A splendid work, Ludwig. A fine symphony. Long, I must say. A long work. But nothing wrong with that.'

Ludwig heard the words clearly. He remembered his anger when Haydn had made the same criticism of his piano trios so many years ago. It was different now. It no longer mattered what other people – even Haydn – thought.

'It had to be. There was no other way.'

'I understand. You sustain the length well. Most of it is in the first movement, isn't it? You are sending your message with those chords, aren't you? Not just the opening two, but those repeated chords – I should say discords – during the movement. They crash like – like – you do when you disagree with something I say.' He laughed.

Ludwig pursed his lips.

'A small word of warning,' Haydn said. 'You will be criticised for those opening chords. Too abrupt, they will say. Unnecessary. Too blatant and so on. I will not say that. I understand why they are there. I understand the message you are conveying. I understand, too, that with this work you have embarked on a new path. But my word of warning is,' his eyes suddenly acquired a mischievous glint, 'do not ever expect that the members of an orchestra will be able to play the first chord in perfect unison!'

A man Ludwig did not know tugged at his sleeve. 'Seebaum, Herr Beethoven. *Berlin Freymüthige*. You have subjected the audience to a test of endurance, have you not?'

Ludwig heard his words, but could not grasp their meaning.

'Such a long piece. And, in my opinion, for the musical cognoscenti only. The applause tonight is from your friends. I doubt many others will applaud as vigorously.'

'Long? Yes. But . . .' He looked to Haydn for support, but he had moved away.

Another man Ludwig did not know approached. 'Herr Beethoven. May I offer my congratulations? Haflinger, *Musikalische Zeitung*. Startling and beautiful passages. But rather spoiled by . . . how shall I put it? . . . losing itself in lawlessness. Yes, lawlessness. Good word.'

'Good word, Haflinger,' said Seebaum. 'Lawlessness. A certain lack of discipline, Herr Beethoven, of which Herr Haydn could never be accused.'

'Gentlemen, will you permit me?' The Archduke, Kinsky close behind, moved forward, the two critics yielding instantly and bowing as they retreated. 'Herr Beethoven. No dominant sevenths this time. You send your message in altogether more important ways.'

'Splendid, Beethoven,' said Kinsky, 'most splendid piece I have ever heard. No equal. No equal.'

'With this piece of music, Beethoven,' said the Archduke, 'you have begun a new era. I thought you had done so with your famous dominant sevenths. But I was wrong. Important as they were, as that piece was, it is nothing compared with this. With those two chords at the opening you have ushered in a new period in music. A new age.'

Prince Lobkowitz, standing with Prince Lichnowsky, said, 'You are right, Your Imperial Highness. The Symphonia Eroica will stand at the forefront . . .'

He moved aside as Countess Erdödy came forward. 'Forgive me, but I must – Your Imperial Highness, are we not fortunate tonight? Ah, Ludwig, such wonderful, such powerful music.' She reached forward and wrung his hands.

Ludwig suddenly felt tired. He took the glass of wine Ries held out to him and sipped it immediately. He wanted the wine to work its wondrous effect swiftly, to calm him, to allow him to cope with the babble around him.

He looked meaningfully at Ries, and was thankful to hear him say, 'Will you excuse Herr Beethoven, Your Imperial Highness? He . . .'

Ludwig smiled at his patrons and turned away. There was the kindly face of Stephan Breuning, talking to the woman he had seen earlier. He wanted to say to Stephan that they should leave, return to the Rothes Haus. But he knew they could not.

He saw from Stephan's expression that he was talking about him to the woman. She turned. Ludwig wanted to move away. A woman he had not met before, whose voice might be soft, who might ask him a question that he could not hear.

He stood stock still. His mouth had fallen slightly open. She was beautiful, the most beautiful woman he had ever seen. She was smiling, a welcoming, inviting smile, and he felt himself move towards her. Her skin was pale, but for a touch of colour on her cheekbones. Her eyes were wide, deep-set and shone joyously. Her auburn curls were burnished by the late-evening sun as it danced around her face with every slight movement of her head. Deep in his mind recognition stirred.

'Ludwig,' said Stephan, 'do you remember Antonie? Antonie

Birkenstock, as she was, now Brentano. You met her at Jahn's restaurant – how many years ago was it?'

'Seven or eight, I think,' she said. 'I was with Leni Willmann. Poor Leni. You performed your quintet. Oh, it was wonderful. I was so pleased – and privileged – to be there.'

Ludwig found himself smiling. It was her voice. So unexpected. Soft and gentle, like balm on his ears. He remembered how he had been struck by her beauty before and had wanted to speak to her more. But there was something different. It came to him suddenly. Before, there had been a sadness in her eyes, an inexplicable melancholy, which was missing now.

Again Stephan provided the information he sought. 'Antonie was about to leave for Frankfurt to marry her husband Franz.'

'Yes, but I am back in my home city now, and it makes me so happy. Even if I am only here for a short while. I will be so sad when I leave.'

And Ludwig saw the cloud fall over her eyes. 'I am glad you were here tonight. What did you . . . ?'

'Ludwig,' said Stephan, 'if I may say so, with my limited understanding of music, even I can see that you have composed something exceptional, something truly remarkable.'

Antonie nodded. 'I agree. I have never heard music like it. I feel as if you are talking in your own special language, and I seem to understand it. What a marvellous composer you are. I cannot tell you how happy it has made me to be here and listen to your music. And meet you again.'

Ludwig found that he was smiling at her.

BOOK FOUR

Chapter 1

Ludwig pulled at the white cravat tied tightly round his neck. It was causing small beads of perspiration to break out on his forehead. He stretched his arm again, hand open, and frowned as the muscles in his arm complained. His left hand rested on the back of a chair, which was lying on its side.

'Really, my dear Beethoven, if you will not sit still, if you insist on moving your arm, I cannot guarantee the result.'

'Mähler, I write music without a piano in front of me. I hear the music in my head. Why can you not paint my portrait from your head? Come and look at me whenever you wish, then take the image away in your mind and paint.'

He relished the look of frustration that settled on Mähler's face as he brought a cotton cover down over the canvas, making sure it hung clear of the wet paint. He moved the easel to a corner.

'I shall not need to put you through this agony again, my friend. I have all I need now.'

Ludwig picked up the chair his hand had been resting on and, letting out a long painful sigh, collapsed on to it. He took a handkerchief from under his sleeve and wiped his damp forehead.

'Do you feel quite well?' asked Mähler, concerned.

Ludwig nodded, but without conviction. He was unduly hot: his forehead was burning and his muscles ached, but he was not sure whether he was ill or whether his body was complaining at the contortion Mähler had made him put it through.

'Can I bring you a glass of water?'

Ludwig let out a contemptuous sigh. He was wondering how shocked Mähler would be if he asked him to go out for a carafe of wine when the door opened and Stephan Breuning entered. 'My dear friend,' he said, immediately troubled. 'You look unwell.'

'I'm just a bit too warm. I need air.'

Stephan's face brightened. 'Ludwig, it is Sunday. Let us go to the Vienna Woods for the day. Take two horses. From the riding school in the Garnisongasse. It is a lovely day. The air will do you good.'

The idea appealed to Ludwig, and the pair took their leave of the painter and his airless studio.

The two walked in silence towards the stables. Music revolved in Ludwig's head. Voices. But there was a high-pitched whistle too that would not go away. Suddenly the smell of horses assailed his senses and he screwed up his face. 'Ugh! Too strong. No, Steffen. Not horses. The stench! It makes my stomach turn.'

Stephan's face betrayed his disappointment. 'You will soon become accustomed to it, Ludwig. You will not notice it. Especially in the countryside.'

His tone grated and Ludwig's head ached.

'No,' he said sharply. 'Walk. We will walk.'

'To the woods?' asked Stephan, hardly able to believe his ears. 'It will be nightfall before we get there, and I am not sleeping under a tree.' But Ludwig had already set off. He had turned into the Alstergasse before Stephan caught up with him.

'Just out of the city, Steffen. Just to the beginning of the woods.' He stood silently for a few moments then strode on. The stop had made his head pound. He would not pause again, he decided, at least, not before lunch.

An hour later the clustered roofs of the village of Dornbach were visible to their right. Ahead, the first trees of the Vienna Woods stood on the gradually rising slopes.

'The air, Steffen. Do you smell the air? How different it is from Vienna. Here in the countryside I can breathe.' Ludwig mopped his brow. Within seconds the perspiration stood out on it again. 'Come. We will have lunch in Dornbach. And some wine.'

At the first inn they came to on the outskirts of the village, Ludwig threw himself on to one of the wooden benches arranged around a few tables outside. He braced himself for the throbbing to begin in his head, and brought out his handkerchief once more. 'Sodden. Do you have one I could borrow?' Stephan passed him a clean dry one with a wry smile.

Ludwig sipped the wine that had arrived without their asking for it. He closed his eyes, leaned his head back and heard the sounds of his music. He pulled a notebook from his pocket and scribbled in it. He listened again, and scribbled some more. He sipped the wine and cursed when a drop of perspiration fell from his nose into the glass.

'What are you working on? May I ask?'

Stephan's voice irritated him – so tuneless after what he had just heard.

'Opera. Finally. A new text. French story.'

'Whatever happened to the opera you were writing in Bonn? Do you remember, the Rhine legends? You had the manuscript with you that day we climbed the Drachenfels together.'

The Drachenfels. The Rhine. So long ago. Another life, it seemed. He said nothing. After a few moments he heard Stephan's voice again. 'I have a message for you. From Antonie. Antonie Brentano. She said she was sorry she did not see you before she left. She wanted me to tell you how much she enjoyed meeting you again.'

Ludwig's mouth was dry. In his mind he could see her dancing curls and glowing eyes, the pallor of her skin and the pink curve of her lips. But he could not put them all together; he could not remember her face. He tried to conjure it up. He heard the gentle, soothing sound of her voice. But her face would not come to him.

'I'm hungry, Steffen. Order some fish. And more wine.'

He heard Stephan's voice again. He could make out the words but not follow their sense. Lobkowitz . . . symphony . . . Eroica . . . performance . . .

'Nothing will be the same after that,' he said quietly, conscious that Stephan was leaning forward to listen. 'It is a departure. Not just for me. For music. Never the same again.'

'Why, Ludwig?'

Ludwig gave his friend an exasperated look. At first he did not reply. Then he said, 'It is more than music. It is a depiction of life. It explains life. That is the purpose of music.'

He looked down at the plate in front of him. The whiff of the fish entered his nostrils and his stomach turned. He could not eat. He broke it with his fork. It was dry. He threw down the fork and the anger welled up in him. Anger at his deafness, at the noises in his head, at the sweat on his forehead . . . the pain that Antonie had left Vienna, that she was beyond his reach, truly beyond his reach . . .

Unthinking he put a piece of fish in his mouth. It was dry, like leather. He tried to swallow it but could not. 'Waiter! Waiter!

Come here! This fish! It is old! Are you trying to poison me? Take it away!'

'The fish is fresh today, sir, I assure you.'

Ludwig's head was thumping and he did not hear what the waiter had said, but knew that the man was arguing, protesting. He could not suppress his fury. He did not want to. 'I said take it away, man! Did you not hear me? Are you deaf? How would you like to be deaf, eh?'

Before Stephan could stop him, Ludwig picked up his plate and hurled it at the waiter. It struck him full on the chest and dropped to the ground, smashing into pieces. The fish and vegetables stuck to the man's waistcoat, slowly sliding down and dropping off. His face was a mask of shock and horror.

The proprietor of the inn, hearing the commotion, came hurrying out.

Stephan leaped out of his chair. 'I'm sorry. So sorry. My friend isn't well. Forgive him.'

'You'll pay for this,' said the proprietor.

Stephan took money out of his pocket. 'Here. This will cover everything. I apologise.'

Ludwig scowled at the two men, but allowed his friend to pull him away.

'Come, Ludwig,' Stephan said. 'Not another word. We will take the coach back to the city.'

The next morning Ludwig was woken by the pain in his head. His skin was sore and the sweat cold on his forehead. He had a fever.

It took hold swiftly and, for several days, Ludwig drifted in and out of a fitful sleep. More than once he was roused by someone dabbing his forehead with a cooling cloth. He thought he saw Nanette once, looking down at him, her brows knitted. Certainly he saw Stephan many times. He often heard muffled voices. If he forced his eyes open he saw lips moving, but he could not make out the words.

The bald head of Doktor Schmidt peered into his face, the palm of his hand warm against the cold sweat on Ludwig's forehead. But under the sweat his skin was burning and Schmidt's hand made him uncomfortable. He tried to shake it off.

As his senses slowly began to return, he felt an arm round his head, gently lifting it, and a glass cool against his lips. The taste of water first, then thick broth, which he could feel giving him strength as it flowed down into his stomach.

Gradually his strength returned and his temperature returned to normal. But the pain in his head remained and the whistling in his ears worsened when he tried to sit up.

'My damned ears,' he said hoarsely one day to Stephan, who sat by the bed.

'The fever has gone,' said Stephan, speaking clearly. 'You're looking better. Do you feel better?'

'Yes. My skin no longer feels as if it is raw and my forehead does not burn.'

'You must stay in bed a day or two longer. Doktor Schmidt wants to see you again before he allows you up.'

Ludwig did not know how long it was after that conversation that Doktor Schmidt came to see him. He had slept soundly, he knew, better than he had slept since the fever began, and he awoke refreshed. And, even better, the throbbing and whistling in his head had lessened.

At last, Schmidt came into the room, accompanied by Nanette who hurried to the side of the bed. 'Dear Ludwig. How much better you look. Andreas will be so pleased. Are you feeling better?'

Ludwig managed a faint smile. 'Yes. Did you come to see me before? I think you did.'

Nanette nodded. 'I had to help Stephan. He was so good to you, you know. He stayed at home to nurse you, when he should —'

'Stayed at home?' There was a note of annoyance in Ludwig's voice. 'Why did he do that? He did not need to. I am not a child.'

'Do not talk so, Ludwig. He is a dear friend. Often he sat by your bed in the night, rather than sleep himself, in case you needed help.'

Ludwig sighed. 'Am I to be grateful all my life to other people? I do not ask for such help. I do not need it. When I was a child with smallpox, my mother left me alone. I did not need help.'

'Well, young man,' said Doktor Schmidt, in a stentorian voice, 'you have had quite a strong fever. Now, if you will allow me . . .' He lifted up Ludwig's nightshirt, took an ear trumpet from his case and placed it at various points on Ludwig's chest. Nanette disappeared to make coffee.

'Sounds fine. Good strong heartbeat. I think we can safely say you have recovered.'

'Why was I ill? What happened?'

Schmidt frowned. 'Several factors. You were weakened after the concert at Prince Lobkowitz's. That made your stomach pains worse, didn't it?'

Ludwig nodded.

'It is my belief that the strain of the concert, the worry of it, lowered your resistance to outside infection. I cannot prove it, but I regard it as highly likely. Then, Breuning has told me you went for a long walk together into the countryside and became very hot, that you cooled down too fast. That was what brought the fever on, I am sure.'

'And my ears? My hearing, Schmidt? It seems worse.'

'Well, I would expect that after a severe fever, since you already have a weakness there. I think it might improve as the effects of the illness wear off.' He paused. 'There is something else, and you will not be grateful to me for telling you.'

Ludwig raised himself slightly on the pillow.

'You are drinking too much wine. That is almost certainly the cause of your stomach pains. It hurts up here, doesn't it?' Schmidt pressed under Ludwig's right lung.

He grimaced, but said nothing.

'The liver. Too much wine damages it. Cut down on the amount you drink. If you must drink, drink only in the evening. And one other piece of advice. Take a rest. What are your plans for the summer?'

'I'll get away. I must. Ries will find me somewhere.'

'Go to Baden. Take the waters. Enjoy the countryside.'

'Anywhere is preferable to this wretched apartment. It's like a prison. I don't know how Steffen can live here. I must get out.'

'Show a little gratitude,' said Schmidt, slapping him on the arm and standing. 'You have fine friends, you know. Breuning and Frau Streicher. They care about you very much.'

Ludwig sat at the dinner table while the housekeeper bustled around, putting bread, water and a carafe of wine on the table. He was hungry and the saliva flowed in his mouth as he watched the drops of condensation run down the outside of the carafe. Where was Stephan? He should be back by now. He poured himself some wine and cut a piece of bread. They tasted good.

He looked round the small room. He was ready for the sweet smells of the countryside. His body was weak but the fever had gone, and although his ears were plaguing him, they were not dulling his creative urge. He needed to be away from the city, with a piano he was allowed to play, so that he could work on *Leonore*. ('No need for the accent,' Ludwig had told Sonnleithner, 'it's not French any more.')

He did not hear Stephan come in. The first he saw was his friend's face, red with anger.

Stephan put his hands on the table and leaned forward. 'I have just been with the landlord. He said you left your apartment without giving notice. Can it be true? I asked you at the time, and you said you had done it.'

Ludwig wished he could plead deafness, but Stephan knew how to speak to be sure Ludwig could hear.

'Ries should have done it. Ries –'

'Ries!' Stephan exploded. 'Always someone else's responsibility! It was up to you, not Ries. And you did not do it.'

Ludwig looked at his friend. Behind the anger Stephan's face wore its usual smugness: I always do everything correctly, I always obey the rules, it said, why can't you? What right did Stephan have to speak to him like this? What was Stephan anyway? A clerk in the War Office. Doing what? Reading reports. Writing them. His head throbbed harder. 'I cannot be bothered with – with trivialities. I cannot be bothered. Do you hear?' He brought his fist down on the table, knocking over his glass of water.

Stephan burst out, 'You cannot be bothered! Do you know how much other people do for you? Do you know what would happen to you without them? That business at the inn in Dornbach, for instance. Who do you think you are? God? To hurl your food at the waiter. Anyone else doing that would be arrested. But there is always someone there to get you out of trouble. You're ill? There's always someone there. And it's usually me. And now you've cost me my deposit. *My* deposit. The money I put down for *you*.'

Anger boiled over in Ludwig: Stephan was shouting at him, his head was throbbing badly and his ears were ringing. He shot up from the table, knocking over the chair. The sound of it clattering to the floor hurt his ears even more.

'I have had enough of being insulted. You were once my friend, Steffen. No more. Do you hear? You are so petty. I am going to Baden. I will not be returning to this apartment. Our friendship is over.'

Chapter 2

The spa town of Baden lay a day's carriage ride south of Vienna, at the southern end of the huge swathe of the Vienna Woods, which stood to the west of the capital city like a protective blanket. The river Schwechat ran through the centre of Baden, before it turned north to empty its waters into the great Danube. But it was the hot sulphurous waters which bubbled up from deep in the earth below that had brought people to Baden since Roman times.

Ries had taken a room for Ludwig in the Johannesbad, a bath-house that stood on a small island in the river. Two narrow bridges of wooden slats connected the island with each bank. On the south bank, set a little way back from the river, stood the Sauerhof, another bath-house, larger and grander than the Johannesbad but showing signs of decay. Ries had established that one of the public rooms in the Sauerhof possessed a piano, and for a small fee the management was prepared to give Ludwig exclusive use of the room for an hour a day.

The lodgings Ries had found for him were well placed, slightly to the west of the town centre, and Ludwig could walk between the Johannesbad and the Sauerhof unnoticed. The room with the piano was to the side of the main building. Ries had instructed both establishments that on no account was Herr Beethoven to be disturbed by anyone.

Ludwig wanted to be left alone in Baden. He knew word would quickly spread of his presence in the town, which would soon lead to invitations to perform on the piano. He still felt weak from his fever, and the altercation with Breuning, and the deterioration in his hearing meant that every time he met someone new he felt a frisson of anxiety that he might not be able to hear them.

He wanted to be alone, to continue work on *Leonore* and to enjoy the solitude and calm of the countryside. To the west of the town lay the vast valley of the Helenenthal, its tall thick trees clustered together on the slopes that ran down to the Schwechat. High up on top of the hill that rose above the valley stood the jagged ruins of the medieval castle of Rauhenstein, its central fragmented turret pointing like a broken finger towards the sky.

The first time Ludwig saw it, Rauhenstein reminded him of the Drachenfels, and he had barely been in Baden a day before he had climbed to it through the dense undergrowth. Soon he established a regular pattern of taking the waters in the Johannesbad, then walking in the Helenenthal and climbing to the Rauhenstein ruin, returning to compose at the piano in the Sauerhof.

One morning as he followed the familiar routine, he found himself thinking of Stephan Breuning. He was alone in the bath, for which he was grateful. He lay back, allowing his head to sink into the water until it bubbled around his chin. The smell of sulphur filled his head. At the beginning of his holiday he had found it unpleasant but now he was used to it. A strange sensation came over him, that his life was repeating itself. That he had been in this position before. It was true: in Heiligenstadt two years before – was it really only two years? – he had sat in a sulphur bath shortly after a breach with his old childhood friend. I should not have shouted at him, Ludwig thought. I really should not. He heaved the top half of his body out of the water and sank immediately down again, the hot water coursing over his shoulders. But it did not really matter, he thought. In the long run the friendship would be restored. It had happened before and, no doubt, would happen again. But it had left him with an immediate problem. He would have to summon Ries to Baden and tell him to look for new lodgings. Friends or not, Ludwig knew he could not go back to living with Stephan.

He sank his head lower, opened his mouth and allowed the water to bubble into it, closing the back of his throat so as not to swallow it. The sound of the natural bubbles was loud in his ears. The water was going into them and beating against his eardrums – a constant, steady sound, no sudden shrieks or laughs, nothing unexpected that his ears would refuse to accept. Consoling, comforting almost.

He stood up suddenly, sending the water cascading over the edge of the bath. He dried hurriedly, took a drink of the sulphurous water from a metal cup hanging by a chain next to a small fountain, rinsed his mouth and spat into the drain with a grunt of displeasure at the taste, dressed swiftly and strode out.

He crossed the wooden bridge to the north bank of the Schwechat, turned left on to the Helenenstrasse and walked towards the western edge of the town. The Schwechat stretched in front of him, carving its way through the Helenenthal, the steep sides of the valley thick with the foliage of its mass of trees. To begin with, at the entrance to the valley, the river was broader and its low banks gave way to expanses of meadow on either side. Here was where the people of Baden came to stroll, sit and eat lunch from wicker baskets. A few cows grazed. At one point there was a small natural waterfall where the river, flowing towards the town, crashed over a natural ridge of rocks and stone. It was no more than a few feet high, but the rushing sound was pleasant and if the weather was fine the sun cut through the spray, making the drops of water glitter like diamonds in the air.

Walking on, in the deep still patches of water directly under overhanging trees, Ludwig could see the motionless dark shapes of trout basking. Occasionally one would rise languidly to the surface, snap at an insect and sink slowly back to its resting place. Up to his right was a high formation of rock, the beginning of the spur on which the Rauhenstein ruin stood, vast and menacing, surveying the land around it yet no longer able to protect it.

Ludwig increased his pace, striding along the river bank then turning to the right and beginning the steep climb to the ruins. Easier than the Drachenfels, he thought, but in his mid-thirties now and lacking the limitless power of youth, he quickly found himself breathing harder than he ever had when he had climbed the familiar rock by the Rhine.

The path, heavily overgrown but well defined, ran in broad sweeps with sharp bends. Bored by its regularity, Ludwig cut up to the side, clambering over rocks that jutted out from the ground. Some were not fixed and he nearly missed his footing, which gave him a sense of exhilaration. When, finally, he came to the outer wall of the castle, he paused for the first time in his climb, propping himself against the wall and resting his head against its cool stone. Then he walked inside the ruin and was struck by its size. From the floor of the valley it looked small, just a few pieces of jagged tower left. But inside there was a labyrinth of walls, some higher than others. The castle must have had dozens of small rooms.

And here . . . he moved forward. Obviously the main hall: the grand fireplace was still identifiable against the far wall, the stonework above it blackened with soot. How long had it been here? How many hundreds of years? Had defenders stood in these turrets, their bows pointed out through the slits in the walls, raining death down on marauders?

His ears felt heavy from the climb, and his head was pulsating but not painful. If he screwed his eyes tightly closed, could he hear men's screams, the jumbled discord of a battle to the death? Or were they sounds of music, chaotic and orderless at first, but slowly forming into harmonies?

He took a notebook and pencil from his pocket. A theme for his opera. Something fierce, to reflect the ruin in which he stood, the dungeon in which Florestan was imprisoned. But the notes would not come. Only the sweet sounds of Leonore singing of her love for her husband.

So be it, he thought. He walked into one of the turrets and looked up. The staircase had gone. It was just a dark empty place. A sudden flurry of movement high under the roof of the turret startled him. It was a bird. He had disturbed it.

He hurried outside and watched the hawk soar effortlessly into the sky. It circled a few times, as if it was looking down at him. Then, in a long swoop, it descended to the ruin, perching high above him, looking down at him, angry at the intrusion but safe, where no human being could touch it.

Why had Ries brought Czerny? At first Ludwig was irritated but he felt guilty too. He had promised the boy lessons and had given him only a few. He was impressed with him. He was a capable, if uninspired, player. Ludwig did not know how old he was, but he could not have been far into his teenage years and he had a remarkable facility with piano exercises. He could play scales, broken chords, arpeggios with ease. Surprisingly he seemed to enjoy it, even more than playing whole pieces. Quite the opposite to the average piano student. Quite the opposite to me!

'Herr Ludwig,' said Ries, 'I'm glad you asked me to come. Your friends are concerned for your welfare. They insisted we come down – two of us – to find out how you were and report back. Ignaz Gleichenstein was going to accompany me, but this young man insisted on coming in his place.'

'Sir,' said Czerny, eyes bright, 'I have been practising every day. I would like to play for you.'

Ludwig smiled. The boy's voice was high-pitched and quite shrill, for which he was thankful. It was Czerny who had brought Ludwig's deafness into the open, when he had remarked on the cotton soaked in yellow oil in his ears.

'See?' said Ludwig now, surprised at his own good humour. 'No cotton any more. No more messy oil running down on to my collar. The doctors have given up on me.'

Czerny stared at his feet, embarrassed.

'Carl has something to tell you, Herr Ludwig. A funny story, which he thinks will amuse you.'

'First, wine,' said Ludwig. 'I suppose not for you, young man. But, Ries, tell the caretaker to bring up a carafe. Or, better still, let's go to the Braunen Kuh on the Weilburggasse.'

'I think, Herr Ludwig, it would not be appropriate with Carl here.'

'Then Luigi's café in the Hauptplatz.'

'Herr Ludwig, in the centre of town, people might . . .'

Ludwig was already at the door. He was in good spirits. The country air, the invigorating walks in the Helenenthal, the warming baths . . . And work on the opera was progressing.

At Luigi's Ludwig ordered strong coffee for himself and Ries, and an almond milk for Carl Czerny. They sat at a table outside. Behind them, in the centre of the square, stood an ornate memorial to the Great Plague, its gold leaf glinting in the sun. It was less ornate than its sister monument in the Graben in Vienna, and the hollow-eyed skulls at its base gave it a more sombre appearance.

'Go on, Carl. Tell Herr Ludwig what you have to do in Vienna.'

The tables around them were occupied and people milled around in the square, through which carriages passed, more slowly than in Vienna, less pressed for time. The sound of horses' hoofs clashed with the shouts of carriage drivers. Ludwig regretted his sudden impulse to come to Luigi's, but the coffee tasted good. 'You'll have to speak up, boy. Remember my wretched hearing.'

'Of course, sir,' said Czerny, with a mischievous grin. 'His Excellency Prince Lichnowsky has noticed that I play your pieces for piano with a certain . . . rather –'

'Extremely well,' cut in Ries. 'Do not be modest. Herr Ludwig, Carl has learned several of your sonata movements, as well as variations. He plays the Prometheus variations from –'

'Daa-daa-daa-daa,' sang Ludwig. 'E flat, B flat, B flat, E flat. You play that, do you, boy?'

Carl looked down modestly. 'His Excellency's wife, Princess Christiane, is not in good health. She is confined to her room for long periods and I play the piano for her. Often His Excellency sits in the room and listens. He likes to choose what I play. Now what he does is just call out the opus number and I play it.'

'Just the opus number? And you play it?'

Ludwig looked at Ries and Czerny suspiciously, wondering if they were having fun at his expense. But it was clear that they were not. 'Thirteen,' he said.

Carl looked quickly at Ries, who nodded. He stretched his small hands over the table and brought them down in the huge C minor chord that opened the Pathétique sonata. He moved them up in the dotted crotchet and quaver chords that followed. Ries reached forward hastily and moved a cup.

'Twenty-six, Marcia Funèbre.'

With barely a hesitation, Czerny's hands played the rhythmic chords that opened the funeral march of the piano sonata in A flat, which he had composed around five years earlier.

'Hah! Do you know who that is dedicated to?' asked Ludwig.

Czerny looked up. 'Well, yes, sir. His Excellency the Prince. That is why he often calls on me to play it. In fact,' he glanced at Ries to check that he was not speaking out of turn, 'he once said he wished you had composed something a little more . . . a little less sad than a funeral march, since it was dedicated to him.'

'No, no. Who is it *really* dedicated to?'

Czerny shook his head; Ries looked puzzled.

'A criminal. A man whose nation trusted him, who carried the hopes of his people on his shoulders, and who is nothing more than a tyrant like the rest of them.'

Ries smiled. 'The new Emperor of France.'

'Emperor Napoleon,' said Czerny. 'The coronation takes place at the end of the year, I read.'

'Frimaire,' said Ries. 'Le onze frimaire.'

'What?' asked Ludwig.

'The revolutionary calendar, Herr Ludwig. He was proclaimed Emperor on the twenty-eighth of floréal, and the coronation is on the eleventh of frimaire.'

Ludwig frowned and intoned in a deep voice, '"Marcia Funebre sulla morte d'un Eroe". I chose the title of the movement well, did I not?'

The two younger men laughed.

'Thirty-five.'

Czerny played the E flat chord that began the Prometheus Variations, and Steibelt's four upside-down notes.

Ludwig finished his coffee. 'Come,' he said suddenly. 'To the Sauerhof. I need to feel real keys under my fingers.'

The two young men followed in his wake as he strode down to the Josefplatz, crossed the main bridge over the Schwechat and turned into the Weilburggasse towards the Sauerhof. He went straight to the room with the piano, while Ries hurried off to tell the management they were not to be disturbed.

'Now listen to this,' said Ludwig, his fingers playing the keys before he had completely sat on the stool, which Czerny hurriedly moved underneath him. He played a gentle lyrical theme, just the right hand in the treble and only eight bars long. Then the left hand, again in the treble, the same theme, as the right hand played a development of it. The right hand then played only the developments, as the left hand took up the main theme again. It was a canon, four distinct voices, each coming in to state the main theme as the one before it moved on. As if to confirm the vocal element, Ludwig began to sing as he played. He had a tuneless, harsh voice – Czerny and Ries exchanged a conspiratorial smile. 'Mir ist so wunderbar,' he sang. 'Es engt das Herz mir ein. Er liebt mich, es ist klar. Ich werde glücklich sein.'

Soon Ludwig's singing became little more than a tuneless hum, but his hands continued to shape the beautiful theme. A quartet for voices. A canon, allowing each voice to come in individually. That was what Sonnleithner had wanted. 'All four characters need to express their emotions at this point. But how can you do it?' It had been his suggestion and Sonnleither had immediately agreed. After the introductory numbers, the opera needed a serious, reflective piece, to set the tone for the drama that was to unfold. He had thought about it for a long time, but the idea had come to him fully formed. A quartet as a canon. The theme had not come so quickly. He had made several sketches, ideas, fragments. Then one day the theme was in his head. Entire and complete. He had his quartet. Four separate characters, yet each dependent on the other. Leonore,

Rocco, Marzelline and Jaquino – yet only Leonore aware of the danger ahead.

He brought the quartet to its *fortissimo* unison close. I must see Sonnleithner, he thought. Discuss the opera. How far is he with his translation?

He turned round. He had not forgotten that Ries and Czerny were there, but now he needed to work, to be left alone.

'A beautiful melody, Herr Ludwig. It is for the opera, is it not?'

Ries's words jarred in Ludwig's head. 'Wait, Ries. Do not talk to me yet. The music is still in my head.'

He looked at the two sitting there. Suddenly he envied their youth. Ries, what, no more than twenty and Czerny still a boy. So much ahead of them. And both talented musicians, gifted enough to earn their living by music.

He turned back to the piano and began the second movement of the sonata he had dedicated to Count Waldstein – the lengthy Andante Grazioso. He had wondered when he composed it if was too substantial to sit as the middle movement. He had played it to Ries – and he had made Ries play it to him. Ries was in no doubt: Ludwig should publish it as a separate work, entire in itself, and compose a new, smaller movement for the sonata. Ludwig had resented the suggestion and Ries had not mentioned it again. But even as he played now he realised that that was how he was treating it, as a single, self-contained piece. The slow passages he stretched so that they were even longer. The bouncing descending rhythm that acted as a link between the two halves of the piece he played with an added jauntiness. And the furious passage close to the end he played in a whirl of notes, a stunning display of virtuosity.

Eventually he turned; both young men were applauding vigorously.

'Sir, if I may say so,' said Ries, 'such a fine piece. It really would stand alone.'

Ludwig frowned. 'Wait, Ries, damn you. Wait till the notes leave my head. Your voice hurts.'

He stood up and walked to the window. A small group of people stood outside on the grass. They turned away quickly as they saw him, but their faces were smiling and one man clapped briefly before he scurried away.

Despite his irritation, Ludwig, smiled. I have brought pleasure to them, he thought, not just by my playing but with my music.

Anyone can play my music, they just have to learn the notes, anyone with talent, Ries, Czerny, Hummel, Cramer, Wölffl . . . But who can compose like me? Who in Vienna, or Europe, or the world?

'Damn you, Ries. You and your damned fool ideas. Do you hear? I said damn you.' But he grinned as he spoke. 'Go and see them at the Kunst-und-Industrie. Tell them to publish the Andante separately. I will compose a new second movement for the sonata.'

'Oh, yes, sir. Certainly. I will. I know it is the right decision. The Andante will become instantly popular. Now, sir, Carl and I will leave. It has been so rewarding for us to see you and know –'

'When you get back, find me somewhere else to live, Ries. Ask Nanette Streicher, she knows of places. And you, Czerny. Remember it takes more than scales and arpeggios to make a pianist. Now go on, both of you. I have work to do.'

Chapter 3

Ludwig followed Ries up the steep stairs, breathing heavily and envying the younger man the ease with which he climbed. He knew Ries was talking to him – he could hear a constant stream of indecipherable words coming from above him – but he paid no attention. By the time he reached the fourth floor sweat was glistening on his forehead and his ears were ringing: he knew he could not take this apartment. Ries should have known better.

The door was already open and Ries bounded in. Ludwig followed him, his eyes scanning the room for a chair. Bright sunshine filled it and the air was cool. It smelled of cut grass. His breathing steadying, he walked to the open window.

The view made him gasp. He looked out over the Bastion and across the broad Glacis towards the northern suburbs of the city, Nussdorf, Heiligenstadt and Grinzing, and beyond the tall peaks of the Vienna Woods, their upper slopes covered in thick fir trees as far round to the left as the eye could see. He wanted to look to the right but the side wall had no window. He leaned out and craned his head round. There was the Augarten, and further to the right the great Prater park, the wide, stately Danube and the beginnings of the Hungarian plain to the east.

He turned back and sat in the chair Ries had pulled up for him. Only now did he realise that Prince Lichnowsky and another man were in the room. The Prince was speaking to him. 'Wonderful, isn't it, Ludwig? Perfect for you. And available now. Baron Pasqualati has been so kind. The bedroom is nice too. Views to the east, without having to lean out of the window. It occupies the whole fourth floor. The top floor. No one above you stamping around. The servant is in a room next door. And the Baron has agreed a very favourable rent.'

Ludwig wanted him to stop talking. There were too many words coming at him, too much information. He looked at

Ries: the young man wore a look of expectancy, his mouth hanging open.

'So fortunate, Herr Ludwig. So fortunate,' he said. 'I spoke to His Excellency, hardly daring to hope. But Baron Pasqualati just happened to have this apartment available.'

Ludwig turned to the stranger, who was smiling at him. 'A piece of good fortune, Herr Beethoven. The previous tenant was forced to leave unexpectedly. I am delighted – and honoured – to have you resident in my building. I am sure you will be happy here. The Mölkerbastei is one of the quietest parts of the city.'

Ludwig looked at the three men, all gazing at him with such expectation. He glanced at the side wall. 'Will you put a window in that wall, so I can see the river?' He delighted in the change of expression on their faces.

The next day Ries arranged for Ludwig's possessions to be moved from the Rothes Haus. Nanette Streicher sorted his clothes, organising them in drawers and the cupboard in the bedroom. Some shirts and socks she took away to repair.

Ludwig told Ries to put all his manuscripts, papers and notebooks on the long table underneath the window, but to place all the work on *Leonore* to one side. There was a dresser along the windowless wall. He told Ries to make sure there was always a full carafe of wine on top of it. Ries passed on the instruction to the servant.

Finally Ludwig's piano was brought in – four men sweating and cursing at the climb to the top of the building. Ries directed them to put it against the left-hand wall, looking continually to Ludwig for approval.

'My grandfather's portrait,' said Ludwig, when he and Ries were alone. 'Hang it above the piano.'

Over the following days friends and colleagues came to see Ludwig. Ignaz Schuppanzigh collapsed in a heap into a chair and complained that Ludwig had deliberately chosen an apartment on the top floor to force him to lose weight.

To Ludwig's satisfaction Stephan Breuning came to see him and drank a glass of wine with him, making no mention of their quarrel. It was as though it had not happened.

One early evening Nikolaus Zmeskall, breathing heavily, came into the room clutching a handful of quills. 'There.

From the Chancellery. One day they will find out and I will get the sack.'

Ludwig smiled, poured two glasses of wine and passed one to his friend.

'How is the work going?' asked Zmeskall, removing his spectacles and rubbing them on his shirt tail.

Ludwig sighed gustily. 'Much to do on the opera. Braun is pestering me to finish. He wants to open the spring season with it. I have told him it is impossible.'

'Ludwig, I envy you. Europe is about to come apart at the seams and you are able to pursue the nobler calling of art.'

'What do you mean?'

'I'm not surprised you haven't heard. You have only musical notes in your head. A certain emperor – and I do not mean our own revered Imperial Majesty – has announced his intention to declare himself King of Italy. It is a direct challenge to the Habsburg Empire's interests there.'

'War again?'

'Inevitably. Only this time victory is certain. The talk is,' Zmeskall leaned forward, as if worried he would be overheard, 'that Austria will join forces with Britain and Russia. Napoleon may be able to defeat a single army, but three he cannot.'

Ludwig lifted the carafe, but Zmeskall put his hand over his glass. 'Enough, Ludwig. For both of us. I have come here for a purpose and I do not want your mind befuddled with wine. I want you to meet a friend of mine, Franz Brunsvik. Hungarian, like me. Fine family. Has sisters. He's a cellist – again like me, only better.'

'No, Nikola. I do not want to meet anyone. It's my hearing. It is not improving. I find it difficult in company . . .'

A concerned look crossed Zmeskall's face. 'I was going to ask you about that. Have you heard of Pater Weiss? A priest at St Stephansdom? A remarkable man. He cures people of deafness.'

Ludwig's eyebrows shot into his hairline. 'Cures people?'

'Yes. They go to him in the crypt. He puts something in their ears – a special fluid – and it cures them. I have heard it from several friends. They said I should mention it to you.'

'A miracle cure in a cathedral. Preposterous!'

'I shall make enquiries anyway. Now, come on. You'll like Franz. And afterwards, shall we not indulge in some relaxation?

You are working hard. You need to relax. The Walfischgasse. A fortress to be stormed.'

A frisson of anticipation ran through Ludwig and he followed his friend down the stairs and into a carriage, which took them to the Rothenturmgasse, north of the cathedral.

Ludwig wished he had resisted Zmeskall's urging. But it was true – he had been working hard and he welcomed an opportunity to leave his apartment. He had not responded to Zmeskall's suggestion that they go to the Walfischgasse, but he knew he would not refuse and the idea excited him.

His heart sank as soon as he entered the house with Zmeskall and saw not only the man who must be Franz Brunsvik, but two women, presumably his sisters. His ears had their usual dullness and he knew he would find it hard to hear the women if they spoke to him. He wished he had not come.

He shook Franz Brunsvik's hand, immediately taking to his kind open face, and he had a firm strong voice, too. Ludwig followed his hand gesture towards the women.

'My sisters, Therese and Josephine. We call Josephine Pepi. Poor darling, barely twenty-five and already a widow.'

Ludwig found himself almost staring at a small woman with a pale face and restless black eyes. He knew she was returning his gaze, but fleetingly, her eyes flitting between him and other things. Her face was framed by black ringlets, which quivered with every slight move of her head. Ludwig was struck by the hollowness of her cheeks and the darkness beneath her eyes.

Another face swam into his mind – fuller, less pale, with auburn curls that danced and deep sparkling eyes. Josephine was not beautiful in the way Antonie was, but she had a certain quality that drew him to her. Maybe it was pity that she was a widow and Ludwig's awareness that she was trying, without appearing too obvious, to look at him.

He forced himself to acknowledge Therese. She had an altogether stronger face, broad and high-cheekboned, and a self-confidence that matched her brother's and was missing in their younger sister.

'Mind you,' Franz continued, 'Count Deym was not an ideal husband. He was not kind to poor dear Pepi. Now he has left her with four small children, the youngest not yet a year old. But we will look after you, won't we, Pepi? We shall be taking her back to Martonvasar soon. She will be so much happier there.'

'I am not going back there,' Josephine said, with surprising vehemence in her voice. 'I am staying here, where I belong.'

Franz looked awkwardly at Zmeskall and Ludwig. 'Now, my friends, so good of you to come and see us. I will order some coffee and cake.' He walked to the mantelpiece and pulled on a bell cord. He directed Zmeskall and Ludwig to chairs.

'We are truly privileged to meet such a great musician. A great composer.' It was Therese, and Ludwig found that her words easily penetrated the dullness in his ears. Maybe, he thought, with just a hint of a smile, it is because she used the word 'composer' rather than pianist. He saw a piano in the corner of the room, and knew it was only a matter of time before someone suggested he play it.

He nodded in acknowledgement but said nothing. He was content to let Zmeskall carry on the conversation, because it allowed him to study Josephine. More than once she glanced at him, saw his look and lowered her eyelashes, a touch of red in her cheeks.

Ludwig sipped the strong black coffee, preparing himself for the moment when the conversation – which at the moment dwelt on the Brunsviks' widowed mother and the family estate at Martonvasar south of Budapest – would turn to him.

It was Josephine who spoke. Her voice was higher than he expected and shrill. It did not have the same soothing effect on him as Antonie's, but he could hear it. 'Herr Beethoven, you must fear that every time you step into someone's salon they will ask you to play the piano for them.'

Ludwig smiled at the aptness of the remark.

'Oh, Pepi,' exclaimed Therese, 'you have quite spoiled it for us. How can we ask Herr Beethoven to play for us now, after you have said that?'

'Therese, my dear,' said Franz, 'Herr Beethoven is our guest. We should not expect him to behave in any other way. I do apologise, sir,' he continued, turning to Ludwig. 'My sisters have something to learn about salon manners.'

Still Ludwig said nothing. All faces, though, were turned to him. He could see that even Zmeskall was expecting him to respond.

He coughed and said, gesturing towards Josephine, 'I understand. Fräulein Brunsvik is correct. It is usual for a request to be made. I prefer it when it is not.'

'Of course! There, didn't I tell you?' exclaimed Josephine.

'Well, I have a better idea.' With a flurry of her full dress she rose and walked determinedly to the piano. Ludwig saw Franz and Therese exchange a concerned look.

'Pepi, dear,' said Franz firmly, 'I am sure Herr Beethoven does not wish to hear your efforts. Why do you not come and sit down again?'

But Josephine stretched her hands over the keys. Ludwig waited for the sounds to reach him. He was looking forward to hearing them, whatever they were. Musical notes – any musical notes – were preferable to conversation. Then he recognised the opening quavers and semiquavers of the Andante grazioso.

'*Tempi*,' he said, under his breath. Then, louder, '*Tempi. Andante*. Not too fast. Good,' as Josephine steadied her playing.

She played just the main opening section of thirty bars, closing with a chord before the development began.

There was polite applause, which Ludwig did not join, and Josephine returned to her chair, not daring to glance at him. He knew he should say something. She had played the piece well, if unsubtly, ignoring several of the dynamic markings.

The music still revolved in his head, but he decided to speak. 'It was going to belong to a sonata, but I decided to publish it separately. You played it well.'

'No, no,' Josephine contradicted him, 'I wish I could learn it properly. Will you teach it to me?' she asked, suddenly staring at Ludwig, her coal-black eyes wide open.

Again Franz and Therese exchanged a look.

'Herr Beethoven is very busy. He is composing an opera for the Wien,' said Zmeskall.

'Of course,' said Josephine. 'But just a little of your time, Herr Beethoven. Will you permit me to visit you?'

Ludwig's pulse quickened. Her face was appealing: to say no would wound her. In any case he was flattered by her attention. As he nodded she gave a little yelp of pleasure.

Soon after, Ludwig and Zmeskall took their leave of the Brunsviks. Josephine extended her hand to Ludwig, and as he took it she darted forward and brushed his cheek with her lips. He caught a whiff of her perfume.

In the carriage Ludwig was tense, his skin hot and his mouth dry. Neither he nor Zmeskall spoke.

Still no word passed between them as they walked along the dark Walfischgasse, the narrow street that ran parallel to the Bastion and in its shadow. The sign of the Blauen Säbel – the hussar with his priapic sabre rising from between his legs – swung forlornly in the night breeze, dimly illuminated by a single light fastened to the wall. The two men climbed the stairs to the door with a grille set in it, through which Zmeskall muttered a few words.

Ludwig's body was on fire, as if his tension was doubling in the certain knowledge that it would soon dissipate.

Inside, figures floated in the dark red light. Candles flickered high in corners, throwing shadows across the room. The perfumed aroma, accentuated by the warmth of bodies, flooded over Ludwig's senses.

Silently, masked faces floated by him. He felt soft moist lips brush against his cheek, but he did not respond. In the constantly moving light he saw flashes of naked breast, nipples erect and rouged red. A hand took his and placed it on a breast. Two fingers induced his thumb and forefinger to squeeze a nipple. His breathing was quick now and his chest tight. He felt the soft contours of a woman press against him and a hand rubbed his groin. A mask was moved to the side and a tongue pushed between his lips. The tongue explored further and the hand rubbed harder on his groin. Then it reached up, took his hand and led him to a door at the back of the room. Down a short corridor, through another door and into a tiny room.

The single small candle was not enough to reveal the girl's face. He closed his eyes and tried to conjure up the face of Josephine Brunsvik, but it would not come. In its place were the dancing auburn curls of Antonie Brentano. He wanted to stop, but he knew he could not. He forced Antonie's face from his mind and in its place, suddenly, was the pale image of Josephine. He felt a hand behind his head, pulling him down on to a face that was soft and sweet-smelling, with lips that were hot against his and a tongue that spread moisture over his mouth and chin.

With her other hand the girl reached expertly inside his clothes and held him, emitting a small gasp as she felt the full length of him. Try as he might, he could not prevent the ecstatic flood of sensations that swept over him, forcing him to strain his groin forward. With a gasp he poured out all the tension, all the strain, all the anxiety within his body.

He heard her whisper in his ear, but he did not know what she said. He buried his face in her neck, wishing she were not a stranger but a woman who had chosen to spend her life with him. But how could that ever be?

The muscles in his body began to soften and where her neck had been there was now a soft cushion. Almost imperceptibly the girl rose and left and Ludwig knew he was alone.

Should he feel guilt? He lay still. Who had he hurt by coming here? No one. He had had a need and this had satisfied it.

He sat up and reached for the towel that he knew would be lying by the mattress. He summoned the face of Antonie into his mind, dismissed it and replaced it with Josephine's. In the darkness he smiled to himself. He even felt a sensation of triumph, as if he had achieved a conquest.

Chapter 4

Ludwig and Nikolaus Zmeskall walked across the square which, only twenty years before, had been a churchyard, and into the vast interior of St Stephansdom, the cathedral that had dominated the centre of the city for five centuries and had twice withstood a Turkish invasion. There was a smell of incense, and sounds echoed off the high, vaulted walls. Ludwig pressed his arms against his sides; he shivered slightly at the sudden stony chill.

He wanted to put his hands to his ears. He could almost feel the vast empty space in them, and the random noises – a chair scraping, the cough of a worshipper – seemed to explode in his head. He wanted to tell Zmeskall that Wolfgang Mozart had married Constanze here, but he did not know how loudly he would need to speak and he was certain he would not hear anything his friend said in reply.

He followed Zmeskall past the first sets of pillars decorated with elaborate statues, and down the stairs to the left of the nave into the catacombs. It was suddenly warmer in the narrow passages underneath the great church and, after a few moments, Ludwig felt his ears adjust to its closeness.

Zmeskall knocked on a door off one of the main passages and, without waiting for a reply, opened it. A candle burned on a table, throwing a dim light on the face of a monk sitting at it, a Bible open in front of him, a quill and paper to his side.

'Same quills I bring you,' Zmeskall hissed in Ludwig's ear. 'From the Chancellery.'

'Hah! My dear friend,' said Pater Weiss, regarding Zmeskall over his spectacles. 'Come, sit down. And allow me . . .'

He stood up and walked to a sideboard on which sat a carafe of wine and glasses. Ludwig smiled. Was it communion wine? Would he offer wafers as well and bless them? As the irreverent thought went through his mind the monk spoke, in a booming voice. 'Not communion wine, I assure you. Indeed, I cannot promise it is as good as you are used to. Herr Beethoven, what a great honour to make your acquaintance.'

Weiss had a large head, which seemed weighed down by the thick white beard falling like a frozen shaft of water from his chin. In contrast the hair on his head was thinning and unruly. He was corpulent, his girth emphasised by the cord tied around his habit.

'"And the Lord said, Let there be light,"' he said, with a laugh in his voice, as he lit a number of candles. 'Now, gentlemen, sit at my table. Enjoy my wine, and I will enjoy it with you. I have worked enough for one day.'

Ludwig felt the sharp taste at the back of his throat and enjoyed the aroma that flooded into his nose. He had realised quickly that he was having no difficulty in hearing Weiss and it was obvious why not: Zmeskall had told the monk why they were there and he was making allowances. But he was doing it without seeming to. Ludwig wished more of his friends could achieve the same result so effortlessly.

'So, Herr Beethoven,' said Weiss, 'your hearing causes you a problem, and you are a musician. A sad fate. As if a priest like me had lost the facility to pray, or a politician the ability to weave words into elaborate sentences which have no meaning.' He laughed and Ludwig, laughing with him, saw his face redden. 'We will see what we can do for you, with the help of the Lord. Tell me first. Is it in both ears, your deafness?'

Ludwig nodded.

'Which ear was affected first?'

'The left.'

'And the right followed soon after?'

Ludwig nodded again.

'When did you first notice the signs?'

'Five or six years ago. I can't remember exactly.'

'And what was happening in your ears?'

Ludwig sipped the wine, as if to give himself strength to go through it all again. 'Humming. Buzzing. Whistling. My head throbs. Sometimes I hear words, but cannot make them out. If someone shouts I can't bear it. In company it is worst. Here, talking just to you in a small room . . . But in the theatre. Or if I have just played music . . .' He drained his glass.

Weiss stroked his beard with his right hand, his left under his right elbow. 'Do you know how the ear is made up? Has any of your doctors ever explained it to you?'

'Vering said the canals were full of fluid. It was trapped in there. He put bark on my arms to draw it off.'

Weiss shook his head. 'I shall not criticise any practitioners of medicine. They are far cleverer than I. But it did not help, did it? Nor the warm baths, the almond oil.'

Ludwig looked at Zmeskall, who smiled.

'I know your history, sir,' said Weiss. 'Now, let me explain to you what I believe the problem to be. Inside your ear, deep inside, where we cannot reach, there are tiny bones, so small they are invisible to the eye. Only after death can the surgeon extract them and examine them under a glass. These bones vibrate very quickly, and in so doing conduct sound to the brain. Now, the most common cause of deafness is when these bones are unable to vibrate, or do not vibrate sufficiently.'

'What causes that?'

'A sticky fluid secreted by the brain, which surrounds the bones, making it impossible for them to vibrate properly.'

'So you need to get rid of that fluid?'

'Precisely.'

'That is no different from what Vering said.'

'Ah, there is a difference. He believed the fluid to be in the auditory canals, where it is relatively simple to dislodge it. I believe it to be deep inside your ear, from where it is very difficult to remove it.'

'How do you do it, then?'

'Similar technique to what you have done before. But not the bark to raise blisters, do not worry about that. Again, I will insert fluid into your ears. But it is a different fluid. I have concocted it after years of experimentation, using herb extracts which are particularly good at absorbing liquid. This fluid will slowly absorb the sticky solution that is causing your problem, then expel itself from your ear, taking the offending fluid with it.'

'But how will it . . . ?'

'Let me refill your glasses. Not a bad wine, eh? As you can imagine, it is very important that the fluid I insert is allowed to descend as deep as possible into the ear and remain there. It means I can only treat one ear at a time.'

'You mean I will have to have this treatment every day?' asked Ludwig. 'I will not be able to live a normal life. How long will it take?'

'Difficult to say. If you have been experiencing this for five years, or thereabouts, it means that the sticky fluid has had time to solidify. It will take time. But weeks, rather than months.'

'What will I have to do?'

'Come to see me each evening. Late. I will insert the fluid into one ear. You go home, being careful to keep your head tilted to the side so the fluid remains inside. Go to bed, sleeping with that ear uppermost and cotton firmly implanted in it. The next day you can behave normally, with the cotton still in place. The next evening I will treat the other ear, and so on.'

Ludwig sat back in his chair. 'Will it really work?' he asked. 'Will it cure my deafness?'

'Pater Weiss has had great success with his treatment. Particularly with children. Apparently this condition is more common in children, isn't it, Pater?'

'But not unheard-of in adults,' the monk added.

'Will you tell me to drink less wine, keep more regular hours, stop working so hard?'

'I do not believe such matters are important – they do not affect your physical condition. You can lead the holiest life in Christendom and still have such a problem in your ears. Why else would poor innocent children suffer?'

'Do your trickery on me then, Herr Priest,' said Ludwig. 'The worst that can happen is that you add your name to the growing list of quack doctors who have failed to cure me.'

With a renewed feeling of optimism Ludwig worked on the opera, and also, almost by way of diversion, set a poem by Christoph Tiedge to music. It bore what he hoped was the prophetic title 'An die Hoffnung', To Hope. And he made sketches for a new piano sonata.

His mood was further lightened when Sonnleithner told him Baron Braun had decided to postpone the opening of *Leonore* until the autumn.

Was he imagining it, or was Pater Weiss's treatment working? Every evening Ludwig went to the crypt of St Stephansdom and Weiss put in the thick sticky liquid. Nanette Streicher, whom he told about the treatment, came every third day to his apartment to put a clean pillowcase on his bed and take away the soiled one.

There was another reason for his mood. Ludwig was falling in love with Josephine Brunsvik. The small face, the darting eyes, the vulnerability attracted him. There was something else. He was convinced that she was attracted to him. Could it be? Josephine had made several visits to his apartment, and she alone, of all his visitors, had never complained about the arduous climb. She entered his rooms, hesitantly at first but then with growing confidence, strode to the piano and sat waiting for him to instruct her. 'Teach me the piece,' she had said on the first occasion. 'The piece I played for you. That is all I want to learn. Then I can say I am able to play a composition by Ludwig van Beethoven.'

He began by playing it for her right through, taking the sudden furious passage in the coda faster than he had intended, his fingers moving in a blur across the keys.

'Oh!' she exclaimed, her fingers over her lips. 'I shall never be able to play that. You are so clever.'

She made little progress, but Ludwig looked forward to her visits. The fleeting movements of her head, the ringlets that seemed to dance of their own accord . . . and the way she touched him. She thought nothing of placing her fingers on his forearm when she spoke. Or when she played a wrong note one hand would go to her lips in confusion, the other to his arm. And always in the air there was the sweet scent of her perfume.

When Josephine came to see him one warm summer's evening he had the proof he needed of her feelings for him.

'Who's that man?' she asked, looking up at the painting that hung above the piano.

'My grandfather. Kapellmeister Beethoven.'

'Your grandfather? You don't look at all like him.'

Ludwig's mouth fell open in dismay. The spontaneity with which she had said those words had hurt him to the core.

She registered his pain. 'Oh no, no. I didn't mean that,' she said. 'You do look like him, really. You do. And what's this? Is it another portrait of him?'

She pointed to a picture frame leaning against the wall, covered by a blanket.

'No. It's . . .' He walked over to it and lifted off the blanket off. She let out a little cry, followed by a cadence of laughter that sounded to him like tiny bells.

'Ludwig! It's you! It's . . . wonderful.' She stood looking at it, both hands held to her face.

He had been in two minds about Mähler's portrait. He considered the setting slightly absurd, but appreciated its seriousness.

Mähler had depicted Ludwig as he sat, his right arm extended as if to indicate the beat, his hand open, the palm facing the viewer. The overturned chair on which Ludwig had rested his left hand was now a lyre. His back was arched forward – Ludwig could still feel the ache the pose had given him at the base of his spine – and his eyes looked slightly to the left. Behind him was an Arcadian scene, a thickly leafed tree, two smaller fir trees and the pillars of what might have been a Greek temple on the left of the picture. Above him the sky was heavy with storm clouds – the single passionate element in the picture. His hair fell in wisps over his forehead, but was otherwise neat. His nose was long and slender, his lips curved sensuously almost like a woman's, and Mähler had highlighted his cheekbones with pink, as if he was blushing from the country air. The skin of his face was unblemished. Mähler had miraculously rid him of the smallpox scars. The cravat, which had stifled him and at which he had continually pulled, was tied in a knot neater than Ludwig had ever achieved.

The overall effect, Ludwig thought, was of a sophisticated, elegant young man, given to strumming the lyre while reciting Greek verse – not a composer driven by passion.

'Oh, Ludwig, can I have it? Borrow it, I mean? Oh, do say I can. Just for a short time. I love it so.'

The next day, almost furtively, Ludwig took the portrait to the Brunsviks' house on the Rothenturmgasse.

It was the first of a series of visits. Josephine asked him if he would come to her house to give her lessons and he readily agreed.

He was in love with her and she was in love with him.

With an elation he had not felt before, he wrote on the title page of 'An die Hoffnung' 'To my beloved Josephine, in celebration of our love'.

He looked at his words. Had he gone too far? He pushed the manuscript to the back of the table. He would choose the right moment, then present the song to her.

Chapter 5

Ludwig forced himself to face an uncomfortable fact: the treatment from Pater Weiss was no longer doing any good. He told the priest this but received little comfort or encouragement. 'Takes time. What d'you expect? A miracle?' He pushed Ludwig's head roughly to the side and poured the oily liquid into the funnel in great gurgles. The outside of each ear was sore where the end of the funnel had torn the skin.

Pater Weiss became more impatient as it became increasingly evident that Ludwig's hearing was not improving. The caring pastor had become a medical practitioner confronted by the fact that his treatment was failing.

One evening, at the time he should have left for the cathedral, Ludwig poured a glass of wine and stayed in his apartment. He resolved not to visit Pater Weiss again.

Ferdinand Ries was worried. It was August 1805 and the Habsburg empire was once again at war with France and his father had written to him from Bonn, warning him that the French authorities there had asked for his address in Vienna to conscript him into the army. 'Can you imagine?' he said despairingly to Ignaz Gleichenstein, as they sipped wine in Stephan Breuning's apartment. 'I'd be in French uniform, fighting against my own people. I pray God you don't suffer the same fate.'

'My parents said they're not conscripting in Freiburg. In fact there is hardly any French presence there at all. We're too far south. It is in the Rhine valley that it is worst because the French have occupied all the cities there – Cologne, Koblenz, Wiesbaden and, of course, Bonn.'

'Can you not leave the city?' asked Stephan. 'Go into the country?'

Ries shook his head. 'They'd issue a warrant for my arrest,

apparently. They have spies everywhere. Someone would re-cognise me and give me away. Also, if I do not obey I will expose my father and family to risk. Anyway, there is one silver lining in it all. I would have to return to Bonn. That is where I would join the army. And that gives me the chance to see my family again. Without conscription papers, I wouldn't be allowed to go.'

The three friends sat in silence for a few moments. Finally Ries spoke: 'I am worried about Herr Beethoven. Ignaz, would you help him out while I'm gone? He needs help, organising his manuscripts, speaking to his publishers and so on. Frau Streicher looks after his domestic needs, but he needs a secretary.'

Gleichenstein understood. 'Of course. But don't look so depressed. You surely won't be gone long. The war will quickly be over.'

Stephan chuckled morbidly. 'What does that mean, Ignaz? That we will soon be victorious, or soon be defeated?'

Gleichenstein did not reply.

'How is Ludwig, Ferdi? You say you're worried about him, but he is well, isn't he?'

Ries drew a deep breath. 'I hope so. I'm not sure. He doesn't confide in me the way he once did. I don't think his hearing is improving. Zmeskall told me he has stopped going to see the priest at the cathedral. I was never in favour of it anyway – he is not a doctor. But it improved his mood. It gave him hope. The let-down, of course, was all the worse. And . . . and there's something else.'

His two friends looked at him intently.

'I hope I am not breaking any confidences, but I feel you should both know. He has become very fond of Countess Deym, Franz Brunsvik's sister. She is a widow with four small children. Nikola says he is in love with her and is contemplating marriage.'

Stephan's face brightened. 'But isn't that good?'

'Nikola says not. He says she is a rather . . . what word did he use? . . . yes, unstable woman. She can be very emotional. She always has been. Now that she's a widow it is worse. Apparently she has given Herr Ludwig cause to believe his affection is reciprocated. You know she borrowed Mähler's portrait of him? It convinced Herr Ludwig she was . . . And another thing – I saw a song he has composed. To Hope, it's called, and he has inscribed it to her in very affectionate terms.'

'I still don't quite see –'

'Her family is absolutely against it. They have spoken to her and she has assured them they have no cause for worry. She says she is fond of him and no more than that. But Nikola believes that if she means it, sooner or later she will reject him and that will hurt him badly.'

'He needs something to occupy him,' said Stephan, 'something to take his mind off her.'

'He has that,' said Ries. '*Leonore*. He is working hard on it and soon rehearsals will begin. And he has composed an extraordinary piano sonata. So passionate. I played a passage of it to Herr Sonnleithner at the Kunst-und-Industrie. He suggested naming it the Passionate Sonata. Appassionata, he said. I don't know what Herr Ludwig will think of that. But at least he's composing, which, given his hearing problem, is a relief. My worry is that if Countess Deym hurts him it will affect his work.'

'Have you spoken to anyone else about it? Prince Lichnowsky, for instance. He might have a suggestion.'

'I have to go and see him. He has asked me to call on him. But I don't know whether . . . I feel rather as if I am betraying confidences,' said Ries, uncertainly.

'Yes. Better to say nothing for the moment,' Stephan agreed. 'See how it works out. Give my regards to the Prince when you see him.'

Ferdi Ries found Prince Lichnowsky in ebullient spirits, despite the renewed war and the effects Ries knew that it was having on his financial resources.

'Ries, my dear boy. Come in, come in. I'll ring for some wine.'

'Sir, if you do not mind I will not stay long. I have to go to the Landstrasse to give a lesson. I am working as hard as I can before I . . . I will have to leave Vienna soon. I am to be conscripted.'

'Yes, yes, I heard. Sad business. Soon be over, though. Now come here to the piano, young man. There is something I want you to do for me.'

'May I ask what, sir?'

'There is a new piece by our friend Herr Beethoven. Everyone is playing it. I want you to teach it to me.'

Ries looked confused. 'The sonata?'

'No, no. Here. I know the first few bars. Let me sit down. It starts like this.'

Ries immediately recognised the gentle dotted rhythm of the opening of the Andante Grazioso, just published by the Kunst-und-Industrie.

'There, you know the piece, don't you?'

'Yes, sir. Herr Ludwig intended it to be the middle movement of the sonata he dedicated to Count Waldstein, but I persuaded . . . some of us thought . . . he decided it was a substantial enough piece to stand on its own.'

'It's wonderful. Marvellous. Everyone is playing it. Do you know why?'

Ries looked at him questioningly.

'Because they can, Ries. Apart from that furious section near the end, which I believe he put in just to upset people. They leave that out. Hah! Good thing he doesn't know. Now, teach it to me, Ries.'

'Leave that section out, Josephine,' said Ludwig, 'if you find it too difficult. Go straight to the coda.'

He watched her small white hands playing the notes he had written. The black curls swung against her cheeks and her lips were slightly parted with the effort of reading the notes, her tongue occasionally moistening them.

He wanted to kiss her. He was going to kiss her. His mind was made up. It was time to declare his love for her. Had she not given him enough signs that she, too, was ready? His heart beat harder and his muscles tested in anticipation. And after the kiss? What then? My years of loneliness are about to end, he thought. I will share my life with someone who will care for me and look after me, who will be by my side when I need help with . . .

Panic shot through him. She was aware of his deafness, he knew that. Would she still . . . ? Of course. Why else would she have borrowed the portrait? Why else would she have allowed him – encouraged him – to come to her house to see her?

He watched her hands stroke the two *piano* chords that closed the piece. His heart was beating so hard now that he feared his chest would burst. He could hear the pounding in his ears but it did not hurt. He could already taste the softness of her lips.

She sat with her hands on her thighs, looking down, as if she sensed the importance of the moment. There was no going back. How should he do it? What should he say?

He reached out but, to his horror, discovered that he was

not close enough to touch her hand. He pulled his chair forward but in that instant Josephine sprang to her feet. He stood up too and put his hands on her shoulders. He did not give himself time to contemplate the startled look – not fear, surely? – on her face. He moved his head forward, tilting it and breathing heavily. His lips touched her cheek, as she turned her head.

Bewildered, he pulled back. He looked at her moist lips, leaned forward and again found himself kissing her cheek, then a moment later the other.

'There, dear Ludwig,' she said, steadily. 'Like the French do.'

He heard her words through the delicious throbbing in his head. What did they mean? What was she saying to him? He wanted to kiss her again, but he wanted to kiss her lips, feel their moisture and softness, part them with his tongue and explore the warmth and wetness of her mouth. But she had stepped back from him. 'My dear sister will be here soon. She so wants to hear you play. You will play for her, won't you?'

'Josephine, I must talk to you. There are things I want –'

She put her finger to her lips. 'Do not say anything, Ludwig. It is better you don't. You know I am leaving soon?'

Her words cut through him. Had he misheard? Were his ears playing tricks again? No. If only they were. He did not know what to say.

'Because of the war we are all going back to Martonvasar. I have to think of the children. I have no choice.'

In a flash of inspiration he remembered something. 'I have composed a song for you. I have written a dedication to you on the title page.'

To his surprise her face clouded. 'I know. You should not have done that.'

He felt a weakness in his knees. Did she really say he should not have done that? Why? *Why?*

'I did it because I . . . Josephine . . . I want to tell you –'

'People saw it. Your friends. They saw it and read it and started saying things about me. Unkind things.'

'My friends? Impossible. If they did, I will find out who and –'

'It doesn't matter. It is not true anyway. Ludwig.' She came towards him and took his hands, but her grip was determined rather than affectionate and the space between them was a chasm. 'I am fond of you. I admire you greatly. I will think of you while I am away. Now you must leave, before Therese and Franz come back.'

Chapter 6

Ludwig instructed the servant to make sure he had ample supplies of wine, and to admit no one, no visitors, with the sole exception of Joseph Sonnleithner.

Leonore was all but complete. Sonnleithner had delivered the final section of the libretto, all but the last number, the finale of townspeople and prisoners as Pizarro's evil designs are foiled.

Ludwig looked at the pile of manuscript papers. His first opera! A story of imprisonment, revenge, freedom. And love. For the hundredth time he picked up Sonnleithner's words for the final duet between Leonore and Florestan. *O namen-namenlose Freude!* Oh, joy beyond words! He had already composed the ecstatic opening – the reunion of the doomed prisoner and the faithful wife who had risked her life to save him. Slurred rising quavers, *pianissimo* rising through *crescendo* to *fortissimo* in just five bars. How fittingly I have expressed their love in music! he thought. My language. Through music I can talk of love. Music takes the place of the words I cannot find.

Me, the Spaniard, with my pockmarked face. Ugly. Mozart called me ugly. 'You are ugly and I detest ugliness.' Tears pricked his eyes and he rubbed his face, feeling the stubble, the indentations, the irregularities. How could a woman ever love me? She will love me for my music. I will always be loved for my music. But who will ever love me for myself? Not even my mother . . . my poor dead mother . . .

He looked up at the portrait of his grandfather. Only you, Grandfather. You understood.

Ludwig heard voices outside the door. His heart sank. He drained the last drops of wine, staggered to the table and refilled his glass. His head was hurting. It throbbed in time to his heart-beat and the heaviness in his ears made it feel as if it were filled with lead and that his shoulders lacked the strength to support it.

When he turned, his heart sank further as he saw Prince Lichnowsky and Ferdinand Ries standing before him. Lichnowsky wore a broad, expectant smile. Ries stood slightly behind him, his good eye blinking nervously and his fingers interlaced.

'I told the servant to admit no one. I am working.'

'Hah, Ludwig!' exclaimed Lichnowsky. 'We had to come and see you. Ries has some news for you. Sad news. And I have some good news. So that way you will not be dismal. Now, will you offer us some wine?' He called to the servant to replenish the carafe.

Ries moved instinctively to the table against the far wall and began to arrange the papers.

'Leave them!' said Ludwig harshly. 'I know what's there. Take wine if you want it. But be quick. I am working.'

Ries glanced at Lichnowsky, who nodded encouragement. 'Sir. Herr Ludwig. I have come to bid you farewell. I am leaving.'

Ludwig craned forward to hear the young man's words. Why was he speaking so quietly? 'What is it, Ries?' he said impatiently. 'Speak up, man, for God's sake.'

'I am leaving, Herr Ludwig,' Ries said, sharply. 'I am returning to Bonn.'

Ludwig took a moment to digest the words. 'You are returning to Bonn?'

'To join the French army. To fight against my own people.'

'What are you talking about? Have you taken leave of your senses?'

'No, sir. It is true. There is conscription. I have been told . . .' Ries's voice trailed away.

Ludwig felt a surge of exasperation at his weakness. 'Well, go, then!' he said bluntly. 'If they've ordered you to go, go! I have no further use for you here.'

'Sir, Ignaz Gleichenstein will serve you in any way he can.'

Ludwig gulped his wine. He wished he wasn't always so unpleasant to Ries, but sometimes he felt that the boy needed to be shouted at, like a puppy being given orders.

'Climb the Drachenfels for me,' he said, trying to inject a little familiarity into his voice.

Lichnowsky bounded forward, rubbing his hands. 'Now, Ludwig, I said I had good news for you. I have composed a piece of music. Yes, my very own composition. For the piano. Would you like to hear it?'

Ludwig gazed at the eager face beaming at him. Lichnowsky had become jowly, his soft white skin quivering under his chin. His face was almost that of a child, the skin smooth but unnaturally so, as if it had been stretched. One of the city's most senior aristocrats, friend and confidant of the Imperial family, was looking at him now with the eagerness of a child anxious to please its parents.

Ludwig said nothing. He looked into his wine glass, gently swilling the deep red liquid that brought such comfort to his tired, overworked brain.

From somewhere he heard the gentle dotted rhythm of the opening theme of the Andante Grazioso. At first he hummed with it, then he leaped to his feet, spilling wine over his clothes and on to the floor. 'Where the devil did you learn that? And you called it your composition? *Your* composition? Who taught you?'

Suddenly Ludwig understood it all. He turned on Ries with incontrollable fury. 'You, you damn puppy! You taught it to him, didn't you? And it was you who saw the title page of "Hoffnung" and told everyone, wasn't it? You tried to ruin my life. It's your fault she – Get out of here! Get out now!'

Ries shrank away from him and Lichnowsky hurried over. 'Ludwig, calm yourself. I asked him to teach me. It was my fault. If you have to be angry with someone – and I don't see why you have to – then be angry with me.'

'You did it then, Ries. That's proof of it. Get out! You too, Lichnowsky. I don't want either of you in here. Go on. Go! Go and fight, Ries. It's all you're good for. Don't ever call yourself a musician again.'

Ludwig was in despair. The city was caught up in the war. There was talk that the French army would not stop until they reached the Bastion, the gates of Vienna. He tried to find out from Stephan Breuning what was going on, but Stephan did not reply to his notes. Zmeskall had stopped coming to see him. Even Gleichenstein had not been, merely sending a short letter saying that if Ludwig required anything, he should contact him.

He wanted to get in touch with his brothers, but could not bring himself to. If he saw Carl, he knew it would degenerate into argument, and although Johann was more easy-going, what had Ludwig to say to an apothecary? The two of them simply did not speak the same language.

It was the quarrel with Ries that was responsible, Ludwig knew that. He had behaved unreasonably. But did no one understand? Did no one realise what pressure he was under?

The opera was complete. That was part of the problem. He had finished composing. But instead of a weight being lifted from his shoulders, he felt the burden of not knowing what to do next. He should be throwing himself into rehearsals, but with the war no one was making any decisions about dates. Baron Braun had said loosely 'in a month or so'. But what did that mean?

And there was the matter with Josephine. Thank God no one seemed to know what had happened. They did not even know how he felt about her and what his intentions had been. She had left Vienna with her brother and sister. At first he had been distraught. Now he felt it was a good thing she was gone. It was one area of strain that had dissolved.

He thought constantly of Ries: he should make amends. That was the only course of action – and his friends might behave normally towards him again.

'Müller!'

The servant hurried in.

'You know Ries? Young Ries? He was here recently. Find out if he has left Vienna yet.'

'He has not, sir. He was here this morning.'

'Here?'

The servant nodded. 'He asked to see you. He said he had come to bid you farewell. But I told him you had given instructions not to be disturbed.'

'Imbecile! Idiot! In future, ask me first. I am writing a note to him. Deliver it right away.'

'Another man came, sir. Herr Sonnleithner. I sent him away too.'

Ludwig wanted to shout at the man, throw something at him, shake him by the shoulders at the least. But he controlled his anger. 'If he comes again, I want to see him. In fact, go and –'

'He left a note for you, sir.'

Ludwig did not know why he was immediately anxious. It could only be good news. A date, perhaps, for the first performance of *Leonore*. Yes, that was what it must be. A date from Braun, at last.

He tore open the seal almost before the envelope was out of Müller's hand.

Herr Beethoven
I have dire news to report. The censor's office, having read my libretto, has refused to allow the opera *Leonore* to be performed. He considers it to be subversive.

  I await further developments.

Yr servant
J.F. Sonnr

Wearily Ludwig went to the table. He took a piece of paper, dipped one of Zmeskall's quills in ink and wrote:

Dear Ries
My words were too harsh. There is bad news about my opera. Let me know when you will be in the Schwan. We will drink some of their vile wine together.

Wholly your
Beethoven

An hour later the servant returned with the news that Herr Ries had left Vienna. He handed the note back to his master.

The *Wiener Zeitung* had put out a special edition. Everywhere in Vienna – on the Bastion promenade, in the inns and coffee houses, on the Graben, in the Augarten and Prater parks – the talk was of the advancing French army. Nothing, it seemed, could stop its advance on the Imperial capital. Those who had the means – and somewhere to go to – left the city. Prince Lichnowsky and Princess Christiane went to their country estate at Troppau in Silesia. Prince Lobkowitz went to Bohemia. The Emperor himself pledged to remain in Vienna, but ordered the Empress and the rest of the family, including Archduke Rudolph, to leave.

The *Wiener Zeitung* consisted of a single sheet, starkly printed, with just two items. The main one was topped by a banner headline in heavy black print.

OUR BRAVE FORCES FACE IGNOMINY!

On 20th October 1805, outside the city of Ulm in southern Bavaria, some twenty thousand of our brave Imperial soldiers, fighting for the honour of His Imperial Majesty, stood and faced the forces of the French imposter Bonaparte, His Excellency General Mack von Leiberich in command.

By an entirely dishonourable manoeuvre, against all the rules of war, the French succeeded in surrounding the Imperial Austrian army.

It is our sad duty to report that General Mack was forced to surrender his army of twenty thousand to the French, handing over the illustrious colours of our brave forebears. The French have taken forty-nine thousand prisoners, whose release His Imperial Majesty is making strenuous efforts to secure.

The latest intelligence from the battle front is that the French are marching east towards our border.

We call on all able-bodied citizens to make preparations to resist the army of the French. The same Bastion which resisted the Turkish invader a century and a quarter ago is being made secure and our civil forces are drilling on the Glacis in readiness to repulse the invader.

At the bottom of the page, in considerably smaller print, there was a brief item, which was largely ignored by the people of Vienna.

One day after the ignominy suffered by our forces at Ulm, a Franco-Spanish fleet was defeated by a British fleet under the command of His Lordship Nelson off the Cape of Trafalgar.

This victory for the allies, inglorious and shameful as it is for the enemy, will have no effect on the progress of the war on land.

BOOK FIVE

Chapter 1

Maréchal Joachim Murat and Maréchal Jean Lannes, the bright sun of a chilly November morning in 1805 glinting off their breastplates, rode across the Glacis at the head of a symbolic detachment of fifteen thousand French troops. In honour of their shared Gascon heritage they held their black gold-trimmed bicorns under their arms and wore instead the flamboyant broad-brimmed hats of King Louis XIII's troupe of musketeers of two centuries before, the front turned up, red cockerel feathers streaming out at the back, quivering with every step their white warhorses took.

Knots of children stood in the shadow of the Bastion, cheering and shouting, challenging each other to run towards the horses, touch them if they dared, then scurry back to the safety of the great fortress wall.

Adults went about their business, streaming through the Bastion gates, sacks over their shoulders or bags in their hands, purposefully refusing to look admiringly at the victorious enemy, glad only that no shots had been fired and that the French had decreed that business and commerce should continue uninterrupted.

The first battalion of cavalry was separated from the ensuing infantry by a military band. The harsh sounds of the brass instruments echoed off the smooth sheer sides of the Bastion. Each piece by Méhul and Lefèvre, which had echoed through Paris in the years of the Revolution, was followed by a rendition of 'La Marseillaise', the stirring tune composed by Joseph Rouget de Lisle in the year that the Great Terror began, and which had been adopted as the anthem of the Revolution and the symbol of the victory of the ordinary men and women of France over the hated monarchy and aristocracy. The soldiers astride their horses and the foot soldiers with muskets on their shoulders sang the words of the anthem at the top of their voices, as if exhorting the people of Vienna to rid themselves of the Habsburgs as the people of Paris had rid themselves of the Bourbons.

Two days after the entry of the French forces, the Emperor himself, Napoleon Bonaparte, astride his black Limousin charger Marengo – named for a famous defeat of the Austrian army in 1800 – and accompanied by twenty-two horsemen of the regiment of Chasseurs who formed his personal bodyguard, rode across the Paradeplatz behind the Hofburg palace to inspect his troops.

Then he rode south-west at walking pace out of the city, along the banks of the Wien river, towards the Emperor's summer palace at Schönbrunn.

Small knots of people gathered to watch his triumphal procession. An occasional cheer was raised, but mostly he was greeted with the sullen faces of the defeated. Napoleon Bonaparte stared straight ahead, making no attempt to ingratiate himself with the crowds.

On arrival at Schönbrunn he made his headquarters there, selecting the late Empress Maria Theresa's bedroom at the rear of the east wing as his own, taking his meals in the Small Gallery, and establishing his war office – consisting of a large desk and huge round table strewn with maps – in the Great Gallery.

In the days that followed, the French army made its occupation of Vienna complete. Maréchal Murat, the senior of the commanding officers, took over the Amalienhof, the suite of rooms in the Hofburg palace that had been Archduke Rudolph's. He sent word to Emperor Franz that he could continue to occupy the main part of the palace. Maréchal Lannes billeted himself in the most splendid of the aristocracy's palaces in Vienna, that owned by Prince Lobkowitz. He gave his aides-de-camp strict instructions that the palace was to be treated with respect and no damage done to it. Junior ranks were quartered within the city walls and the foot soldiers in the suburbs beyond the Glacis.

Soon the sight of uniformed French officers strolling in the city, on the Bastion boulevard, along the Graben, gazing into the shop windows on the Kärntnerstrasse and the Kohlmarkt, their heavy black greatcoats fully buttoned against the winter cold, or drinking in the coffee houses and taverns became familiar. The people of Vienna knew the French had been ordered to be civil to them. They went about their business as if the soldiers were not there.

To show their disaffection in the only way they could, the Viennese began to remain at home in the evening. It was as if an unspoken directive had been passed round the streets of the city and it was swiftly taken up. Soon restaurants and taverns found themselves serving only French officers, and then with an ill will. More symbolically the people of Vienna stayed away from the entertainment they loved, the theatre. Within a week of the occupation the audiences, which never filled more than half the house, were made up entirely of French officers.

Ignaz Seyfried, music director of the Theater an der Wien, asked, 'Can you not postpone it for a month, Baron?'

Braun shook his head impatiently. 'Impossible. It is too close. It opens on Wednesday the twentieth for three nights. Since the censor, in his wisdom, performed the unprecedented feat of reversing his decision, it would merely arouse his suspicions if we cancelled. Where does the main problem lie? Beethoven again?'

'Up to a point. He keeps making changes, but that is to be expected. The real problem is some of the singers. Demmer, the tenor, is simply not up to the part of Florestan. His main aria, in the dungeon at the opening of Act Three, does not have the power . . . pathos that it needs. Joseph Röckel would have been perfect, but he's not in the city. And Rothe makes Rocco too weak. He's the gaoler being manipulated against his will. He needs more –'

'Do the best you can, Seyfried. The audience will not be the city's connoisseurs. What do soldiers know of opera? Especially French ones. Has Beethoven composed an overture?'

'He wrote one but scrapped it. He wouldn't let me have it. So I decided to do without an overture.'

'No,' said Braun, exasperation in his voice. 'You must have an overture. It settles the audience. And this audience will need that. Tell him to compose a new one. Shorter. Damn man. Scourge of my life.'

Ludwig knew the wine would make the stomach pains worse, but it would help his head. He emptied the glass, refilled it and returned to the piano.

The overture was not causing problems. He was pleased he had abandoned the earlier one; it had not been right – too insubstantial for the drama to follow. The new one was progressing. But by the time Schlemmer and his team had copied out the parts it was unlikely that the orchestra would have time for more than one run-through.

When the servant said Prince Lichnowsky was outside waiting to see him, his first reaction was to tell him to send him away. Instead he nodded, suspecting that Lichnowsky might have news about the opening night.

'Ludwig, Christiane and I hurried back from Troppau as soon as word reached us that all was calm here, and that the date for *Leonore* had been set. Is all going well?'

Lichnowsky irritated Ludwig. He wanted to shock the Prince, just to see his crestfallen look. 'No. The orchestra is incapable of playing my music, the singers incapable of singing it. So it will fail.'

'No, no, no, Ludwig. Do not say that. It will not fail. How is the overture coming along? I heard you were composing a new one.'

Ludwig shrugged. 'I need Ries. For the first time, I really need him. And he chooses to go off and become a soldier.'

Ludwig savoured the Prince's sudden change of expression, from childlike eagerness to horror. 'Oh, Ludwig. You were so unkind, cruel even, to that young man. You should never have behaved like that. If it was anyone's fault, it was mine.'

Ludwig's head hurt and he did not want to talk to Lichnowsky. He wanted to get back to composing. 'What are the plans for the twentieth? Tell me quickly, then I must work.'

Lichnowsky smiled, clearly glad of the change of subject. 'Of course, the occupation has changed things. The Imperial family is not here. Prince Lobkowitz is away and young Kinsky. But Christiane and I will be there, of course. I hope Fries and Schwarzenberg will come, and Herr Würth the banker. And your friends are coming. Breuning, Zmeskall, Gleichenstein. Your brothers, too, I hope. But I rather regret,' Lichnowsky said, lowering his voice, 'that the bulk of the audience will be made up of French soldiers. Pray God that is about to change and we can get back to normal life.'

'What do you mean?'

Lichnowsky looked quickly round the room and lowered his voice. 'There are plans for the Austrian army to join forces with the Russians – a hundred thousand soldiers, double the number of French. There will be a huge battle and the French will be defeated once and for all. Our forces are already massing.'

'Where?'

'North of here. In Moravia. Near Brünn. In a small town. Austerlitz I think is its name.'

Chapter 2

Wednesday, 20 November 1805 was a cold crisp day; frost coated the Glacis, resisting the weak sun. Ludwig woke early with stomach pains and knew from the moment he got up that this would be one of the worst days of his life. The opera was not ready. Neither the singers nor the orchestra had mastered the music.

And what of the music? The overture was too long and Seyfried had urged him to cut it, particularly the wind section the musicians said was unplayable; he had refused. Then give us back the first version, Seyfried had said. Again Ludwig had refused.

There were pieces in the score that Ludwig knew were right. The quartet for Marzelline, Leonore, Jaquino and Rocco in Act One. That was practically the first piece he had written, and it had remained unchanged. Leonore's dramatic aria, 'Komm, Hoffnung', in Act Two was good, and Milder's voice suited it. The Prisoners' Chorus and the final duet 'O namenlose Freude' both worked well. But Florestan's great aria at the opening of Act Three, 'Gott! Welch' Dunkel hier', was unsatisfactory. Ludwig was unsure why. It certainly needed a stronger voice than Demmer's: his opening cry of despair, which was supposed to embody defiance with vulnerability, was nothing more than a shout.

But something more fundamental worried Ludwig and he could not see what it was. He discussed it with Sonnleithner, who strove to put his mind at rest. Ludwig believed it was to do with the structure. But it was too late now.

By the time he left the Mölkerbastei to walk to the Wien, Ludwig was beset by a gloom as heavy as any he had known. He knew he should take a carriage but the icy air cut into his lungs and he enjoyed the sensation.

The colic was still in his stomach and he wondered how soon

he would be able to secure a glass of wine at the theatre. His head throbbed and he knew the music would fight with the other sounds to penetrate his head.

Alone he walked across the Glacis, his boots crunching the frosted grass, alone in body and mind. Few other people were crossing the wide expanse that ran around the Bastion. Those who did, bundles under their arms, hurried along face down, their breath turning into instant shafts of white.

Ludwig thrust his hands deep into his coat pockets. An image floated into his mind, of auburn ringlets and a smile. But he could not call to mind the face. He knew it was Antonie, but her features would not take coherent shape in his mind. He wondered if, should she walk up to him this very moment, he would recognise her.

And he thought of his friends. Do I have any real friends? he wondered. Stephan Breuning, Nikolaus Zmeskall, Schuppanzigh. The Streichers. Are they my friends? Do I turn to them when I need comfort? And my brothers? Are they there when I need them? He knew the answer was no. But it was not really their fault, he knew that too. He could not turn to them. He was different from them. Not *normal*, as his mother used to say. She was right. I am not normal. I am different from other men. I am destined to be alone, always. Why was it my fate to be the way I am? A musician who has nothing in life but his music. A musician who is going deaf.

The amphitheatre of the Theater an der Wien was half empty. Only the second parterre and the first tier of boxes were occupied. Ludwig saw the Lichnowskys, Breuning, Zmeskall and his brothers. But the bulk of the audience was indeed made up of uniformed French soldiers, chatting animatedly.

Ludwig acknowledged the nods of those he knew. They all looked apprehensive: they knew the rehearsals had not gone well and they could see that the audience was not appropriate – Vienna's opera lovers were at home.

Ludwig sat on a chair near the front of the side wall of the theatre, so that he could watch the action on the stage, see the orchestra clearly and, with a small turn of the head, the audience.

With a sinking heart he watched Seyfried weave his way through the music stands to the front of the orchestra pit. The diminutive *Kapellmeister* did not make the customary bow to the audience, but instead turned to his musicians and raised his arms. Ludwig braced himself for the first *fortissimo* chord of the overture. It cut into his ears a full second after Seyfried's arms came down and the players sounded the note, a unison G. Ludwig tilted his head back, eyes closed, relishing the music – his music, his harmonies – that filled his mind to the exclusion of all else. Slowly, Seyfried, he wanted to say to him. Do not hurry it. Obey my *tempi*. *Fortissimo*, then immediately *piano*. Slowly, *crescendo*, allow the tension to build.

He opened his eyes and watched as the violinists – in the massive runs of semi-demi-semiquavers, which presaged the Allegro – played only every ninth note, with the exception of the leader Franz Clement, whose fingers raced across all four strings. And later, in the passage the wind section had declared unplayable, the musicians held their instruments away from their lips. Rather that, Ludwig thought ruefully, than play it wrong.

He glanced towards the audience. The French soldiers were talking among themselves! He wanted to leap to his feet and call for silence. He looked across at his friends. Nikolaus Zmeskall, palms outwards, was gesturing at him to remain calm; Stephan Breuning looked worried.

Ludwig turned his gaze back towards the players. Thank goodness for the trumpet, he thought. That will win their attention. But when the solo trumpeter stepped from behind the curtain on to the front of the stage and sounded his call, a perfect presentiment of the drama that was about to unfold, Ludwig saw a soldier rise to his feet, put his closed hand to his mouth and pretend to make the call himself: the company bugler entertaining his laughing colleagues.

Soon the familiar throbbing began in Ludwig's head, painlessly at first, then with the ache that intensified with every heartbeat. His ears were ringing, as if they were trying to compete with the singers. Anna Milder's soprano rang through the cavernous auditorium. Haydn was right: she did have a voice as big as a house. When his ears adjusted to the sound, he realised she was singing beautifully.

Ludwig strained to hear the *piano* chord – *pizzicato* in the bass – that opened the quartet half-way through Act One. It was a crucial moment in the opera. All four characters on stage – Leonore, Rocco, Marzelline and Jaquino – were expressing their emotions and hopes for the future in the canon. Rothe,

the bass, had complained about his entry on high D and sure enough he fluffed it now. His voice cracked before it dropped to the B below.

Ludwig glanced at the audience. The soldiers were laughing, digging each other in the ribs.

Throughout the next number, Rocco's Gold aria which was intended to introduce levity into the plot, the soldiers sat still and impassive. Why did they not find his glorification of money amusing? Rothe was now in his element, rolling his eyes and waving his arms in emphasis. The swift quavers suited his voice – few sustained notes to test it.

The performance was turning into a disaster and a humiliation. The only time the dreadful audience of smug uncultured soldiers paid any attention to what was going on was when errors were made. In the interval after the First Act Ludwig wanted to shout at them, to make them understand they were witnessing the first performance of his first opera – and that they were ruining it.

Because the scene change was swift the curtain soon rose again. The orchestra played the march that preceded the entry of the governor Pizarro and his military escort. Ludwig heard laughter. He turned his head and saw a small contingent of French soldiers marching up and down the aisle of the parterre in time to the music. He put his hand to his forehead, hot and damp under his fingers. Sebastian Mayer, Mozart's brother-in-law, whose conceit had upset the other singers and the orchestra, was acting furiously as Pizarro to cover his inability to sing the part as Ludwig had composed it.

There was more laughter from the audience, but less overt this time. Ludwig looked at the faces: they had undergone a subtle change. The smiles had frozen.

During Leonore's great aria, 'Komm, Hoffnung', the soldiers in the audience paid no attention, whispering to each other. Occasionally they glanced at the stage, but the conviction and power with which Anna Milder was singing passed them by.

Moments later, a turning point in the plot, Rocco, succumbing to the pleading of Marzelline and Leonore, unlocked the bars of the gaol and allowed the prisoners out into the sunlight. Ludwig listened to the fine words Sonnleithner had written, extolling the virtues of liberty. But take care, one of the prisoners sings, there are eyes and ears everywhere, ready to take away our freedom from us again.

There was movement in the audience. Ludwig saw a soldier – an officer clearly, judging by his uniform – stand up and motion to another to do likewise.

The curtain fell on Act Two and small groups of soldiers were standing, their faces serious. Others were talking and beckoning to each other, getting to their feet.

Ludwig understood what was happening. *Leonore* was more than a love story, more than the willingness of a faithful wife to risk her life to save her husband. It was the story of the triumph of freedom over oppression, of the vanquished over the victor. The senior officer who had stood first barked a command and walked down the aisle out of the auditorium, followed by his men.

At the opening of Act Three Joseph Demmer's strangled cry from the depth of the dungeon reverberated around an almost empty auditorium.

With the departure of most of the audience, the singers seemed to take heart, as if the tension had dissipated. Ludwig, too, was able to concentrate on the performance. Now the drama unfolded well, Milder perfectly executing her mighty leap to top B flat as she revealed her true identity as Florestan's wife. The singers put all the more effort into the arrest of Pizarro – Mayer acting even more forcefully, given that the threat of retaliation from the French soldiers had been removed.

The love duet – 'O namenlose Freude' – would have been fine, if Demmer's voice had been any match for Milder's, but Ludwig heard enough to know that with the right pairing it would work well.

The final curtain fell to a smattering of applause from Ludwig's friends. He wanted to leave. He did not want to talk about the performance, its faults, the insulting behaviour of the soldiers – or that the next two performances would play to empty houses.

As quickly as he could he took his leave. To his displeasure, no sooner had he taken more than a couple of steps in the cold night air than Zmeskall joined him, patting his shoulder. 'Don't talk to me about it,' said Ludwig.

Wordlessly they crossed the Glacis, ignoring the sentries at the Kärntnertor gate who shouted a challenge at them and half raised their rifles. Zmeskall said something to them, Ludwig did not know what, and they walked under the Bastion. Then Ludwig felt his friend tug his sleeve and jerk his head. He understood. The Walfischgasse stretched off to their right, dark and narrow, just a few flickering flames of candlelight high on the walls. Ludwig felt his heart thud inside his chest. But a group of drunken French soldiers was walking towards them along the Walfischgasse, their arms round each other, laughing and singing, their dress in disarray. Ludwig felt anger and revulsion. He turned away from Zmeskall, directing his steps instead towards the Herrengasse and the walk home to the Mölkerbastei.

Chapter 3

It promised to be a bleak Christmas. The street-sellers offering hot punch and sweet cake had vanished, the decorations in the shop windows were muted with none of the usual children gazing in expectantly. The coffee-houses and taverns were empty save for a small handful of regular customers, and the theatres were shut. No one knew how long it would last. The most optimistic voices said not more than a few weeks; others said months or even years. It all depended on the French soldiers and their desire for revenge.

'The defeat at Austerlitz is enough. They have had their revenge,' said the optimists.

'Defeat on the battlefield is only the start,' said the pessimists. 'They have destroyed the Austrian army, now they must destroy the people.'

In the event the optimists won the day. Having demolished the combined forces of Austria and Russia on the Moravian plain outside the town of Austerlitz, Napoleon turned his attention to other enemies. To the even greater relief of the Viennese, he ordered all but a small contingent of French soldiers to leave the city and join the rest of his army in Germany. Three weeks after the decisive battle Napoleon imposed a humiliating peace settlement on the Austrian Empire, whereby it ceded to France practically all its possessions outside its own borders.

Ludwig was lying in the bath, moving gently so that he could still feel the heat in the rapidly cooling water, cursing silently when he moved too much and water spilled over the side. He cursed more as the servant approached him.

'Gentleman to see you, sir. Says it's most important.'

Ludwig wondered whether he should pretend he hadn't heard, but decided there was no point. 'Send him away.'

'It's His Imperial Excellency Prince Lichnowsky, sir. I can't –'

'Send him away,' Ludwig said, louder, hoping it carried into the hall, and closed his eyes.

When he opened them, the Prince was standing beside the bath. 'Oh, Ludwig, such good news,' he said excitedly, wringing his hands. 'Baron Braun is prepared to stage your opera again at the Wien.'

Ludwig sat up quickly, sending more water on to the floor. 'What did you say?'

'Baron Braun came to see me to discuss the new season at the court theatres and he said he would put *Leonore* on again at the Wien in the spring. March or early April. He says you will need to make a few changes – nothing major – just to shorten it a little.'

'No changes.'

'Ludwig, will you come to my apartment and discuss it? Will you? Christiane would so love to see you. Also, there is someone I would like you to meet. A fine dramatist who is doing some work for Baron Braun. I am sure you and he would have much to discuss. You will come, won't you? Tonight at six. And we will dine together.'

'I must have a new Florestan. Demmer was no good. Tell Braun that. If he gives me a new Florestan, maybe I will agree to some cuts – but in the dialogue only. Not in the music.'

Ludwig and Stephan Breuning walked along the broad Herrengasse, their coat collars turned up against the cold January air.

'Have you seen Princess Christiane lately?' Stephan asked, his voice carrying clearly on the wintry air. 'She has been very ill. The Prince took her to his estate at Troppau, but brought her back here as soon as he could to be near her doctors. The travelling was not good for her.'

'I knew she was unwell. How ill is she?'

'The surgeons operated on her some months ago. The Prince says they made her worse. She is very frail.'

They walked along the narrow alley to the side of the Kärntnertor theatre, almost in the shadow of the Bastion, and turned up into the Kärntnerstrasse, immediately turning right into the Krugerstrasse. Ludwig had not been to the building in the Krugerstrasse since he had had dinner there with the Lichnowskys, George Bridgetower and Countess Erdödy more than two years before. He had been struck then by how much both the Prince and Princess had aged, and how nervous and highly strung Princess Christiane had seemed.

'Be tolerant with her, Ludwig,' said Stephan. 'If she says something that offends you, do not let it upset you.'

'Does that go for everyone else, Steffen?'

Stephan smiled but said nothing.

They climbed the brightly lit stairs and walked along the corridor towards the double doors that already stood open to the Lichnowskys' apartment. Just inside two servants were hurrying out of the main salon, carrying trays piled with china cups and saucers.

'We have missed coffee and tea,' said Stephan.

'Then it will have to be wine,' said Ludwig. 'I hope the Prince serves his finest.'

'I am sure he will.'

A tail-coated servant bowed low to them and extended his right hand as an indication to the two men to follow him. 'Herr von Breuning and Herr van Beethoven,' he said, imperiously.

Immediately Princess Christiane rushed over, her arms held out, like a bird with damaged wings. Her face was drawn, the skin gathering in folds beneath her chin. Her eyes, though, blazed. 'My dear Ludwig. And dear Stephan. Now the evening is complete. Come in, come in. It has been so long, Ludwig. Are you well?' She touched his cheek lightly. 'You must both have some wine. Let me fetch Karl and he'll introduce you to everyone.'

Ludwig looked round the room and saw, to his surprise, that most of *Leonore*'s cast were there – Anna Milder, Mayer and Rothe, Seyfried and Clement – and some faces he did not recognise. He was relieved that he could not see Demmer. So, he thought, we are to perform the opera and then dissect it. He took a glass of wine from the tray proffered by a servant and drank a sizeable gulp.

Suddenly Prince Lichnowsky was at his side. 'My dear Ludwig. So glad you have come. So glad. It'll be a successful evening, of that I'm sure. Good to see the damn French no longer plaguing us, mmh? Come, I want you to meet someone.'

Ludwig felt the familiar anxiety shoot through him. Someone new, who would not know of his deafness, who might have a soft voice . . . Lichnowsky led him to a man of slight stature, with thinning hair and a lively, alert face. Ludwig estimated he was around the same age as himself.

'Ludwig, this is Friedrich Treitschke from Leipzig, the dramatist I was telling you about. He is about to take up a position at the Kärntnertor theatre. Or maybe you already have, Friedrich? May I present Ludwig van Beethoven, of whom you have heard me talk often?'

Ludwig braced himself for the new voice which, to his relief, proved firmer than he had expected.

'Herr Beethoven, a pleasure and an honour. I will not presume to join in the discussion this evening, but I hope you will allow me to hear you talk of your sublime work.'

Ludwig smiled at him and inclined his head. He was searching for an appropriate response to the well-turned compliment, but Lichnowsky spoke immediately. 'And come. You must meet young Röckel.'

Ludwig sighed, but allowed himself to be led away. Another stranger, presumably the young man he had seen standing with the singers. He saw the young man look down as he realised he was being approached and immediately took to his modesty. He was tall and thin with a long narrow face. His eyebrows were arched, as if in search of knowledge, and his mouth was half open with eagerness. He must be around twenty, Ludwig thought, certainly the youngest in the room. He was not drinking, in common with the other singers. Instead his hands were clenched tightly in front of him.

'Ludwig, this is Joseph Röckel. He is from Salzburg. He is your new Florestan.'

Ludwig gasped. He knew immediately that the young man was wrong for the role. The quality Florestan needed above all was heroism: starving to death, and knowing that he was the victim of evil revenge, he must rise above the baseness of his position. He must be possessed of inner strength and virtue. Joseph Röckel had the demeanour of a servant rather than that of a hero.

'Only if you approve, Herr Beethoven,' Röckel said, in a voice whose strength belied the slight frame from which it came. 'If not, I shall return to Salzburg forthwith, pleased only to be able to say I have met Europe's greatest composer.'

'Salzburg,' said Ludwig. 'A name that brings another immediately to mind.'

'Yes, sir. To mine, too. I am proud to have been born in the same city that gave birth to Herr Mozart.'

'Now, gentlemen,' said Lichnowsky quickly, 'I have laid a buffet in the dining room next door for later. But why do we not get down to work? Mmh?'

Ludwig took another glass of wine from the servant. It was sweeter than he would have liked, but he knew from its thickness and the depth of its colour – almost orange – that it was strong and would soon begin to relax him. It would not have the same effect on him the next day as the rough red wine from the Schwan so he could indulge himself. He made a mental note to keep an eye on a servant so that his glass could be replenished at a nod.

'I am grateful to you all for taking the trouble to be here this evening,' said Lichnowsky. 'How fortunate we are that this noble work by Herr Beethoven is to be performed again at the Theater an der Wien. The purpose now is to go through the sublime work and see if it is possible to improve on the perfect, shall we say?'

Ludwig saw Röckel clap his hands in agreement. The boy had a strong speaking voice. Could he have an equally strong singing voice? If he did, it was just possible, just possible . . .

'I shall ask my dear wife to take her seat at the piano, and let us begin.'

Ludwig settled back in his chair, emptying his glass and summoning another. He watched the singers take their places in a semi-circle in front of the piano, while Princess Christiane adjusted the piano stool. Only Röckel remained seated. Ludwig caught his eye. Poor young man, he thought. He has a long time to wait. Two acts.

He watched the concentration on all the faces. Lichnowsky had a notebook and pencil and frequently made jottings. Stephan Breuning sat next to him, glancing across to see what he wrote. Occasionally Seyfried would lean across and whisper something to Clement. Treitschke sat with his eyes half closed and his hands folded neatly on his crossed legs.

A better audience than at the Wien, Ludwig thought wryly. This small group was infinitely more appreciative than a hundred French soldiers.

He listened to his work. The quartet, ah, the quartet. He knew the singers were nervous – he could see it in their faces: the audience was not a real one, the sort a performer needed to feed off, and the composer was sitting a few feet from them, listening to them intently.

No wonder poor old Rothe still could not get that high D entry in the canon. He'll ask me to lower it by an octave, Ludwig thought, but I will tell him to go and swim in the Danube. Yet how well he sang the Gold aria, a few moments later, seeming to relish the comedy in it.

Ludwig expected everything to stop at the end of the first act, but after a short pause the Princess began to play the march that opened the second act and presaged the entry of the villain Don Pizarro, sung with menace by Mozart's brother-in-law Sebastian Mayer – so much better than he had sung it at the Wien.

The action picked up now. The plot began to unfold. Pizarro tries to draw kindly Rocco into his plot to murder Florestan, but Rocco balks at it. Leonore, disguised as the gaol boy Fidelio, overhears the plot and swears to risk her life to save her husband. And finally, the chorus of prisoners, that hymn to freedom that had so upset the French soldiers.

Act Two was good, and Ludwig knew it. The problem lay with Act One. What would they suggest? They would want him to cut numbers, obviously. No, he thought smiling inwardly. Not a note.

Suddenly everyone was looking at him. They were not going to proceed with Act Three. As if by some prearranged cue, they were going to discuss the first two acts before singing the last.

Prince Lichnowsky pulled his chair forward a little and addressed the whole room. 'Such wonderful music, we all agree. Ludwig, you have never written more powerful music. Do we not all agree?'

Ludwig saw the unanimous nod. It was all proceeding according to a plan, he could see that. He wanted to tell them he could see their plot, and that he would not alter a note.

'The music is perfect. What we need to discuss is structure. Shape and structure.'

Treitschke took up his cue. 'Herr Beethoven,' he said, 'forgive my impertinence, but we have now heard two acts, more than two hours have passed and we have not yet reached the climax of the piece. The act which contains all the drama is still to come. It is asking too much of the audience.'

Ludwig cleared his throat. Though he resolved not to say it, Ludwig knew Treitschke was right. The length was a problem – it always had been. 'You are wrong, Herr Treitschke,'

Ludwig said. 'An audience of French soldiers is not a judge of a work of art.'

Treitschke paused before he replied. 'I will concede you that point, sir. Allow me to say, though, that for your friends in the audience it was also something of an ordeal.'

'What Treitschke means, Ludwig,' Lichnowsky put in, 'is that in order to appeal to the general public, the opera needs to be shorter. They need to be able to grasp more quickly what is happening.'

A flurry of activity caught Ludwig's eye. It was the Princess. 'Oh, come, it is so simple. Why does no one say it? My dear Ludwig, the first two acts should become one. One single act. Cut the unnecessary numbers. Allow Act One to set the scene, unveil the plot. End with the prisoners' temporary freedom. Open Act Two in the dungeon with Florestan, as you have now, and the drama unfolds.'

There was silence in the room. Combine the first two acts into one. Unable to stop himself, Ludwig nodded slowly. Of course that was the answer. Tighten the plot. Damn Sonnleithner for making it so long.

'That would mean cutting several numbers,' said the Prince.

'No!' said Ludwig sharply. 'My music stays. Cut all you like, but my music stays.'

There was laughter, but it was not unkind.

Treitschke leaned forward in his chair and said, 'Herr Beethoven, the fault does not lie with your divine music. It lies with the structure of the libretto. Your main villain, Don Pizarro, does not appear until the second act. Your hero, Florestan, does not appear until the third. So what happens in the first? Mostly it is Jaquino wooing Marzelline, which is subsidiary to the main plot. There is the wonderful quartet, in which each character sets out their own personal drama. Then the tension is lost by Rocco singing a comic aria about gold. At the end of Act One, the audience has heard a lot of music, but nothing has happened.'

Nothing has happened. Treitschke is right, Ludwig thought again. He said, 'Your wine is excellent, Lichnowsky. My opera is excellent. Now give me my music and I shall take my leave of you.'

He held out his arm towards the Princess, who had the score on her lap. His head swam and he balanced himself with a hand on the back of his chair. Princess Christiane let out a small cry and clutched the thick folder to her chest. 'Oh, divine practitioner of the most noble art!' she twittered. 'I shall guard this fruit of your genius with my very life, so that the world shall know it.' Her face was flushed and she was breathing heavily.

Prince Lichnowsky hurried to his wife's side and stroked her shoulder. 'Calm yourself, my dear.' He turned to Ludwig. 'She has been unwell. She cares so much for you, you know.'

Ludwig sat down again. Remorse flashed through him, but he dismissed it instantly.

'Shall we not call a halt to the proceedings?' the Prince said. 'It is past ten o'clock. We are all, perhaps, a little tired.'

'No! No!' said the Princess. 'We shall hear Act Three. Poor Florestan has not sung yet. I shall play the introduction.' And with barely a pause to open the music on the stand, Princess Christiane struck the portentous minor chords that opened the dungeon scene.

Young Joseph Röckel walked to the centre of the room, clearing his throat nervously. Ludwig, to his shame, enjoyed the young man's discomfort. He could not possibly play Florestan, who needed to be a large man, capable of bearing the suffering and humiliation inflicted on him by Don Pizarro.

Röckel sang the opening words of the huge aria that began Act Three, Florestan's first appearance in the opera. 'Gott! Welch' Dunkel hier!'

Ludwig sat up and stared at him. The word 'Gott!' echoed round the room, softly at first, then increasing in intensity. Princess Christiane waited, just as Ludwig had envisaged, while the voice sustained the note. Then the cry of despair at the all-enveloping darkness. He had never heard it sung like this. Exactly the way he had always wanted. The slim figure of Röckel seemed to have increased in stature. His eyes were blazing with defiance and determination, yet there was vulnerability too. He felt tears rise. His music, his notes, brought to life, leaping off the page, made real by this young man.

He reached for his glass, his hand trembling. Röckel sounded the dying note and Ludwig called out, 'Again, Röckling. Again.'

He heard the minor chords and then the perfect expression of 'Gott!'

Yes, they are right, they are *all* right, damn them. This *is* the high point of the opera and we must reach it sooner. But I shall not tell them. I shall not agree.

He sat back and listened to the drama unfold. Mayer's sinister, almost deranged Pizarro dominated briefly, a man who had allowed his judgement to be distorted by the desire for revenge.

'Ich bin sein Weib!' Anna Milder sang, as she threw herself between the murderous prison governor and her husband. Yes, I am his wife. I love him. I will risk my life for him. Her voice was huge. She executed the leap on the word 'Weib' magnificently – neither hysterically nor with a shriek, but a controlled, determined cry of defiance.

The trumpet call came at exactly the right moment, halting the action – picked out by the Princess with the little finger of her right hand. The *dénouement*.

'O namenlose Freude,' Leonore and Florestan sang, their love triumphing over all adversity.

In unison they all sang of the overthrow of Don Pizarro, only Mayer remaining silent, allowing himself to be dragged away, his face registering the shock that his plot had been foiled, his career ruined, that instead of taking Florestan's life he was condemned to lose his own.

Applause echoed round the room – for Ludwig's opera. He could see it in their faces. He nodded to them, half smiled. He held up his hands to quieten them. 'Thank you. You have sung well. Princess, your powers as a pianist are formidable. Let us eat and discuss what is to be done.' He stood up and everyone else stood with him.

'Capital idea,' said Lichnowsky. 'It is after midnight and we must reward our brave singers for their endeavours.'

The servants hurried to the double doors and opened them to reveal a large table laden with cold cuts of meat and bottles of wine uncorked and ready. Fruit was piled high in bowls.

Everyone sat down. Ludwig slumped heavily into a chair, reaching for a fresh glass of wine. It was red this time, smooth and velvety on his tongue.

'May I help you to food?' asked Prince Lichnowsky, beside him.

Ludwig nodded and turned to Stephan Breuning, who had sat on his other side. 'Well, Steffen, will you allow them to butcher my opera the way they have butchered the cow and the pig to get this meat?'

'Hah!' exclaimed the Prince, as he forked up slices of pork.

'The poor animal that gave us this meat has not survived, but your opera will survive and be even more glorious.'

Ludwig looked across the table. Röckel was immediately opposite, the other singers to either side of him. He was eating at a furious speed: in less than a minute his plate, which had been piled high, was empty, and he was helping himself to more.

Ludwig said loudly, 'My dear Röckling, you eat like a wolf that has not seen food for a week. What did you choose?'

Röckel's fork arrested in mid-air. 'I – I was so hungry, famished. I did not even notice what I ate.'

Ludwig let out a cry. 'Hah! Now I know why you were such a perfect Florestan. It was not only Florestan who was starving. Well, always see to it that you do not touch food for a week before a performance, and then you will be sure of success!'

There was a burst of laughter, clear relief at the composer's good humour. Prince Lichnowsky took advantage of it. 'So, Ludwig, will you allow our friend Treitschke to rework the libretto for you? Condense it into two acts, to speed up the action?'

Before Ludwig could answer, Treitschke, on the other side of Stephan, said, 'You must forgive me, Your Highness. I cannot. My duties at the Kärntnertor forbid it. I would not be able to do it justice. I have so many other tasks.'

Ludwig felt Stephan's hand on his shoulder. 'I will do it for you, Ludwig. Will you allow me? I will speak to Sonnleithner. I know he will not mind. He is working on his new libretto.'

'Yes, for my theatre,' said Treitschke. '*Faniska*, music by Cherubini. Allow Herr Breuning to do that for you, sir. And I, if I may, will advise you if you require it, Herr Breuning.'

'Excellent. Perfect. What do you say, Ludwig?'

'I will not cut the music.'

'Very little is required,' said Treitschke, diplomatically. 'It is the text that is at fault. Only the Gold aria. That sits uncomfortably in an opera of such drama.'

Ludwig sighed and said nothing.

Prince Lichnowsky interjected, 'Enough talking now. Let us enjoy the food and wine. Stephan, you may set about your task. All final decisions, of course, rest with our friend here, the greatest practitioner of his art in Europe.'

There was a chorus of approval from around the table. Ludwig ate, and drank his wine. Two acts would be right, he knew that. Let Stephan do it. At least with Stephan he could say exactly

what he thought. No need for politeness. If he does not do it
properly, I will tell him so. And maybe Treitschke was right:
maybe the Gold aria should go.

Licknowsky tapped his shoulder. 'I have spoken to Baron
Braun. The date for the opening is fixed. March the twenty-
second. A Saturday. Just one week before Holy Week starts.
That gives you two months. A little more.'

Ludwig raised his glass to his lips, savouring the taste of the
wine. My opera will be performed again, he thought, with
satisfaction. Two acts.

He heard Lichnowsky's voice again, quieter this time but
even more distinct. 'The Baron is prepared to share the profits
with you. A percentage. He has never done that before. If it
is a success – and I know it will be – it will be very much to
your advantage.'

Chapter 4

While he was waiting for Stephan to complete the revised libretto, Ludwig began a new symphony, his fourth, choosing the key of B flat. It was related to E flat, the key of the Eroica. He was pleased. The symphony would be a coda to that great work, less intense, more sprightly, a piece to turn to after the monumental work in E flat. He also sought out sketches he had made some time before for a new piano concerto and began serious work on it. Once he had its shape clear, he turned to a form of composition new to him. It had been in his mind for a while, and it was Franz Clement, leader of the Theater an der Wien orchestra, who had given him the idea. 'So many sonatas for my instrument, Herr Beethoven, and yours among the best of them. But how many concertos for violin and full orchestra? The good Mozart left us five, but nearly thirty for piano. Herr Haydn only four. When will you join their ranks, sir?'

He had chosen the key of D and was soon well advanced in its composition. He frequently sought Clement's advice, and over a glass of wine in the Zum Weingartel, a tavern close to the Wien, had promised that he would dedicate it to him.

Stephan came to see him with the completed libretto of *Leonore*, and the two men sat over it for several hours. Ludwig was gratified to find that he needed to make fewer changes to the music than he had feared. For the most part it was the dialogue which was shorter and more dramatic.

Pizarro's entry was now brought forward to the first act. Ludwig would need to write a longer march to allow the scene change to be made behind Pizarro's soldiers, who would largely obscure it from the audience. The trio near the start of the first act, between Rocco, Marzelline and Jaquino, was moved to later in the act where it provided more of a contrast with the prisoners' chorus that followed; and Leonore's great aria 'Komm, Hoffnung' came forward to increase the pace of the drama. The entry of the governor, Don Fernando, at the crucial moment became more dramatic.

Regrettably Rocco's Gold aria had to go, Stephan explained patiently: it did not fit in with the new intensity of the drama, but the single interval would induce less ennui in the audience.

Ludwig knew that the new shape was good and told Stephan he would start work right away. When he had finished, he said, he would write another overture.

'Why?' asked Stephan. 'The one you wrote is fine.'

Ludwig shook his head. 'The end is wrong. After the trumpet call. Too abrupt. It needs a proper coda.'

'Time is short, Ludwig. Remember, the date is fixed. March twenty-second. Baron Braun is about to put out posters.'

'Tell him there is one more change. I want to rename the opera. I want it to be called *Fidelio*.'

In a frenzy of activity Ludwig worked on the symphony, the piano concerto and the violin concerto. He also needed to do some revision on the piano sonata in F, which the Kunst-und-Industrie intended to publish as his opus number fifty-seven under the name Appassionata.

Finally, he turned to *Fidelio* and immediately the work did not go well. He was adapting his music at the direction of other people, and it did not come easily to him. It had seemed that little alteration was required, but Braun, Seyfried, Lichnowsky, even Breuning had told him to shorten as many pieces as he could, and simplify the orchestration so that the players – and singers – would have less difficulty.

How could he adapt his music on demand? His art would not let him. Neither, it became increasingly clear, would his health.

On the date that he had promised to deliver the revised manuscript to Baron Braun, he was in bed with a fever. Nanette Streicher was in his apartment, bringing him sips of water whenever he wanted it and mopping the cold sweat from his brow. She forbade visitors, sending away Baron Braun's messenger each time he called, except for Doktor Schmidt. Several times Ludwig heard him tell Nanette that the fever would pass without any long-term deleterious effects, as long as he was sensible and did not undertake any activity afterwards that was too strenuous.

As the fever began to wane, Ludwig found himself wanting

it to remain. He knew what would happen when it left him. 'My ears, Nanette,' he said, as he sat up in bed and drank the chicken broth she had made for him. 'My damned ears. All I hear is noises and they hurt me.'

Nanette tried to convince him that the effect on his hearing was temporary, that as the effects of the fever lessened, his hearing would improve. But he knew she was wrong. Every time he succumbed to serious illness, his hearing worsened.

When he was well enough he returned to the opera, but with a heavy heart. He formulated a plan that he would agree to make more changes if they would reinstate Rocco's Gold aria. Then he abandoned the idea. He did not have the strength to fight them.

Baron Braun's messenger brought him a note.

Herr Beethoven
Your tardiness in executing the necessary work on the opera has left insufficient time for rehearsals. Therefore I have postponed the first performance for one week.

You shall have Saturday March 29, the last night before the theatre closes for Holy Week. As you know, it is considered to be the best night of the season. The second performance – if the work meets with the public's approval – will take place 12 days later when the theatre reopens.

Please believe me, Herr Beethoven, when I say that if the work is not ready for the 29th, it will receive no performance at all.

I trust your health is restored.

Brn Braun
Director, Imprl Crt Thtrs

Ludwig slapped the palm of his hand on the table. If the work meets with the public's approval!

At that moment the servant announced that Baron Zmeskall of the Hungarian Chancellery was waiting in the anteroom to see him.

'Who?' asked Ludwig, momentarily confused, trying to filter the words through the dullness in his ears. But before the servant could repeat it, he had understood. 'Yes. Send him in. Be quick, man.'

When Ludwig's eyes fell on his old friend, he sighed with relief. 'Come in, Zmeskallovitch. Baron Muckcart Driver.

Zmeskall of Zmeskalls. Look at you, blind behind those pebblestone spectacles. You blind, me deaf. Between us, the perfect musician. Wine, Nikola. Pour us both wine.'

He sprawled in a chair and took the glass from Zmeskall, who sat down beside him.

'Frau Streicher told me you were better, Ludwig. I kept away while you were ill. She guarded you night and day, you know. She is a fine friend. But I had to come to see you. How are you?'

Ludwig was grateful that his friend was speaking in a strong, clear voice. 'Wretched, Nikola. My hearing is worse. The fever damaged it, I know. Every time I am ill, I pay for it with my hearing. And Braun, damned man – read this.'

Zmeskall took the note and read it. 'But that is good news, Ludwig. You have more time. A whole week more.'

'What is a week? Always people push me. Do this now, do that now. Have it ready by tomorrow. I will not work like that. I cannot.' The anger was mounting in him. 'I am an artist. I will not respond to threats. Schmidt tells me to stop drinking wine. More orders.'

'Come, Ludwig, do not upset yourself. Your opera is to be performed again, and it will be much improved. I will help you. Have you made changes?'

'Some. Enough. The prisoners' chorus is shorter. Pizarro's entrance march longer. Rocco's Gold aria has gone. I was going to fight them over it. But the opera will be shorter, two acts instead of three. More dramatic.'

'Good. *Leonore* will succeed this time, and you will once again be the toast of Vienna.'

'*Fidelio*, Nikola. That is what it is now called. At least I managed to persuade the Baron of that.'

'No, Ludwig.' Zmeskall took a rolled-up sheet from his bag. 'There. *Leonore, ou l'Amour Conjugal.* Same title as before.'

At last Ludwig turned his attention to the overture. He tightened the opening bars, and he shortened by half the huge semi-demi-semiquaver runs that so upset the string players. But he made most changes to the final section, after the trumpet calls – a full-scale recapitulation in place of the swift coda in the earlier version. And the main motif in the Allegro he gave to the cellos and violins in unison, so at least the woodwind players would stop complaining. This was the third overture Ludwig had composed to accompany his opera. He had had enough. It had come to symbolise his whole experience with the opera: too many people involved, making too many suggestions. There was the orchestra to contend with – at least he was used to that. But there were also the singers, some wanting small changes, some wanting big ones. Ludwig did not attend rehearsals. He was not well enough, true, but it was the prospect of hearing opinions, arguments, discussion of changes, that he knew would be more than he could bear.

And there were the directors. Not just Baron Braun, but the small army, it seemed, of men prescribing the singers' movements, instructing them on the positions for their hands and arms, planning the climactic moment of the attempted murder. On several occasions, Röckel reported that after hours of movement rehearsal, the singers still made mistakes. There was the scenery, too. Ludwig had not gone to look at it because he knew instinctively that it would be wrong.

Röckel brought him the news that confirmed all his fears: 'We had two or three rehearsals for the singers with just piano accompaniment,' he told Ludwig. 'They were satisfactory, because the singing parts are not much changed. But with the orchestra, it was not good.'

'What is the problem?'

'They complain – the woodwind especially – that the music is too difficult. Also, they play too loudly. They are nervous, I suppose. But it is difficult for we singers to project our voices sufficiently. In the rehearsal room it is easy but on stage it is a different matter. We have had only one full rehearsal on stage. There is time for only one more. And, sir, may I ask? The new overture?'

'Yes, yes. It is nearly ready.'

'Will you come to the final rehearsal?'

Ludwig shook his head wearily. His ears hurt and the fever, coupled with his enormous workload, had left him weak.

'No. Seyfried will have to do it.'

The truth was that he had had enough of composing the opera. Mozart had been right all those years ago. Do not write operas, he had said. His reason had been that, since there was no copyright on operas, Ludwig would make no money.

At least that was the one area in which, Ludwig knew, he had nothing to worry about. Baron Braun had promised him a percentage of the receipts.

Chapter 5

The Theater an der Wien, lying beyond the Bastion, was more decorative and its atmosphere more relaxed than the other two more traditional court theatres, the Burg and the Kärntnertor. The fronts of the boxes were embossed with the heads of characters from famous dramas, and the two chandeliers were ornate, each reflecting the light of two dozen candles off its multi-faceted crystal. The curtain that hung across the top of the stage and down the sides was of heavy velvet, festooned with golden tassels.

When Baron Braun had bought the Wien from Bartholomäus Zitterbarth, he had understood that it catered for a different section of society from that of the Burg and the Kärntnertor, which, within the city wall, could always rely on an aristocratic – even Imperial – audience. They were the theatres at which the city's nobility met most frequently. At the first performance of a new play or opera, one of the Emperor's eight brothers or, at least, one of their wives – perhaps even the Emperor or Empress – could be counted on as guest of honour. The audience was seated according to its seniority within the aristocracy: the more elevated would have their own box, for which they would pay an annual fee of up to a thousand florins. The cheapest seats, in the Paradies high above the auditorium, were – even at ten kreuzer – out of the reach of artisans.

The clientele of the Wien were ordinary Viennese who were prepared to spend hard-earned money for an enjoyable evening. Whole families might attend a performance of a new work, and the audience was less deferential, more discerning.

Baron Braun did nothing to alter the balance. To the contrary, he fostered the informality of the Theater an der Wien. He could also take more risks at the smaller theatre beyond the Bastion, for although the audience might be more critical, their reaction was a good indication of the worth of

Cherubini's latest opera or a production of one of the late Karl Dittersdorf's pieces.

Braun was aware of the esteem in which Beethoven was held in the highest circles in Vienna. His music had been played, and well received, in the Burgtheater. Had he not dedicated his Septet to a grateful Empress, and had he not visited the Amalienhof to tutor the young, gifted Archduke? Difficult as he might be to deal with, he was – as Braun well knew – a force to be reckoned with in the artistic and aristocratic circles of the city. It was for that reason that he had decided to allow Beethoven to restage his first opera at the Wien, despite its previous embarrassing failure. A more charitable person might have attributed that solely to the French occupation of the city and the unresponsive audience, but Braun was in no doubt that the work was flawed.

But improvements had been made – although Beethoven had delivered them late and rehearsals had been few – and young Joseph Röckel was a strong Florestan. Even the new overture had arrived – at the last moment, of course, but it *had* arrived. The wind musicians had been piqued to discover that the composer had given the 'unplayable' passage to the strings.

Advance bookings were good, and Braun was confident that the planned second performance on 10 April would go ahead. If the opera was well received, he was prepared to let it run for several weeks. He knew he had upset Beethoven by refusing to change the name of the opera. But what did the man know of business? It was to his advantage that the opera that had been forced to close by the detested French was now reopening before a native audience; that the faithful Leonore, having dispatched Pizarro to face justice, was once again reunited with her beloved Florestan, just as the Viennese, having seen the French depart, were once again tasting freedom.

There was only one decision Baron Braun had made that he was now regretting. He knew that Beethoven had been unwell, and from what he had heard the illness had not been trivial. Given that, he should never have agreed to let the composer direct the performance.

On the night of 29 March 1806, the Theater an der Wien was full. Baron Braun, with an obsequiousness that few had seen him adopt before, walked along the parterre aisles and in and out of the first tier boxes, greeting the more elevated figures among the audience. 'What a pity Their Imperial Highnesses have not yet returned to the city,' he said to Prince Lichnowsky. 'Still, splendid to see the house full. A great compliment to Beethoven's music.'

Lichnowsky's eyes narrowed a little.

Meanwhile Ludwig craved wine; several glasses. Red wine from the Schwan, that burned the back of his throat as he swallowed it. His head hurt and the sharp stomach pains were back. No amount of white powders had had any effect.

'Seyfried, can you find me some wine?'

Ignaz Seyfried put his hand on Ludwig's shoulder. 'No, my good friend,' he said, speaking close to Ludwig's ear. 'This is a big night for you. The auditorium is full – not an empty seat, I am told. Now, listen, permit me to ask you one more time. Yield the baton to me. Particularly if you are not feeling too well.'

Ludwig took a deep breath. Maybe Seyfried was right. But then he remembered the work he had put into this opera. The music he had had to rewrite; the three overtures. The meeting at Prince Lichnowsky's, where everyone had had a view to express, as if somehow the opera belonged to them. Well, they were wrong, he thought. It is mine. Mine.

'No, Seyfried. I will direct. And if it fails again I will withdraw it. And it will still be mine.'

'It is not going to fail, my friend. As I said, the house is full, and you will earn a considerable amount of money. I shall not expect to be buying my own glass of wine for some time.'

Ludwig managed a small smile. He stood at the back of the orchestra pit, raised himself on his toes and looked out across the sea of faces. The steady hum of conversation swept over him. The orchestra were filing past to take their seats. He looked up towards the Paradies. Seyfried was right. Even from there people were looking down expectantly.

Then the stage manager signalled that all was ready. Ludwig mounted the podium. He knew he should turn and bow to the audience but he wanted the performance over and done with. He tapped his baton sharply on the music stand and raised both arms to bring the orchestra to attention. With a supreme effort he forced the pain in his stomach out of his mind, screwed up his eyes to shut all noises from his head, and in their place he summoned the opening chord of the new overture, a unison and *fortissimo* G, sustained by the woodwind and brass.

It took a moment for the sound to reach his ears, and when it did, instead of jarring in his head as he expected it to, it filled him with relief. At last, after all the talking, all the arguing, all the work, the sound of his music. And when the strings began their slow descent to an unexpected F sharp, what did it matter that they were still playing *forte* and not, as he had clearly marked on their scores, *piano*?

As soon as Louise Müller, singing Marzelline, began her speech that opened the opera Ludwig realised that the structure was still wrong. *The opera began with a speech*, a dozen lines of prose, before she sang her introductory aria about her love for Fidelio. Who should he blame? Sonnleithner? Breuning? What did it matter?

Müller sang sweetly, and Caché gave Jaquino the right amount of frustrated longing. Rothe's reliable bass endowed Rocco with the sensitivity he needed. Ah, how Ludwig regretted having dropped the Gold aria, the touch of levity in this early part of the first act.

Anna Milder strode on to the stage, dragging the chains she had brought up from the prison and which she now put down in a heap by the door. Dialogue again. Too much dialogue.

He brought the orchestra in for the stroked dotted minims that introduced the quartet, the canon that was the first important piece of music in the opera. It went well, and Ludwig cursed again at the extensive dialogue that followed it. The quartet set a musical mood. Only music could follow it, or the spell was broken.

The orchestra was beginning to play sluggishly. Ludwig tried to move them on, but they seemed to be holding back. He would be able to correct that with the march that opened the fourth scene, the entry of the villain Pizarro and his escort.

It happened as he wished. The march, which he had marked *vivace*, was not technically difficult, and the players seemed to relish it. Once more, though, they ignored the sudden change from *fortissimo* to *piano*, which Ludwig had carefully put in to allow a *crescendo* leading to Pizarro's *fortissimo* top D at the start of his aria. So much work still to be done, Ludwig thought. At least Sebastian Mayer now seemed to understand his character, giving Pizarro the jealous venom he warranted. But while Pizarro spat out his plans for revenge, the soldiers on stage behind him jostled for position. Some were standing in the wrong place and were trying to correct this inconspicuously. They were not succeeding.

Ludwig wanted to wave at them to keep still, but as they moved clumsily in their heavy armour, their shields clashed. There was a ripple of laughter from the audience. Mayer sang on valiantly.

Rothe, suddenly, was misreading Rocco's role as he quaked at Pizarro's plan for murder. He was supposed to be frightened of Pizarro, while summoning up his last ounce of courage to defy the Governor and refuse to commit murder for him. But Rothe had seen the audience laugh at the soldiers' antics, and played the scene in a way calculated to draw more laughs. He knocked his knees together, shaking his head and rolling his eyes. No, no, no! thought Ludwig. You are supposed to be a righteous man, *like my grandfather*, and you would not commit an immoral act. *You are not a clown, damn you.*

Milder restored the drama with her aria 'Komm, Hoffnung!' which the audience applauded enthusiastically. He nodded to her and she sang it again as an encore.

Yet more wretched dialogue, then the duet between Leonore and Marzelline, which, Ludwig knew, was better placed now than it had been in the original libretto when it had come midway through the second act.

The first act would soon be over, with the prisoners being given temporary freedom, and singing of their joy at breathing pure air. He knew that was right, and that the audience would see in it an allegory of their freedom from the French invaders.

Suddenly he was struck by the crucial mistake in the revised opera. The prisoners do not return to the gaol! Pizarro comes on stage, unaware that they have been wandering in the prison garden. He leaves after delivering his threats, but the prisoners are still at large as the curtain comes down. Act Two begins in the dungeon, so the status of the prisoners is never satisfactorily resolved. Why had no one seen that? Breuning, or Braun, or Seyfried?

He was still shaking his head in disbelief, as he heard the applause behind him. It was loud and there were cheers. The singers were coming out from behind the curtain. He let them take their bows, then motioned to the orchestra to stand. While they acknowledged the applause, he left the rostrum and walked out of the pit.

Seyfried was waiting for him in the wings. 'Excellent, Ludwig. Superb. You must be thrilled.'

Ludwig frowned. As he had known it would, Seyfried's voice had cut into his head. 'Will you find me wine, Seyfried?'

'I will not, sir. I will not. You have enough to do, still, with coaxing a second act out of them as good as what we have just seen. And I will not put that at risk.'

Ludwig sighed. 'You do not understand, Seyfried. No one does. It is still not right.'

'Hah! Tell that to the audience.'

Ludwig knew the opera was going to be a success. That was obvious. The first act was the most difficult: nothing much happened in it; the characters had to establish themselves and explain their emotions and motives. Act Two provided the action, the attempted murder, the dramatic intervention of Fidelio and his unmasking as the disguised wife of Florestan. If Act One had succeeded, Act Two certainly would, particularly given the fine quality of Joseph Röckel's voice.

His confidence in Act Two was justified. Röckel sang out beautifully from his dungeon. His opening aria expressed all the strength and pathos it demanded.

Rocco and Fidelio descended into the dungeon, and Milder calculated her recognition of the prisoner perfectly. But there is too much dialogue, Ludwig thought. This, one of the most important moments in the opera: Fidelio, at last, sees what she longed for and what she also dreaded, that the lone prisoner in chains, dying of starvation, is indeed her husband Florestan. The murder she overheard Pizarro plotting is the murder of Florestan. But he is alive! Music should accompany this moment, not words.

Pizarro's entry was well judged, Mayer's face distorted with the thought of the act he was about to commit, Rocco fearful, Fidelio determined. And at the climax of the opera, when Fidelio unmasked himself as Leonore, Pizarro's horror was almost tangible, Florestan's face frozen with wonder, Rocco's with confusion.

Leonore draws a pistol, but for how long can she hold Pizarro at bay? Suddenly, from the ramparts, the trumpet sounds. The governor has arrived. They are saved. Pizarro's plot has failed.

Ludwig drove the orchestra on as husband and wife embraced. 'O namenlose Freude!' they sang out, extolling the virtues of married love. The sounds washed over Ludwig, and he wanted them to continue. But suddenly the chorus was on stage, the minister singing of virtue. It was too quick, Ludwig realised. Florestan and Leonore should rejoice with each other for longer.

And Marzelline should acknowledge that although fate had been cruel to her what had happened was for the higher good. The ending was all wrong and Ludwig wanted to stop and tell the singers to do it differently. But he could not.

He brought the final note of the last chorus to an end with a sigh of relief. So much work still to do, he thought. He heard the cheers from behind him. He saw the musicians motioning him to turn round. For a moment he thought of leaving the orchestra pit without facing the audience. But he knew he must not do that: he owed it to the performers to stay. So he turned and saw the sea of cheering faces, the blur of clapping hands. He made himself smile. Whatever its shortcomings the performance was a success. His reputation had not suffered. And he could expect a good income from the Baron.

Two days later, leaving his apartment in a hurry, Ludwig nearly collided with a stand on which stood a plaster head-and-shoulders bust. He had not seen it before. He looked at the head and recognised the likeness immediately.

He tore open the sealed letter propped against it.

My dear Beethoven
Forgive my immodesty, but accept this token as a memento of a great success in which I pride myself in having played a small part.

Lichnowsky

Ludwig threw it down and ran out. He wanted the orchestra and singers to rehearse more but Seyfried had told him it was not necessary and when he had asked Ludwig to yield the baton for the second performance at the end of Holy Week, he had not demurred. He wanted to watch the opera as a member of the audience. One day he would return to it.

The second performance left him profoundly depressed. The damned soldiers still raised a laugh and Ludwig suspected that this time it was deliberate. How better to ingratiate themselves with the audience? The singers did their best, but several of their movements were wrong. At one point Jaquino sang from the wrong side of the stage to Marzelline, who had to hurry to the right position. The plot worked dramatically, but it was slowed fatally by the dialogue. Ludwig noticed that in long stretches people in the audience whispered to each other. If they wanted to go and see a play, he thought, they could go to the Kärntnertor theatre. This was supposed to be opera, and in opera the performers sing, not talk.

Worst, though, the orchestra played *forte* throughout. It was as if there were no dynamic markings in the music at all. Why did that so often happen to his music? Pianists played his sonatas and singers sang his songs like that. When would musicians grasp that the dynamic markings were what gave his music its most distinctive quality?

As he sat in his apartment the next day he was wondering what to do about it when the answer was provided by a note from Baron Braun.

Herr Beethoven
I am pleased to inform you that the receipts from the first two performances of your revised opera will amount to a figure in the region of 200 florins.
Your servant, sir, P. von Braun (Baron)

Two hundred florins! Ludwig could scarcely contain himself. The figure should be much higher. Braun was a thief. Two hundred florins!

In that instant he decided that Vienna had heard the last of his opera. His 'revised' opera. Without putting on his coat, although the rain was falling hard and vertically, bouncing high off the cobbles, Ludwig strode down the Herrengasse towards the Kärntnertor gate and across the Glacis. Entering the Theater an der Wien he brushed past Josef Röckel, whose words of congratulation went unheard. Without knocking he opened Baron Braun's door and was gratified to see the look of surprise on the man's face.

'Braun, I have come for my money. All of it. Not just two hundred.'

'My dear Herr Beethoven, do sit down. I –'

Ludwig heard Braun's words through a fog, as if his head was stuffed with wool. 'More than two hundred, Braun. You cannot deceive me.'

'I assure you, sir,' said Braun, in a firmer voice edged with sharpness at the implied accusation, 'I would do no such thing. I resent your implication.'

'You are deceiving me, Braun. You have always resented my music. Now you are taking advantage of me.'

'Herr Beethoven.' Braun leaned forward on the desk, clasping his hands. He spoke firmly, clearly and calmly. 'Let me remind you that I have agreed to share the profits of your opera with you. A percentage, that is. You are the first composer for whom that has ever been the case. Herr Mozart did not receive a percentage. Nor Abbé Vogler. Nor Cherubini.'

Braun's reasonable tone was infuriating and Ludwig snapped, 'The theatre was full, Braun. On both nights.'

'Let me correct you, sir. It may have appeared to be full, but it was not quite so. Nearly, I grant you. The front parterre and the boxes were full. But the rear parterre, where the masses sit, was not full. Difficult to see from where you were positioned. I have the figures if you wish.' He pushed some papers towards Ludwig, who ignored them.

'Seyfried told me the theatre was full. I could see it for myself.'

'Herr Beethoven,' said Braun, 'such was the success of your opera that I have no doubt even the rear parterre will be full for the next performance.'

'I do not compose for the rear parterre, Braun. I write for the cultured.'

'My dear sir, if we relied on the cultured to survive, there would barely be a single theatre in this whole – uncultured – city. We need the multitude to bring in money.'

Ludwig's head began to throb. He did not want to go on arguing. But there was Braun's voice again. 'I can assure you, my dear Herr Beethoven, that your predecessor understood what you do not. He wrote for the multitude. If we had given Mozart the same percentage of the receipts that we have given you, he would have become very rich.'

The second mention of Mozart's name and Braun's infelicitous comparison of Ludwig to him was the last straw. 'I have heard enough of your snivelling words, Braun. Give me back my score. At once. Now!'

Braun looked at Ludwig open-mouthed. 'But – but we need it – to –'

'Now, Braun. I want my score.'

Baron Braun rose slowly from his chair and pulled a bellrope. A servant entered immediately. 'Bring the score of yesterday's opera, *Leonore*, for this gentleman. Herr Beethoven, what —'

'You will not have it again, Braun. It will not be shown again. Cancel all future performances. I am withdrawing it.'

'Sir, I beseech you to reflect calmly on what you are saying. I assure you the success . . .'

The servant entered, holding the thick bundle of manuscript, held in stiff covers by a black ribbon. Ludwig snatched it. 'You have seen the last of my opera, Braun. *Fidelio. Fidelio*, do you hear? That is its name.'

He strode out of the room and descended the stairs. Outside he paused, adjusting his eyes to the glare and wrinkling his nose at the smell of fruit coming from the market just across the Wien.

He smiled to himself. That really had been an inspiration to use the name he had always wanted to use. He clutched the papers to his chest and strode towards the Bastion.

BOOK SIX

Chapter 1

Ludwig did not want to see Prince Lichnowsky or Count Razumovsky. He wanted to be left alone. In the last few weeks, months even, there had been a constant stream of visitors to his apartment. There had been a pattern to the meetings: amicable words, enquiries after health, then disappointment that he had withdrawn his opera.

It was a conspiracy, that was obvious. First, his friends: Breuning, Zmeskall, Schuppanzigh, Clement, Seyfried had all stressed what a fine work *Leonore* was and how enthusiastically it had been received. His patrons, Prince Lichnowsky, Prince Lobkowitz, who had returned to Vienna, and Countess Erdödy congratulated him on its success, pointing out that his receipts would increase with every performance. Even Archduke Rudolph wrote to him bemoaning the fact that his short enforced exile from the city had robbed him of the chance to see the opera.

But his mind was made up. It was withdrawn. Stephan Breuning, who as the author of the revised libretto was keener than most to change Ludwig's mind, brought a copy of the balance sheet of receipts. Ludwig dismissed it imperiously. For a time he considered explaining to them all what really lay behind his decision but he decided not to: it would be difficult to articulate and they would find arguments to counter it.

The opera needed more work certainly, but the truth was that Ludwig felt his music had been taken out of his hands. He wanted to reclaim it, as a father might reclaim the son who had fallen too much under the influence of others. And with that went a desire to return to composing pure music for the voices of instruments.

'Send them in,' he said defeatedly to the servant, and went to stand by the window, looking out towards the Vienna Woods, his back to the room.

He heard Prince Lichnowsky's cough, delicate at first, then louder. He turned. 'Prince. Count. Sit down. I will tell the servant to bring wine.'

'No, no, dear Ludwig, thank you, but we will not stay long. I hope you like my small gift. A little immodest of me, I admit. But I'm pleased to see it displayed outside.'

'If you have come to talk about the opera, you may as well leave now.'

'That is in the past, Ludwig,' Lichnowsky said soothingly. 'The work is yours. It is for you to decide what to do with it.'

Ludwig wondered now what the true purpose of the visit was.

'Count Razumovsky asked me to bring him here, Ludwig.'

'Herr Beethoven,' said Razumovsky, 'first, allow me to congratulate you on *Leonore*. I know you have withdrawn it. That is your prerogative. I look forward to hearing it again, whenever you deem the time right.'

Ludwig walked across the room and sat down, pleased that the Russian spoke fluently enough to give him no difficulty in understanding him.

'I mentioned to you once before my grand project. I am building a new palace to house my embassy. In the Landstrasse suburb, overlooking the Danube Arm. It would give me the utmost pleasure – indeed, it would be a privilege beyond words – if you would compose a new piece to celebrate its opening. A commission, of course, on your own terms.'

Ludwig sighed. He liked Razumovsky. He knew the Count was a competent violinist and that he frequently played second violin to Schuppanzigh in the performance of string quartets. Ludwig had heard his own set of quartets, the six that comprised Opus 18, played by Schuppanzigh, Razumovsky, Weiss and Linke at Prince Lichnowsky's matinées. Furthermore, the Russian ambassador had always been supportive of his music and unstinting in his praise. 'I will turn again to the string quartet,' he said.

Razumovsky's face lit up. 'Is it not the purest form of music? Just four voices, engaged in conversation. Discussion, agreement, dispute, one moment laughing and joyful, the next angry and quarrelling.'

Ludwig said, 'Yes, you are right.'

'No room for error,' the Count continued. 'A single wrong

note and the harmony is destroyed, as I know only too well.'

'Yes, yes,' said Ludwig. 'In an orchestra a wrong note can be hidden but in a quartet each note must be perfect. How many do you want, Count?'

Razumovsky's face relaxed into a grin. 'A set of three?'

'And I suppose you will demand Russian themes in them?' Ludwig said, quirking an eyebrow.

'My dear sir, I would not presume . . .'

'You shall have them, Razumovsky. I will work on them during the summer. I will get away, though God knows where to. Everywhere is too close to this infernal city.'

Lichnowsky's face lit up. 'Ludwig! I have to go to Grätz this summer, my castle in Silesia. Come with me. You can have your own quarters, your own music room. You will be undisturbed. You can work in peace.'

Ludwig's initial instinct was to say no: he did not want to be beholden yet again to Prince Lichnowsky. But the thought of getting away – far away – to where he could work uninterrupted, to where no demands would be made of him, was an attractive proposition.

After the two had left, mouthing effusive thanks, Ludwig went to the table on which lay piles of manuscript paper and notebooks. He searched through them until, with a gasp of pleasure, he found the one he was looking for. The decision to tell Razumovsky he wanted to return to the string quartet had been a moment's inspiration – for some time he had had a new set of quartets in mind. But there was something else too. He leafed through the notebook until he found what he wanted. A simple musical statement, so simple that anyone looking at it – a musician, even – would dismiss it as a mere jotting. But Ludwig knew it was as portentous as the four notes that had dominated his thinking for so long, E flat, B flat, B flat, E flat. This was just four notes, too. The opening to a new symphony.

He went to the piano, taking a sheet of manuscript paper with him. He wrote at the top Symphony in C minor and scribbled the four notes on the stave.

Ludwig heard from Zmeskall that Josephine Deym had returned to Vienna and wanted to see him. His stomach lurched at the thought of her. He wanted to see her. He had not forgotten how she had rejected him. But then she had still been grieving for her dead husband. Perhaps it would be different now.

'No, no, Ludwig,' said Zmeskall. 'Take my advice. Do not try to see her. She ... I have spoken to her brother Franz. She is still frail and unwell. She weeps for Deym. Therese has her children. She is too ... unpredictable to look after them. She is a very emotional woman, Ludwig. You would be better not to persist.'

Ludwig thought about Zmeskall's words. Why, he wondered bitterly, was he fated to desire unattainable women? Magdalena Willmann, Giulietta Guicciardi, Josephine Deym ...

Alone at night, standing by the window and gazing over the rooftops towards the dark hills, candles flickering in windows, he felt a surge of despair. The woman I desire most, with the auburn hair and sparkling eyes, is the most unattainable of all. Married and far away, in Frankfurt.

Married. He shuddered. He had wanted to ask Josephine to marry him. Do I really *want* to be married? he wondered. Does marriage *really* bring happiness?

His brother Johann, accompanied by Stephan Breuning, came to see him unexpectedly.

'Have you seen Carl?' Johann asked.

Ludwig stared at him. 'I never see him. I do not wish to.'

'We do not know where he is,' Stephan said. 'He is not at home and no one has seen him for a week. He has not reported for work at the Hofburg.'

'Maybe he has gone away,' Ludwig suggested.

'He must have,' said Stephan. 'We wondered if he had told you anything.'

'No. I wouldn't expect him to.'

'When do you leave for Silesia?'

'Two weeks.'

'Will you be away all summer?'

Ludwig said that he would. 'Peace. Away from here. Demands.'

'Will you revise *Leonore*?' asked Breuning.

'No. The symphony in B flat. Final revisions. The piano sonata, Appassionata – though I hate the name – corrections. Quartets. And a new symphony. C minor. So much to do.'

There was silence. Ludwig wished they would leave. He thought about offering them wine, but that would only delay their departure.

'There is bad news from our homeland, Ludwig,' said Stephan, gently. 'Napoleon has turned it into a new state belonging to the French empire.'

Ludwig did not understand at first what he was saying. His mind was full of the work he had to do on his compositions. He allowed the words to sound again in his head. 'What do you mean?'

'Bonn is now part of the Confederation of the Rhine. All the electorates, the principalities, belong to the new Confederation, and the Confederation belongs to France. We are now French subjects.'

'Bah!' said Ludwig. Then, anxiously, 'Any news of Ries?'

Stephan managed a small smile. 'He wrote to me. He is in Bonn with his father. In the end he did not have to join the French army, because of his bad eye. They rejected him.'

'It must have been the only time he was grateful for his disability,' said Johann, conscious of his own imperfect eye.

There was silence again and Ludwig was grateful when Stephan stood up, encouraging Johann to do the same.

'If you hear from Carl, you will let us know?'

Ludwig nodded distantly, his mind elsewhere.

Chapter 2

Carl's note was brief and when Ludwig read it he could scarcely believe the words. His hands trembled. He screwed the paper into a ball, squashed it even smaller between his palms and flung it into the grate. Then he picked it up, unravelled it, read it again, and tossed it back.

He went to the table and lifted the carafe. It was empty. 'Wine, man! Why do I always have to remind you?' he shouted at the servant.

He read the note for the third time while the servant poured him a glass of wine.

> BROTHER!
> You should come to the rooms I have taken on the Rauhensteingasse, corner of Ballgasse, at the earliest opportunity, to meet Johanna, my wife.
>
> Carl, yr brthr

Johanna my wife! So that explained Carl's disappearance. He had sneaked off and married in secret. Ludwig felt the anger rise up in him. I, the elder brother, head of the family, knew nothing. Carl did not come to me for advice, he did not introduce me to his fiancée. Why?

He gulped the wine and as he began to feel its first effects a clarity came into his mind. The answer was obvious. Carl did not want me to meet the woman, because he knew I would disapprove of her. So what sort of woman could she be? He shuddered at the thought. Who would want to marry Carl – an unattractive man with a poor job and no hope of advancement?

He felt the anger rise in him as the implications became clearer. Something had happened – who could know what? – leaving Carl with no choice. Maybe the woman had tricked him. Yes, that had to be it. Somehow she had tricked him.

By the time Ludwig left his apartment he had convinced himself that Carl had married a woman of devious – almost certainly immoral – character. He had married her and so it was too late to prevent certain catastrophe. And worst of all, the thought of which sent a chill tremor down Ludwig's spine, there would be children – children who would bear the name of Beethoven.

He walked through the wide Freyung and into the broad Graben as if in a dream. He did not look up at the monument to the plague of a century before, nor towards the welcoming sight of Taroni's, from which the aroma of freshly ground coffee wafted. He ignored the stone walls and great Gothic spire of St Stephansdom as he walked along the Singerstrasse and turned down the Rauhensteingasse. For a moment the temptation to turn into the Ballgasse and walk down to the Alten Blumenstock almost got the better of him, but he had to confront his brother – and this woman Johanna.

'Erdgeschoss, v. Beethoven C. u. J.', the sign read. So he had taken the ground floor apartment. Ludwig ground his teeth at the sight of the family name linking his brother with this terrible woman. It was dark and cold inside the building, which smelled of damp. At the front door, he paused briefly, closed his right hand into a fist and banged it twice on the door, causing it to shake slightly on its hinges.

His ears were ringing with the effort of the walk and he tried to steady his breathing, but even as he did so the pounding in his head turned to pain. Damn, damn, damn, why did I come? He put out a hand to steady himself against the wall when the door swung open.

How he loathed the sight of Carl! That pale pinkish face covered in smudged freckles, and the dusty red hair looking as if it had faded permanently, had always made him recoil, and the brief time the two brothers had lived together, at the Theater an der Wien, had not brought them any closer. But, thought Ludwig, as he followed Carl into the room, this is my brother. He is my blood.

'How are your ears, Ludwig? Will I have to shout?'

The sound of Carl's voice cut into Ludwig's head. He walked to the nearest chair and sat heavily in it. His eyes swept round the room. There was no sign of Johanna.

'You came sooner than we expected. My wife is in the bedroom. She will be out in a moment. So, do you have nothing to say to your brother? Not even congratulations? You will like Johanna.' He prodded his brother. 'She comes with a good dowry. Two thousand florins. I've done well, don't you think?'

Ludwig looked up wearily. Arrows of pain flew through his head and his ears were dull and heavy. 'I need a glass of water.'

A few moments later he realised that a woman's hand was proffering a glass to him. He sipped at first, then took a long draught. What was he going to say?

When he looked up, Johanna was sitting in the easy chair opposite him, her hands demurely folded on a cushion that lay on her lap. Carl stood by the chair, his arm across the top of it. It was a tableau, the sort that an artist like Mähler might paint. Neither of them was smiling. Instead, as if by some unuttered agreement, they wore a look of defiance.

Ludwig gazed at Johanna. She was not beautiful, but her face was strong and well defined. Her hair was pitch black and hung straight down. Her eyes shone with an intensity that immediately unsettled him. He wanted to look more closely at her face, study it, to see if he could detect the wickedness – the immorality – he knew must be behind it.

'Will you welcome my wife into our family, Ludwig? Frau van Beethoven.'

Ludwig caught his breath at the sound of the name, with the prefix he had not heard since childhood.

'Johanna is the daughter of Herr Reiss, the upholsterer, of the Alserrorstadt, a fine citizen. And a most popular and sought-after young lady. I am extremely fortunate to have climbed to the top of the heap.'

Johanna put out a hand to stop Carl. Ludwig saw her mouth turn up slightly. He saw her mouth open. He did not want her to speak. What will her voice be like? Perhaps I will not be able to hear it. And I will not want to hear what she says.

'It is an honour for me, Herr Beethoven. I know of you and your music. I am proud to call myself your sister-in-law.'

Sister-in-law! What was the woman talking about? He scowled as the throbbing in his head intensified. 'No!' he said forcefully. 'Do not call yourself that.'

He enjoyed the sudden transformation of the defiance in their faces into shock.

'You have married my brother. He has chosen to marry you.

You will carry our name. But –' He set his jaw. He knew he should not say what he was about to say. But it had to be said, and if he did not say it now it might never be said. 'You will never be a Beethoven.'

Carl started towards him but Johanna restrained him. 'No, no, Carl. It is a shock for your brother. I can understand why he feels like that. It will take time. We must be patient.'

She looked back at Ludwig. Her face seemed stronger now, the defiance returned and all the greater. Her eyes were fixed on his. Gritting his teeth, he turned away, angered at the weakness his movement showed.

He heard her voice again, strong and firm. He did not want her to say anything else. He wanted only silence.

'You will have to get used to there being more Beethovens,' she said. 'I am carrying a child. Your brother's child. You will be its uncle.'

Chapter 3

Grätz Castle, near the town of Troppau in Silesia, stood at the top of a wooded rise, which gave it commanding views of the countryside around it. It was an imposing building, four-sided with a large courtyard within. At the back a curved row of pillars created a marble passageway that faced out on to ornate, formally laid-out gardens, beyond which lay a plateau thick with trees. In the Prince's absence the castle was run by a team of servants and gardeners, who kept it immaculate both inside and out.

Prince Lichnowsky came to the castle, which had been in his family for generations, as often as he could. The continuous wars against the French had made his visits less frequent, given the length of the journey and the dangers involved, as had his wife's poor health. Since the major surgery she had undergone, which had involved the removal of her breasts, she could no longer withstand the rigours of travel. The Prince was looking forward to when she would be well enough to return to the castle for a prolonged period of recuperation. He found it lonely in the castle without his wife. The local people, who lived in humbler surroundings, left him to himself, never failing to doff their caps when his carriage passed. His most frequent companion was Count Oppersdorff, whose own country seat was at Ober-Glogau less than a day's carriage-ride away. The Count maintained his own small orchestra, which allowed the two noblemen to indulge their passion for music.

The Prince's delight at Beethoven's acceptance of his invitation was boundless. He knew that the atmosphere of the Silesian countryside, away from the noise of the city, away from meaningless conversation, the opportunity to relax and work in the music room, with its splendid piano made by Sébastien Erard of Paris, would suit Ludwig's mood perfectly.

Almost from the moment he set foot in it Ludwig disliked the castle. It was cold and characterless, and servants in starched uniforms moved silently, almost stealthily about, their eyes never wavering from some fixed point in the distance.

Ludwig had a suite of rooms in the west wing, which looked down the hill on which the castle stood to the countryside beyond. And what a dismal countryside it was, Ludwig thought, the first time he saw it. It stretched as far as he could see, occasionally broken by the odd cluster of trees or small settlement of dwellings. In places the ground rose, but the hills it created barely merited the name. There was a darkness that he had not expected: the foliage of the trees was a deeper green than he had seen before and the only birds that seemed to want to make it their home were lustrous black crows, which cut haphazardly across the sky as if they wished they were somewhere else.

Ludwig even found the silence oppressive. He could hear it: it hung in his head like a weight. In the music room the sounds from the piano echoed off the walls. He mentioned this to the solicitous Prince Lichnowsky, and the next day the room was hung with thick tapestries, one depicting the Judgement of Paris. Ludwig complained to the Prince that he found the three goddesses, portrayed as voluptuous nudes, distracting. The next day, to his amusement, he found that it had been replaced by an even larger picture of the rape of the Sabines.

Ludwig had not expected to miss the noisy, overcrowded atmosphere of Vienna. Perhaps for the first time he realised that what he liked most about the city was the ease with which he could get away from it. A short carriage-ride and he could be in Heiligenstadt, Döbling or Grinzing to the north, Mödling or Baden to the south, and once there he could walk for hours in the countryside. There were streams, woodland, hills and valleys. There were the Rauhenstein ruins in the Helenenthal and the rushing Schwechat. Here, it was not practical to take long walks. It meant descending the hill down a gravel track, and there was little in the featureless landscape to interest him. Instead he walked in the castle grounds for hour upon hour.

His mind was in turmoil. He wanted to compose – he needed to compose – but he could not rid his mind of the image of Johanna. Johanna van Beethoven – and the child she was carrying. The discovery that she was expecting a child had confirmed his direst suspicious about her. Even Carl's off-hand remark about her popularity had added to it. She had to be a woman without morals, a wicked woman who had selected Carl as her victim.

God, what a fool Carl had been! The child had obviously been conceived before he married Johanna. She must have tricked him! So easy to trick a man as stupid as Carl. Striding along the path towards the thick woods, his shoes crunching on the gravel, he came to understand it all. He could see it in her face. The defiance, the triumph. She had achieved her aim. She had lured Carl and secured what she wanted. Now the Beethoven family was to be for ever different. A child – a Beethoven child – conceived out of wedlock by trickery.

Day after day, Ludwig insisted on being left alone by the Prince and headed straight through the formal gardens to the woods beyond. There, he could lose himself in their wildness. This was nature's creation, not the gardeners', the workings of God, not man.

And all the time he walked his head rang with four notes, the simplest sequence he had ever composed. Furiously he scribbled them again and again in his notebook, slowly coming to understand their portentousness, the ominous and prophetic message they held that he would unlock.

Da-da-da-daaa, he sang to himself as he walked, pounding the air with his fists, careless of the rain that matted his hair and ran down his forehead.

His clothes still wet, he sat for hours at the piano in the music room, pounding the simple theme on the keys and scribbling on manuscript paper. He rarely played more than the four notes, yet he completed stave after stave. What he wrote he heard in his head.

The servants learned to bring him food and wine wherever he was. If he was outside they brought him a hamper of cold meats and put it silently on an iron table they had moved to the bottom of the garden. If he was in the music room, they set a tray on a table there.

Soon he had the outline for all four movements of the new symphony. How differently he was composing now, compared to the last symphony, the Eroica. With that, he had begun with the last movement, the four notes and the theme that grew from them, then composed the first, second and third movements, showing how that great final theme grew organically from the earlier movements. Now, the four simple notes, three quavers and a minim, opened the first bar of the first movement and would be there at the end of the fourth. They were the driving force of the entire work. In them lay all the passion, anger and pain of his life.

For some days Ludwig had known that Prince Lichnowsky wanted to speak to him. He had seen him standing at the edge of the gardens, clearly unable to bring himself to attract Ludwig's attention. He saw him in the doorway of the music room, hands clasped before him, leaning forward expectantly. At first Ludwig ignored him, then he took to seeing him and dismissing him with a wave of the hand. He began to revel in the humiliation he was inflicting on the Prince, suppressing the guilt that accompanied his wilful mistreatment of his benefactor. Finally he could endure the Prince's mute entreaties no longer. He was ready for the interruption. He had sketched the framework of the new symphony and was content to let it rest, for the ideas in his head to take root.

In the meantime, almost as an outlet for the energy that rushed through him, he brought to fruition the three quartets for Count Razumovsky and made final corrections to the piano sonata, which Sonnleithner had named Appassionata.

'Ludwig, my good friend Count Oppersdorff – you have met him in Vienna, I believe.'

The name meant nothing to Ludwig.

'You will like him, I know. I have just received word that he has arrived at his estate near Ober-Glogau, a short carriage-ride from here. We are to go and stay with him for a few days.'

'I have work to do here.'

'The break will do you good. And another thing – he has his own orchestra who have been rehearsing your music. You will not disappoint them, will you?'

Almost from the moment the carriage left Grätz Ludwig was pleased that he had agreed to go. Away from the austerity of the castle the countryside seemed to lighten. They crossed the Oder. What a difference a river made, he thought. It softened the foliage, colouring it a richer green, attracting birds, smaller and with more vibrant plumage than the dismal crows. Looking at the flowing water caused a tug at Ludwig's heart, a pining once more for the restless, magical waters of the Rhine.

He took to Count Oppersdorff immediately. The man had a modesty about him yet lacked the servility of Prince Lichnowsky. He introduced Ludwig to the members of his orchestra, who in turn showed him the utmost respect and spoke of his music in awed tones. Ludwig noticed that, although the familiar dullness hung heavily in his ears, he had less difficulty here than he had expected in carrying on conversation, and the pain that had riven his head at Grätz was absent here in Ober-Glogau.

He even sat back and enjoyed listening to the orchestra playing his second symphony in D. So long ago, he thought, and so painful to write. Heiligenstadt, and the realisation that his deafness would not improve. And only I understood that, he thought. An inevitable, inexorable, relentless decline. Until one day I will be able to hear nothing more. Not even my music.

On the evening before their return to Grätz, Ludwig and Lichnowsky sat by the Count's roaring fire, sipping a heady sweet white wine. Ludwig marvelled at the sensation of calm it induced in him.

'Herr Beethoven, I cannot tell what pleasure it has given me to meet you and hear your music. I hope you have enjoyed your stay.'

Ludwig raised his wine glass in acknowledgement.

'I do hope you will not think me presumptuous, but it would give me the greatest pleasure to commission a new work from you, which I hope you would allow my musicians to perform.'

Ludwig felt the familiar sinking in his stomach, but it passed quickly. The Count's eyebrows were raised expectantly. Lichnowsky, next to him, was looking between the two of them, mouth closed slightly more firmly than usual. Was he envious? Ludwig wondered. 'What did you have in mind?' he asked.

'A symphony,' the Count said. 'A new symphony. Similar to the one in D we performed for you.'

'Similar to . . .' Ludwig frowned. The C minor symphony he had been working on was unlike anything else he had composed. As different from the Eroica as the Eroica had been from the second. Instinctively Ludwig knew it was not the work for Count Oppersdorff. He would be bewildered by it – it was likely the whole of Vienna would be bewildered by it. It was probable that they would reject it.

He detected a tiny shake of Lichnowsky's head, as if the prince was encouraging him to refuse.

The Prince, emboldened by Ludwig's glance, spoke. 'My dear Count, I don't think Herr Beethoven –'

Ludwig gestured angrily and the Prince's words froze in the air. 'Do you have a figure in mind?'

'Would five hundred florins be acceptable?'

'I will compose a new symphony for your orchestra,' said Ludwig. 'I will start on it now and complete it before I return to Vienna.'

As soon as he returned to Grätz, Ludwig felt the old depression settle on him. Lichnowsky had told him he must stay in Silesia for another month, which disheartened him all the more.

He threw himself into composing the new symphony for Oppersdorff and found it easier than he had expected. Sitting at the piano, he composed straight on to the manuscript paper. The notebooks that lay on the table by the piano, replete with jottings for the symphony in C minor and other works, remained untouched.

The first movement, after a slow and expectant opening, took flight in a flurry of semiquavers. The music flowed out of him almost too quickly for him to write it down. He threw open the windows of the music room to allow it to soar out into the air. He wanted to shout at the crows, in their leaden flight, to listen and learn and follow the music – to fly as the little coloured birds of Ober-Glogau flew.

The second movement, which he marked *adagio*, gushed fully formed from his head to the keys and on to the paper. He found himself writing a gloriously tender tune, a hymn to love which brought into his mind dancing auburn ringlets and banished the image of pitch black hair that hung straight down. Descending crotchets, ascending again, turning and coming to rest in the movement's warm home key of E flat. He scribbled the outline on the paper. He did not need to write more. He knew exactly what he wanted. Clarinet now, answering the opening theme with another, equally poignant, ascending again, turning at the top and falling. Tunelessly he mouthed the notes as they streamed from his brain. 'Pum pum-pum pum-pum pum-pum,' he sang, and his fingers picked out the staccato semiquavers and demi-semiquavers that separated the two themes.

After the interlude of calm, the third movement echoed the energy of the first, deriving its impetus from the theme being off the beat. Difficult to play, he knew that. But Oppersdorff's musicians were not only uncomplaining about the challenges in his music, they were good instrumentalists. They would be able to play this, he knew. A trio section to vary the pace – so simple, a turning phrase of crotchets and minims. So simple that he extended it – lilting, flowing – before the offbeat main theme re-emerged, brought to a final crashing end with a unison *fortissimo* chord of B flat.

The finale, again like the first movement, became almost a blur of semiquavers. It was if Ludwig could not restrain his energy. 'Timpani!' he called out, scribbling trills, knowing that there was not a timpanist in Vienna who would be able to play them. He drove the music on, alternating *fortissimo* passages with *pianissimo*, sprinkling it with accidentals and key changes until, exhausted, he allowed the music to resolve itself through a series of chords, lower strings emitting a last flurry of runs, into the home key.

The symphony in B flat had taken him no more than a week to compose. After he had finished it, he took time to tidy the manuscript, alter certain passages, adjust the instrumentation. But Count Oppersdorff's symphony was all but complete, needing only the copyist Schlemmer to produce it in legible form.

Ludwig expected to feel drained. Instead he felt invigorated, as if the work had given him the outlet he needed to draw off his surplus energy.

It was time now to return to the symphony in C minor, so different from what he had just composed that people would ask how the same composer could have written both. Even as he thought of that symphony, which would be his fifth, he felt the portentousness of what lay ahead, the passion and the pain that must follow the almost frivolous utterances of the B flat work.

That was the mood he was in when Prince Lichnowsky, tiptoeing silently into the music room, left a letter on a silver platter.

Even as he recognised Carl's handwriting Ludwig let out a low cry. He did not need to read the letter – he did not *want* to read it. All the anger and frustration that had so built up over Carl's marriage would, he knew, come flooding back.

He ripped open the seal, sending shards of wax to the floor.

BROTHER!
My wife Johanna and I are proud to inform you of the

safe birth of our son, to whom we have given the name Karl.

He will, we have no doubt, bring honour to the name of Beethoven.

Yr brother
Carl

Chapter 4

The autumn of 1806 had slipped prematurely into winter, the overcast Silesian sky matching the look on Prince Lichnowsky's face. He put an arm round his friend and led him to an easy chair. 'Dreadful news, Oppersdorff. The Prussian Army defeated. It is almost unbelievable.'

'Another name to add to the gravestone of Europe. Jena, along with Hohenlinden and Austerlitz. And now Napoleon is marching to Berlin. Berlin! Where will he stop? Moscow?'

'Russia is already defeated. I heard that after Austerlitz young Tsar Alexander sat among the Russian dead on the battlefield and wept. It is small wonder that the Russian army did not arrive in time at Jena. The thought of another defeat was too much for them.'

Lichnowsky handed him a glass of wine. 'Good of you to come, Oppersdorff. I'm not looking forward to tonight. But it has to be done. We have to obey French orders,' he added wryly.

'How many do you expect?'

'At least six – the General and his immediate staff. I am told he is a cultured man. In fact, that is why he has invited himself to dinner. He heard that our friend was here and wanted to hear him play the piano. He admires his music.'

'Good. Then we shall all benefit.'

A worried look crossed Lichnowsky's face. 'I'm not sure. He is behaving a little strangely. It began soon after we returned from visiting you. He won't talk to anyone. Not me, not the servants. He spends all day in the music room or walking in the woods at the bottom of the garden. Frequently he returns drenched to the skin. I'm rather worried.'

'Maybe he is working on my new symphony and doesn't want to be disturbed,' said Oppersdorff, with a smile.

'I know he is doing that. I have heard him playing passages.

No, it's to do with a letter he received. From his brother Carl
in Vienna.'

'Bad news?'

Lichnowsky frowned. 'That's the strange thing. Excellent
news.' He lowered his voice. 'I found the letter in his room
and read it. I know I should not have but I wanted to know
what had upset him. Carl and his wife have had a son. Ludwig
is an uncle.'

'But that's excellent news.'

'I know. Yet it has upset him.'

'Let me speak to him,' said Oppersdorff brightly. 'We got on
so well. And I can ask him about my symphony.'

Ludwig was tired. He had thrown himself into the composition
of the C minor symphony, which had sapped his strength.
And it was far from complete, not much more than a series
of sketches and ideas. But so different from the other piece.
Da–da–da–daaa, da–da–da–daaa. How could such a simple motif
carry such portent within it? At first he had found it easy
to develop, but then he found himself going deeper behind
the notes.

He wanted to return to Vienna – he had had enough
of the dark, tenebrous countryside of Silesia, where the air
seemed always heavy with the damp of an impending storm.
He found himself longing for the green of the Helenenthal
valley, the white-flecked water of the Schwechat cutting joyously through it. He needed to be back in his apartment
where he could devote himself to the C minor symphony,
the familiar keys of Andreas Streicher's piano under his fingers.

Sitting at the piano, he felt rather than heard the footsteps
approaching and the small cough barely penetrated his ears.
What could he say to Lichnowsky? How could he make him
grasp that he wanted to be left alone?

'I need to return to Vienna, Lichnowsky,' he said, gruffly.
'We must leave soon.'

'My dear Ludwig,' Count Oppersdorff said, in a strong clear
voice, 'I shall tell my friend the Prince. I am sure he will be
leaving soon.'

Ludwig was only slightly less vexed to find it was Oppersdorff,
not Lichnowsky, speaking. He nodded curtly. 'The symphony is
done. It needs to be copied.'

'I shall arrange immediately with my bankers for our contract to be honoured. You do not know how grateful I am.'

Ludwig took a deep breath. 'I need to be alone. Will you leave me now?'

'Ludwig, I understand, but will you allow me to ask you a favour on behalf of the Prince?'

'A favour?' Ludwig's voice rose. 'Always the man wants favours from me. Always asking me to do this, to do that. He wants me to play for him, doesn't he? Ever since I have known him, he has asked me. No. Tell him, no favours.'

He faced the keys, but before he began to play he heard Oppersdorff's voice. 'He cares very much for you. He and the Princess both do. He is under a lot of strain now. His wife's health is poor and the war is draining his resources. You must be understanding.'

Ludwig turned on the stool. '*Understanding!* Do people understand me, Oppersdorff? I am a musician and my hearing is leaving me. Do they know what that means? I am a musician and they treat me like a . . . a circus performer.'

'Ludwig, you are the finest piano virtuoso in Europe.' Oppersdorff spoke quickly, allowing no interruption. 'Tonight the Prince has important dinner guests. The French General, who is in command of this district, and his staff. He is a great admirer of your music. He has asked especially to meet you and hear you play. He —'

'French!' Ludwig exclaimed. 'You expect me to play for French soldiers? Who serve under that tyrant? That so-called emperor. Do you know something, Oppersdorff? That Frenchman Kreutzer did not even acknowledge the sonata I sent him.'

'You will at least join us for dinner. Please do that, Ludwig.'

The tiredness had not left him, and all he wanted to do was sleep. He was finding it difficult to follow the conversation at the dinner table. The French General – a Gascon called Daguin – was talking about success on the battlefield and how the shape of Europe had changed for ever.

He had a fine, sensitive face, but he held it at a slight upward angle so that he appeared to look down on those to whom he was talking, which made him seem arrogant. The six or so staff officers around him rarely spoke, but made the most of the liberal flow of wine.

Ludwig, too, had drunk a quantity of wine – Lichnowsky

was clearly so pleased he had attended the dinner that he made sure the servant did not allow his glass to remain empty for a moment. But he waited in vain for it to have the liberating effect on his brain he so desired. It was serving only to increase his fatigue.

'Murat and Lannes, who led our forces into Vienna, are both Gascons. Maréchal Murat led the cavalry at Jena, under the direct command of His Imperial Majesty.'

'Is General Bernadotte not also a Gascon?' asked Lichnowsky, in a compliant, almost fawning, tone.

'We allow him to say he is. He is from Pau, to the south. In the foothills of the Pyrenees. Strictly speaking, he is a Béarnais.'

Then one of the staff officers, sitting several places to the right of the General, spoke. He was drunk. 'Hah, Gascons! Do you know, Monsieur Beethoven? In France we have a word, *gasconnade. Une gasconnade.* It means an exaggeration. Do you know why a *gasconnade* is an exaggeration? Because all Gascons exaggerate.'

Despite warning looks from his colleagues, the soldier spoke again. This time he looked directly at Ludwig. 'If you want to meet a true Frenchman, Monsieur le musicien, you should go to Paris. Only in Paris will you meet a true Frenchman. I, Monsieur, am a Parisian. These Gascons,' he sneered, 'know only the land. Their souls are dark, like the soil they were brought up on.'

'The same soil that produces Armagnac,' said Daguin, with a smile that defused the tension.

Emboldened, the soldier turned again to Ludwig. 'Lejeune,' he said, 'à votre service, Monsieur le musicien.' The smirk in his voice was obvious to everyone at the table.

Ludwig's breath quickened. He caught the expression of shock on Lichnowsky's face. He was about to say something, but General Daguin spoke first. His voice was sharp. 'Enough, Lejeune. You will curb your tongue. That is an order. Do you understand?'

'Mon général,' he said. A slur had replaced the smirk. 'Tell me, Monsieur le musicien, it is said you play the piano. To be a real musician you must also play the violin, like our divine Monsieur Kreutzer.'

Ludwig put down his glass and glared at the arrogant young man.

'Lejeune!' said Daguin. 'You will report to me tomorrow at seven in the morning. For now, you will not utter another word.'

Ludwig finished his wine. Lichnowsky, taking his cue from him, announced, 'Gentlemen, will you follow me to the music room, where we will have coffee and Armagnac, of course, in honour of our distinguished guest. And it is my profound hope that Herr Beethoven will do us the honour of exhibiting his noble art.'

Ludwig felt a mixture of anger and frustration. Play the piano for these – these . . . For a brief moment he considered pleading that his deafness made it impossible.

He stood up and was pleased to see that the rest of the company stood with him. He caught Oppersdorff's eye. The Count nodded encouragingly. Him too! Ludwig thought.

He hung back as the soldiers, led by Lichnowsky, walked towards the music room, their gait made awkward by the high leather riding boots they wore. He grimaced as the heavy tread of their steel-tipped boots made a cacophony in his head.

Silently, with all eyes turned away from him, he peeled off from the group and mounted the wide staircase. Without looking back he went along the corridor to his room, entered it, closed the door behind him and bolted it.

For a moment he sat on the edge of the bed, his head in his hands. How it hurt! How the whistle in his ears cut through his head! The wine was making his head spin, too, and with it came renewed anger. Play for French soldiers! The enemy of my country!

He stood up again, swaying slightly and supporting himself on the bed head. He looked round the room. Clothes were strewn on a chair, papers in random piles on the table. Was there anything in the music room? Had he left any papers down there? No. He congratulated himself on that.

He began to scoop up his clothes. Da-da-da-daaa, da-da-da-daaa. The four notes. He could not get them out of his head. Round and round they revolved. He could hear how the orchestra would play them, develop them, vary them, weave themes around them. Roughly he pushed his clothes into the single leather bag he had brought. He heard the fist banging on the door. 'Ludwig! Ludwig!'

'Go away! D'you hear? Go away!'

'Ludwig! You must come down. Please come down and play for my guests. You must!'

He carried on pushing his clothes into the bag. Then the papers. Where was the folder? He found the leather folder, untied it and began to gather up the papers.

There was a banging on the door. Louder this time. Not a fist. The door shuddered. Suddenly it burst open, the bolt flying out in pieces. Ludwig was transfixed. The servant who had burst the bolt scurried away and Lichnowsky stood red-faced, his eyes bulging with rage. 'How could you do this? After all I have done! You ungrateful, wretched –' Lichnowsky took a step towards Ludwig, his fists clenched.

Ludwig's anger swelled in him uncontrollably. 'Now I see you for what you are!' he shouted at Lichnowsky. 'You want to control me. Use me like a servant. A circus performer. I will not do it! Now get out!'

Unable to stop himself he reached for the back of the small wooden chair that stood by the table and lifted it in the air. Suddenly he felt a firm hand on his shoulder and saw another hand take hold of the chair and force it down.

'Calm yourself, Ludwig,' said Oppersdorff, in a firm but kindly voice. 'There is no need for violence. Stay here, if that is what you want. We will leave you alone.'

He sat Ludwig on the edge of the bed. Then he put an arm round Lichnowsky and led him away, pulling the door closed behind him.

Ludwig struggled to control himself. He stood up again and continued to put papers into the folder. Finally, leaving several pages stuck out at an angle he tied it, then fastened the strap round the bag.

A single scrap of paper remained on the table. He foraged in his pocket for a pencil. On the paper he wrote:

Prince! What you are, you are by circumstance and by birth. What I am, I am through myself. Of princes there have been and will be thousands. Of Beethoven there is only one.

I am leaving this moment for Vienna. Do not try to stop me.

He opened the door with his foot. He did not pause to close it. He hurried down the stairs and into the front hall. Clasping the bag clumsily under his arm he hauled open the heavy front door.

He shivered as the cold air hit him, and started as the noise of a hundred marching soldiers struck his ears. It was pouring with rain; big bulbous drops pounding on to the gravel, like the heels of so many soldiers' boots. He lifted the bag up higher under his arm and pulled his coat up higher round his neck.

He walked around the side of the house to the stables. Troppau was only an hour away by carriage, maybe less. He would stay the night there and catch the first post to Vienna. He rattled on the door of the stables but it was locked. The building was in darkness. He looked around him. Everywhere was total darkness. After a moment's hesitation, he walked down the drive as swiftly as he could, clutching the bag and the folder. The rain fell on him with such force that, despite the thickness of his hair, he could feel the drops pounding against his scalp. The water ran in rivulets down his face.

As he went down the thickly wooded hill away from the castle he was careful not to slip. At the bottom he paused briefly to catch his breath, sheltering under a tree. It was pitch black. His sodden clothes were heavy and lay icily against his skin. He had to keep moving. He strode out on to the main road and turned towards Troppau. The mud squelched around his boots, and he tried to keep out of the carriage ruts in which the rainwater lay deep.

He walked on, breathing heavily. The effort warmed his skin and soon the chill left him. Still the rain pounded mercilessly: the noise of it splashing on the road filled his ears. He listened to it as he walked, haphazard, a sudden gust of wind lightening or strengthening it. In the distance he could see the few twinkling lights of Troppau. It could not be long now. Ten minutes, maybe fifteen.

He walked on. His legs felt heavy as the lights danced in the distance, seeming to come no nearer. The rain began to ease off, leaving his head filled with a whooshing noise, as if water was cascading in torrents around him. He looked up to see if, by some freak of nature, a river had burst its banks and he was about to be submerged in raging waves. With a sinking heart, he understood that his ears were playing tricks on him again.

It must have been another hour before he was in the main street of Troppau, a few lights flickering but not a single window illuminated. He walked up and down the street, looking for the inn. When he found it he hammered on the door until he heard bolts being drawn back on the other side. A face, blinking angrily behind a candle, peered out at him. 'A room. And hot water.'

The man turned without speaking and Ludwig followed him up a small flight of stairs. He opened a door, put the candle on a chest of drawers, said something and left.

The room was tiny and freezing cold. Ludwig was shivering violently. It was clear that he was going to get no hot water. What could he do? He knew that if he took his clothes off and got into bed the cold would overwhelm him.

He threw down his bag and folder, peered around the room and saw an upright chair in the corner. He walked to it, cursing as his soaked clothes pressed against his skin. He sat, leaned his head back against the wall and prayed for sleep to overcome him.

He was woken by voices. Every muscle in his body complained. His neck hurt most – his head had fallen to the side as he slept and he nearly cried out with pain as he lifted it upright. The shivering began immediately. His head ached and the sound of rain still filled his ears.

He tried to respond to the knocking on the door, which grew insistently louder, but could not find his voice. Finally the door opened. The face that had peered out at him in the night was still set in a long scowl, but behind the landlord was Count Oppersdorff.

Ludwig wanted only to get away, to leave for Vienna, without speaking to anyone.

Oppersdorff pushed past the landlord and hurried over to him. 'My dear friend, you are ill. Your clothes are soaked. You will catch a chill, maybe even a fever.' He turned to the landlord. 'Here, take this,' he said, thrusting money into the man's hand. 'Bring hot water and towels. And hot coffee and bread. And be quick, do you understand?'

Ludwig heard what he said through the noises in his ears, and the effect of the words alone was warming. He braced himself for what he knew would follow.

'Ludwig, we were so concerned about you. Prince Lichnowsky is so sorry to have upset you. He pleads forgiveness. He –'

Ludwig did not want to talk, to explain. His head was hurting, his skin – icy cold only a few moments ago – was burning. He wanted to be in Vienna, in his apartment on the Mölkerbastei. 'Oppersdorff, I want to leave by the next coach for Vienna. When will that be?'

'Not yet, my friend, not yet. I am bringing a doctor to see you first and we will let him decide.'

Ludwig concentrated on the Count's words. He did not hear them clearly, but he heard 'doctor'. 'No!' he said sharply. 'I must leave.'

A worried look crossed Oppersdorff's face. 'Ludwig, Prince Lichnowsky wants to come to see you. He told me –'

Ludwig took a deep breath. 'Oppersdorff. I want to leave. You cannot stop me. You must not. I do not want to see anyone.'

Oppersdorff turned to the tray the landlord had put down. He handed Ludwig a cup of coffee. Ludwig took it, warming his hands around it, trying to quell his shivering so that the coffee did not spill over the sides. The pungent taste flooded through his senses and he relished it, burning his tongue. Immediately his head began to clear and warmth returned to his body. The shivering subsided. 'I am grateful to you,' he said. 'But I must leave. I do not want to see anyone. Especially not Lichnowsky. Will you find out when the next coach leaves for Vienna?'

Oppersdorff smiled. 'I am afraid it is not as simple as that. Remember, the French are in control now and you need a pass to travel. If you try to go without one you will be arrested. It will take some time to get one.'

Ludwig could hear him clearly now. 'They know who I am. I am Beethoven, the musician. I am not a soldier or diplomat or spy! They will have to let me through. I live in Vienna. I am returning to my home.'

'If only it were that easy. I will try my best. Do not worry. In the meantime I am sending a change of clothes for you and I will ask the landlord to prepare a hot bath.'

He threw a smile at Ludwig as he left.

Ludwig poured himself more coffee and ate the bread hungrily. This damned war, he thought. These damned French.

Later that day Ludwig sat in the same chair, warm again and wearing a fresh set of clothes. A deep tiredness had overcome him. He wanted so much to lie on the bed and sleep. But no, he had to get back to Vienna. He clenched his fists with determination.

The knock on the door startled him, but he was pleased to see Oppersdorff enter with another man behind him. 'Ah, Ludwig. You look a little more comfortable now.'

Ludwig flinched at the effect of the words on his ears. The sudden sound of speech hurt them, and his head began immediately to thump. It was the familiar pain. He knew it would not go away.

Oppersdorff seemed to sense this and spoke gently but clearly. 'I have brought Doktor Weiser with me. Don't complain. It is important he makes sure you are well enough to travel.'

Ludwig acquiesced. He did not feel well. Apart from his head, his skin was sore and when he took a deep breath it hurt his lungs.

The doctor moved into the room and smiled at him. Without speaking he untied Ludwig's shirt at the neck and pulled it open. He placed the end of an ear trumpet on his chest and listened, moving it to several places. Then he reached round and placed it low on Ludwig's back. Satisfied, he lifted Ludwig's upper eyelids, each in turn. Then he reached into his bag and pulled out a spatula. He opened his mouth to indicate to Ludwig to do the same and placed the spatula on Ludwig's tongue, flattening it, and peered into the back of his mouth.

Finally he left the room, beckoning to the Count to follow him.

Ludwig wanted to go over to the small window. Was it pouring with rain again – it seemed always to rain in Silesia – or was it just his treacherous ears? But he knew that the effort of standing would hurt his aching muscles and cause the clothes to chafe against his skin.

Oppersdorff's face told Ludwig what the Count was going to say.

'Ludwig, Doktor Weiser says you must not travel for two days. You have the beginnings of a fever. To travel would be folly. Come back to Grätz Castle with me. My carriage is outside. There you will be warm and comfortable.'

'Oppersdorff, I am leaving today. Have you a pass for me?'

The Count said nothing, but tightened his lips.

'You have it, haven't you?'

Oppersdorff nodded. 'Prince Lichnowsky arranged it for you.

He spoke to the head of police. He said if that was what you wanted, you must have it. He is a kind man.'

'Give it to me. What time is the next coach?'

'This evening. Eight o'clock. But you must not travel through the night. It would be madness.'

'Eight o'clock?'

Oppersdorff, resignation in his eyes, said, 'You must promise me that you will stay the night in Brünn. Before the last leg to Vienna.'

'Get me the necessary tickets. I will leave this evening.'

The journey was dreadful and Ludwig regretted his decision almost from the moment he left Troppau. It rained incessantly. The coach frequently became stuck in mud and had to be pulled clear while the passengers stood in the rain watching helplessly. On one occasion the male passengers were asked to help push. Ludwig hung back and stood under the cover of a tree.

There were frequent stops for papers to be checked. French soldiers were everywhere, demanding papers in French, refusing to listen to any German.

Several times new passengers attempted to engage Ludwig in conversation, but failed.

Ludwig clutched his bag and folder on his lap, staring out of the window at the desolate countryside. He was shivering again and his skin was so sore that every movement of the carriage hurt. And he was cold. His coat sleeves, already damp from the rain, were soon even more so from his constant efforts to dry his dripping nose.

In Brünn, almost without thinking, he walked straight to the Vienna stage, which was due to leave in four hours' time. It was early morning, too early even for anywhere to be serving coffee. He sat motionless, his head pounding, his ears dull and heavy, his breathing laboured, his skin sore.

After a final stop at a French checkpoint north of the city, the stage entered Vienna through the Schottentor. Ludwig got out only a street away from the Mölkerbastei. It was the earliest moment of dawn, the sun beginning to rise to the east across the Hungarian plain but not yet throwing any light on the city.

He trudged up the four flights of stairs to his apartment. The effort hurt: he could not draw deep enough breaths to give him the strength he needed.

He had the presence of mind to bang on the servant's door

as he walked towards his own. He stood patiently, leaning against the wall for support, while the servant pushed past him, unlocked the outer door and turned away.

Ludwig almost fell into his apartment. The chill air hit him, causing him to gasp. No heat. The damned servant had not even heated the place. Then he remembered he had not told the man of his return. Damn, he thought. Damn, damn, damn. He stumbled as he crossed the lobby and knocked into something. He heard a slight rocking sound but could not immediately see what it was.

It was the plaster bust of Prince Lichnowsky. The pedestal was steadying itself.

Lichnowsky! What an odious, obsequious . . . Play for French soldiers! No more, he said to himself. Then, 'No more!' out loud. 'No more playing to order! No more obeying orders. No more!'

With a roar of anger he dropped his bag and the folder, snatched the bust off its pedestal with both hands and dashed it to the floor, where it smashed into a thousand pieces.

BOOK SEVEN

BOOK SEVEN

Chapter 1

There was a weariness inside Ludwig that he could not shake off. It followed him everywhere, deadening his mind and pulling at his feet. Inside his head the noises were worse. A constant ringing, sometimes in one ear, sometimes in the other, made him hold on to the back of a chair for balance. If the ringing subsided it was replaced by the sound of waves breaking on sand. If there was silence in his head, he knew that the sound of a voice – or worse, a piano key struck – would jar and jangle and bring on the throbbing pain.

'It's not surprising,' said Doktor Schmidt. 'You were very ill. You behaved, if I may say so, somewhat stupidly. You allowed yourself to become soaked to the skin, you carried on wearing the same clothes. It is hardly surprising you developed a fever. You are fortunate you did not damage your lungs. There is consumption in your family, is there not?'

'My mother died of it.'

'Then you should take extra care. Instead of that, you mistreat yourself.'

Ludwig waved him away and returned to the only medicine he knew would work. Somehow, after two glasses of wine – sometimes it needed more – the heaviness in his head lightened and the noises in his ears subsided. And the piano keys sounded pure and sweet.

'Look at that wall, Gleichenstein. Dreadful. Just blank. Beyond, the Prater, the river, the plains of Hungary, and all I see is a blank wall.'

Gleichenstein, opening the folder on his lap, said, 'May I suggest a picture, sir? Perhaps the portrait of your grandfather. Why not move it to there? It would look very fine.'

Ludwig filled two glasses with wine and put one on the table near Gleichenstein. 'The portrait stays above the piano.

What have you got there? Are you going to hurt my ears with figures?'

'Essential, I am afraid, sir. I will go through it as swiftly as I can.'

'If I don't want to hear it, I will plead deafness.'

Ludwig liked the brightness of the young man's face. His hair, combed forward, swept up as it reached his forehead, giving a permanent lift to his expression. And Ludwig knew he had reason to be grateful for Gleichenstein's attentiveness.

'The violin concerto first, sir. The score is with the Kunst-und-Industrie. Herr Sonnleithner is asking if you wish to put a dedication on the title page. Herr Clement, perhaps, for whom you composed it?'

Ludwig thought for a moment. 'No. Give it to Steffen. Stephan Breuning.'

'Herr Breuning, sir?'

'He is an old friend. We had a disagreement.'

Gleichenstein wrote on a piece of paper. 'I have good news from London. The firm of Clementi wishes to secure publication rights for your symphony in B flat, the piano concerto in G, as well as,' he turned over a piece of paper, 'the set of quartets for Count Razumovsky.'

'What is he offering?'

Gleichenstein pulled another sheet of paper from the folder. 'Two hundred pounds sterling. That is roughly two thousand florins, maybe a little less. A handsome sum, sir. Oh, and he asks one more thing. He would like you to make a piano transcription of the violin concerto.'

Ludwig was unsure that he had heard correctly.

'Strange, I know, sir. Apparently London boasts more pianists than violinists.'

Ludwig sipped his wine and shrugged.

'Just a few more matters, sir, which I would like to deal with while I am here. Count Oppersdorff wrote to me from Silesia. He asks me to remind you how much he admires your music. He says he believes you began work on a new symphony while you were in Silesia. He wishes to make the same payment to you as for the previous one – five hundred florins – for its exclusive use for six months. He also says he hopes the good memories of your stay will outweigh the bad.'

Ludwig said nothing. Since his illness he had tried to shut out from his mind all remembrance of the trip to Grätz. He glanced across at the table near the piano and saw the pile of manuscripts for the symphony in C minor, his fifth. Not yet complete but destined, he knew, to be a monumental work.

He nodded briefly. 'But do not tell him when it will be ready. I do not know myself.'

'Of course, sir. And, sir, Prince Lichnowsky has asked to see you.' He uttered the final words in a rush.

Ludwig clicked his tongue. Even the sound of the name made him frown. He knew, in the cold light of day, that he had treated Lichnowsky badly. But even so. 'No, damn it!' he said curtly. 'I do not want to see him.'

'I will tell him, sir.' Gleichenstein shuffled some more papers. 'Finally,' he said, brightly, 'your brother Johann . . .'

Ludwig heaved a deep sigh. Lichnowsky, Johann, could they not just leave him alone?

'While you were ill, sir, he made across a considerable sum of money to you. Five thousand florins. I did not bother you with the details. He said he was purchasing an apothecary shop, and he wanted to put money aside. He did not want it in his bank account because he believed they might reveal to the vendor that he had it. Now he wants it back. I only require your authorisation to make the transfer.'

Ludwig struggled to digest the words. What had Johann done? Music, he thought, that is what I understand. Apothecary shops, money, transfers . . . He wanted to shout, but there was no point in shouting at Gleichenstein. He wanted to shout at Johann, at Carl. His two imbeciles of brothers. One ruining his life financially, the other ruining it with the wrong woman. Why could they not have stayed in Bonn?

He heard Gleichenstein again. '. . . simple, sir. I will arrange the necessary paperwork.' He gathered up his things, smiled at Ludwig and left.

Ludwig might not have responded to the note that arrived from Stephan had the Rothes Haus not been so close – a pleasant stroll across the Glacis on a warm, sunlit evening. He was not troubled at the thought of returning to his friend's apartment and the unpleasant memories it held for him. That was in the past and he and Stephan had known each other long enough for their friendship to be unaffected.

What he found hard to come to terms with were Stephan's words, '. . . to come to meet my fiancée Julie.'

Stephan to be married! Ludwig wanted to reason with him, ask him if he understood what he was doing. But he knew Stephan would not have blundered into this unthinkingly as Carl had into his marriage. It was the thought that calm, logical Stephan had made the right decision and was about to enjoy long years of happiness that caused the loneliness to sweep over him.

Stephan welcomed him into the apartment that the two had once – briefly – shared as if they had never quarrelled. Ludwig noticed at once how the other man's face had lightened. 'Steffen,' he said, using the version of the name he had used as a boy in Bonn, 'I have to congratulate you.' He glanced quickly round the room: he was a little nervous of meeting Julie.

'Believe me, Ludwig, I am as surprised as you are, and I can tell you are by the expression on your face. You were never very good at disguising your feelings.'

'She must speak up, Steffen. My hearing is not good.'

'Do not worry, my old friend. Her voice is as clear and distinct as the voices of angels in heaven.'

A whiff of coffee floated into the room and a young woman entered. She put down a tray on which coffee steamed and there were plates of sweet cake, too, covered in ground almond.

Ludwig gasped as the woman – little more than a girl – smiled beatifically at Stephan and walked towards him, slipping her arm through his. He had thought at first she was a servant but this was Stephan's intended bride.

'Ludwig, I would like you to meet Julie, my darling Julie, who has taken total leave of her senses and agreed to marry me.'

Ludwig bowed and smiled. She had the prettiest face he had ever seen. It was open and honest, her large eyes betraying her innocence. Unlike Johanna there were no hidden depths that concealed – who knew what? She had a freshness and vitality that were completely beguiling. It was difficult to tell, but Ludwig thought she could not have been more than seventeen or eighteen – only a little more than half Stephan's age.

Ludwig groped for the right words. 'I – I have known Steffen for many years. He is – a fine man. I – wish you both happiness.'

'Oh, Herr Beethoven,' said Julie, rising on her toes, 'it is such an honour to meet you. Stephan talks so much about you.'

Stephan was right: her voice was clear and she spoke more slowly than he had expected. Stephan must have told her, he thought. My disability, the cross I bear, the infirmity that sets me apart . . .

'Ludwig, Julie is Professor Vering's daughter. He treated you once.'

Ludwig's mind raced. Vering, with the florid face and full white beard. Army doctor, rooms in Hetzendorf. Even as he thought of him, the prickling sensations began on his arm. The bark of *Daphne Mezerium*!

'And my friend Giulietta,' said Julie. 'Giulietta Guicciardi. Do you remember her?'

Ludwig caught his breath. Giulietta. Julia, as she insisted on being called. Sadness swept over him. How often was he to be reminded of his failures? Stephan has a young fiancée and she is a friend of the woman I wanted to marry, he thought, bitterly. The woman I intended to propose to, whom I taught and with whom I . . . *with whom I fell in love.*

He turned away and walked to the table, took a cup of coffee and sipped it. Rejected by Julia, rejected before her by Leni, since her by Josephine . . . He sipped again, half closing his eyes.

Julie had come across to him and was talking again. 'She is in Italy with her husband, Count Gallenberg. In Naples. He is a composer too. He composes for the music festivals. I hear from her often.'

Ludwig looked at her young, eager face. She was unaware of his painful thoughts and he struggled to hide them.

'I told her in a letter that I was going to meet you. She said I should tell you she still has the piece of music you wrote for her, but she still cannot play the final movement.'

Ludwig smiled at her. 'I remember,' he said, the strong coffee giving his voice an edge. 'She didn't like the piece. She said it was too gloomy.'

Julie let out a high laugh. 'I'm afraid she likes only what makes her happy.'

Stephan came over. 'Ludwig, Julie would be too shy to tell you, but she is a fine pianist herself. She –'

'Hush, Steffen. Compared to Herr Beethoven I am worthless.'

'No, Julie. You are very good indeed. In fact, Ludwig, I happen to know that Julie is one of the few pianists who can play that movement.'

Julie's cheeks reddened and she lowered her head modestly.

Ludwig was drawn to her unassuming nature and lack of pretension.

'Do you see what I have had installed, Ludwig?' Stephan pointed to the corner of the room. A screen stood across it. Stephan walked to it and folded it back. A small upright piano stood against the wall.

'For my modest future wife,' he said. 'Come, Julie, play the final movement. For my old friend.'

'No, no, Steffen. Not in front of Herr Beethoven. I wouldn't presume. Herr Beethoven, would you do us the honour of playing for us?'

How sweetly she smiled, he thought. He found himself smiling back. 'No, Julie. But it would give me great pleasure to hear you play.'

She flushed again but walked hesitantly to the piano. From the top she took several sheets of music, turned to the page she wanted, propped the music on the stand and sat down.

Ludwig lifted his head and closed his eyes. *Presto agitato*, swiftly moving semiquaver runs in the treble, quavers in the bass. Difficult to play, he knew.

Julie's fingers flew unerringly over the notes. He smiled. The sound of my music, he thought. And it was not hurting his ears. Julie was obeying the *piano* marking. This is how I meant it to sound.

He opened his eyes and watched her, her small body moving as her hands spanned the keyboard. The staccato chords, the sudden *sforzandos*, perfectly performed. And after the final massive descending octave runs in both hands, the two *fortissimo* chords of C sharp minor, her body lifting clear of the chair in her effort to give them the right force.

A jarring sound assaulted his ears, and he winced. At first he could not understand what it was, but he saw Julie's face, the broad smile, and followed her gaze.

He could not help the sigh of disappointment. The noise was applause, coming from the group of people that stood by the door. Carl and Johanna, Johann with a woman Ludwig did not know, and in Johanna's arms a bundle of blankets that must contain the infant Karl.

Stephan moved swiftly over to them and greeted them, ushering them into the room. Ludwig caught a movement from the other side of the room. It was the housekeeper bringing in fresh coffee and cakes, more cups and plates. He recognised her from the brief time he had lived here with Stephan. She gave him a reproving look, turned quickly and went back to the kitchen.

Suddenly he felt more alone than ever. The housekeeper's unmistakable expression was the catalyst. Stephan with his fiancée, Carl with his wife and child, Johann with a woman . . . In his mind, memories of Giulietta Guicciardi, her face melding with the music that still sounded in his head, then the dark bouncing curls of Josephine Deym seeming almost to mock him. He felt a hand on his arm.

'Well, brother, I was wondering if you had left Vienna, it has been so long.' Johann was grinning at him. 'This is Milli.' He pulled the young woman forward. She stood, one hand on her hip. Ludwig clenched his teeth as he looked at her. Her dress was flowery and full, of a kind seen more in the countryside than in the city. Her bosom was large, the pale flesh rising provocatively above her bodice. Ludwig thought immediately of the Walfischgasse where this woman would surely feel more at home. Johann reached up and pinched her cheek. She slapped down his hand with a coquettish giggle. 'I have employed her as a shop assistant,' he said. 'Do you not admire my good taste?'

Ludwig turned to Carl, disliking the arrogance that sat so conspicuously on his face. 'We thought, Johanna and I, that you should see your nephew.'

Ludwig looked at Johanna and unease flowed through him, tightening his stomach and running down his legs to his feet. Her face had changed since he had last seen her, but it was difficult to tell exactly how. There was a greater depth to it, an added maturity, the result of having given birth. But it had, too, a look of insolence, accentuated by the way in which she stood now, the baby in her left arm and her left hip cocked out to support it. It was as if both she and her husband were defying Ludwig. With growing disquiet he watched her fold back the blanket to reveal the baby's face.

It was smaller and more fine than he had expected. The lips were pursed and glistening from a thin trail of saliva that fell on to a delicate, pointed chin. The eyes were tightly closed and Ludwig found himself wishing that they would open and look at him.

A wave of yearning swept over him and with it a giddiness. He saw himself suddenly as his grandfather, looking at himself as an infant. This was a Beethoven, the next generation. He knew that the child would be a musician, just as surely as his grandfather had known it of himself. He felt himself drawn irresistibly to the tiny figure. He looks nothing like his parents, Ludwig thought, with that tinge of mischief showing at the corners of his mouth. His face had none of the shiftiness and restlessness of Carl's, and none of the ambiguity of Johanna's. Yes, Ludwig thought. A Beethoven. Like my grandfather – and like me.

He put out his arms but Johanna took a step back. She gripped the bundle tightly, holding it close to her.

Emptiness flooded over Ludwig, and he felt a constriction in his chest.

Stephan's voice cut into his thoughts. 'My good friends, what a marvellous occasion. Julie, my dear, you are meeting some of my oldest friends. We grew up together in Bonn. There is a bond between us that is almost a bond of blood. We will drink wine together.'

He went to the sideboard and brought out a bottle. 'Here, a Johannisberger from the banks of the river by which we all grew up.'

Ludwig heard the noise of conversation. No face was turned to him; no one was talking to him. At first he minded – he wanted to be part of the celebrations – but he was not *normal*, as his mother had often said. How it had hurt him! It had hurt him all the more when he discovered she was right.

The conversation became animated. The men were looking at Johann with astonishment. Stephan smiled broadly and Carl clapped his brother on the back. Ludwig heard the word Linz. What were they talking about?

Stephan, with a look of kindly concern, walked over to him. 'Good news about Johann, Ludwig,' he said. 'He is about to buy his own apothecary shop in Linz. In Upper Austria. Two day's carriage-ride from here.'

Ludwig did not really take in the words. Then Julie handed him a glass of wine – he wanted to talk to her, thank her for the way she had played his music, but now she was talking to the young woman with Johann. What could he say to Johann? As his elder brother he had a duty to tell him that he was consorting with a woman of low character.

He studied Carl and Johann almost despairingly. He resented their happiness. Could they not see that they were ruining their lives?

Johann came across and sat on the arm of his chair. 'Fine-looking wench, is she not, Ludwig?' he said close to his brother's ear.

Ludwig wanted to tell his brother to stop. He did not want to hear words like that.

'She is very . . . obliging,' Johann continued. 'Why do I not send her to your apartment? When I have gone to Linz you could –'

'No!' Ludwig had shouted and all eyes were suddenly on him. He was tempted to repeat what Johann had said, to shame him.

But Johann spoke first. 'I am sorry, everyone. I have upset my brother. I was just talking about an old flame of his – the Countess Deym. She has returned to Vienna. That's right, isn't it, Milli? You served her in the shop the other day, and she asked about my brother, didn't she?'

Chapter 2

Ludwig paced up and down his room. He threw open the window and took great gulps of air into his lungs. Then he sat at the piano and played huge crashing chords, the sounds jangling and colliding in his head until finally they faded to nothing. His skin was hot and his chest was tight, and when he closed his eyes he saw, to his disgust, the soft flesh of that despicable girl who worked for Johann, rising in mounds above the top of her dress.

Nor could he rid his mind of what Johann had said to him. Had Josephine really asked after him? He had wanted to question his brother further but knew he could not. If she had returned to Vienna, why had she not written to him?

He gazed at the carafe of wine on the table. Already he could taste the sharpness and imagine the good it would do him. The afternoon sun streamed across the room and lit it up, piercing the deep red with a shaft of light. Ludwig got up and left the room, slamming the door behind him.

He walked across the broad Freyung into the Hof square, across the Judenplatz, barely glancing at the small houses squeezed together like too many books crammed on a shelf. He ignored the men in long black coats, black hats pushed back on their heads, arms waving in argument, and went on through the Hoher Markt, with the thick sweet smell of vegetables laid out in the sun, to the Rothenturmgasse, where the salty odour of fish hung in the air from the market stalls that stood under the northern section of the Bastion wall, fading slowly as he walked on.

He felt agitated but he tried to remain calm by telling himself this was perfectly logical behaviour: why should he not call on an old friend who had once asked him to give her piano lessons? Nothing had ever happened that should cause him shame. If once he had pressed his suit and she had not responded positively, what did it matter? That should be of no consequence.

And if it was true that she had asked after him, perhaps it meant that there might be a grain of truth in the suspicion he had always had that maybe her reaction to him had been dictated by her family and not her heart?

He approached the house on the opposite side of the Rothenturmgasse, though there was no need to. The curtains were drawn and all seemed still behind them. He crossed the street and banged on the door twice. A few moments later he knocked again.

The door opened and a servant stood before him. Before Ludwig could speak, the elderly man said, in a heavy voice, 'There is no one at home, sir. Do you wish to leave a message?'

'No,' Ludwig said, turning away. Then, 'Yes. Tell Josephine – Madame Deym – that Beethoven called.'

'I shall inform the Countess Deym, sir.'

Ludwig's initial feeling of disappointment gave way to a certain relief, which by the evening, and fortified with wine, had become boldness.

The next morning he retraced his steps to the Rothenturmgasse. The same servant intoned the news lugubriously that the Countess had left early to spend the day in the country with her sister.

'Will she be at home tomorrow?' Ludwig asked gruffly.

'I have no idea, sir. Shall I tell the Countess you called?'

'I will call tomorrow at noon. Tell her that.'

Later he wished he had not said he would call again. Another rejection would send a clear message to him. He considered writing her a letter. No, it was better that he knew. His mind was in turmoil. He had committed himself to calling again. She would have to see him. Why should she not, anyway? Had he ever done her any wrong? She would see him, she would have to, since she would know he was coming at an appointed time. He would speak coolly and calmly to her. He would ask her if she returned any of the affection he felt for her. If she said no, then so be it.

The following day he allowed the temptation of the wine to overcome his resistance. Not too much, he said to himself, just a glass to lighten my head and help my ears to behave.

By the time he reached the house in the Rothenturmgasse he

had built up a certain defiance. The wine had had exactly the effect he desired, emboldening him and smoothing the edge off his nervousness. Another glass and he would have been unsure of his words.

'The Countess very much regrets that she is indisposed today, sir. She fears she caught a chill in the country and has taken to her room.'

Ludwig strode away. On an impulse he turned into the Braunen Hirschen and ordered a small carafe of wine. He drank it quickly, ignoring the small pieces of salted herring that had accompanied it and dismissing the waiter, who bore a menu. 'The special dish is carp, sir. Fresh from the Baltic.'

Ludwig threw some coins on the table and walked towards the massive dark bulk of St Stephansdom, round the cathedral and down the Kärntnerstrasse. He thought for a moment of going to the Alten Blumenstock for more wine, but that would take him too close to Carl's apartment. He shuddered at the thought. He wanted anonymity. He wanted to be alone. Away from anyone he knew.

His skin was on fire now and his head pounded, but with expectation not pain. He looked at his feet as he walked. He did not want anyone to see him or recognise him. He did not want to talk. He did not want to listen. More than anything, he did not want rejection. Was it so bad, what he was about to do? He had wanted to berate his brothers – Johann, with that cheap and brazen young woman, Carl with an immoral wife who had used him and tricked him. Was he behaving any differently? Of course I am, he thought. Of course. There is no comparison. This is necessity. With no complications. I am benefiting from a service that is available. The women are not immoral: they choose to be there. They will not argue with me or reject me.

Already as he turned into the Walfischgasse his heart was hammering and his knees felt weak.

Minutes later his senses reeled from the aroma of sweet perfume and the tips of his fingers tingled from the sensation of softness. Softness giving way to sudden firmness. Tension and tautness building inside him until he thought his body would burst. The small soft hand over his mouth to stifle his cry and the hand on the back of his head guiding it gently on to a shoulder and patting it, as if to say, 'All the pain is gone, there is no need to worry any more.'

*   *   *

The next morning, woken by the sunlight pouring across his bedroom, he listened for the familiar sounds in his head but they did not come. He felt confident and reassured.

He called to the servant to bring him coffee, then went to the table and pulled a sheet of writing paper towards him.

> Dear J,
> Since I almost fear that you no longer *allow yourself to be found by me* – and since I do not care to put up with the refusals of your servant any longer – well then, I cannot come to you any more – unless you let me know what you really think – Is it really *a fact* – that you do not want to see me any more – if so – do be *frank* – I certainly deserve you should be frank with me.

He scribbled a few more perfunctory words and told the servant to deliver it immediately.

He did not expect a reply. He even began to hope that she would not respond, and felt a twinge in his stomach when he saw her writing on the note that the servant handed him later in the day.

> Dear Ludwig,
> Of course I care for you very much, as a sister cares for a brother. I leave soon for Hungary again and trust you will keep me in your thoughts.
>
> Yr loyal friend
J. Deym

So there it was! Plain as if she were standing here in front of him and telling him. He expected sadness to engulf him, but it did not.

Gleichenstein and Zmeskall came to see Ludwig. He was at first frustrated by the interruption, pushing away the manuscript of the symphony in C minor, but the beaming faces of his friends softened him. 'More glasses!' he called to the servant. Then, 'Listen to this.'

He went to the piano, taking a sheet of the manuscript with him and played a soft chord of E flat. '*Piano pianissimo,*' he called. With his left hand he tapped out a beat on lower C. '*Pianissimo. Sempre pianissimo.*'

The beat, da-da-da-daa, da-da-da-daa, became a continuous

beat, da-da-da, da-da-da, da-da-da. With his right hand he played an arpeggio in E flat, pausing on C, then a curious falling phrase, da-daa-da, da-daa-da, da-daa-da, da-daa-da . . . '*Pianissimo.*' The falling phrase continued, off the key, off the key again, climbing step by step, E flat, E natural, F, G, A, B . . . as if from darkness slowly and steadily into light . . . C, D, E.

'*Crescendo, crescendo.*' He played a chord in both hands, an unresolved chord, then played it as swift quaver chords, taking it through two key changes, firmer with every beat, until with both hands he played a mighty chord in C major. He paused, his hands on the keys, his arms stretched straight, his back arched and his head thrown back. The pure, beautiful sounds rang in his ears. He sat still, eyes closed, allowing them to fade slowly from his head, praying that they would not be replaced by other familiar sounds.

Finally he put his hands on his thighs and turned round smiling weakly. He stood up, took the glass of wine that Zmeskall held out to him and sat heavily in a chair. He braced himself for the sound of voices and was gratified, when they came, that they caused him no pain.

'Very mysterious,' said Zmeskall. 'Eerie. Then, slowly, the darkness fades . . .' He held out his hands, moving his arms as if pushing away the gloom, his eyes open wide in wonder and expectation.

'What is it, sir? A sonata?' asked Gleichenstein, his eyebrows raised in expectation.

'The symphony. Leads from the third movement into the finale. Tension. I need to build tension. Through the darkness of distant keys to the blazing light of C major. The cleanest key, do you not think? The most open. No sharps or flats. And then I add trombones – three – to blaze out and bring light.'

'Trombones? For the last movement only?' asked Zmeskall, amazed. 'What will they do while they wait? They must sit through all the previous movements to await their moment.' He had not really needed to ask. 'They will revolt. Or put a book on their stand to amuse themselves. You know what trombonists are like. They believe their instrument is the most important in the orchestra.'

Ludwig smiled and shrugged.

'Anyway, here. So you can write more music to upset the musicians,' said Zmeskall, reaching into a bag and pulling out a fistful of quills. 'I do not know why I risk my job for you,

Ludwig. One day they will ask why my office uses more quills than any other in the Chancellery, and that will be that.'

Ludwig took them and shook his friend's hand in gratitude. 'Have some more wine. Fill my glass.'

Gleichenstein said, with a lively and infectious lilt in his voice, 'I bring good news, sir, that I am sure will please you. The new Director of the Imperial Court Theatres called me to see him. Court Councillor Joseph von Hartl. He wants to offer you a benefit concert in the Wien.'

His ears must be playing tricks again. 'A benefit concert? My own music only?'

Gleichenstein nodded. 'Your own music only. You may choose the pieces. Profits to be split equally between you and the theatre after the deduction of costs.'

'When?'

Gleichenstein took a sheet of paper from the folder he had laid on the table. 'Well, at the end of March there is a special performance of *The Creation*, in the presence of Herr Haydn, to honour his birthday. We will all, of course, attend. That is in the university hall. Herr Hartl said we should allow a decent interval after that. He suggested the end of April.' Gleichenstein looked at him expectantly.

Ludwig allowed himself to smile. 'Then you will hear that passage I played for you as it should be played.'

Chapter 3

Ludwig stood uncomfortably in the throng of people in the Great Hall of the Old University. The pianist and composer Johann Nepomuk Hummel was with him, for which he was grateful. The city's leading musical patrons were there. Prince Lichnowsky smiled at him, but did not come over and Ludwig bowed curtly. It was 27 March 1808. Four days short of Joseph Haydn's seventy-sixth birthday.

His heart sank when he saw Prince Lobkowitz on his way across the hall. He did not want to talk, particularly since the crowd was buzzing with conversation and his ears felt dull. But he knew that he could not avoid all contact with other people, so he braced himself.

Lobkowitz did not look well. He seemed to have aged since Ludwig had last seen him: he was leaning heavily on his crutch and the pain of his hip was etched on his face, which was less fleshy, the skin hanging loose at his jaw. Walking alongside him was a tall, stout young man in military uniform, whom Ludwig recognised but whose name he had forgotten.

'Beethoven, dear boy,' said Lobkowitz, with a dip of the head. 'Hummel, good day to you too, sir. Bring my distinguished friend Lichnowsky's greetings to you,' he said to Ludwig. 'Understand you won't see him. Your privilege. But he speaks highly of you. You should reconsider.'

Ludwig wanted to respond brusquely, but he thought better of it and said nothing. He looked at the young man at Lobkowitz's side, who snapped his heels and bowed low from the waist.

'D'you recall Kinsky, sir? Prince Ferdinand Kinsky. Lately distinguished himself on the battlefield.'

Ludwig remembered the young man who had been with his father when he had first met him. Kinsky was now in his mid-twenties, tall with an erect bearing, and an enormous girth around which a maroon sash was tied. He had inherited his father's figure along with the title.

'Great honour, Herr Beethoven, sir. As you know, I have been an admirer of your music from my earliest days. Still am. None more so than me. Herr Hummel. A pleasure.'

Ludwig wanted the pleasantries to cease. His ears were starting to ring and the griping in his stomach that seemed to accompany any public gathering had taken hold. He stared at the imposing figure of Kapellmeister Salieri. Not a large man, slight almost, but given stature by his exalted position. Salieri was in charge of the event, and he stood with his hands clasped before him and his head held high.

Suddenly Ludwig was aware that all those who had been seated were getting to their feet. The nobility lowered their heads, lesser men bowed from the waist and their ladies curtsied.

Salieri raised his baton and a fanfare sounded. Prince Esterhazy, grandson of the Prince who had been Haydn's patron for nearly thirty years, entered the hall, the Princess on his arm. With his free hand he acknowledged the obeisances of the gathering. The royal couple took their seats of honour in the front row.

Conversation resumed, until the fanfare sounded again and the audience stood, heads craning. Ludwig saw the double doors at the entrance to the Great Hall open. He gasped, along with practically everyone else in the hall. Four university students, dressed in the medieval uniform of the original students, were carrying aloft a chair, bars to the front and back of it resting on their shoulders. Seated in the chair, gripping its arms, was the venerable old composer Joseph Haydn. The fanfare continued to sound, accompanied now by a roll of drums. Someone shouted, 'Long live Haydn!'

'Long live Haydn! Long live Haydn!' The words echoed round the vast hall. Ludwig found himself joining in. The crowd parted in the middle, creating a gangway for the chair to be carried down the centre of the hall to join Prince and Princess Esterhazy in the front row.

Ludwig was struck by Haydn's appearance. His face was now thin and gaunt, his skin pallid with a film of perspiration, and his wig had slipped, which gave him a rather comical appearance.

The applause and the fanfare continued until Haydn's chair was lowered in ungainly fashion to the floor and the students removed the poles. Immediately two women fussed around the old man, adjusting his frock-coat and wig and putting shawls over him, one on his shoulders and another covering his legs.

Ludwig felt Hummel tug his sleeve. 'Come on,' he whispered. 'Time to pay our respects.'

Ludwig followed him to the front of the hall, where a line of young men had formed. Ludwig spotted Schuppanzigh, Clement, the young violinist Joseph Mayseder, Kraft and Weiss and a number of other musicians. He looked at the face of the man whose pupil he had been. He knew he had been intolerant of him, sometimes impolite. But Haydn had criticised his work – the third of his opus one piano trios – and Ludwig had known even then that he was wrong.

'Ah, my dear boy,' said Haydn, taking Ludwig's hand in both his. 'How well you have done. I always knew you would make your mark, since I first saw you in Bonn and looked at your cantatas. Mozart said so too, poor man. He told me to watch out for you.'

Ludwig bent low to be sure of hearing him. He did not want to interrupt his old teacher.

'I have heard talk of your new symphony,' Haydn continued. 'Will we hear it soon? I hear the opening is different. Dramatic. Puh-puh-puh-puuuh,' he intoned, dropping Ludwig's hands and bringing one fist down on his thigh. 'So much passion in your music, Ludwig. And anger. I often wondered what it was that made you so angry. Hah! Anyway, I shall continue to wait for the words "pupil of Haydn" to appear at the top of one of your pieces. In vain, no doubt. But I am proud to have taught you, my boy. Most proud.'

Ludwig saw that Hummel was waiting to lead him to their seats so he bowed to Haydn and went after the other man. He settled into his chair and looked up at the splendid vaulted ceiling, paintings of pastoral scenes adorning it, noblemen and their ladies strolling by Greek colonnades, cherubs and angels serenading them from the blue, cloudless sky.

The stirring sounds of the opening bars of *The Creation* swept over the hall. They were comforting to Ludwig's ears after the conversation he found so difficult.

Joseph Haydn's glorious music. Music that would endure. But music, Ludwig thought, of the last century, not of the one that had so recently begun.

Ludwig looked at the man with envy. He was roughly dressed,

his heavily stained trousers stopping short of big black boots laced above his ankles. He had taken off his shirt and thrown it in a heap on the floor. His muscular torso was coated in a film of sweat and dust. His tousled hair was like coiled springs that jerked in different directions every time he moved. The man's build was not unlike his own: he was about the same height, and the predominant impression he gave was of powerful stockiness. Ludwig watched his back and shoulder muscles ripple each time he drove the hammer on to the chisel.

But the noise was dreadful and Ludwig sat pressing a cushion to each ear. The window on the back wall was open and Ludwig watched as the dust, pink-hued in the sunlight, was sucked outside, now and then blown back into the room by a gust of wind. The floor and bookshelves were becoming coated with a layer of brick dust. It would be worth it, though, he thought, a window in the side wall giving out across the city to the Danube, the Prater park and the Hungarian plain beyond. It would give the room a feeling of spaciousness.

Baron Pasqualati would approve, he knew. The new window was such an obvious improvement to the apartment.

'I'm telling you,' said Mähler, putting down his glass with emphasis, 'the French emperor has made his first serious mistake.'

'Lower your voice, Willi,' said Stephan Breuning, nervously. 'Whether he's made a mistake or not, this city is still full of his spies.'

'Then I hope the Schwan's wine makes them suffer. They should go home and drink some real wine from Bordeaux.'

There was laughter at the table, and Carl van Beethoven said, 'I believe you're wrong, Willi. Spain will present less of a problem to him than Prussia. If he can squash the Prussian Army like a gnat —'

'It is to do with terrain,' said Mähler. 'He fought Prussia on the plain. Flat, open country, where he could manoeuvre his troops. Spain is rugged, mountainous, and the problem will come from the hills, from bandits. They strike at random. He has never confronted that kind of fighter before.'

'I hope you are right,' said Nikolaus Zmeskall. 'In the meantime we must become accustomed to new kings of Europe. All with the same family name. And a wretched name it is.'

Stephan Breuning again held up his hands to lower the voices.

'Please. You must believe me. Ignaz and I will have to leave otherwise.'

'We who toil in the Hofburg must remain loyal,' said Gleichenstein quietly. 'And, at the moment, we are at peace with France.'

'It will not last, from what I hear,' said Andreas Streicher. 'Is it true Austria is mobilising?'

'Archduke Charles is establishing a new army,' Stephen said, barely above a whisper. 'Service will be compulsory for all Austrians and Hungarians over eighteen.'

'Unless they are blind like me!' said Zmeskall, blinking, and his chuckle broke the tension.

'King of Westphalia, Jerome Bonaparte. King of Spain, Joseph Bonaparte. Why do we not simply rename Europe the continent of Bonaparte?' asked Carl cynically.

'It cannot endure. It cannot,' said Stephan emphatically, surprised at his own vehemence and looking round quickly to make sure he had not been heard beyond the table.

'It is sad about Westphalia. So close to our own homeland, and a Frenchman is made king of it. It is absurd!'

'Well,' said Zmeskall, lifting his glass, 'let us drink to defeat in Spain, and victory for the new Austrian Army.'

Ludwig registered the horror on Pasqualati's face. 'Have a glass of wine, Baron. It will calm your nerves.'

'Herr Beethoven, I regret that what you have done is in breach of our agreement. You leave me no choice –'

'Bah, Pasqualati! Do not be so small-minded. Can you not see what an improvement it has made?'

'Sir, what I see is dust everywhere and a hole in the wall that will need to be repaired.'

Ludwig looked at the wall. The hole in it, visible through the sheet nailed over it, was about half the size required for the window. The floor was thick with dust and jagged pieces of masonry. 'The mason said he would be back to finish it. He had something else that needed his attention.'

'It is always the way with masons. I will need to get my own mason to fill in the hole again. You should not have done this, sir.'

Ludwig waved contemptuously. 'It is an improvement. Can you not see –'

'Sir,' said Pasqualati, 'allow me to explain the predicament in which you have put me. I have received complaints from other tenants, first about the noise the work caused, and second because they found out what you were doing and demanded similar "improvements" to their own apartments. I have, of course, refused and they have in turn demanded that your "improvement" does not go ahead. I am afraid they are within their rights.'

Ludwig could not understand what Pasqualati was saying. His ears were ringing and he wanted his landlord to leave. He knew that he was upset – and for a brief moment he thought of invoking Prince Lichnowsky's name, but rejected the idea immediately.

Pasqualati must have sensed his difficulty: he came up to Ludwig and spoke clearly and directly to him. 'I am afraid, sir, I have no choice but to ask you to leave the apartment. You will have to make other arrangements for accommodation.'

Ludwig was staggered. 'Baron, I have a benefit concert to give. After that I will go away for the summer. To the country. That will give you time to –'

'Sir. Herr Beethoven. I must make myself clear. You have to leave. I have no choice. I have my other tenants to consider.'

'Baron!' Ludwig said, anger rising. 'I have work to do. Do you not understand that? Speak to Gleichenstein. He will explain.'

Pasqualati sighed. 'I will allow you to stay until after the concert. Then you will have to leave.'

After Pasqualati had gone depression descended upon Ludwig. This was a complication he had not foreseen and did not want. He needed to prepare for the concert. It had to be a success. For his reputation – particularly after the fraught circumstances that had surrounded *Leonore* – a success was essential. It was also important that this new man, Hartl, should see that his music was popular, otherwise it might be hard to secure future performances, and a benefit concert was a risk: with no other music but his own to be played, there could be no excuses.

Ludwig slammed a fist into the palm of his other hand. It will be a success, he said to himself. I will make sure of it.

Later that day the servant brought Ludwig a letter. He walked across to the window, breaking the seal as he went.

Herr Beethoven
There is an unavoidable change in the theatre schedule. Your

benefit concert at the Wien must be delayed until July. The summer period will be more suitable. A firm date will be set soon and you will be informed.

Yr servant, Jsph Hartl
Intdnt, R.I. Court Theatres

Chapter 4

The familiar colic pains were plaguing Ludwig, made all the worse by their unpredictability. He called in Doktor Schmidt, who prescribed some powders, and asked about his hearing. Ludwig refused Schmidt's request to test him with tuning forks. 'It's not getting better,' he told the doctor. 'I'm used to it. Even the noises. They're becoming like friends.'

'Have you taken my advice and cut down on the amount of wine you drink?'

'It's the only medicine that works,' Ludwig expostulated. 'I've told you that before. It eases the pain in my head and the noises in my ears so why shouldn't I continue?'

'Because it is not doing the rest of your body any good. One day you will pay the price. What are your plans for the summer?'

'I will go to the country. I have no choice. I have to leave my apartment.'

'Where will you live when you return?'

'Gleichenstein will find me somewhere. Or Frau Streicher.'

'When do you leave for the country?'

'Not till late July or August. I have a benefit concert in July. An important concert. That is why my stomach hurts me so.'

Some days later another letter came from Joseph Hartl. The concert would have to be postponed a second time. A new comic opera at the Wien was proving very popular and Hartl could not afford to take it off. He promised Ludwig a date in the autumn.

Ludwig exploded. Damn Hartl. Damn, *damn* him.

Gleichenstein was smiling more broadly than Ludwig had ever seen.

'What is it, Gleichenstein? I do not want to be disturbed, especially if you are going to grin in such a fatuous manner.'

'Ferdinand Ries is returning to Vienna, sir.'

Ludwig felt a slight churn of guilt in his stomach. 'He is all right, then? He had to join the army, didn't he?'

Gleichenstein nodded. 'The French Army. Terrible. I was lucky to escape that. But he has written that all is well. His eye saved him from active service. He wrote to Herr Breuning. He did not know about his marriage – he will have a lot of news to catch up on. We were so worried about him when we heard about the dreadful fighting at Austerlitz and Jena. But he is well.'

Ludwig was barely listening to him. 'I have to leave this apartment, Gleichenstein. Will you find me another for after the summer? Or ask Frau Streicher.'

'I heard, sir. I will make enquiries but it will not be easy. Now that we are no longer at war, people have flocked back to the city.'

'And I need somewhere for the summer. To prepare for the benefit concert that imbecile Hartl has postponed again.'

'Yes, sir,' said Gleichenstein, with an edge to his voice. 'I will see what I can do when I have a moment to spare from my own work at the Hofburg. By the way, sir, Herr Sonnleithner at the Kunst-und-Industrie asks if you would go to see him. He has some questions about the symphony in B flat, your fourth. Final corrections before they publish it.'

Ludwig walked along the Graben and turned down the Kohlmarkt. He entered a building on the right and walked into the new offices of the Kunst-und-Industrie publishing house – new, at least, in comparison with the offices of the city's leading publisher Artaria on the opposite side of the Kohlmarkt and a little further down.

Joseph Sonnleithner welcomed him warmly and took him through to his private office. 'Thank you for coming, Ludwig. Just a few small points I want to clear up before we build the plates for the symphony. The dedication is for Count Oppersdorff, is that right?'

Ludwig agreed that it was.

'You know,' Sonnleithner continued, 'it's good to see you again. I've never had the chance to talk to you about *Leonore*. I thought Breuning made a good job of the libretto. He improved considerably on my feeble efforts.'

Ludwig did not want to talk about the opera because he knew that sooner or later the conversation would lead to an entreaty from Sonnleithner to revive it. 'It was better at two acts,' Ludwig said. 'Three made it too long. I will look at it again one day. Not now.'

'You should, you should. Such good material in it.'

To Ludwig's relief, the other man changed the subject. 'I have heard that you have completed a new symphony, and from what I hear it is rather extraordinary.'

'It is not complete. Nearly. It is different from the B flat. Very different.'

'May I hope that you will ask the Kunst-und-Industrie to publish it too?'

Ludwig shrugged. 'Gleichenstein handles that. I think it is going to Breitkopf and Härtel in Leipzig.'

'Pity, pity. Maybe something else, then. Do you have plans for the summer? Are you going away?'

'I want to. To the country. I have to – there's some trouble at my lodgings and I have to leave the Mölkerbastei.'

'Really? I'm sure you'll find something else just as convenient. On a lower floor, maybe, thus saving all our hearts some strain.' He chortled at his own joke. 'And where are you staying in the country?'

'I don't know. I've asked Gleichenstein to find somewhere.'

Sonnleithner thought for a moment. 'I know of a place. I think it would suit you perfectly. My sister has taken rooms in a house in Heiligenstadt. She is going there with her boy. He is seventeen. She told me there are other vacant rooms in the house. You know Heiligenstadt, don't you?'

Ludwig nodded slowly. 'I've stayed there before. But I don't want to be disturbed. Tell your sister that, if I decide to go.'

When he returned to his apartment, Ludwig told the servant he was not to be interrupted. He walked across to the table and poured himself a glass of wine. It tasted bitter and made him suck in his cheeks. The servant had obviously not replenished it as he had ordered him to. For the first time Ludwig felt exhilaration that he was leaving the apartment. He would not be sorry to leave behind the worthless man.

He went into the bedroom and sat on the edge of the bed. He opened a cupboard in the bedside table, reached down and drew out the wooden panel that lay just above the base. It ran roughly in the grooves and he had to pull it in jerks, favouring one side and then the other. When it was out far enough, he reached behind it and took out a piece of paper. Carefully he unfolded it, ignoring the words he had scribbled on the outside, and looked at what he had written.

For my brothers Carl and   Beethoven

He remembered how he had at first left out both his brothers' names, then after their long talk by the stream, he had inserted Carl's name. But he had not been able to write Johann.

Should he add it now? He rejected the idea as soon as it entered his mind. I may call him Johann now, he thought, but when he reads this one day, let him understand then how I felt.

He lowered his eyes, searching for three tiny words.

I am deaf

I knew it then. When the doctors were still saying it would be fine, I knew it.

He folded the document quickly, not wanting to read any more. It was enough. What else mattered but those three words? He put it back where it had come from, pushed the panel roughly into place, closed the door and went back into the main room.

He looked round for the wine glass, found it and drained it. He thought of the work he had done since writing his testament. So many pieces, but most of all there was the symphony he had named the Eroica and the symphony in C minor, his fifth. They were his true statements to the world, worth so much more than words; worth so much more than that document.

For a moment he considered getting it out again and burning it in the grate, but he decided not to.

He poured himself more wine. He would return to Heiligenstadt. Why not? He would return there and compose again.

Who knows? he thought, with a rush of passion and determination. Maybe another symphony, as different from the fifth as the fifth had been from the fourth.

Chapter 5

Ludwig was disappointed with the house in Heiligenstadt. The rooms he had taken were on the front of the two-storey house and looked over the main road to Grinzing; the carriages passed with monotonous frequency right under his window and sometimes he could smell the sweat coming off the horses' flanks. However, his rooms faced towards the Kahlenberg and the hills of the Vienna Woods – practically the same view he had had from the apartment on the Mölkerbastei, only now it was much closer and without any roofs in the way.

The house had a large archway in the front façade and its four walls surrounded an inner courtyard. A flight of wooden stairs led up to a landing that ran round the house at first-floor level. Sonnleithner's sister and her son occupied the larger apartment at the back of the house overlooking the garden, which led down to a small stream.

Two streets away, on the Herrengasse, was the small house Ludwig had stayed in six years before, and soon after he arrived in Heiligenstadt he went to look at it. It was smaller than he remembered. He could see the linden tree in the courtyard, but he did not go in. The front of the house seemed unfamiliar. It took him a moment to realise that the windows had changed; the curtains were different. There was a sign in one window. He peered at it: 'Farm eggs for sale.' Julie and her mother must have left, he thought, with a rush of nostalgia. Then he turned away and retraced his steps to the house on the Kirchengasse.

Slowly the peace of Heiligenstadt began to soothe Ludwig's nerves and he slipped into the routine he had established on his previous visit. He would walk towards the Kahlenberg hill, striding along the banks of the stream. Some days he would climb the lower slopes, walking between the vines that grew heavier with grapes almost daily.

The stream he had come to know so well was smaller than he remembered. In his mind it was wider and the water raged down from the hills of the Vienna Woods to disgorge into the Danube. Now it seemed placid, flowing gently, rippling benignly over the stones and small rocks that stood in its way. Every day he had lunch in a tavern, in Nussdorf or Grinzing, and in the evening he dined in one of the small inns on the Kirchengasse, a short walk from the house.

There was a piano in the larger of his rooms, which was on the first floor – Sonnleithner must have arranged that. For hours he would sit at it, improvising mostly, and as the days passed the dullness in his ears abated and the pain in his head went away. He no longer thought of Hartl and the benefit concert; he forgot that he had to find new lodgings.

Occasionally he heard movement from the other apartment: when the mother or her son walked round the wooden landing, he felt the vibrations. But they did not disturb him, for which he was grateful.

On his walks he listened to the sounds of nature. Bird calls, the water in the stream, occasionally the distant rumble of thunder. God's music, he thought to himself. He would sit under a tree and empty his brain of everything but the sounds of nature.

At the piano he found he was trying to re-create in music the bird calls, the water, the thunder. He played the notes and tried to hear behind them. Sometimes just a few at a time, sometimes just one. An occasional chord, a gentle run. He heard the sounds the notes made, but if he concentrated he could hear *behind* them. He could hear the sounds of nature in his music.

He was speaking in the language he understood. It was the only way he could communicate with other people. His task now, he knew, was to bring the sounds of nature to them. It was the reason he was alive. It was the work entrusted to him by God.

One afternoon, notebook in hand, eyes half closed and cast down as he listened again and again to the tones that revolved in his head, he almost collided with a figure walking down the steps of the courtyard landing.

He looked up. It was a young man of seventeen or eighteen with thick curly hair and a fresh face. Ludwig was about to push past him but the sudden stop, after a long, strenuous walk, threw him off balance. He put out his arm to steady himself on the wall of the house.

He felt the young man take his other arm firmly and ease him down to sit on the bottom step of the staircase. For a moment he was annoyed – he could easily have gone on into his apartment. Instead he was sitting on a step, looking up at a stranger young enough to be his son. He knew the young man would speak, and more than anything he did not want to hear words. They would cut into his thoughts, into the sounds of nature that filled his head.

'Grillparzer, sir. Franz Grillparzer, poet, at your service.'

Ludwig screwed up his eyes, in a vain attempt to lessen the harshness of the man's voice, and lowered his head, hoping he would go away.

'My mother sends her compliments, sir. She would be most honoured if you would play the piano for her, in return for which I will read you some of my verse.'

Ludwig stood up, holding on to the staircase railing. 'Tell your mother I am not to be disturbed. She is not to interrupt me.'

After that Ludwig did not see the young man or his mother. Occasionally he heard footsteps stop outside his room, and whenever that happened, he played crashing discords on the piano and did not resume playing until he heard the footsteps going away.

A shape for a new symphony was forming in his mind. He had expected it to be different, but did not know in what way. Slowly, now, it was coming to him. He would translate the sounds of nature into musical tones and give them form and substance. But there would be more to the music than just the notes. More than just calls and rippling water and rumbling thunder. To discover what more there was the listener would have to listen *behind* the music. Only then would they understand what he was trying to do – to bring the sounds created by God to the ears of all mankind.

He had begun to scribble sketches in a manuscript book, fragments, snatches of phrases. Late one afternoon, as the sun sent slanting rays through the window and across the room, he pulled the manuscript book towards him. There were two empty staves at the bottom of the first page. He wrote:

Sinfonia caracteristica
or recollections of country life

He played a gentle sequence on the piano, quavers then semi-quavers, rising then falling, coming to an end on a sustained minim. He played it again, this time prefacing it with a single note in the bass. He reached for the manuscript book. This time, at the top of the page, on the right immediately underneath the sketch of the sequence he had just played, he wrote:

It is for the listener alone to discover the meaning.

The sun was warm on his face and he longed then for the clear air. He stood up quickly and left the room, almost running down the stairs and out into the street. He strode towards the Kahlenberg, and looked up at the sun, squinting to protect his eyes. It was almost possible to look directly at it: the harshness of high summer had gone and it hung now like a burnished globe, bringing the grapes, the wheat and all growing things to final ripeness before the harvest.

He turned left along the stream, hearing in his head the sounds of his new symphony. He crossed a narrow wooden bridge, his heavy footsteps becoming the regular beat of the timpani. On he walked, away from the stream, down the steady incline and on to the path that led towards the village of Grinzing. It would take him an hour or more to get there. That was fine, he thought. Dinner and wine in Grinzing and then the long walk back, or maybe a carriage if it was late.

Occasionally he stopped, leaned against a tree, took a note-book from his pocket and scribbled in it. Tunelessly he sang phrases, marking time with his hand, and then walked on, the heat of his body warding off the chill as the sun slowly lost its strength.

In his head he heard music. At first it fitted in with the sequences that he was creating in his mind, but then it seemed to acquire an existence of its own. He stopped and listened. He *could* hear music.

He walked towards the sound, which grew harsher as he drew nearer. He stopped again, closed his eyes and allowed his ears to become accustomed to the clamour. There was something strange – impure – about the music, which he could not at first identify. Then he realised it was shouts and whoops and laughter, and sudden joyous cries.

On the outskirts of Grinzing he walked along a path that ran beside the wood he had come through. The music filled his head now. He turned a corner and saw a village square, surrounded by stunted trees. The short branches, all heavily pruned and trained upwards, were festooned with bunting, streamers joining one tree to another so that the entire square was ringed with ribbons. An inn dominated the scene and tables and benches were set out around the clearing. Seated in front of the inn was a small orchestra, its members playing as if their lives depended on it. The square swirled with the merry dancing of country folk.

A broad smile spread across Ludwig's face. He propped himself against one of the trees to catch his breath and a woman beckoned him, pointing to a small table with a single chair by it.

Ludwig walked across and sat down. Before he had had time to look round a tankard of beer was put in front of him by the woman, a smile permanently on her face, along with a carafe of red wine, the glass upturned on the top of it. Moments later she brought a large plate with several pieces of sweet cake and biscuits. He nodded his thanks, but she had already turned away.

The music was rough in his head, but it was good. Sometimes it was difficult to hear it above the shouts and laughter, the dancing and the swirl of voluminous dresses. Little clouds of dust sprang up whenever the men stamped their feet.

Ludwig drank some beer, the cold bitter flavour bringing tears to his eyes. He watched the musicians. There were five of them: two fiddlers, two pipe players, and a bass player. They were smiling constantly, and the pipe players sometimes had to stop blowing their instruments to laugh at something they saw or heard. One of the fiddle players was the lead: he would nod or call to another player to take a solo. Frequently one or more at them would stop for a mouthful of beer or wine.

Ludwig found himself tapping his foot to the rhythm of the music. It was in two-four time, he thought, lively, rollicking music, the fiddle players bending their bodies in time to it.

Suddenly, as if at a hidden command, the musicians stopped playing. The lead fiddler gave a nod and in unison they played a fanfare. The dancers formed two straight lines leading out from the entrance to the tavern and, amid much cheering and clapping, a bride and groom emerged, their faces wreathed in smiles.

Holding hands the young couple walked to the middle of the square. The groom wore short leather trousers and a flowery shirt with billowing sleeves. His bride wore a full dress decorated with flowers, the bodice gathered up into folds of fine linen. She motioned to others to join them, but they simply cheered more loudly. The orchestra played a sustained unison chord, then broke into a favourite local tune. The bride and groom clasped hands high and began to dance. After they had held the square alone for several minutes, others rose to join them. Soon the entire square was a mass of gyrating bodies and laughing faces.

Then Ludwig knew what it was about the music that had struck him. Its rawness went straight to the heart of these people. Its roughness, its unsophistication exactly answered their needs. These musicians – with all their wrong notes, their untutored playing – were providing the people with the merriment they sought, the outlet for their emotions. What could be higher or more worthy than that?

The beer and wine were making him light-headed. Vienna and its problems seemed far distant. He poured more wine from the carafe, and wished there was a piano where the orchestra sat so that he could play for these people, bring more laughter and happiness to them. So different from the salons of Vienna. These people would listen to the music because it spoke to their souls, not because they were indulging in some social ritual.

He felt an unexpected droplet on his forehead, then another, and he watched several more stain the wood of the table and spread into a dark blotch.

The merrymakers turned up their faces to the sky. Ludwig followed their gaze. The blue had vanished and in its place loomed a huge grey cloud.

The dancers squealed and bustled into the tavern to escape the impending storm. Huge globules of water splashed off the dust of the square. Ludwig was partly shielded by the tree, but soon the rain was heavy enough to penetrate the leaves. He raised his face, and let the drops fall on it. The rain was warm and he enjoyed the sensation as it trickled down his forehead and cheeks.

A distant rumble came to his ears, and he looked across to the doorway of the inn. The woman who had brought him the wine and cakes was gesturing to him to come inside. He stood up and nodded his thanks, but walked away from the square, back towards the woods, unmindful of the rain that soon penetrated his clothes. In his mind the swirling music ran round and round, mingling with the laughter and cries of the merrymakers. The joyous gathering of country folk.

Chapter 6

There was no seal on the envelope, and Ludwig tore it open. He took out the single sheet of cheap paper.

> Herr Ludwig, Sir
> I trust this letter will find you in good health. If it does not inconvenience you, I will come to you in Heiligenstadt. I have news regarding your lodgings. Gleichenstein has given me your address.
> I am now returned to Vienna. I pray you will not have harsh memories of me.
>
> Yr friend
> Fd. Ries

Ferdi Ries! Ludwig remembered how harsh he had been to him. At the time he had felt justified: the boy had taught a piece of his music to Lichnowsky and Lichnowsky had pretended it was his own composition. He remembered Lichnowsky's pleadings on Ries's behalf.

Yet now he found, to his surprise, that he was looking forward to Ries's visit.

He did not have to wait long. The day after the letter arrived Ludwig returned from a long walk to see Ries in the courtyard, pacing round the perimeter, his hands clasped behind his back.

'Ries! So you have returned to the civilised world.' He hoped the friendliness of his greeting would dispel any lingering resentment Ries might harbour towards him. The breadth of Ries's smile gave him the assurance he sought.

'Come upstairs. We will drink some wine.' Ludwig led Ries up the wooden staircase and along to the room with the piano. He poured two glasses of wine, waved the young man to a chair and sat down himself.

He studied Ries, who still had the same pitch black tousled

hair he had had as a young child when Ludwig had taught him the piano to repay old Father Ries for the kindness he had shown him. But there was something different about him, something Ludwig could not quite fathom.

'You have changed, my boy. I can't say exactly how. How long has it been?'

'Three years, sir. It hardly seems possible. You . . . you were about to . . . your opera, sir, you were about to stage it at the Theater an der Wien.'

'French soldiers killed it. Steffen rewrote it.'

'I heard it was very good the second time. Excellent audiences.'

Ludwig said nothing. Then, with a smile, 'Remember my hearing problem, Ries. I don't hear anything I don't want to hear!'

Ries laughed. 'Well, sir, if I might say so, you do not appear to be troubled by your hearing.'

'It's no better. Worse in fact. But I am becoming better at reading people's lips. And here in the country there is no other noise. And my head is not hurting. As soon as I return to Vienna the noises will come back. It will never improve. I know that. I knew it that afternoon on the Kahlenberg slope. The shepherd's pipe.'

Ries said nothing. Suddenly Ludwig exclaimed, 'Your eye! That's what is different. Where is your patch?'

Ries smiled. 'Gone, sir. I owe a lot to my useless eye. The French said that because of it I couldn't be conscripted into their army. Then the army surgeon heard about it and decided to experiment with me. In Paris they have developed a glass eye, which they make any colour you need and fix in place so you appear to have two normal eyes. Almost normal. It doesn't move, of course. But it is far better than having to wear a wretched patch.'

Ludwig was curious. 'You mean, one of your eyes is glass?'

'Yes. See, I'll demonstrate for you. Watch my eyes.' He looked sharply to the left. His left eye moved but the right one remained motionless.

Ludwig could not restrain a small cry of delight. 'So you cannot see through it?'

'No, no, sir,' said Ries, in an indulgent tone. 'It is just a ball of glass. Like a child's marble. Occasionally it weeps a little.' He pulled a handkerchief from his sleeve and wiped under his eye.

'But I am very pleased with it. It's the only good thing I can say about the French.'

Ludwig refilled their glasses. 'And tell me about Bonn. How are things at home?'

'Quiet, but tense. We are part of the French empire now. The Confederacy of the Rhine. For the most part the French soldiers have left. It is said that Napoleon needs them in Spain. But it is sad to see our own people – school friends of mine – wearing French uniforms.'

Ludwig took a mouthful of wine. 'I want to go back. One day I'll go. How is your father?'

'He is well, thank you, sir, but he can barely feed the family. The electoral orchestra, as you know, was disbanded some time ago. He earns what he can by teaching. Now that the mail coaches are running again, I will send him what I can from here.'

'And the Breunings?'

Ries grinned. 'Frau Breuning successfully waged a personal war against the French. They wanted to take over her house on the Münsterplatz for their officers because it is the grandest in Bonn. But she succeeded where the entire Austrian army failed. Eleonore, I am sure you know, is married to Franz Wegeler and they have moved to Koblenz, where he has a good practice. They have two children, I believe.'

'At least there is no more fighting there.'

'No. In fact, we are in more danger of that in Vienna than Bonn. Apparently,' instinctively he lowered his voice, but made sure he still spoke clearly, 'the Austrian army has been put in the hands of Archduke Charles. He is reorganising it, modernising it, creating a new officer corps. The word is that, when he has completed that, Austria will declare war on France again. Again! And . . . well, I shouldn't say it, but another defeat is inevitable.'

'Bah!' Ludwig put down his glass heavily and strode to the piano. 'Listen to this, Ries.'

As soon as he sat down his fingers struck the keys. He repeated a D rapidly in the bass, with flying staccato quavers in the right hand. Then, triplet quavers in the bass, slowly becoming louder and louder and suddenly a massive *fortissimo* chord in the treble. Swift demi–semiquaver runs in the bass, more shattering octaves in the treble. Higher and higher in the treble. Then swift descent. Up again and swift descent. And again. Quieter now, quieter still, *pianissimo*, a few final upward bursts, but quieter, calmer. Final rumblings in the bass. And the music brought to a halt.

Ludwig arched his back, lifting his fingers from the keys. He waited for the music to die away in his head. Then he turned to Ries. 'It will be longer than that, but that is its outline.'

'A storm!' cried Ries enthusiastically. 'A Steibelt storm. I heard how you –'

'No, damn you, Ries!' shouted Ludwig. He snatched up a pencil and hurled it at him. 'Imbecile! Do not let that name ever cross your lips again. That man was not a musician, he was a charlatan. What I played was a real storm. I witnessed it. Here. In Grinzing. I am re-creating it in musical tones. God, Ries, sometimes you make me so angry.'

'I apologise, sir,' said Ries, casting his face down.

Ludwig returned to his chair, breathing heavily. 'You said something in your note about my lodgings.'

'Yes, Herr Ludwig,' said Ries, brightening. 'Good news. I have spoken to Countess Erdödy. She says she has a self-contained suite in her apartment on the Krugerstrasse, which she would be very pleased to let you have – rent free – until you find – I find you – something more permanent. I –'

Ludwig shut his eyes and waved at Ries to stop talking. 'Erdödy, did you say? Countess Erdödy? You have arranged for me to stay with her? Ries, have you taken leave of your senses?'

'Sir, I understood there was some urgency –'

'Ries, I am not living with Countess Erdödy, do you hear? I can't do it. It will be like living with the Lichnowskys. Dinner at six. Play for us afterwards. We have guests. I cannot do it, Ries. Do you understand? Tell her I will not.'

Ludwig could not rid his mind of Ries's stupidity. How could he have done such a thing? Why had he not spoken to Gleichenstein, or Nanette Streicher?

Ironically he found that his bad temper did not hinder his composition. He made certain decisions about the new symphony that he knew were right. He would give each movement a name, a description. Let no one be in doubt, he thought, as to what I am trying to do. But once they know, then let them listen further and try to understand. I am not *describing* nature, I am *creating* it in sound. It is not like a painting; it is an expression of emotions.

There would be five movements. Five movements! Had any composer written a symphony with five movements before? They will tell me I cannot do that, that I must cut one. No! I will not!

Some days after Ries's fateful visit, and a week before he was due to return to Vienna, Ludwig received a curt note.

Sir!
I have made a multitude of enquiries on your behalf, without success. I stress that the Countess's act of kindness should not be rejected. All your friends counsel this course of action, at least temporarily.

Trusting that you will not reject it, I have made arrangements for your piano and other effects to be moved to the Krugerstrasse.

Yr servant
Ries

Ludwig howled in exasperation; he stormed over to the piano and began to play. It was nothing in particular, a theme that came into his head. He varied it, changing the key and structure.

He gritted his teeth as, during a soft section, he felt the vibrations of footsteps on the landing outside. They stopped and he noticed that they neither proceeded to the stairs nor went away.

It has begun already! I am playing for an audience. Like a hired servant to play as directed. That is what will happen in Vienna, and that is what is happening now.

Quickly he strode to the door and flung it open. Frau Grillparzer sat bolt upright in the chair she had put in place on the landing. Ludwig could scarcely contain himself. She was sitting on the landing, an audience of one, being entertained!

He glared at her, groping for the right words, but they would not come. He strode back inside, went into the bedroom, reached on top of the cupboard for the black stove-pipe hat, which he had not worn before, went back out on to the landing where Frau Grillparzer was now standing, her arms held out in a conciliatory fashion. Without looking at her Ludwig pushed the hat hard on his head and trod heavily down the staircase.

When he returned from a long walk, he found a note under his door. He read it quickly. Frau Grillparzer assured him that she would never again sit outside his door or even walk along the landing. She would use the ground-floor entrance and would instruct her son to do the same. She would lock the upper door so no mistake could be made . . . if only he would resume his divine playing.

He screwed up the letter and hurled it to the floor. Then he went to the piano and slammed the lid shut. For the rest of his stay he did not play another note.

BOOK EIGHT

Chapter 1

Ludwig's ears were ringing and his head ached agonisingly. He was in the living room, a large room with windows that gave out on to the Bastion, on a level not much higher than the people walking along the Bastion promenade. He could almost see their expressions.

He examined the portrait of his grandfather, which Ries had hung above the piano. A deep melancholy settled on him. He was living once again as a house guest, expected to obey summonses to the dinner table . . . Countess Erdödy had stressed that he need not feel under any obligation to do so, but never failed to make it clear how disappointed she was when he refused. To make matters worse, Prince Lichnowsky's apartment was upstairs. Several times the Countess had tried to persuade Ludwig to join her and the Lichnowskys for dinner, but he had always managed to find an excuse. This time he knew he had no choice.

He watched the people on the Bastion. Some walking alone, purposefully, some in pairs, arm in arm, chatting. He wished he was one of them, with no more cares on his shoulders than those of ordinary people. Instead, he thought, I am driven by this force inside me. I have to create music, give to these ordinary people music that will excite them and calm them and inspire them, and do the same for their children and their grandchildren.

And I have this disability to overcome – the worst disability a musician can have. And I have to put up with people who throw obstacles in my path, who do not understand that ultimately nothing, *nothing*, will stop me.

He looked in a mirror, flattened his hair with the palms of his hands and walked through to Countess Erdödy's rooms. It occurred to him as he entered the salon that he had been last in this room with that despicable man Bridgetower. He thought now of the unkind way in which the mulatto musician had imitated the Countess's ungainly walk, as she came over to him with her arms outstretched. He had felt sorry for her then; now, he had to admit, her impediment irritated him.

He kept his arms to his side, bowing curtly to her. Then he bowed to Prince Lichnowsky, pointedly failing to return the Prince's smile. He was struck by the physical change in his former patron. His face was careworn, gaunt almost, his skin, which Ludwig remembered as smooth and pale, now lined and tinged with grey. 'My wife asks me to give you her fond greetings, Ludwig. She is unwell most of the time now, since I allowed the surgeons to practise on her.'

His voice had a weary quality. Ludwig heard it clearly enough, the ringing in his ears providing an accompaniment to it rather than blunting it. It was not the first time he had seen Prince Lichnowsky since the unhappy trip to Silesia, but he had barely exchanged words with him since then. At first he had refused to allow him to come to the Mölkerbastei, and when he had relented, he treated him brusquely, making it clear that their relationship had changed irrevocably. He was determined not to do anything this evening to alter that, so he nodded again but said nothing, and took a glass of wine from the tray a servant held out to him.

'You have composed a new symphony,' the Prince said. 'I have heard about it from Ferdi Ries.'

Unable to restrain himself, Ludwig said, 'Has he taught you to play it, so you can claim it as your own? As you did the Andante Grazioso?'

'Now, now, now,' said the Countess. 'Let us go and eat. I know how you like to return to your room early, Ludwig.'

At the table Ludwig produced a notebook and pencil from his pocket and laid it beside his plate. Occasionally he scribbled in it. In the early stages of the meal he responded to questions with a nod or shake of the head, and soon found that the Countess and the Prince were content to talk together, the Countess occasionally glancing at him protectively.

Ludwig ate quickly. He listened without interest as the conversation centred on the French emperor and his exploits.

'So now he has Spain to add to his conquests,' said the Countess.

'Yes, but it is the beginning of the end for him. He has overstretched himself. Too many French soldiers have been lost. And he has had to take charge personally. He is too far away from his seat of power. And while the cat's away . . .'

'Oh, I do hope you are right. Otherwise all of Europe will become his kingdom.'

'It will not last. It cannot,' Ludwig said, roused despite himself. 'The people will never stand for it. Ries told me there will be another war.'

'It is possible. Our army is preparing. But . . . I don't know. That man seems invincible on the battlefield. And every time we go to war, it drains our exchequer. Drains mine, too, I have to say. And I'm not alone,' said the Prince.

'You poor dear man,' said Countess Erdödy. 'You're doing so much for our empire. You and Prince Lobkowitz, and Schwarzenberg and the others. Spending so much of your own money to help our emperor. You will be rewarded one day, I am sure of it.'

'You are very kind, Countess. But it will not be necessary. I am a patriot. I do not require a reward. But do not let us talk about such gloomy matters. Ludwig, I hear you are preparing for a benefit concert at the Kärntnertor. Or is it the Burg?'

'The Wien,' said Ludwig.

'No, no,' said Lichnowsky. 'The Wien is closed. I know it is. Until November or December. I was speaking to Hartl only the other day.'

Ludwig was astounded. 'He promised me a date in the autumn!'

'Well, the theatre is closed. And he told me that there are new plays at the other two which will run till the end of the year. So it means . . .' His voice trailed away.

'Damn it, Ries!' roared Ludwig, 'I will not accept it. I don't know how many times he has now put back the date.'

'I know, Herr Ludwig. I am afraid he is under a lot of pressure.'

'I don't care how much pressure he is under. Go and see him and get a statement in writing from him. With a firm date, do you hear? And if he breaks his promise once more, I will take him to court.'

'I will speak to him, sir. I will do my best. I will speak to Herr Salieri. Maybe –'

'Salieri? Why Salieri?'

'As *Kapellmeister* at court he might be able to exert some influence on Herr Hartl.'

'He will do the opposite! Are you insane? He is jealous of my music. I know it. I have been told.'

'No, sir, I am sure that is not true.'

Ludwig flapped his hand. 'Do something anyway, Ries. I must have my benefit concert. I need the receipts it will bring. I also want my new symphonies to be heard. It is important. They will quell voices like Salieri's once and for all.'

'I am sure they will be well received, sir.'

'And when that's over, Ries,' Ludwig sounded exhausted, 'I think I will go away.'

'To the country again, sir?'

'No. Far away. I have had enough of this city and its intrigues and its jealousies and its broken promises.'

'Where to, sir?'

'I really do not know, Ries. Somewhere where my music will be appreciated and I will be treated properly. Not Paris. I am sure of that – not with that monster still usurping power. Maybe Moscow. Or London. I do not know. But away from here.'

Countess Erdödy's servant stood in the doorway. 'There is a gentleman to see you, sir. The Countess said I was to show him in. And would you be so good as to see her afterwards and tell her what he wanted.'

The impertinent sneer on the servant's face made Ludwig want to shout at him that he would not go to see the Countess, that she had no business questioning him about anything. But, with an effort, he held his tongue.

A small immaculately dressed man walked in, resplendent in a uniform Ludwig did not recognise. His jacket was scarlet velvet with gold tassels hanging from the sleeves. His breeches were tied below the knee above white stockings. Under his arm he carried a plumed hat, and across his chest was a broad yellow sash. He executed a formal bow, sweeping the hat low across his body.

Ludwig was taken aback, and wondered what to say. He decided to wait for the man to speak and hoped his ears would allow the words to filter through, unimpeded, to his brain.

'Most distinguished tone poet and artist *sans pareil* . . .'

The man had a high-pitched voice which, in the quiet of the room, presented Ludwig with no difficulty. Of more concern to him was the man's unfamiliar accent and frequent mangling of the language.

'I have been sent here on the orders by His Majesty the King of Westphalia –'

'The King of Westphalia?' echoed Ludwig slowly.

'None less, sir. His Majesty King Jerome, brother of His Supreme Majesty the Emperor of France.'

Ludwig sat back in his chair. The distaste he had felt on hearing reference to Napoleon was outweighed by this man's comic appearance and behaviour.

'Count Truchsess-Waldburg, Chief Chamberlain to His Majesty, at your disposal, sir. I shall come straight to the matter, in order not to waste your hours.' He pulled a rolled parchment from a leather pouch that hung from his belt, made a great show of untying it, coughed self-importantly and began to read. Ludwig motioned him to speak slowly.

'Sir, I am commanded of His Majesty to offer to you the position of Chief *Kapellmeister* to His Majesty at the court of His Majesty in Kassel. The conditions, which His Majesty trusts you will find acceptable, are following. You will be in sole charge of all musical activities at court. You will appoint and dismiss musicians to His Majesty's orchestra as you see fit. You will compose music for special occasions, as requested by His Majesty. You will be required to demonstrate your genius as a virtuoso for His Majesty, but such would be a request from His Majesty not a command. You are to state your salary, which His Majesty will guarantee for life. Finally, all expenses incurred in removing yourself and your belongings to the city of Kassel will be met in advance.'

He rolled up the parchment, tied the ribbon round it and handed it to Ludwig, bowing as he did so.

Ludwig's mind raced. An offer of a permanent position, at a salary that was his to command, all musical activities to be at his discretion. He must be dreaming. The man was looking at him expectantly.

'Where is Kassel?'

The Count coughed again. 'The capital of the kingdom of Westphalia, sir. Elevated above Hannover, Frankfurt and Cologne, all of which, I am pleased to say, sir, are but a day's carriage-ride away.'

'Cologne?'

'Yes, sir. A fine city.'

'You do not need to tell me about Cologne. I was born a short distance away. Tell your . . . the King –'

'His Majesty, sir.'

'– His Majesty that I am grateful for his offer and will give it my consideration.'

'His Majesty understands that you will need time to decide, sir. He awaits your reply only at your most early convenience.'

Chapter 2

Prince Lichnowsky's jowls were quivering. 'I hate to bring up unpleasant memories, Ludwig, but I remember well how you reacted to my request for you to play for French officers. Now you are considering taking a position at the court of a French king. Brother of Napoleon, no less.'

Countess Erdödy wailed, 'Ludwig, it cannot be true. You must tell us it is not true. You are not going to leave us? Leave Vienna?'

Ludwig was sitting at the piano, his fingers drifting idly across the keys. He was playing nothing in particular, just allowing the sounds to waft through the air. The events of the last few days had amused him. Obviously Countess Erdödy had questioned the absurd Chief Chamberlain, whose name Ludwig could not remember, as he left and had ascertained the purpose of his visit. Within no time at all, a steady procession of his friends and colleagues had arrived to persuade him to reject the offer.

Prince Lobkowitz and young Prince Kinsky had appealed to his public spirit. 'The city would simply not survive your departure,' Lobkowitz said, emphatically.

'Herr Beethoven, my late father told me you would one day be the finest musician in Vienna. I only wish I was able to tell him he was right,' said Kinsky, squaring his shoulders military style, which strained the leather belt around his corpulent belly.

His friends had taken a different approach. Stephan Breuning had pointed out that Kassel was a remote city where he would soon become lonely and isolated. 'You will have no friends, Ludwig. You will lose those who have known you for years, who understand your needs and who help you. Do you believe these new people would be as tolerant if you had trouble conversing with them?'

'You will not be among musicians, Ludwig,' Schuppanzigh

had reasoned. 'Provincial fiddlers, that is all. You will soon tire of their uselessness. You will miss being able to talk about music. And, Ludwig, how will you be able to give concerts?'

It had been the hapless Schuppanzigh who took the brunt of Ludwig's fury. 'Concerts, Schuppanzigh! Do you believe I can give concerts here? In Vienna? Ask Hartl. He will tell you how simple it is. Here's a date, Herr Beethoven. Oh, no, not that one. Here's another. And another. No one will be able to do that to me in Kassel.'

Ludwig stopped playing now, stood up and walked away from the piano, holding up his hands so that voices would not interrupt the slow fading of the notes from his mind. As he sat down he glanced up at the portrait on the wall: he was sure he had seen a glint in his grandfather's eye.

'We are all so fond of you, Ludwig dear,' said the Countess. 'Here in Vienna we can look after you. You have such good friends. There, you would be alone.'

Ludwig drew a deep breath and sighed. 'I have heard enough arguments. From you, from everybody. If my life here in Vienna is as wonderful as you say it is, tell Hartl to give me my benefit concert.'

On a day when she knew Ludwig was in the Landstrasse suburb, seeing his old friends Nanette and Andreas Streicher, Countess Erdödy asked Prince Lichnowsky, Prince Lobkowitz and young Prince Kinsky to come to see her. 'Gentlemen, so good of you to give me your time. I fear we will lose the battle over our mutual friend if something is not done.'

'But what, Countess, eh?' asked Lobkowitz. 'We can hardly appoint him Chief *Kapellmeister* in Vienna.'

'Signor Salieri guards his job with his life,' said Lichnowsky.

'Ludwig would never take an appointment like that anyway,' said the Countess. 'He is too . . . independent.'

'He will take this one, though, in Kassel, eh?' said Lobkowitz.

'It is different,' said Lichnowsky. 'I have known him since his earliest days here and he will take this wretched job just to show he is beholden to no one. He will regret it in the long run, but he doesn't look that far ahead.'

'My worry,' said the Countess, her face clouding, 'is that he will suffer enormously there. They will not make allowances for his deafness the way we do. They will get frustrated and angry. And he will never have compositions ready on time. It will just annoy them.'

There was a moment's silence. Then Prince Kinsky spoke. 'Forgive my presumptuousness, but it seems to me there is a fairly simple solution. What he wants more than anything is the benefit concert Herr Hartl keeps promising him. Somehow pressure should be put on Hartl to give him a date and keep it.'

'You are right,' said Lichnowsky. 'And I know who could do that. The perfect person. In fact the only person.'

Archduke Rudolph listened to Prince Lichnowsky, nodding slowly. 'I understand exactly, my dear prince. To lose him would be a disaster, not just for us but for the cultural life of our great city. I will speak to Herr Hartl. I am sure there is something he can do.'

Ferdi Ries could hardly contain his excitement. 'Herr Ludwig, it is set. The date for your benefit concert. December the twenty-second.'

Ludwig's eyes rolled to the ceiling. 'No, Ries. I will not believe that rascal of a man ever again. He does not keep his word.'

'Sir, this time it is true. Look, I have a letter here from him. "Kindly inform your master that a concert of his music will be held in the Theater an der Wien on the twenty-second of December next. He is to let me have a programme of music to be performed at the earliest opportunity so the musicians can be retained and rehearsals begin. I am pleased to announce that His Imperial Highness Archduke Rudolph will be guest of honour." There, sir. It is going to take place.'

'Then we have work to do, Ries. A lot of work.'

'Yes, sir. Do you know what music you will perform?'

'The two symphonies, C minor and F. Such a contrast. I suppose I have that at least to be grateful for. If Hartl had kept to the original date, the symphony in F would not have been written. My symphony to nature.'

'I will make sure Schlemmer has copied all the parts in time for rehearsal. Which piano concerto will you perform, sir?'

Ludwig thought for a moment. 'The most recent, in G. Also the concert aria I composed in Prague. Ah! *perfido*. Tell Anna Milder. She will sing it.'

'That is four major pieces, sir – the concert will be very long. Perhaps the aria is not necessary.'

'I will have the aria,' Ludwig insisted. 'This is my opportunity, Ries, and I have waited a long time for it.'

Ries was making notes. 'Let me know, sir, when you have decided on an order.'

'The C minor last. It will be the finale.'

When he heard the date of the benefit concert Prince Lichnowsky put his head in his hands – it was the same day as the annual concert for the Musicians' Widows and Orphans Fund at the Burgtheater, which was to be conducted by Kapellmeister Salieri.

The Prince made a few discreet enquiries and established that most of the city's best orchestral players had been hired for that. Seyfried and Clement, under contract to the Wien, were not involved, but they were almost alone. Ludwig's music was difficult enough for even the most proficient players, but for those of second rank it could prove impossible.

Word quickly spread about Ludwig's concert. His friends, naturally, were pleased, hoping that it would put an end – or, at least, cause a fatal prolongation – to the possibility of accepting the offer from Kassel.

His aristocratic friends congratulated themselves on the successful outcome of their strategy and made sure that others of their rank would attend the Wien rather than the Burg. The determination of the Archduke to be guest of honour – even when it was pointed out to him that Signor Salieri was by far the more senior musician – ensured the widest attention, which annoyed Salieri. He took his revenge in a simple but highly effective way: he wrote to every musician on the city's payroll threatening to suspend them if they agreed to play at Ludwig's concert.

When Archduke Rudolph discovered this, he ordered Salieri to withdraw the letter, but the damage had been done. The orchestra that gathered under Ignaz Seyfried for the first rehearsal was made up of musicians of whom only a few had played together before, and even fewer had attempted music by the city's most demanding composer, Ludwig van Beethoven.

Chapter 3

'No, Seyfried. No! Do you hear? I will direct. This is *my* concert.'

The sharp pains in Ludwig's stomach were unaffected by Doktor Schmidt's powders. His ears rang and his head throbbed. He had begun the rehearsals with such optimism, but it seemed that with each one the musicians, instead of improving, became worse.

'Allow me, then, to direct the rehearsals, and you direct the performance.'

Ludwig thumped the table. 'I know how I want my music played, Seyfried. The problem is not me, it is the musicians.'

He stormed out on to the stage. 'We will take the end of the second movement again,' he snapped at the players, tapping his baton on the music stand. 'The birdcalls. They are important. They must be right. Just woodwind. First beat silent. And –' He brought down his arms. The flute played the nightingale's chant. Ludwig concentrated on the sound. It was wrong, he knew it. And the oboe with the sharp chirp of the quail. Where was it? In the silence the clarinet's cuckoo. There should not be silence. They should overlap each other. 'No! No! No! Can you not read what is written in front of you? Flute, last beat oboe, first beat of the next bar clarinet. How many times do I have to rehearse it?'

The flautist said something Ludwig could not hear. There was a burst of laughter.

He struck the music stand again and the baton snapped. More laughter. He lifted his arms quickly. 'Again! And – off the beat,' he called. 'No! Off the beat!'

The flautist put down his instrument. The oboe was held away from its player's lips. The clarinettist was shaking his head.

'Animals would play better!' Ludwig shouted. 'Do you hear? Animals, I said.'

A raucous sound hit his ears. The trumpet had played a growl and another player barked like a dog. As he watched, the orchestra stood up slowly and walked off the stage.

Ludwig sat at a table in the large room behind the stage, Seyfried and Ries with him.

'I am sorry, Herr Beethoven,' said Seyfried, coldly, 'but the musicians say they will not continue if you take rehearsals. I cannot persuade them otherwise. I have tried.'

Ludwig felt sick. How could this have become so dreadful? He had his concert, at long last. But the musicians could not play his music and were now refusing even to try. He said, 'Then it is over. Ries, tell Hartl we cannot continue. I –' He was unable to contain his grief.

'No, sir. There is a solution.' Ries looked at Seyfried. 'If you allow Herr Seyfried to direct rehearsals, he will work hard with the orchestra, and you will be able to direct at the concert.'

'But I . . .'

'It is the only way, Herr Beethoven.'

The concert date was only two weeks away, and Ludwig, with Ries's assistance, had established a pattern. He would stay in the room behind the stage with the door open, listening to the rehearsal. He made comments and Ries wrote them down. Every so often Seyfried would appear to discuss progress.

Ludwig paced up and down. The birdcalls now approximated what he had in mind. The storm sequence in the fourth movement, he said to Ries, still sounded more like a light shower, but Ries told him it would improve.

Seyfried turned next to the symphony in C minor. To Ludwig's frustration, it took a whole rehearsal just to get the opening bars right. He knew they were difficult – Seyfried even asked him if he would consider changing the first movement to four-four time, with the three quavers played as triplets on the fourth beat. 'That way I can be sure the players will come in together,' he said.

Ludwig looked at him without speaking. The *Kapellmeister* did not raise the point again.

As he listened to the C minor being rehearsed, and the musicians becoming more confident, an idea began to take hold in Ludwig's mind. 'Ries. We can no longer end the concert with the C minor.'

'But, sir, it is the perfect finale, as you yourself said.'

'No. It is too . . . too . . . there is too much there. The audience must hear it with a fresh mind.'

'Should it open the concert, then?'

'No. The orchestra would not be ready for it. Open with the symphony in F. Then the piano concerto. Then the aria. After the interval we will perform the C minor. And we will end with a new piece.'

Ries's mouth fell open. 'A new piece? Sir, Herr Ludwig, you do not mean an entirely new piece?'

'Yes, Ries. An entirely new piece. I will compose something entirely new. As a finale. Yes. That is the way.'

'Sir, it is less than two weeks to the concert. There is no time. The orchestra would not be able to rehearse and –'

'Ries. Tell Seyfried I need a chorus. Not a large one, say six of each voice. Salieri is not using a chorus, is he?'

Ries thought not.

'Good. Get the Burg chorus. I will compose a piece for orchestra and chorus. To be opened with solo piano. I will play the piano.'

'Sir, Herr Ludwig. Forgive me for saying so. You are asking the impossible.'

Ludwig spent the next few days in his apartment working on the new piece, which he entitled Choral Fantasia. He would give it a rousing finale which – whatever had happened in the previous pieces – would induce the audience to huge applause, thus putting the seal of success on the concert. Because time was short he worked only on the orchestral part and the choral accompaniment. The piano solo – a lengthy opening that would justify the title Fantasia – he would improvise on the night. There was no need for the orchestra to be bothered with it. An obvious starting point and a nod of the head would bring them in.

An unexpected hitch interrupted him briefly. Ries arrived at his apartment, accompanied by Anna Milder, whose face was set, her arms folded imperiously under a capacious bosom.

'Herr Beethoven, I cannot work like this,' she said, her voice cutting into Ludwig's head. 'Herr Seyfried tells me I will have only one rehearsal, and with him, not you.'

Ludwig put down his pen. 'Then, Madame, you will have one more rehearsal than I will have for the piano concerto. Now leave me, I am working on a new piece.'

'Herr Beethoven, it does not become you to make light of the matter. If I do not have more rehearsal time, I will not perform.'

Ludwig looked at Ries. 'Explain to Madame Milder the problems we have. I must continue working.'

'If you have no more to say on the matter, Herr Beethoven, I have no choice but to withdraw my services.'

Ludwig thought no more of it, and continued to compose the orchestral and choral parts of the Fantasia. The main theme came to him easily: it was almost childlike in its simplicity. He wanted it to take flight – he knew it could – but time was short. In the final days before the concert, he gave each sheet of music to Ries as he completed it, Ries corrected obvious errors of harmony and passed it on to Schlemmer, who had a team of copyists standing by.

The problem of the aria remained.

'Madame Milder is not to be persuaded. She fears her reputation will suffer.'

'Take the lead soprano from the chorus,' Ludwig replied.

'We have tried. In fact, we have spoken to almost all the city's leading sopranos, who all say that without adequate rehearsal they are not prepared to perform. Sir, would you consider cancelling the aria?'

'No! Find a soprano.'

'We have, sir. She is Ignaz Schuppanzigh's sister-in-law. Fräulein Killitzky. She is very young and rather inexperienced. I still believe –'

'Rehearse with her, Ries. We will use her.'

Chapter 4

There was a heaviness in his head that Ludwig could not shake off. His ears, mercifully, were quiet but he knew how often that heaviness was a portent of pain to come, the noises, harsh and irregular, that fought each other, blotting out the sounds that were his lifeblood.

His stomach, though, had calmed down, as Doktor Schmidt had told him it would. If the tension of rehearsals had brought on the pains, the arrival of the concert date had stilled them.

He looked round the auditorium of the Theater an der Wien. It was filling slowly. People were rubbing their hands from the December cold, their breath still white from the icy air outside, but there was a chill in the great theatre, made worse by the open doors. People kept their coats on and their scarves round their necks.

He saw Prince Lobkowitz in his box in the first tier, talking animatedly with Prince Lichnowsky. Countess Erdödy sat in another box towards the centre. Towards the rear of the parterre were his brother Carl and Stephan Breuning. Ludwig could not suppress a stab of envy. His brother and his childhood friend, now both married men, Carl a father and Stephan soon to become one. Such normal lives. He watched as Willi Mähler and Nikola Zmeskall joined them.

Ries tapped his shoulder. The young Carl Czerny was with him. 'Good luck tonight, sir,' said Czerny.

'Schuppanzigh sends his heartfelt apologies, Herr Ludwig,' said Ries. 'He had no choice but to play for Signor Salieri tonight. He wishes you every success.'

Ludwig's stomach lurched. He breathed deeply to quell it.

Seyfried came over to him, looking worried. 'The musicians are about to go on to the stage, Herr Beethoven. Sir, the flautist is concerned about the birdsong. He implores you to cut it. He has the support of the oboist and clarinettist. They say it would be simple enough to do.'

Ludwig frowned. 'Tell them to play what is on the page in front of them, Seyfried.'

Seyfried and Ries exchanged glances, then Seyfried walked back to the musicians, said a few words and ushered them to their seats.

Ludwig stood to the side of the stage, alone now, as Seyfried took his position in front of the orchestra, waited for a cue from the back of the auditorium, then raised his hands. The trumpeter sounded the fanfare to signal the arrival of the guest of honour, Archduke Rudolph.

Ludwig felt the tension in his stomach increase. He waited for the audience to seat themselves once more, then walked on to the stage. He looked out over the sea of faces. The audience looked uncomfortable, huddled in their coats. Many women had blankets over their legs and shawls round their shoulders – irritated, no doubt, Ludwig thought, that their fashionable clothes were hidden. With so many hands deep in coat pockets or under blankets, there was no more than a smattering of applause.

Ludwig turned to the orchestra, closed his eyes and conjured up pictures of green fields and trees, corn swaying in a gentle breeze, hills rising towards clear blue skies. But they were not the hills of the Vienna Woods, they were the hills of the Siebengebirge, and the sound of water rippling over stones was the brook meandering its way down to feed the mighty Rhine.

He brought up his arms and, without waiting to see if all the players were giving him their attention, brought them down to begin the symphony in F, his musical representation of nature.

It took a moment for the sound of the strings to reach him, and when it did it was muffled. Had the damned players put mutes on their instruments? No. It was his damned ears. Instinctively he beat harder to try to make the sound louder, but it did not change.

He had written *pianissimo*, he remembered, and they were certainly obeying that. But it was to be followed by a *crescendo*. A vitally important *crescendo* that led naturally to a *forte* passage. The players were ignoring his dynamic markings. The essence of his music. Do they not see that? Did Seyfried not tell them that?

He looked at them and saw that they were following Clement, the leader. Clement was doing his best and occasionally glanced at Ludwig to check the beat. But the result was not what Ludwig wanted.

They were playing too fast, and now that his ears had adjusted he realised that they were playing *forte* throughout. Where was the contrast? The infinite variety of nature, which he had tried so hard to represent, was lost.

He wanted to look at the audience, but he knew he could not. He could not even glance at Lobkowitz's box. A noise was coming from behind him, from the first rows of the parterre. It was a buzz, a hum. His ears playing tricks again? No. People talking.

Scene by the brook, he thought wryly to himself. It sounded more like waves crashing on the shore. The second violins were sawing at the notes as if their lives depended on them. Ludwig had marked the passage slurred, three quavers at a time slurred, the way water ripples and ebbs, over stones and round rocks. *What* was he hearing instead?

The same was true of the semiquaver passages – second violins, violas and cellos, in unison to represent the *perpetuum mobile* of the water. But they were not in unison and their bows were bending with the effort when they should have been stroking the strings.

He braced himself for the birdcalls that ended the second movement. The flautist raised his instrument to his lips, half raised himself from his seat and blew so hard that his cheeks puffed out. The oboist, with the quail call, did the same; so, too, the clarinettist, the cuckoo.

The string players laughed, and Ludwig heard more laughter from behind him. He turned round. Heads in the audience were nodding and faces laughing.

The three players repeated their comic turn, as Ludwig had written it, but this time even louder and raising themselves a little higher from their seats.

The laughter behind Ludwig was now unrestrained. What should he do? What *could* he do?

He conducted the next two movements without inspiration. The piece was ruined. What did it matter if the dance of the country folk – so lovingly transcribed from the wedding dance he had witnessed in Grinzing – was played with as much vivacity as a funeral dirge? Or that the thunderstorm had as much menace as a light sprinkling of summer rain – little different from in rehearsal, except that the notes were right.

The shepherds' song of thanks for the passing of the storm –
a serene moment of peace – was doomed by the solo clarinettist,
who kept missing the F sharp at the top of the phrase.

Ludwig was in despair. He conducted mechanically to the
end of the symphony, the two *fortissimo* chords that closed it
so unlike any other ending he had composed that the audience
did not realise the piece was over.

He turned to them and they returned his look, smiling.
From somewhere towards the back of the second parterre
Ludwig heard a cuckoo call. Then another, and another. A
few people applauded, his friends mostly, but the cuckoo calls
and the accompanying laughter smothered it.

He raised his arms to quieten them, and heard the silencing
hisses run round the audience. They expected him to speak,
to explain himself. But he shook his head and faced the
orchestra again.

Ludwig felt ill. The sharp stomach pains had given way to a
dull nausea. His symphony had failed.

Before he had time to assimilate the thought, a nervous young
woman, her hands clasped tremblingly in front of her, took a
small step out on to the back of the stage. Josephine Killitzky,
sister-in-law of Ignaz Schuppanzigh.

Ludwig nodded to her but she stood still, wringing her hands.
Exasperated he walked to the back of the stage. Holding her arm
a little too tightly, he led her to the front of the stage. He could
feel her shaking.

'I need you to sing well,' he said into her ear, and released her.
She swayed slightly and he feared she might lose her balance, but
she steadied herself.

The oboe gave the A and the players tuned their instruments.
Ludwig looked sideways towards Josephine. Her face was a mask
of fear. God, how he wished Anna Milder were standing in her
place. Or even Josefa Duschek, for whom he had composed the
aria in Prague.

He raised his arms to begin the orchestral introduction.
The sound flowed over him and it was good. He saw the
concentration on the faces of the musicians, who were playing
unexpectedly well.

To his left he heard Josephine's voice – thin, delicate and
trembling, barely audible above the orchestra. There was a
purity to it and a vulnerability: exactly the opposite of what
was required for a spurned woman calling down the wrath of

the gods on her faithless lover. Worse than that, Ludwig knew immediately that she would not be heard further back than the first half-dozen rows of the parterre. He wanted to spur the orchestra on, to reach the end as swiftly as possible. But to do so would make Josephine's task all the more difficult. The chromatic passage that lay in wait almost like an ambush would be nothing more than a tuneless *glissando*. He decided, nevertheless, to increase the speed. The orchestra followed him. Josephine's frail voice became little better than a slithering sound and she gave up the attempt to reach the high notes.

'*Moriro. Moriro.*' 'I will die. I will die.' Hold the word, sustain it, he had told Josefa. Make the orchestra wait for you. And how wonderfully she had.

Josephine almost spoke the words, which were smothered by the orchestra.

Ludwig swiftly brought in the orchestra for the final turbulent passage. By now he could no longer hear Josephine's voice. Was it his ears? Was she, by some divine miracle, singing with glorious power and his ears deceiving him? He knew it could not be so.

During the final *tutti* for the orchestra, during which the soprano usually stands, her hands clasped, eyes turned upwards, awaiting the roar of applause, Ludwig caught a fleeting movement. Josephine was hurrying to the back of the stage. He quickly lost sight of her. He knew he should turn to the audience, but he did not want to see their faces. He heard applause, but as it reached his ears it was superseded by the murmur of voices and cackles of laughter.

He walked to the back of the stage just in time to see Josephine Killitzky vanish towards the stage door, her mother's arm reassuringly around her shoulders, her small body shaking with sobs.

He came back on to the stage and saw that in the audience people were standing. Small groups had formed, chatting among themselves. Hands were thrust deep in pockets, shawls were pulled tighter around shoulders, noses were pink with cold, feet were being stamped. Everywhere there were smiles and some laughter, shaking heads.

Ludwig saw Seyfried approaching him. 'Get the piano on, Seyfried. And be quick. The piano concerto will quieten them.'

'Sir, shall I call the interval? It's so cold in the auditorium. Then we could move on to –'

'The piano!' growled Ludwig. 'And hurry.'

He waited in the wings as the piano was trundled into place, feeling the vibrations under his feet. Ludwig looked at the instrument. Such a familiar ally. With a piano I can do anything I wish, he thought. I can make them cry and I can make them cheer. The piano: my lover, mistress, wife. Everything will be all right now.

A boy carried two lamps on to the stage, the candlelight flickering under the bulbous glass. He placed them carefully on the hollowed circles at each end of the piano's wide music stand. Stupid, thought Ludwig. He waved away a second boy who was placing the score on the stand. 'No music. Take it away, boy.'

Ludwig walked up to Clement, who was talking to the players. 'Just follow me, Clement. Do you understand? Tell your musicians. Take the lead from me.'

'Herr Beethoven. If Seyfried directed while –'

'No. I will direct from the piano. Take the beat from me.' He turned away quickly, sat at the piano and struck the A. The players took a few seconds to tune their instruments, and immediately put them down, as if in protest at the solo piano opening to the concerto.

Yes, thought Ludwig, the piano alone. For just five bars. A G major chord, sustained, and a gentle theme arising from it, ending questioningly. *Piano*. Then the orchestra enters – in B major, a key change just five bars from the opening! *Pianissimo*. There had been no opening to a piano concerto like it.

He placed his hands over the keys. He knew he should turn first to see if the audience was settled. It did not matter. He was ready to play his piano concerto. He stroked the opening chord. How soft and gentle the notes sounded in his head. He held it and he held it more, until the last vibration had died under his fingers; then the insistent quaver chords. Ah, yes, he thought. Such a simple theme, yet promising so much.

He lifted his hands to bring in the orchestra. He saw Clement take the lead from him and the strings played the B major chord. The sound reached him. Too loud, too loud! he wanted to shout. But the notes were right. That was good enough.

Pianissimo. Piano. Crescendo. The orchestra alone, preparing the way for the solo piano to re-enter. But this opening section must be *crescendo*. Ludwig half raised himself from the chair, lifting his arms higher.

Follow me, he thought. Follow me. Louder. Louder. He flung out his arms to indicate the *sforzando* chord. The lamps on the music stand crashed to the floor. The audience shrieked with laughter. The players stopped abruptly, arms frozen in mid-bow, wind instruments held away from lips half open in astonishment.

Seyfried and one of the boys hurried on to the stage, stamping out the little flames on the floorboards. Ludwig continued to direct, but no one was paying attention. Seyfried put a hand on his shoulder and pushed him gently but firmly back on to the chair.

'Do not worry.' Ludwig heard Seyfried's voice in his ear. 'You can start again. I will send the boys out to hold the candles.'

'I do not need them.'

'If you are directing the orchestra, they need to see you. It is too dark otherwise.'

Ludwig heard Seyfried address the audience. A ripple of applause – and more laughter – greeted his announcement that the piano concerto would be played again from the start. From somewhere towards the back of the hall Ludwig distinctly heard a cuckoo call, followed by an outburst of raucous laughter. He wanted to shout at them, order them to be quiet and listen. Instead he looked down at the piano keys. How he wished he was alone with the piano. In a room far, far away. Alone, with just a piano and his music.

He felt the vibrations of running feet. The boys were at his side, holding the lamps. He was actually grateful: he could see the keys more clearly.

The stroked opening chord again and the hushed sequence that followed it. Again he raised his hands to bring in the orchestra. It took a moment for their sound to reach him. Yes. It was good. Softer this time. Yes, yes.

He began to raise himself again from the chair and lift his arms to indicate the *crescendo*. Louder. Yes, gradually louder. It was good. He threw out his right arm and cried out as it struck the brass lamp. Again the lamp fell to the ground. The boy leaped on the flame, stamping it out. The other boy scurried off the stage.

This time the laughter from the audience hit him like a clap of thunder. Damn them. Damn them. What should he do now? What could he do? He looked towards the orchestra. They were still playing. *Still playing.* He conducted on. He knew it was pointless. They could not see him. But Clement was nodding vigorously and they were taking their lead from him.

The laughter subsided as quickly as it had begun. He sat back in the chair and listened to the lengthy *tutti*. It was still good. Except for the damned clarinet. He distinctly heard the wrong notes. Wretched, wretched man. But the players at least reached the end of the *tutti* in unison. Ludwig brought the solo piano back in, playing faster than he had intended, so that the semiquaver run, first in the right hand then in both, sounded like a blur, yet each note perfectly struck.

To his surprise the first movement proceeded without mishap, the three closing chords bringing it to a satisfactory end. And did it really matter, he wondered, that the intensely rhythmic opening to the Andante was flattened out so that all the notes seemed to have the same value?

He hunched his shoulders low as he played the dialogue with the orchestra. Then the mysterious chromatic sextuplets, leading into the trills. Alone. No orchestra. Voices, damn them. They were talking behind him. Why did his ears not blot out the sound? This passage was supposed to be heard in complete silence, so every note, each unexpected note, surprised the listener.

In the closing bars of the movement the strings came in to accompany him. The sounds swept over him. He had marked the passage *piano pianissimo*. Could they not see that?

The rising triplets from the piano, and then the strings ushered in the final movement, the Rondo. Staccato! he wanted to shout at them. As I wrote it. Read the music – do not invent it!

He brought the piano in, driving the music along. The orchestra seemed unable to match his pace – they kept dropping behind. He had to adjust it, so that unintended discords did not sound.

He played the solo passages, the huge runs, with fury. At the massive *fortissimo* chords that brought the orchestra to a halt, he played a cadenza, improvising on the main theme. Were they listening? Could they hear? Were they still talking? He played on, pouring out all his frustration and anger and pain into the notes. He knew the orchestra were waiting impatiently. Let them wait. He needed to play. To release his emotions. His passion.

Finally, the trills that were the cue to the orchestra. In they came. On he played. He increased the pace. The wrong notes from the clarinet again. What did it matter?

The chromatic runs and then the chords that ended the concerto.

He stood and leaned on the piano. He turned. Some faces were looking at him. There was some applause, mostly from the private boxes. A small group midway back in the parterre was applauding. Elsewhere groups in the audience were talking, as if his music had been an accompaniment to their conversation.

When they grasped that the piece was over, that the concert was half-way through, the audience rose, flapping their arms around their bodies to keep warm. Large numbers headed towards the exit.

Ludwig walked off the stage and slumped into a chair. He was glad of a few moments alone. After a minute or two Seyfried came over to him and clapped him on the shoulder. 'I have announced that the interval will be only ten minutes,' he said, speaking into Ludwig's ear. 'Otherwise it is so cold many will not return. We will begin with the symphony in C minor. Yes?'

Ludwig nodded.

'I will direct it for you, Ludwig. It is better. Rest here.'

Ludwig assented wearily. He wanted to be alone. He picked up his chair and moved it further back, into darkness. He hoped no one would come looking for him. He pulled a handkerchief from his sleeve and wiped his forehead. He felt suddenly very tired. What was the point? Ordinary people will never really appreciate my music, he thought. The aristocrats, yes. The Lichnowskys, the Lobkowitzs, they will fawn and praise and declare themselves great patrons of the arts. But my music is for ordinary people, to bring art into their lives, to inspire them when their shoulders sag with the weight of their burdens.

He clenched his fists with determination. That is what I am on this earth to do, not to stun audiences with my virtuoso skills but to bring art into the souls of people. One day I will achieve it. People will turn to my music when they need art to touch their soul. Whether they are happy or sad, successful or bowed down with misery, my music will be there for them. But I will no longer be on this earth to see it. They will listen to my music and it will inspire them and give them courage. They will know nothing of me, the passion that is within me, the pain I have endured, the impediment that threatens to destroy me.

He felt the vibrations in the floorboards before he heard the sounds. But he could hear the sounds of his music. Yes, he could still hear them. The three quavers and the minim. The dramatic, yet simple, opening to his symphony in C minor. His fifth.

He was grateful to Seyfried for taking over the direction of the orchestra. He needed to rest. He listened to the music he had composed. Faster, Seyfried, faster. Drive them. This symphony must move forward. At last the orchestra was playing as he wanted. The momentum was there, even the contrast between the movement.

He waited for the mysterious linking section he had written to lead straight into the final movement. *Piano pianissimo*. Quiet, timpani. He wanted to shout to the timpani player to tap his drum more quietly. Just the rhythm, that is all the timpani are supposed to give out. Why else would I have written *sempre pianissimo* in the score?

He stood and walked towards the front of the stage, still in the wings. Unseen, he looked out at the audience. The parterre was half empty. Unable to stand the cold, people had left in the interval and not come back. Those who remained, though, at least appeared to be listening, not talking.

The boxes in the first tier were still occupied. He saw Prince Lichnowsky, chin cupped in hand, a look of expectation on his face. Lobkowitz sat with his hands folded on top of his upright crutch, his chin resting on them, eyes closed, eyebrows raised. Further round, Archduke Rudolph sat tensed, eyes wide open, one leg forward.

Looking round the auditorium again, Ludwig realised that, for the first time this evening, everybody was looking towards the stage – and listening to his music!

That slow mysterious passage was leading inexorably to the climax of the work. Seyfried was observing the *crescendo* perfectly, the musicians for once obeying his directions, as he slowly straightened his body and lengthened his arms.

Fortissimo! Fortissimo! The C major chords rang out across the hall, a perfect climax to what had gone before. Just as he had intended. He saw a flash of movement from half-way back in the auditorium. An old soldier in uniform had leaped to his feet.

'Long live the Emperor!' he shouted, standing rigidly to attention.

Faces turned up to him smiling, but they were benevolent smiles. There was no mocking this old soldier, who had risked his life on the battlefield for the Empire.

Across the hall, someone else stood. More people stood. Soon the whole audience was standing, as the trumpets and horns sounded the motif, the same that had opened the work, three quavers and crotchet, three quavers and crotchet.

Seyfried's arms were now waving wildly, driving the orchestra on. Wrong notes were scattered everywhere and Ludwig winced, but what did it matter? Had he not told Ries and Czerny a thousand times that wrong notes mattered less than wrong dynamics, or wrong speeds, or failure to find the spirit of the music?

The final long sequence of chords sounded, and from somewhere in the audience, in the moment's hush that followed, Ludwig heard a voice say distinctly, 'Bravo, Beethoven.'

Other voices took it up, and soon Ludwig heard his name being shouted from the auditorium.

He saw Seyfried coming towards him, a smile stretching from ear to ear. 'Come, Herr Beethoven. Will you acknowledge the applause?'

Ludwig walked on to the stage. All faces were now looking at him, and hands applauding. He nodded two or three times. Why had they not received the symphony to nature like this? Why had they mocked it?

He turned to Seyfried. 'Now the Fantasia.'

'Sir, already it is late. The auditorium is cold. This is a perfect ending to the concert.'

'No! They will hear more. And let us see whether they laugh or applaud.'

Concern was stamped on Seyfried's face. 'Do you have the score showing the piano part?'

Ludwig shook his head. 'I will improvise it. The orchestra must take their lead from me.'

'Herr Beethoven, as *Kapellmeister* I must tell you I believe the orchestra have played enough for one evening. Their instruments are freezing in the cold. And I have to tell you a lot of the audience are leaving.'

'Damn it, Seyfried. They are with us now, can you not see? Get the piano moved on. And the chorus. We begin as soon as it is ready.'

'Sir, shall I direct?'

'I will direct from the piano.'

'Then may I suggest no repeats? In the second variation, no repeat. The orchestra should play straight through.'

Ludwig nodded cursorily as Seyfried left to instruct the orchestra. He felt every fibre of his body tingling with defiance. He wanted to feel the piano keys under his fingers. He barely waited for the players to tune their instruments and settle themselves. He sat at the piano, glanced at the audience, even more depleted now, and at the players sitting grim-faced. The chorus behind them sat impassive, the women with their arms close to their sides to keep warm.

For a moment he was still, then he reached forward and played a sequence of minor chords spanning the whole width of the keyboard, and repeated it. Into the major, back into minor. And then improvisation. Freedom. He allowed his fingers to roam over the keys, switching constantly from one key to another to keep the music fresh, to make the listener wonder what was coming next. On he played. Chords, arpeggios, major, minor, soft, loud. Yes, let the piano – my instrument – sing, and let everyone hear what I can make it do.

Finally, he slowed the music and looked towards the orchestra: several players, instruments on their laps, were blowing into their hands to warm them.

He continued to play while they laboriously raised their instruments into position. Then he lifted his hands off the keys, half stood, and lowered his arms to bring them in.

The formal part of the work began, the statement of the main theme. Simple, a turning phrase, falling, rising and returning to its starting point. The orchestra played it but it was shapeless, without form. *Legato*, he wanted to shout to them. Now is the time for *legato*. The phrase is the foundation stone of the work. Give it life!

He began the first variation, accompanied by lifeless playing from the orchestra. Wretched, wretched musicians. Why must they always do this to my music? Why could they not play as they had in the symphony?

He increased the pace for the second variation, nodding at the orchestra to follow him. Then, slow, slow, let the notes make their mark, and . . . with a high nod of the head, a repeat of the second variation, a little slower this time to allow . . .

He heard cacophony. The orchestra were playing as if he did not exist. What were they doing? Discord after discord sounded. And then a high shriek, as if an angry crow had swept across the stage. The clarinettist again! He tried to adapt his playing to the jumble of sounds entering his ears, but could not. The piece was running away from him. It was chaos. There was no way to save it.

He leaped up from the piano and strode across the stage to the orchestra. 'No! No! Fools! Imbeciles! You!' He stabbed a finger at the clarinettist. 'Can you not read? Do you not see what is on the page in front of you? Damn you, man! From the orchestra entry, again!' He stalked back to the piano and looked up at the musicians but they were not ready to play. They glowered; their instruments lay in their laps.

Ludwig saw Seyfried walk out on to the stage. He began to talk to the musicians. Ludwig turned to the audience. They were sitting transfixed, staring, gaping, agog to know what would happen next.

Seyfried was gesticulating with his hands, palms down in a conciliatory manner. The clarinettist stood up and spoke angrily to him.

Ludwig was swamped in misery. He wanted to play. Just play. Let the sounds of my music flow over the people, he thought. That is all I want to do. Play my music.

Seyfried came over to him, said urgently into his ear, 'They will play, but only if I direct. Will you accept that?'

Ludwig nodded, the very action causing pain in his head. 'Just play,' he said quietly.

Seyfried leaned forward. 'Herr Beethoven. No repeat in variation two. As we agreed. Do you remember? No repeat.'

The words revolved in Ludwig's head as he saw Seyfried move towards the orchestra. He sighed audibly and tears filled his eyes. Seyfried was right. We had agreed there would be no repeat of the second variation. So it was my fault, he thought. My fault. He looked around him at the expectant faces. You have had your amusement at my expense, he wanted to say to them. But I have had enough of all of you. And of this accursed city.

He played again, but the spirit had gone out of him. The sounds washed over him and he allowed his fingers to go wherever they wanted. Let the orchestra play, let the chorus sing. It really does not matter.

More swiftly than he expected the coda began, the headlong rush towards the end. Orchestra and chorus, the simple theme, sounding almost magisterial, runs on the piano, *crescendo* from the players and singers, a chromatic rise, a huge chord and the music hangs suspended, resolves itself and gallops *fortissimo* to the final chord.

Ludwig leaned forward, his head bowed and his hands flat on his thighs. He heard the harsh sound of applause, looked at the audience but they were directing their appreciation to the orchestra.

Seyfried brought the players to their feet. The clapping continued, louder. Seyfried indicated individuals and, finally, the clarinettist, bringing a roar of approval. Ludwig's jaw clenched. He wished he had not spoken so harshly. But what else could he have done? The music could not have gone on. But it was my fault, he thought to himself. My fault.

He saw Seyfried walk towards him, his face set in a smile. He stood up and Seyfried beckoned him to turn to the audience. Reluctantly he did so, but the clapping died away, people rose from their seats and made for the aisles and the exits.

Ludwig walked off the stage and round to the large back room, which had been set with cold meats and quantities of wine. Swiftly he poured himself a glass and relished the taste against his dry throat.

Seyfried was soon by his side. 'Sir, forgive me for saying so, but you – you humiliated the players. You should not have done that.'

Ludwig took another gulp of the wine. Despair creased his forehead. How he could tell Seyfried about the pain of hearing his symphony to nature mocked, the pain of hearing the Killitzky girl mangle his music? The pain of hearing the clarinet screech like a raucous crow, even if the catastrophic mistake in the Fantasia had been his?

Where was Ries? Or Breuning? He needed a sympathetic face by his side.

'They did not play as I wanted. They were too –'

'Herr Beethoven,' said Seyfried, 'you demanded too much. Too many difficult pieces. The concert was too long. And it was so cold. You should have played just the symphonies and the concerto. Everyone would have been happier. The players and the audience.'

Ludwig let out a long sigh. 'Bring the musicians to me.'

'They are here. Behind you.'

Ludwig felt the dullness in his ears. He sipped the wine again: lightness was beginning to penetrate the fog in his head. He turned. The players, all holding glasses, were looking at him. The clarinettist stood at the front, his face a mask of anger.

'You are all musicians,' Ludwig said, 'the highest calling. I realise . . . It was difficult tonight. I am grateful. To all of you.'

He held out his glass to the clarinettist and drank what remained in it.

With relieved looks sliding over their faces, the players began to talk together.

Ludwig felt a hand on his shoulder. 'At last. Ries.'

'Sir. His Imperial Highness invites you to his box, where wine is being served. The Princes are there. He wishes to . . . to . . . congratulate you on the concert.'

'No, Ries. No. Tell him – I have to go back to my apartment. I shall leave by the back way. I need to be alone.'

BOOK NINE

Chapter 1

Ludwig told Countess Erdödy to let no one disturb him. For once he was glad to be living in her apartment: it meant no one could come to see him without first persuading her.

For several days he did not go out, pacing round his apartment, with one issue revolving in his mind.

What had Vienna given him? Nothing but heartache. Why, he wondered, was it always such a struggle? A struggle to have my music heard, a struggle to have it appreciated and accepted.

He thought back to *Leonore*. Poor singers, a libretto that was not right despite everyone's efforts, threats from Baron Braun – and then cheated of my money! Braun goes, replaced by Hartl, and what do I get? Almost a year of promises, all broken, until finally I am given a date in freezing December on the same day as the widows' and orphans' concert.

One day, on a whim, he allowed Gleichenstein to see him.

'We are concerned about you, sir. Is there anything any of us can do?'

Without thinking, Ludwig said, 'Yes. Tell them to match the offer from Kassel, or I will go.'

To his astonishment Gleichenstein pulled a piece of paper from his pocket, almost as if he had been prepared. 'Tell me what is required, sir.'

'I – I haven't thought about it. But a salary equal to what they are offering me in Kassel. Whatever that is. Freedom to compose. A title. It doesn't have to be *Kapellmeister*. But freedom, above all else.'

A little over two weeks after the concert, a copy of the newspaper *Der Sammler* was pushed under Ludwig's door. It was open to an inside page and a small piece had been circled in red crayon.

The last days of Christmas week were dedicated to concerts. On 22 December the Society of Musicians presented
for the benefit of widows and orphans an oratorio of the
immortal Joseph Haydn. On the same day Herr von
Beethoven organised a concert for his benefit in the
Theater an der Wien in which he presented to the public
the youngest offspring of his inexhaustible talents. All
the pieces were by him. Unsurpassedly beautiful was a
description of a storm in the first, *Pastoral Symphony*. A
second new symphony was performed, which caused an
old soldier of the Empire to rise to his feet. Otherwise the
piece had difficult passages for players and listeners alike.
His Imperial Majesty the Archduke Rudolph honoured
this concert with his presence.

He tossed the paper aside. 'Von' Beethoven; he shook his head.
What was Gleichenstein up to? Why hadn't he heard from him?
It was too late. His mind was made up.

'Bring writing paper,' he shouted to his servant. A plan was
forming in his mind.

HIS EXCELLENCY THE HIGH CHAMBERLAIN TO HIS
MAJESTY THE KING OF WESTPHALIA

I wish to accept your offer of the post of Chief Kapellmeister
to His Majesty. I will write again shortly with terms.

Yr humble servant
L. v Beethoven

As he wrote the image of a beautiful face framed by tumbling
auburn curls floated into his mind. He remembered Stephan
Breuning telling him that Antonie Brentano lived in Frankfurt
with her husband. Frankfurt was not far from Kassel and only a
small detour on the route from Vienna to the north-west. She
was married – he allowed himself a wry smile – but he would
still like to see her, and meet her husband. He remembered how
she had enthused over the Eroica, after its first performance at
Prince Lobkowitz's palace. If only she could have been there
to hear the new symphonies, he thought, and to comfort me
afterwards.

Doktor Schmidt sent him a note, saying it was time he saw him.

'There is no point, Schmidt,' he said, as the doctor unpacked his bag. He flexed the muscles in his jaw as the doctor held the tuning fork first to his ears, then pressed it against the back of his head. 'In my head, Schmidt. That is where I hear it. Hardly at all in my ears. I told you before.'

'So you do hear a bit?'

'Like I hear your voice. Through a – a – blanket. Muffled. Smothered. Use any word you like. It is as if there is a bundle of wool in each ear, stopping the sounds getting through.'

'And other sounds?

'Sometimes whistles, bells, humming, buzzing. Sometimes nothing. When there are noises there is nearly always pain in my head.'

'Does anything relieve it? Sleep, for instance. Or peace and quiet in the countryside.'

Ludwig grinned. 'The only doctor I listen to. Doktor Wine.'

Schmidt hesitated briefly. 'Then, like all medicines, you should only take it in small doses. No, no, don't get angry. I will not pursue it. There is something else I want to talk to you about.'

'I have had enough talking, Schmidt. Enough of voices.'

'There is a new technique which we are studying at the hospital. Invented by an Italian physician. Or Swiss, I'm not sure. Called galvanism, named after its inventor. It's said to cure deafness.'

Ludwig raised his eyebrows. 'Schmidt, one day you will believe me when I say there is no cure for deafness. Not for *my* deafness. How does it work, anyway?'

'It involves inserting a piece of wire into the ear as far as it will go and passing an electrical current along it.'

Ludwig shuddered. 'You will not try that on me, I assure you.'

'It has been used on a young girl in Berlin who had been deaf since birth. Gradually it restored her hearing. I have tried it on myself in our experiments at the hospital. It jolts the brain but it induces a remarkable sensation of – how can I put it? – clarity in the head.'

'It certainly doesn't cure baldness,' Ludwig said, pointing at Schmidt's shiny pate. But he kept Schmidt's words at the back of his mind. A girl, deaf since birth, had been gradually cured. Was it possible?

*   *   *

Countess Erdödy was beside herself with worry. She hurried upstairs to the Lichnowskys' apartment and poured out her fears to the Prince. 'He has accepted the appointment and he will go. I honestly believe he will not survive there.'

The Prince replied sadly, 'I fear you are right, my dear Anna. But what is there to be done? If he has made up his mind –'

'I believe there is only one person with the power, the influence, to alter his decision. The same person who made the concert possible.'

Lichnowsky stared at her. 'His Imperial Highness?'

'Karl, could you not speak to him? It would at least make me happy to know we were trying to do something.'

'Certainly. But I do not see what he can possibly do.'

Some days later Countess Erdödy was gratified to receive a note from the Archduke, summoning her to his rooms in the Amalienhof. He would send a carriage for her, to save any strain on her poor feet.

'I agree with you absolutely, Countess. But I am not able to offer him a permanent post.'

The Countess's mind had not been idle. 'Your Imperial Highness, I understand that. In my opinion that is not the main issue. I have come to know our friend rather well, particularly since he has been living in my apartment. I believe his decision to go to Kassel is based not so much on the fact that he will be chief *Kapellmeister*, but more that he will be being treated with . . . respect. It is the honour he is being accorded, rather than the position itself. He said as much to one of his friends, apparently.'

The Archduke nodded slowly. 'I understand that. But I still don't . . .'

'If I am right, then the offer of a specific position here in Vienna would not dissuade him. In fact, it might have the opposite effect, since the only position he is worthy of – that matches the Kassel one – is already taken, and Signor Salieri is likely to enjoy many more years in the post. What is required is some sort of gesture that will persuade him – particularly after all the trouble over the concert – that he is valued. Highly valued.'

'A financial gesture?'

Countess Erdödy said seriously, 'I think it would have to be, simply because he has been asked to state his salary in Kassel. But it is just as important that he is left in no doubt of the esteem in which he is held. And that could come from no more exalted person than yourself.'

'Sir,' said the servant, in a lugubrious tone, 'Herr Ries is in the anteroom. I have told him you are seeing no one, but he says he will not go away.'

'Have you asked him what he wants?'

'He says it is a matter of personal importance, and he wishes to convey it to you himself.'

Ludwig suspected that he knew what Ries had come to talk about. It would not have taken long for news of his acceptance of the post in Kassel to have become common knowledge, and with it renewed efforts to persuade him to change his mind. 'Let him in.' It was not that he wanted to listen yet again to the reasoning, but that he had begun to find his self-imposed isolation wearing. He also wanted to find out if anyone else had heard about this new form of treatment Doktor Schmidt had mentioned.

He regretted his decision as soon as he saw Ries's face.

'Sir. Herr Ludwig. I bring you grave news. Doktor Schmidt has died. He suffered a stroke to the brain from which he did not recover.'

'Schmidt? But he was here only a few days ago.'

'It was very sudden, sir. I have heard that it may be connected to some experiment he was carrying out at the hospital. They are not sure but his brain failed. He apparently lived for a short time afterwards, but had lost his faculties. It is a mercy that he finally passed away. That is what I was told. Poor man, he was barely fifty years old.'

Chapter 2

Ludwig sat in a plush chair clutching a folder of manuscript paper. The young Archduke, his frame seeming slighter than when Ludwig had seen him at the Theater an der Wien only two months before, was silhouetted by the bright light flooding in through the windows that looked out on to the busy Ballhausplatz.

'Herr Beethoven, I must thank you for agreeing to come here to see me today. I know how you dislike being drawn away from your work. May I presume to ask if you are composing anything new?'

Ludwig felt surprisingly at ease. The Archduke's voice had a strength that belied the frailty of his body, and the thick tapestries and curtains absorbed the clamour from the street outside. Also, he respected the Archduke's musical talent and interest. 'I have started work on a new piano concerto.'

'Capital.' The Archduke clapped.

'It opens in a new way,' Ludwig continued, 'which will excite interest, but I doubt there is a pianist in Vienna who will be able to play it.'

'I know of one,' the Archduke said, with a chuckle. 'And only one. May I be bold enough to ask you to play it for me? Now?'

Ludwig was on the point of refusing but the Archduke was a genuine admirer of his music and a particularly proficient pianist. He brought out some manuscript paper. There were the opening bars of the new concerto, a mass of semiquavers for the solo instrument. He stood up and walked to the piano, propped the sheets on the stand and smoothed them out with his hands. 'E flat chord. *Tutti*!' he cried, as he played a huge chord. Then his fingers, beginning with a deep E flat, ran the length of the keyboard in rising phrases to turn at the top, hover between B flat and A, descend chromatically to an E flat trill, rise in semiquavers, then descend, more purposefully now, in slurred quavers, to another chord. '*Tutti*! Orchestra alone. Then —' He sang tunelessly as his fingers ascended the keyboard again, to turn even higher this time, descend and rise again, descending more purposefully still in slurred crotchets, to yet another chord. He held the chord, and once again his fingers rose the length of the keyboard, this time in chopping movements between left and right hand, descending in crotchet and quaver chords to a sustained trill, the right hand then rising alone in ever quicker sequences of four semiquavers, finally descending, slowing for greater emphasis, to four chords, resolving in the home key of E flat.

He held the final chord until the sounds died away in his head. His eyes, through habit, were closed tight to protect himself from the noises that would cut into his head. For a moment he forgot where he was, wondering whose voice would invade his ears first.

He opened his eyes and was pleased to see the Archduke, alone, smiling at him. The young man knew better than to applaud or even speak. Ludwig was grateful to him. He got up, a little unsteadily, leaving the papers on the stand, and returned to his seat.

Without speaking, Archduke Rudolph went to the piano, looked for a few moments at the notes, ran along the stave with his finger, looking between the page and the keys as he did so, then played the opening chord of E flat.

He played more slowly than Ludwig had, but there was a swaying, sweeping movement to his hands. Each note was in its rightful place, but in adopting a steadier pace he was giving the music a different character — more reflective, contemplative. As he grew bolder, he increased the pace, but the chord that sounded again did not cause the piano to quake as it had under Ludwig's hands.

His fingers flew up the keyboard again: the chopping movements of notes alternating between the two hands almost became chords. The Archduke winced as the semiquavers defeated him and he played a series of chords to take him to the top of the keyboard. He descended to the A flat trill, playing the final rising sequences at a steady pace, as if the effort was exhausting him. The closing chords he played with a slow, stately deliberation.

Ludwig allowed the sounds to wash over him. The Archduke was not playing it as he had written it, but it did not matter. The important point was that the spirit of the music was there. For a first reading it was remarkable.

The young man handed him the folder and returned to his seat.

Ludwig cleared his throat. 'You did well,' he said, gruffly.

'I would have done better, Herr Beethoven, had I been reading from the printed score, rather than your own manuscript – if you will forgive me for saying so. But, my dear sir, I have never seen anything like it. You have written a cadenza for the soloist at the beginning of the piece. You said that is how the concerto opens?'

'The first bars.'

'Then, as you rightly say, you will find no pianist to play it! It is exposing the soloist right at the start, before he has had time to settle down. A cadenza like that usually comes much, much later.'

'It is what I want. I will not change it.'

'No, no. It will give the pianists of this city something to complain about, and cause to practise. Certainly, I am sure of one thing.' Archduke Rudolph leaned forward purposefully. 'No one outside this city will be able to play it. They will dismiss it as unplayable. Only in Vienna are there pianists capable of it. Hummel, for instance.'

'Maybe. In that case I shall have to perform it myself.'

'Excellent. Now, Herr Beethoven, would you allow me to raise another matter with you? A matter of some importance. I have some news which I hope will please you.'

Ludwig wanted to talk about music, and only music. He had managed to put out of his mind the anxiety about his impending move to Kassel and he did not want to have to think about it.

'I believe that is impossible, your Imperial Highness,' said Ludwig, hoping his formality would put an end to the matter.

'Allow me at least to try. I have been speaking to some good friends of mine. We all share an admiration for your music which knows no bounds. We also admire you very much for the courage you unfailingly show when obstacles are put in your path. I need not explain what I mean, I am sure.' He arched an eyebrow.

Ludwig realised, grudgingly, that the Archduke had won his interest. He liked the young man, who had none of the arrogance to be expected of a member of the Habsburg royal family. He said nothing, but inclined his head to signal to the Archduke to continue.

'We have decided, these friends and I, to take determined action to ensure that no further obstacles shall stand in your way, so that you can devote yourself, without encumbrance or impediment, to your sole task as composer.'

Composer! The Archduke had used the right word. Not pianist or performer but composer. That really is all I want in life, he thought. To be alone to compose. To put down on paper the sounds I hear – my language – so that I can communicate with other people.

The Archduke walked to a desk, opened it, pulled out a folder and returned to his chair.

'I, together with my noble and distinguished friends Prince Lobkowitz and Prince Kinsky, bind ourselves to make over to you a regular salary which, we trust, will rid you of the need for financial worry. The sum will be four thousand florins per annum. I will not bother you with details of how we will share the amount. This sum to be paid to you until you are able to secure an appointment which will yield you the equivalent.'

Ludwig held up his hands to give him time to digest the Archduke's words.

'An appointment?'

'Forgive me,' the Archduke continued, 'but let me finish with the details first. This sum to be paid to you either in monthly or quarterly instalments, as you wish, until, as I said, you secure an appointment with an equivalent salary. But,' he went on quickly, 'should no such appointment be forthcoming, or should any untoward circumstance prevent you from taking such an appointment, the Princes and I will continue to pay you the sum we have agreed for life.'

The final word hung in the air.

'Yes, Herr Beethoven. In effect we are saying you are to be paid four thousand florins a year for life. Now, there are several details that have to be settled. I will talk to your representative about them so that we can draw up a contract.'

'My representative?'

The Archduke said, 'I have already spoken to certain of your friends, who have advised me in this matter. They have spoken on your behalf, with your interests at heart. On the basis of that, I spoke to my aristocratic colleagues, and the result is this annuity which we hope you will find acceptable.'

'You said details. What details?'

'Formalities, nothing more. Conditions, just a few stipulations –'

'No conditions. If people have spoken to you on my behalf and said I will accept conditions, they have no right –'

The Archduke interrupted, 'No, no, Herr Beethoven. Please do not be concerned. There is only one and it is not a condition, more a requirement, and it is not something I believe will cause you any anxiety.'

'What is it?'

'Only that you agree to continue residing in Vienna.'

At the round table at the back of the Schwan the small group of Rhinelanders sat, sipping wine. Breuning and Gleichenstein were raising their glasses to Ferdinand Ries, who was looking down modestly.

'Congratulations, Ferdi,' said Breuning, 'but it means we shall once more have to bid you farewell, and that will cause us pain.'

'And me too,' said Ries. 'You are all such good friends. But I cannot turn the opportunity down. Such a good position, with a regular salary. I have never had that in my life.'

'And rather appropriate,' said Gleichenstein, 'that Herr Beethoven is responsible – even if he does not know it – for your good fortune.'

Ries held up a cautioning hand. 'I hope we are not celebrating too soon. The job is not yet mine. But they have asked me to apply and the letter from Herr Truchsess-Waldburg said it was a mere formality. But there is something I have to be sure of first.'

The other men raised their eyebrows.

'I have to be completely sure Herr Ludwig has turned down the position. I have to hear it from his own lips. Only then will I feel free to write.'

'Don't wait too long, Ferdi,' said Breuning.

The three men clinked their glasses.

Chapter 3

Ludwig poured himself a glass of wine, looked at it for a moment, then held it briefly in the air as an ironic toast to Doktor Schmidt, before raising it to his lips. 'I always told you you were wrong,' he said. 'It'll never get better.'

His head pounded, as it had for days. The high-pitched whistle would not leave his ears and he knew that when it finally subsided his hearing would be worse.

Why? Why? *Why?* He banged the glass down so hard on the table that the stem broke. Just when the triumph of his contract should have lifted his spirits, he found himself dragged down again by his wretched health.

But there were other factors too, which he was loath to articulate. By accepting the contract he was once more bound to others. True, there were no conditions – he could compose what and when he liked – but he was still beholden to three men. And he must remain in Vienna. Lonely though the prospect of living in Kassel may have been, at least it represented a change. It was in Germany, where his accent would raise no eyebrows; and it was not far from Frankfurt, home of the Brentanos. Suddenly all his frustration at living in Countess Erdödy's apartment came to the surface. He wanted to leave. He did not know where he would go. Anywhere. Just to be living alone again. Underlying everything, though, was the knowledge that he had succumbed to persuasion, that his bold initiative, which would have taken him in an entirely new direction, had been abandoned – which, surely, would make him seem a weaker man in the eyes of his friends and colleagues.

His mood, therefore, was far from receptive when Nikolaus Zmeskall became effusive. 'So, Ludwig. You are to stay after all. We keep one friend but we lose another.'

'What are you talking about?' Ludwig snapped.

'Ferdi Ries is applying for the job of chief *Kapellmeister* to

His Majesty King Bonaparte the Younger, which thankfully you turned down.'

'Zmeskall, you are a fool and a drunken fool. You do not know what you are talking about. Does he really think he could fill a position that was offered to *me*?'

Several times over the next few days Ries tried to see Ludwig but each time Ludwig told the servant to send him away. Finally he shouted at the man, 'Do you not understand me? Is my German different from your German? I do not want to see Ries. Is that clear enough?' He could not control his rising temper and the servant was a ready target for his frustration. Ludwig grabbed him by the shoulders and propelled him from the room.

Countess Erdödy came to see him. 'Dear Ludwig, I have heard you are out of sorts. Why?'

Ludwig stood stiffly, his arms clamped to his sides. 'Countess. Do you not understand? Does nobody understand? I am not a – a – plaything for you all to plot over, to pass back and forth between you, like some child's toy.'

'Whatever do you mean, you poor dear man?'

'What are you calling me? God, you are no better than the rest of them, plotting against me, treating me like a – a – I am leaving your apartment. I have decided.'

'No, Ludwig. I would be so sad. Where will you go?'

'Anywhere. Now leave me.'

The next day Ludwig was looking at a copy of the *Wiener Zeitung* when he heard noises coming from outside his room, raised voices. He made a ring round a small announcement in the paper and tossed it on to the sideboard. The voices were louder, shouting angrily. Suddenly there was a crash and the walls of the room shook.

He ran to the door and threw it open. Ferdinand Ries was standing outside, breathing heavily, eyes moist and staring. Ludwig looked down. The servant was lying on the floor, wiping a trickle of blood away from his chin with his sleeve.

'What in God's name–?' Ludwig dug his hand into his pocket and pulled out a fistful of coins. 'Here, man,' he said to the servant, thrusting them at him. 'Take these. Here.' He pulled more from his pocket and gave them to him. 'Forget about this incident. Go on. I will give you more coins tomorrow.' The servant scurried away.

Ludwig looked at Ries: he was trembling, wiping under his glass eye with his handkerchief. 'Come on in, Ries. You had better have some wine.' He put his arm round the young man's shoulder and led him into the room. He poured two glasses and Ries took one. 'Now will you tell me what that was about? And speak clearly, Ries.'

'Sir – Herr Ludwig, I have been trying to see you. I needed to see you, to talk about something urgent. But you kept refusing to see me, and time was running out.'

'I know about it, Ries. You thought you could fill an appointment that was offered to me. You applied for it behind my back.'

'No, sir. That is not true. I would never do that.'

'You applied for it, Ries. You told them you would do the job. A job that was offered to me.'

'No, sir. I did not. I have not applied for the job.'

'You have not?'

'No, sir. My plan was that only once I was certain you were no longer going to take it, would I put myself forward.'

'So you still believe you could do a job that was offered to me? That is insolent, Ries.'

The fire had gone out of Ludwig's voice, but the residue of anger was still in him.

'I would never presume that, Herr Ludwig. You are the supreme musician in Europe. I am a humble – just an ordinary pianist. But I need to earn money, sir, so that I can send some back to my father. But I would only put myself forward for the post in Kassel when I was certain you had withdrawn.'

Ludwig looked at the young man's troubled face.

'That was why I was trying to see you,' Ries went on. 'That was why I kept coming here. Zmeskall and Herr Breuning both told me you had turned down the job, but I needed to hear it from you, sir, so I could be sure. But the servant kept turning me away. Finally, I . . .' His voice tailed off.

'And will you apply now?'

'With your permission, sir. But I fear it will be too late.'

Ludwig stood up and walked to the sideboard. He picked up the newspaper and returned to his chair. 'Misunderstanding, then. That is what it seems like. But, Ries, I have had enough of everyone telling me to do this or that, advising me, sign here, go there. The Countess,' he lowered his voice, 'thinks she is my mother. I am stifled. I am leaving this apartment. Getting out of here.'

'Where to, sir?'

Ludwig held out the paper to him.

Ries read aloud, 'Walfischgasse, number 1087.' His cheeks coloured and his jaw dropped. 'But, Herr Ludwig,' he said, 'you cannot take a room there. The house is a brothel.'

Chapter 4

The main room at least had a view from the back of the Walfischgasse over the Bastion and the Glacis beyond, but Ludwig's new lodgings were far too small for him to consider staying there any length of time. The bedroom had no window and, with a bed, wardrobe and wash-stand, was full. There was no room for a piano anywhere. But Ludwig felt a certain exhilaration at his new-found independence.

It was a short walk to the end of the Walfischgasse, down the Kärntnerstrasse and under the gate on to the Glacis, where Ludwig spent most of the day walking, a notebook and pencil in his pocket. He was composing again, completing work on the piano concerto at the same time as working on a new piano sonata – with no piano in his room! The sounds of his music were as clear in his head as if he were hearing them emerge from under his fingertips. After a while even the occasional cry of a child or the snort of a horse no longer disturbed him. So absorbed was he that he did not notice how the number of carriages crossing the grassy expanse was increasing, luggage always piled high on the roof, heading away from the city.

But soon, as he had feared it would, the thought of walking back along the narrow alley with its guttering candles, passing customers from the Blauen Säbel, began to deaden his spirits.

Only Nikolaus Zmeskall came to see him, and even he berated Ludwig for his choice of accommodation.

'I needed to get away from everyone,' Ludwig replied. 'It's only temporary. I'll get something better soon.'

Zmeskall said, 'You might find it easier than you think. People are leaving the city, taking everything with them.'

'Is it the war again?'

'I fear so. With our new, remodelled and re-equipped army, we will again take on the Corsican and defeat him once and for all. That, at any rate, is what we have been ordered to say in the Chancellery.'

'Will you find somewhere for me? Ask Ries, or Nanette Streicher.'

Zmeskall said he would try, but Ludwig saw concern in his friend's face as he coughed delicately into his closed hand. Ludwig guessed he was about to say something significant.

'Ludwig, do you remember a certain friend of yours? A lady? A countess?'

Ludwig knew immediately who Zmeskall meant, but time had passed and the wound of rejection had healed. In fact, he could not remember when she had last crossed his mind. It was as if she belonged to the past.

'She . . . I have heard she is to marry her children's tutor.'

The word 'marry' caused Ludwig a little pang and he repeated it quietly under his breath.

'I must say, her family is nervous. Franz Brunsvik believes the man is a scoundrel. Stackelberg is his name. But her mind is made up. They are powerless to stop her.'

'A chain of sorrows,' Ludwig said. 'That is what my poor mother used to say about marriage. Nothing but a chain of sorrows.'

'Yes, well, anyway, what I wanted to say was . . . I heard you had tried to see her, that she was away or out . . . I just wanted to make sure you . . .'

Ludwig lifted his hands. 'Do not be concerned, my friend. I have consigned her name to the past.'

Relief crossed Zmeskall's face. 'Wise, Ludwig. Very wise. I know I have told you before. She is a highly emotional woman, sometimes not very stable. Franz worries about her, I know. Somehow she seems to attract misfortune. Maybe Stackelberg will be the right husband for her, but I can't help doubting it.'

After Zmeskall had gone Ludwig found himself thinking of Josephine Deym. What he remembered best about her were her blazing black eyes. But their intensity was disturbing. Slowly the image faded, to be replaced by a feeling of calm. Was it relief that, although he had come under her spell, he had – through her rejection – escaped? He thought about it briefly, but he had more important matters to attend to. His music.

Ludwig was pleased with progress on the piano concerto. Time and time again he looked at those opening bars – the dense mass of quavers and semiquavers that Archduke Rudolph had made such a brave attempt at playing – each time wondering if he was demanding too much of the soloist. and he played the opening sequence over and over, the tips of his fingers striking dully against the wooden surface. Then, with a decisive gesture of finality, he wrote at the top of the first page, 'The opening stays. The concerto to be dedicated to HIH Rudolph.'

A few days later Stephan Breuning came to see him. His face was grim. 'Ludwig, since you no longer care to associate with your friends, I have been left with no choice but to seek you out, even in this dreadful place where you have chosen to live.'

Instinctively Ludwig looked round the room for the familiar carafe of wine and cursed under his breath. He had none, and no servant to fetch some. 'I shan't stay. But I needed –

'We all worked hard on your behalf, to ensure you did not make a mistake about the future. But you repay us by moving into a – a – brothel and treating us as if . . . Ries told me what happened.'

'I apologised to him. I was misled about his motives.'

'He told me, but your apology came too late. He was unable to secure the appointment he so desired – the appointment you toyed with, accepted, turned down. It would have been the making of him. Now he is reduced to giving lessons again, which barely yield enough for him to live on.'

'I will speak to him. He can work for me again, now I have a proper income.'

'I rather think, Ludwig, that he wishes to make his own way, however difficult that might be. He is thinking of leaving the city again, which, given the likelihood of war, is probably a wise decision.'

'I cannot offer you wine, Steffen. I do not have any.'

'I do not want wine. I have not yet told you the reason for my visit. Why I have come to this – this place. I regret to tell you that I . . . I have lost my beloved wife. Julie. She has died.'

Ludwig was stricken. First Schmidt, now Julie. 'I did not know. I am so sorry.'

'Of course you are sorry!' Stephan said, tears starting in his eyes. 'Of course you did not know, stuck in here thinking of no one but yourself.'

Ludwig said nothing. He felt for his old friend and he wanted to say something, to show his sorrow. 'How – why – what caused her death?'

'Fever first. They couldn't quell it. She grew weaker. Finally she had a haemorrhage of the lungs. It was dreadful to see her little face so racked with pain.'

'I am so sorry for you, my old friend.'

Stephan stood up and looked at him. 'You hurt the Countess, too,' he said. 'She cares for you, you know. I suppose you did not know she is leaving?'

Ludwig was shamed by the expression in the other man's eyes.

'The war again – or the threat of it. Her husband has written to her from Croatia. He has taken a post in the provincial government there. It is his home state. He has sent for her. Everyone is leaving, and this time many will not return.'

Ludwig snatched a copy of the *Wiener Zeitung* from the vendor standing in the shadow of the Bastion and tossed a couple of kreuzer into the dented metal bowl.

AUSTRIA DECLARES WAR ON FRANCE!

The glorious forces of His Imperial Majesty the Emperor have taken to the field once more to challenge the French imposter. All patriotic Austrians will pray that His Imperial Highness Archduke Charles will lead our soldiers to victory . . .

Ludwig snorted in disapproval, screwed up the sheet and threw it away.

The streets were teeming with excited people, some hurrying on their way, others standing and chatting, arms gesticulating. Carriages moved swiftly this way and that, criss-crossing the streets, the crack of the drivers' whips accompanied by hoarse shouts.

Ludwig walked under the shadow of St Stephansdom and along the wide Graben, a folder of manuscript paper under his arm, keeping a wary eye open to avoid stepping in the path of a carriage. He had been pleased to receive the note from Ferdinand Ries, asking him to meet him in Taroni's coffee house. Normally such an invitation would have irritated him and elicited an immediate refusal, but he wanted to speak to Ries and heal the rift he had caused between them. He forgot that Ries had written he had news that would be welcome to his master.

Ries, he knew, would gladly return to being his helper, and this time he would offer him a salary. He had brought the opening of the new piano concerto to show him. He wanted Ries to learn it and play it for him.

Taroni's was half empty, for which Ludwig was thankful. He saw Ries standing by a small table towards the rear of the room. The younger man bowed his head and the two of them sat.

'Ries,' Ludwig said quickly, 'I have missed seeing you. Steffen told me . . . I am sorry about Kassel.'

He was pleased to see a small smile – even though it was tinged with regret – on Ries's face.

'In the end I was too late. But you know what they say, sir? From misfortune fortune sometimes comes.'

The atmosphere inside Taroni's was congenial, the smell of strong roasting coffee good, and there were no customers near enough to them to make it difficult for Ludwig to hear Ries's words.

'Here. Look.' Ludwig took the top sheet from the folder. 'The opening to my new concerto. I want you to take it, copy it and learn it.'

Ries's hand came forward quickly. 'Be careful, sir. The coffee.' He whisked out his handkerchief and wiped a stain off the paper, glancing at Ludwig's scribbled notes. 'The piano is solo, sir? Right at the beginning of the piece?'

'Solo, Ries. Can you imagine the effect?'

'It is asking a lot of the soloist. He will have had no time to –'

Ludwig picked up the small cup and swallowed the thick black liquid, down to the heavy sludge at the bottom. A moment later he drunk the chilled water that had accompanied the coffee. 'The rest will be ready soon. Tell Schlemmer to start on this. Now listen, Ries, I want you to help me. With copying, publishers, like you used to. Now I have a contract I can help you a little financially. And there is work to be done.'

Ludwig noticed that Ries's jaw was clenched. He wondered if he should say more, but decided to wait for the younger man's reaction.

When Ries looked at Ludwig his face was solemn. 'I appreciate your kindness, Herr Ludwig. But I have made a decision.
There is nothing for me in Vienna any more. Especially with war
again. Word is that Napoleon is advancing along the Danube.
There will be more fighting. It is unavoidable. My pupils are
all leaving the city. I shall have no income, apart from . . . I
appreciate your generosity, sir, but I have my family in Bonn
to think of. I have to provide them with what I can. My father
has had to retire.'

'What are you going to do? You are not leaving Vienna again,
are you?'

'I have to, sir. I really have no choice. I have heard that there
are good teaching opportunities in other cities. Also, some posts
which I might be able to fill.'

'Where? Where will you go?'

Ries's shoulders slumped. 'Stockholm first. If I fail there, then
apparently there are good opportunities in Petersburg, although
it is a bit far. Also London. But the English are constantly fighting
the French.'

'But are you able to travel with the war?'

Ries smiled wryly. 'It is the sole advantage I have over other
people. Because I returned to Bonn last time and made myself
available for conscription, I was given a French passport. I am
a French citizen. I am no more French than you are, sir, but I
am at least free to travel.'

'I shall miss you, Ries. You have been a great help to me.'

'No, no, sir. I was often too busy teaching. Gleichenstein
will continue to look after your affairs as much as he can.
But now that you have your contract . . . At least I have
the pleasure of knowing that your true worth, sir, has been
recognised.'

'It makes me a slave, Ries. No better than Mozart was, or
even Haydn.'

Ries slapped his forehead. 'Forgive me, sir, I should have told
you earlier. I am too consumed with my own problems. Herr
Haydn is gravely ill.'

Ludwig was saddened. 'I must go and see him,' he said.

The two men fell silent. After a few moments Ries spoke
again. 'Now, sir, I said I had good news for you. I went to
see Prince Lichnowsky, who was most concerned about you.
He knew about . . . he had spoken, obviously, to Countess
Erdödy.'

Ludwig tensed. He wanted to put those events behind him but he did not interrupt.

'He was worried that you had taken rooms in the Walfischgasse. I told him that it was essential we find better accommodation for you.' A gleam entered Ries's eye. 'Impertinent of me, I know, but the Prince is a kindly man. He did not take offence. Quite the contrary. He said he would look into it. Can you imagine who he spoke to?'

'Zmeskall? He said he would find lodgings for me. Or Nanette? Breuning? I don't know.'

'No, sir. Count Pasqualati. Your old landlord. And he has agreed to make your apartment available to you again. On the Mölkerbastei. And from what I understand, it now has a rather good view to the Prater park and the Danube. Though I imagine Schuppanzigh will curse having to climb four flights of stairs again!'

Ludwig's grin almost reached the back of his head. 'I am grateful to you, Ries. You have done well.' He was disconcerted to see the young man's lower lip quiver.

'I . . . Thank you, sir. I am not sure you have ever said that to me before.'

'Then forgive me,' said Ludwig, raising his hands expansively. 'You are a good man, Ries, and a fine musician. And your father is a good man too. You will do well, I have no doubt of it. And I wish you well.'

Ries stood up, squaring his shoulders. Ludwig got to his feet too, and they walked outside into the Graben.

'I shall bid you farewell now, sir. I leave tomorrow at dawn. I am glad to have been able to help you. When this dreadful war is finally over, I will return and come to see you straight away. In the meantime, sir, wherever I am, Stockholm, Petersburg or London, rest assured I will champion your music and make it heard.'

'And when all this is over,' Ludwig added, 'let us return to Bonn. With Steffen, to our homeland. And see the Rhine again.' He took Ries's outstretched hand in one of his, and just as he turned away, clasped the younger man's shoulder with the other.

At first Vienna rejoiced at the news that the Austrian army, under the command of Archduke Charles, had inflicted a defeat on the French forces, under Napoleon Bonaparte, on the Marchfeld, the flat marshy expanse immediately to the east of the city. But as the days passed, word filtered into the city that the victory had not been decisive. There had been massive losses on both sides, and Napoleon had been forced to withdraw to the east. There he had camped, awaiting reinforcements, but Archduke Charles did not have the manpower to challenge him again. Austria had no choice but to wait, knowing that when Bonaparte's forces arrived, he would attack again.

The exodus from Vienna continued. Those who had not left before, trusting in the remodelled Austrian army to inflict a final defeat on the French, realised that their optimism would not be fulfilled. The roads leading out of the city to the south and to the west became rivers of people. Carriages trundled along slowly, their roofs piled high with belongings. Carts, loaded with as much as they would carry, chairs sticking out at odd angles, were pulled by old horses unused to such weight. People with no horses pushed their belongings in front of them in handcarts as best they could.

As Ludwig's friends had tried to persuade him to leave the Walfischgasse, now they urged him to leave the city, as they were doing. The aristocrats had long since left. Stephan Breuning went with Zmeskall to Budapest, to be joined by Gleichenstein a few days later. Carl van Beethoven had intended taking Johanna and Karl to Linz to stay with Johann, but he left it too late.

The servant stammered, 'Sir, th–there is a v–very important p–p–person to see you. From the palace, sir. His Imperial Highness!'

Ludwig looked up in time to see the young Archduke walking into the room, his face a mask of worry. He stood up and bowed.

'Herr Beethoven. I will not disturb you long. I see you are working.'

Ludwig glanced at the manuscript papers strewn on the table and the piano top. 'A piano sonata. I began it some weeks ago, but I put it aside while I was completing work on the concerto.'

'A new sonata by Beethoven. What a gift to us all. And it is good to see you installed again in your old apartment. I see you have restored the venerable *Kapellmeister* to his rightful position.'

Ludwig followed the Archduke's gaze to the wall above the piano. 'I compose better when my grandfather is looking down at me,' he said.

'I trust all is going well with the annuity? Prince Lobkowitz has returned to Prague and Prince Kinsky is once more on the battlefield, but both assured me they had made the necessary arrangements.'

'Yes. Thank you. I am grateful.'

'Herr Beethoven, let me come straight to the point. We are in dire danger in this city. Everyone who remains. As you know, Napoleon's army is regrouping. Reinforcements have arrived. A major battle is inevitable and I fear we will be defeated again. And then Napoleon will take his revenge on the city, in a different manner from last time. You should leave.'

'I cannot leave. Where would I go? I cannot go home to Bonn. It is impossible. Where else would I go?'

'Out into the country. Baden, even. Anywhere beyond the Bastion wall.'

'No. I am content here. I am working. I have no time to look for a lodging anywhere else. Ries and Gleichenstein have gone. I will stay.'

'Herr Beethoven, I have to tell you that I am leaving the city. I have no choice. The Emperor has ordered us all to go. Only he will remain. I leave with the Empress in the morning. We take the southerly route to Budapest.'

Ludwig moved quickly to the piano. 'Then I shall give you a present,' he said. He picked up the sheet that stood on the stand. 'See here. The opening of the new sonata. Three chords.' He played them without sitting down. 'Laa-laa-laa,' he sang as he played. He brought the sheet to the table, snatched up a quill and wrote above the chords, '*Le-be-wohl*. Fare-you-well. There, the first movement shall be entitled *Lebewohl*. While you are away I shall compose the second movement. The third I shall not write until you return.'

The Archduke held out his hand. 'Herr Beethoven, I would rather have a gift of a single bar of your music than all the riches in the empire. I wish you well. Stay safe, and I shall look forward with impatience to our next meeting – let us hope in happier times.'

Events did not proceed quite as Archduke Rudolph had predicted. Napolen Bonaparte, informed by his intelligence officers that barely an Austrian soldier was left in the city, decided to invade Vienna before he engaged the Austrian army in the Marchfeld. He put General Oudinot in charge of the attack and moved his army nearer to the city, camping outside the village of Wagram to await word that Vienna was once again in French hands.

The Viennese mobilised a civilians' militia, whose first task was to burn the bridges across the Danube, the second to build barricades in the streets.

Chapter 5

At dusk on a warm May evening Ludwig leaned out of the window of his apartment and looked north and west to the hills of the Vienna Woods. Small dark shapes scurried over them, hauling longer more solid dark shapes into position. Slowly darkness fell, finally blanketing them in invisibility.

Ludwig could hear the silence outside. An eeriness hung in the air, an expectation that filled him with dread. Occasionally a shout would drift towards him on the night air, but otherwise all was still – an unnatural, oppressive silence.

He jumped as the hills blazed into light. Flashes of fire erupted on the hilltops, one after another. He leaped back in fright. He heard a high-pitched whistle, and another, and another, accompanied by a whirring sound, and he knew his ears were not deceiving him.

Moments later the crump of exploding shells shook the building. He propped himself against the table, ignoring the empty glass which rolled off it on to the floor. He was four floors up, on the top floor of a building that stood high above the Bastion. He had to leave. But how? And where should he go?

He slammed the window shut, eyes wide at the sight of cannon spitting flame. The Kahlenberg, that tame hill at the eastern end of the Woods, had come alive, with its very own dragon at the top. Like the Drachenfels.

The end, thought Ludwig, as he hurried from his apartment and down the round staircase. Any moment now a shell will hit the building and I will be buried under a pile of rubble. They will mourn me. But it is too soon, too soon. So much more work to do.

He stepped out on to the Mölkerbastei. The streets were deserted. The high-pitched whistles continued over his head and the blast of exploding shells seemed nearer. He almost ran the length of the Herrengasse.

The sky above him was turning red with flames. How far to the Kärntnertor gate? He had a vague idea of getting through the Bastion into the Landstrasse and trying to reach Andreas and Nanette Streicher's house. But even as he thought of it he knew he would not make it. The shellfire was unrelenting and he was already panting hard, his face covered in sweat.

He leaned against a wall for a moment, hands over his ears to cut out the dreadful ugly sounds. Then he made a decision. He cut through the narrow streets to the Neuer Markt, past the side of the Schwan and into the Kärntnerstrasse. A huge barricade was in his way – piles of furniture, mattresses and iron bedsteads – but he clambered over it where it was lowest. He ran across the wide street, the ancient spire of St Stephansdom stretching up into the red sky. He hurried down the Himmelpfortgasse and up into the Rauhensteingasse, keeping close to the buildings.

At the corner of the Ballgasse he paused and sat on a low wall, panting so hard that he thought his lungs would explode. The sweat ran down his forehead, and he wiped it away with his sleeve.

His ears were howling, the whistle, whine and thud of shells mingling in such a cacophony that he did not know which sounds were caused by his deafness and which by the destruction going on around him. He covered his ears again but it made no difference – nothing could keep out the din. He forced himself to get up and run on.

When he reached the building he ran up the steps and through the open main door, then hammered with both fists on the door of his brother Carl's apartment.

He leaned against the door frame, supporting himself on his arm. It seemed like an eternity before the door was opened, and he was looking into Johanna's face. His breath came in short bursts and he could not speak.

'Quick. We wondered where you were. Come in,' she said.

He tried to avoid her eyes and flinched as she grasped his arm, but he had to allow her to lead him in. He wanted to sit, but her grip was firm. 'Into the cellar. Carl and the child are down there. We'll be safe. I came up to get water. If I hadn't, I wouldn't have heard you. Quick.' She led him out of the room to a small internal corridor. As she moved, she grabbed a flask from the table.

At the end of the corridor, almost against the wall, was a trap-door. Johanna lifted it. 'Down the steps. Hurry!'

'No,' he said, his breathing steadier now but his chest tense. 'You go. I'll follow.'

Johanna hesitated, then did as he said. Holding her dress close to her legs, she climbed through the opening and down the steps. 'Don't forget to close the door after you,' she called up.

Ludwig waited until he was sure she was down, then climbed on to the top stair. He reached out, took hold of the top of the trap-door and pulled it closed after him.

There were only four or five steps down and he stepped off into a small room. Two candles burned on a table. Packing boxes stood against one wall and empty bottles against another. There were several stools, which Ludwig recognised from the apartment.

There was a musty, damp odour, but they were below ground. They were safe.

For a moment there was silence, then a shell exploded high overhead. The earth shook.

'Sit down, Ludwig,' Johanna said. 'We'll all sit down. It will help relax us.'

Ludwig felt his forehead break out into a cold sweat. His head began to pound and his ears were hurting. Noises clashed with each other, although he knew it was silent in the cellar apart from the distant heavy crump of shells. It was as if now that he knew he was safe, his ears were taking their revenge. The crashing of the shells exploding above him as he ran through the streets had been more than they could bear. Now that he was still, they were sending their own explosions into his brain. He put his hands over them and bowed his head, his eyes screwed tight.

Then he felt a hand on his shoulder and opened his eyes. The candles flared as strong as sunlight.

Johanna held out two cushions to him. He saw her lips move. He did not know what she was saying but her intentions were clear. He took them and held them against his ears. Their softness felt like a soothing balm.

Ludwig knew he must have slept. When he opened his eyes he realised that he was lying on the floor, one cushion under his head, the other over his exposed ear. At one point he thought he had felt someone adjust his head so that it lay fully on the cushion, then take his hand and place it over the other to hold it in place. No, he thought, he must have imagined it.

The silence was occasionally broken by the haphazard thud of exploding shells but they seemed less sharp than before. Or had he become accustomed to the sound? He did not know yet. There was a strong, familiar smell in the cellar, not unpleasant, which he could not immediately identify.

It was an effort to sit up, and when he succeeded pain racked his neck and head. He shivered. It was cold in the cellar and his limbs ached from the damp.

For a moment he rested his head against the wall, reliving his race across the city. The primitive howling of the shells, the destruction and chaos.

The smell, now strong under his nose, was coffee. He felt a tap on his shoulder and opened his eyes. He took the steaming cup Johanna handed him and sipped it, scalding his lips.

Carl and the child were both sitting on stools at the small table drinking coffee, their faces half illuminated in the candlelight. Johanna sat down opposite her husband. She turned round and said to Ludwig, 'We can't leave yet. It's not safe. They're still shelling the city.'

Carl's face, Ludwig saw, was etched with defeat and submission. It contrasted with Johanna's, which was strong and defiant. It bore the mark of an inner strength that Ludwig knew his brother lacked.

Karl began to cry, softly at first, but soon with a piercing edge that bounced off the walls. Johanna hurried round the table to pick him up.

Ludwig noticed the serenity that came over her face as she gazed down at her child, patting his back. He was slight for his age; although he was nearly three, his frame was frail. His legs dangled limply; one of his arms was round his mother's neck, the other hung down loosely. The infant was looking at him. His eyes, though, were unfocused, as if directed at some invisible image between Ludwig and himself.

Ludwig slept fitfully, although his body told him it must be daylight now. Carl, Johanna and their son slept too. Several hours passed like this before Ludwig realised the explosions had stopped. Carl was asleep, his head in his arms on the table, and the little boy was curled up on a small mattress on the floor.

Only Johanna was awake and Ludwig watched her climb the steps and lift the trap-door. She stood there for several minutes, and finally opened it fully, letting a shaft of light into the cellar. Then she went out and closed it behind her.

Ludwig wanted to go after her but he knew he could not: his

legs were aching. He needed to walk but it would take time to prepare his muscles. He thought of waking Carl, shaking him roughly by the shoulders and telling him it was he who should be going outside, not his wife.

He wanted more coffee. How long would Johanna be?

He may have dozed again, he was not sure, but a glare hit his eyes as Johanna lifted the trap-door and came down the stairs. This time she did not close it behind her.

She walked over to Carl and touched his hand. Then she looked at the child, still sleeping, but did not wake him. She turned to Ludwig. The light for the trap-door illuminated one side of her face; the other was half lit by the candles. Once again Ludwig was struck by her strength. He found himself curiously drawn to her, but repelled at the same time. She did not have the face of a wife and mother, he thought, more that of a strong-minded, independent woman, determined to get what she wanted, by whatever means and at whatever cost. Suddenly he felt a measure of pity for his brother.

'It is over,' Johanna said. 'The bombardment has stopped. The white flag is flying from the Hofburg. The streets are covered in rubble. There are French soldiers everywhere. They are tearing down the barricades. Useless, anyway. Matchsticks against cannon. We are occupied again.'

BOOK TEN

Chapter 1

It was May 1809 and for the second time in less than four years the French tricolour flew from Schönbrunn Palace where Napoleon Bonaparte, Emperor of France, was in residence. The people of Vienna moved slowly and sullenly around the city. The usual groups did not form to discuss events. The strollers on the Bastion promenade were French soldiers – laughing and joking, the Viennese knew, at their expense.

But the fighting was over. Most of those who had fled from the city – including Ludwig's friends – had returned.

The soldiers patrolled the main streets, loaded muskets shouldered. For the most part the occupation was peaceful, but unlike the last time when French soldiers had been in the streets, any hint of dissent was ruthlessly put down. A hot-headed student, Friedrich Staps, lunged at Napoleon as he descended the steps of Schönbrunn to review his troops, but was brought down before he could bring his knife anywhere near its target. Napoleon, keen to be seen as magnanimous, offered Staps a pardon in return for an apology. Staps refused. Napoleon ordered him to be shot.

Peter Toll, master carpenter and captain of the citizens' guard, snapped a French officer's sword across his knee. He was put against the wall where he stood, still clutching the broken blade, and shot. Jakob Eschenbacher, master harness-maker and jovial, well-liked local figure, was found to have three guns hidden in his back garden. He suffered the same fate as Toll.

Ludwig shook his fist at the small detachment of French troops marching along the Graben. 'If I knew as much about war as I know about music, I'd give you something to watch out for!'

Gleichenstein took his arm and steered him quickly towards Taroni's coffee house. There was bustle and noise in the large room and Ludwig wanted to resist Gleichenstein's urging, but the aroma of coffee drew him in. He took a small round table near the window, glancing briefly to the back of the room where he had sat with Ries before bidding him farewell.

At tables and in small standing groups, hands were gesticulating, heads nodding and shaking. Voices were raised barely above a whisper, but occasionally one would become voluble, to be accompanied by hissed urgings for it to be lowered. The voices, cups clattering, the occasional burst of nervous laughter reached Ludwig as if through a heavy curtain.

Gleichenstein came across the room with two small cups. He put them on the table, sat down and leaned towards Ludwig, speaking close to his ear. 'We must not talk here. I have been warned. Spies. You should drink your coffee and we will leave.'

'To the Schwan. Some wine.'

Gleichenstein shook his head. 'Will you come to my apartment?'

Twenty minutes later they sat in the small front room overlooking Dorotheegasse, one of the narrow streets that ran from the Graben down to the Hofburg Palace.

'Is there any wine?' Ludwig asked.

Gleichenstein went to a cupboard, took out a bottle and poured a glass for him. He did not take one himself. 'I am sorry to have pulled you away from Taroni's, sir, but it is too risky now. You are well known, and if you were to say something unguarded, who knows what might happen? Most of the men in Taroni's criticising the French were spies, hoping to lure some poor fool into agreeing with them. Then, in the night, the soldiers will come to take him away.'

Ludwig sipped the wine, enjoying the way it mingled with the taste of the coffee still in his mouth. 'Spies. Bah! No better than rats.'

Gleichenstein lowered his voice even though he was in the safety of his own apartment. 'It is said there are now more spies in the city than tradesmen. A spy in every family. No one is safe. And all in the pay of this new foreign minister, who has been given all the powers he wants.'

'Who is he?'

'His name is Metternich. He has an iron fist. And he is not even an Austrian but one of us, from the Rhineland.' Gleichenstein smiled with irony.

'He should wave his iron fist at the French.'

'Unfortunately the French need not be concerned. There is no army for them to worry about, not after the action at Wagram. It is said we may have lost as many as forty thousand men.'

Ludwig said thoughtfully, 'Now the people of Vienna know what it has been like in Bonn these past few years. French soldiers in the streets.'

'We have been fortunate in Freiburg not to have suffered that. You know, sir, we were worried about you during the invasion. You should have left the city with us.'

Ludwig swilled the wine in the glass and gazed into the deep red liquid. 'I thought I was going to die, Gleichenstein, when the shells came over. I was frightened but I was determined to survive. Determined.'

He struck his fist against his thigh. A drop of wine spilled over the glass on to the arm of the chair. He wiped it with his hand. 'It gave me a resolve, a determination. I felt I had to survive. To compose, to give people something to wipe away all this violence. To show them the nobility of the human spirit.'

He looked up at Gleichenstein, who was gazing at him intently.

'Even more so,' Ludwig continued, 'after poor Haydn died.'

Gleichenstein nodded. 'We were all sorry not to have been here.'

'It was only a matter of days after the bombardment. The thirty-first of May. A sad date. I was never able to see him. I regret that, but it was impossible. If only there could have been a proper funeral and memorial service.' Ludwig felt a heaviness descend on him. He spoke more to himself than Gleichenstein. 'He was a fine man. A great musician. Better than I believed. His last two oratorios proved that. When I thought he had finished, he produced his greatest work. Mozart could see it, though. He told me. And I didn't believe it.'

He gave a grunt of dissatisfaction and gulped the rest of the wine. His ears rang. 'Damn my ears,' he said. 'Damn them. Damn the pain they cause me.'

He was startled to feel Gleichenstein's hand on his arm. 'Sir, forgive my impertinence, but there is something I would like to suggest to you. I have become acquainted with a charming family of Italian extraction. Signor Malfatti is a merchant. He has two daughters who, I might say, are delightful. He also has a cousin who is a doctor. He is an excellent doctor. Now that Doktor Schmidt . . . I am only suggesting that should you wish to consult someone about your hearing, I can recommend Doktor Malfatti most highly.'

Ludwig studied him and kept his temper. 'Young man,' he said tightly, 'I have no need of doctors. They can do nothing for me, with their potions and their tuning forks and their talk about a cure. If I need powders for my stomach I will ask your Italian friend. I fear my hearing will never return.'

Ludwig tried to summon the face to fit the name but it would not come. All he could remember were the dancing auburn curls and the deep, wide, dark eyes. But wasn't Antonie Brentano in Frankfurt, where she lived with her husband and children?

Antonie Brentano. She had signed her name with a curly flourish, the line from the final vowel trailing down the page and fading into nothing. The note was short and direct.

> Herr Beethoven
> You would bring me infinite pleasure if you were to call on me at my father's house, 98 Erdbeergasse in the Landstrasse, tomorrow afternoon at 4 o'clock.
>
> > Your admirer
> > Antonie Brentano

In his dream that night her face came to him, as clear as if she were standing before him. But when he awoke the next morning, try as he might, he could not conjure it back into his mind. Just the tumbling ringlets and the deep, dark eyes. And the gentle voice telling him that yes, she understood what he was trying to say with his music. She knew the meaning of the Eroica.

He felt nervous as he took a carriage to the Landstrasse suburb. He had instructed his servant to tell any callers he was going to Döbling to walk by the river. The Erdbeergasse, he was gratified to learn, was further out of the city and in a different area from where Andreas and Nanette Streicher lived. He ordered the driver to stop as soon as they turned into the wide street lined with linden trees, dismounted and told him not to wait.

The house was imposing, built of a dark grey stone with a pillar either side of the wide front door. He felt a moment of panic. He should not have come. He knew what Antonie wanted – it was obvious. She would ask him to give her piano lessons. Why else would she have asked him to come? And he would have to say no. He loathed teaching and had long since resolved never to take on another student.

He could not help the gasp he gave when the heavy door was swung back by Antonie herself. She was smiling broadly and stood back to allow him in. How well he remembered her face now! Still framed by the curls, her eyes wide and shining, her lips parted in a smile.

He bowed and entered.

'Herr Beethoven, I cannot tell you how happy you have made me by coming to see me. Such a long way from the city. I scarcely dared hope you would take the trouble.' He had forgotten how soft her voice was, its purity, its mellifluous tone soothing to his ears.

His eyes adjusted quickly to the gloomy interior. The wide entrance hall to the house was like a museum. Objects stood everywhere – there was scarcely a free space on the floor or walls: antique urns, oil lamps, vases, marble busts, glass-topped cases, telescopes on stands, and on the walls, maps, engravings, drawings, paintings.

'It's terrible, isn't it?' Antonie said. 'Like something from a past era. And look in these cases.'

Ludwig gazed at hundreds of insects, butterflies, moths, and even small birds, all neatly laid out, their wings secured with pins. Other cases held coin collections, ancient artifacts and documents, each neatly labelled with a description and an estimated date.

'And here, the pride of my father's collection,' she said, walking to a tall glass case. 'The sword of the Emperor Carolus.'

'Your father's collection?' Ludwig regretted his words immediately as sadness eclipsed the brightness of Antonie's face.

'Yes. He collected them all through his life. Many of these things I grew up with. My brother and I used to run around in here and he used to scold us and tell us how precious they were and we were not allowed to touch anything. My childhood friends used to find them horrible. They said it was like coming to a museum. But to me they are part of my childhood.'

He looked at her melancholy, beautiful face. 'But now they make you sad?'

'I have to sell them all. My father died a month ago. I nursed him in his final illness. That is why I came to Vienna. Come with me, into the morning room. It is cosy in there.'

Ludwig followed her down a short corridor into a relatively small bright room, the sofas and chairs informal and comfortable. A small piano stood in the corner.

'This is my part of the house,' Antonie said. 'I have three rooms. My father gave them to me when I was fifteen and returned from the cloister.'

'The cloister?'

She walked to a small table where a pot and cups stood, along with several plates of cake. 'I made tea. Do you drink it? I like it so much more than coffee.' She poured Ludwig a cup and brought it to him, along with a selection of cakes. Then she came with a cup for herself and sat down in a chair near him. 'But I did not invite you here to tell you about my dismal past.'

'Tell me. I'd like to hear. But . . .' Ludwig smiled, 'you'll have to speak a little more forcefully. My hearing is no better.'

A look of deep compassion came over Antonie's face. 'Oh, I am so sorry. Of course. Here I am, just talking about myself. I –'

'No, no. Go on. I want to hear.'

She sipped her tea. 'My mother died when I was eight. On my birthday.' He saw her lower lip tremble but she continued, 'My father sent me to a cloister. My brother stayed at home. He could not manage both of us, and I was too young to be of any assistance in the house. I was there for seven years. I missed my poor papa so much.'

Ludwig's heart went out to her. The tears in her eyes made them seem deeper than ever. He broke off a piece of cake and chewed it but the curious dryness at the back of his throat made it difficult to swallow. He drank more tea, and tried to hide a grimace at its watery flavourless taste.

'I was so pleased to return home. But I was not here as long as I wished. My father needed to . . . he needed me . . . it was time I was married. He found me my dear Franz and we were married in St Stephansdom when I had just turned eighteen. He is from Frankfurt and we were to live there. I left my beloved papa and the beloved city of my birth.'

'But you came back. I met you when –'

She nodded eagerly. 'I heard your wonderful music at the palace of Prince Lobkowitz. A new symphony you had composed. I was transported. It seemed to be speaking directly to me. I understood it, in the same way I understand a language. I had never heard any music like it. Herr Beethoven, I –'

'Ludwig,' he said quickly. 'Please call me by my first name.'

'Then will you call me Toni?'

He smiled in agreement. 'So you came back to Vienna?'

'I come back to Vienna as often as I can, but it is not very often. Until now. And this time for the most melancholy of reasons. The house feels so empty, although there is so much in it.' She took a little lace handkerchief from her sleeve and wiped her eyes. 'And soon it will be emptier still, when I have sold everything.'

Ludwig sipped his tea again.

A sparkle came into her eyes. 'But there is no cloud without its silver lining. With so much work to do I will be in Vienna for some time. It will take months to dispose of everything. And soon my darling children will come to join me.'

'Children?'

'Four precious children. The youngest, Fanny, is just four. Oh, I am so sad to be away from them. My sister-in-law Bettina is looking after them. She will bring them to Vienna soon. And Franz has promised that he will consider opening a branch of his bank here. Then I will have even more excuse to return often to Vienna. But, Ludwig, I have been so selfish telling you all about myself. You must tell me. Are you composing?'

'I recently completed a piano concerto, and a new sonata – both for the Archduke. The final movement of the sonata is to be composed when he returns to the city.'

Antonie stirred in her chair. 'Now, my dear friend. You must allow me to tell you the real reason I invited you here this afternoon. You expected me to ask you to play the piano but I shall not do that. I remember your friend Herr Breuning telling me how much you disliked that. *I* am going to play for *you*. If you will permit me, that is.'

Ludwig signalled his approval but braced himself for the impact the piano would make on his ears. He wondered what she would play. Bach, most likely. It was what the ladies of Vienna played most readily: there was a uniformity to his writing that appealed to them.

The last thing he expected to hear was the simple lilting melody that opened the Andante Grazioso. He sighed.

Antonie immediately stopped playing. 'I have offended you,' she said. 'I can see it in your face. I am sorry.'

'No, no. Go on. Play it. Please.'

He listened to the simple melody, followed by its development, the lively middle section of high descending notes. He wondered how she would cope with the difficult, tempestuous passage he had written near the end.

He relaxed at her simple solution: she played it at half speed and, to his surprise, he did not mind. He knew he was being irrational, that if Ries or Czerny or Hummel or anyone else played it at half speed he would shout at them to stop and order them not to play it again until they could do so properly. Why, then, did he not mind Antonie doing that? She played the two final soft chords and he looked at her expectant face. He wanted her to speak first. The sound of his own voice after the music he knew, would, be harsh.

Eventually she said, in a rush, 'Was it . . . ? Did I . . . ? I hope that was all right.'

He nodded. 'I should rename that piece. Andante Favori. Yes, that is what I shall call it from now on. It seems I cannot escape from it!'

She stood up and went back to her chair. 'I shouldn't have played it. I have displeased you.'

'No, Antonie. Toni. You have not. You play with a delicate touch. I am pleased you played it. Now, you will excuse me, but I have work to return to.'

'Oh, of course. I have been so selfish. I am so glad you came. I enjoyed meeting you again.'

'And I you,' Ludwig said. Then he took her hand, lowered his head to it and brushed it with his lips.

Chapter 2

Almost as suddenly as they had appeared on the streets of Vienna, the French soldiers melted away. At the same time, those Viennese who had not thought it safe to return home now did so. The reason was an event so stunning, so unexpected, that the people of Vienna thought a monstrous trick was being played on them. When the *Wiener Zeitung* confirmed the truth of it there was rejoicing on the streets. Street-sellers began to trade once more, the coffee houses and taverns filled and those keen to show off the latest fashions strolled again on the Bastion promenade and in the public parks.

It was inconceivable but true. Emperor Napoleon, conqueror of Austria, destroyer of Vienna, was to marry the daughter of Emperor Franz. The old enemies, Austria and France, were to be united by marriage. Can you believe, voices said amid smiling faces and waving arms, our own emperor is to be father-in-law to the Emperor of France!

While Vienna was coming to terms with the extraordinary development, Ludwig received a piece of welcome news. It was Gleichenstein who brought it. 'Herr Hartl, sir, he wishes you to compose music to accompany a forthcoming production of Herr Goethe's play *Egmont*. He has asked me to give you the text to read.'

'Goethe,' said Ludwig. 'Yes. A better poet for the musician than Schiller. Who can set Schiller's words to music?'

'It is for the next spring season at the Burgtheater, which gives you five months or more. Can I tell him you accept?'

'Hartl? That scoundrel? Yes, I will do it, though he does not deserve it.'

Ludwig quicky read the play about the Flemish Count Egmont who gave his life in the fight against the Spanish oppressors. The theme – and its relevance to such recent events in Vienna – appealed to him. A clear image of the faithful heroine Clärchen formed in his mind. It brought him great pleasure that her love for the doomed Count, her loyalty to the cause of freedom that he espoused, and her determination to accompany him in death brought the image of Antonie Brentano into his mind each time he considered her. Swiftly, he sketched out the central piece of the drama, Clärchen's song. He wanted nothing more than to sit at the piano and hear Toni sing it.

On a cold day in late November, with the rain falling steadily, Ludwig – his head filled with the sounds of Clärchen's words – took a carriage to Heiligenstadt, the rain steaming off the horse's flank and filling his nostrils with a dank odour. He thrust a few coins at the driver, shook his head at the man's offer to wait for him, and strode up through the vineyards of the lower slopes of the Kahlenberg.

The rain beat down on his head, matting his hair and running in rivulets down his forehead. On and up he strode, the sounds he had written revolving in his mind. Soon just the last two lines of Clärchen's song repeated themselves, over and over again.

Glücklich allein	Only the soul that has
Ist die Seele, die liebt	Loved, can know joy

Only the soul that has loved can know joy. Soaked to the skin with the rain, he stood finally on the summit of the Kahlenberg and gazed down on the city, shrouded in a mist that rose from the warmth of the cobbles. The sharp spire of St Stephansdom pierced it like a knife tearing a piece of cloth. To the right of the city, and close to it, pushing the mist up into an irregular shape, was the Spittelberg hill, from which he knew the French howitzers had fired after the initial bombardment from the Kahlenberg. Around him, great brown gashes were cut like scars into the grass where the cannon had been hauled into position, tiny beads of ice coating the frozen mud, like frosting on a chocolate cake. Behind him the trunks of the tall pines were seared white where flames from hidden cannon had blazed over them. Such destruction . . . and for what?

He walked along the summit of the hill, singing at the top of his voice, the rain trickling down his neck and under his shirt. *Only the soul that has loved can know joy.* Toni's face, her soft, gentle, smiling face, swam into his mind. It was there now, clearly.

He did not need to tell himself he loved her; he knew it. And maybe, maybe, it was just possible that she loved him. He did not need to tell himself either that it was a hopeless love, a doomed love. He knew that too. They could never live together, never know the joy of loving one another.

He shook his head and the rain flew off his hair in front of his eyes. The drops of water might have been tears. Fate, again, he thought. My destiny.

The fever took hold with a ferocity that felled him. Its harbinger was the throbbing pain in his head to which he had grown accustomed but no amount of wine would dull it. He wanted to work; he needed to work. But in the end only sleep – a restless, fitful sleep – provided him with any relief. Voices drifted in and out of his head. He opened his eyes occasionally to see anxious faces looking down at him, but before he could focus on them he drifted back into sleep. He was aware of a cold cloth being pressed to his burning forehead, which, ineffective at first, slowly began to reduce the fever. Finally he was able to sit up, and sip the warm soup Nanette Streicher held to his lips. 'You've had a dreadful fever. Doktor Bertolini came to see you. He is a friend of ours. He said there was nothing to be done but to let it run its course. How are you feeling?'

'Nanette, my head is pounding and my ears are howling. I can tell what you are saying because I know you are speaking clearly. But the fever has made my hearing worse.'

'Maybe as you get better your hearing will get better too.'

Ludwig growled, 'Why does everyone always try to tell me that? I need some wine.'

Nanette said, with kindly disdain, 'You certainly will not have any. Doctor Bertolini ordered it. No wine until you are completely recovered, and then only in small amounts. I have told your servant he is not to bring you any.'

After several days, though still weak, Ludwig was able to dress and resume work on *Egmont*. At the back of his cupboard was a carafe of wine he had left there before he had fallen ill. He drank it slowly, savouring the taste.

The ringing in his ears was more intense than he had ever known, and after an hour of work sweat broke out on his forehead and he felt dizzy.

The fever struck a second time – the pounding in his head, the screeching in his ears, and his skin was so sore that even turning under the sheet was agony.

Again faces, voices. In his mind the face of Antonie. But he could never focus his eyes on her.

He tossed in a fitful sleep, eyes screwed tight shut against the pain in his head. When, at last, it began to pass he awoke to see Nanette's loving face. 'Ignaz is bringing a new doctor to see you. Doktor Malfatti.' Ludwig was too exhausted to protest.

He took immediately to the Italian when he came the next day, accompanied by Gleichenstein. He was a tall, thin man, with a long, mournful face. The pendulous bags under his eyes were reflected in cheeks that hung down the sides of his face like sacks.

'Doktor Bloodhound, I shall call you.'

The unsmiling doctor walked towards him and held up his wrist, measuring his pulse.

'Or Doktor Time-waster. Maybe that is better.'

Doktor Malfatti felt his forehead, clammy and hot to the touch. He made Ludwig lie back on the pillow, undid his nightshirt and held a hearing trumpet to his chest. He pulled a wooden spatula from his case, flattened Ludwig's tongue with it and looked to the back of his throat. He took another, slimmer trumpet from his case, inserted it first in Ludwig's left ear, then the right, and gazed in. 'Your hearing troubles you, mmh?'

His voice was deep and strong and penetrated the fog that hung in Ludwig's head like the mist that had hung over the city.

'It always has, it always will.'

'You are probably right,' said Doktor Malfatti.

Ludwig had not expected such a response, and its pessimism was outweighed by his relief that he would not have to argue. He saw the doctor say something to Nanette, who returned a few minutes later with a towel.

'Sit up and lean forward,' said Malfatti.

Ludwig did as he said. Malfatti held an ice-cold towel against the back of his neck. Suddenly the pain in his head seemed to dissipate, to be replaced by an unexpected clarity. 'That's good. That's better,' he heard himself saying.

'Put your hand on it. Hold it there and lean back.'

Ludwig did as he was told.

'It will melt soon, but it will have done you good.'

Ludwig could hardly hear Malfatti's words. His ears felt deadened, as if the cloth he was holding also filled his head, but the dreadful throbbing pain had gone.

'It helps, but it does not cure. Its cold causes more blood to come to the brain, but it is temporary relief only. It will not cure your deafness.'

Ludwig felt the melting ice begin to run between his fingers. Nanette scooped up the cloth, and tossed it into a porcelain basin.

'Rest is the only remedy. For the fever, not the deafness. I do not know what caused your deafness, Herr Beethoven, but I suspect medical science will not be of much use to you.'

'I want to drink wine. I find it helps.'

Malfatti pursed his lips. 'Why not if it relaxes you? It has medicinal qualities we should not ignore.'

'But not too much,' said Nanette. 'It hurts your stomach.'

'Let Herr Beethoven be the judge,' said Malfatti. 'If he is suffering and he finds it helps . . . We doctors should accept readily anything that improves our patients' condition. You were told your hearing would improve, I presume?'

Ludwig made a gesture of assent.

'The first rule for the doctor: assure your patient his health will improve so that when it does you can take the credit. I do not do that. You are deaf, Herr Beethoven. A man of your age – what, around forty? – whose hearing deteriorates over a period of time is unlikely to recover it. I cannot make you any false promises.'

The fever left Ludwig but the weakness remained. He walked to the piano and took several sheets of manuscript paper back to bed. He almost collapsed on it with the relief of taking the weight off his legs. Sitting up in bed, beating time, singing tunelessly, the music clear in his head, he worked on *Egmont*. But the effort drained him and he knew that he could do no more than make notes and sketches until he was stronger.

Slowly his appetite returned. The servant brought him food and wine. At first he could only take small amounts, but gradually he ate more.

One late afternoon, after several hours' composing, he was sprawled at the table, his head on his arms. Imperceptibly at first, then stronger, a wonderful aroma wafted into the room.

He sat upright. It was chicken cooking. Nanette. He went quickly across to the cupboard and put away the wine. He was grateful to her but she would interrogate him about how he felt, how much rest he was taking, and make him promise he was not drinking wine, despite what the Italian doctor had said . . .

He sat at the piano deliberately, and was playing a series of chords when the door opened. When he turned, his heart missed a beat.

'Toni.'

'I made it for you at home, Ludwig. I knew you would need it. It will help make you strong.'

He left the piano and went to the table. 'You are kind. I am grateful.'

She put down the tray, lifted the plate off it, and ladled the chicken broth from a cauldron into it. Carefully she added two dumplings. 'There. That will do you good.'

Ludwig relished the warm broth, and ate hungrily, holding his spoon in the air so that Antonie could refill the plate.

Finally, he sat back, breathing heavily. 'Thank you, Toni. Thank you.'

'Better than any doctor's medicine. I am pleased to have been able to help. Now I must tell you my good news. Bettina has brought my children to me. My babies. Oh, I am so happy to be with them again. And Franz will come soon. I have written to him about you. He is so looking forward to meeting you.'

After she had gone Ludwig felt a well of loneliness in the pit of his stomach. Am I destined, he wondered, for ever to remain alone?

Chapter 3

'It's a strange kind of peace, isn't it, Herr Beethoven?' said Archduke Rudolph.

Ludwig agreed. The sound of church bells no longer hurt his ears. For days past they had rung out across the city, led by the bells of the Augustinerkirche within the walls of the Hofburg itself.

'My aunt mounts the steps of the guillotine in Paris, now my niece marries the Emperor of France in the Hofburg, with my brother who fought him on the Danube plain standing as proxy. And the people of Vienna,' he gestured through the tall windows with his arm, 'line the streets and cheer as if all the fighting and all the killing amount to nothing.'

'The peace will not last. That is what Breuning says.'

Hurriedly Archduke Rudolph put his finger to his lips. 'Even here, Herr Beethoven, we should not talk so. Neither of us would wish to offend His Excellency Count Metternich. Who knows what punishment he might inflict on us? Safer by far – and more enjoyable – to talk of music. But before that, is all well with your contract? Are the payments being made regularly?'

'I believe so. Gleichenstein has not told me otherwise.'

'Good.' The Archduke was silent for a moment. 'Will you let me know if there are any problems? I am slightly concerned. I believe that prices will soon go up and money will be short – the effect of war. The effect no soldier considers when he talks of the glory of battle. But let us talk of music. What work are you doing?'

'I was ill for some time. Longer than usual. Twice I had the fever. It has put me behind. But Hartl will soon have his *Egmont*, and I have in mind a new trio, piano, violin and cello.'

'Remarkable,' said the Archduke, his pleasure evident. 'While I was away I composed some pieces myself. Will you look at them?'

'If I have time,' Ludwig said, masking his reluctance. He was beginning to find conversation difficult. The heaviness in his ears was markedly worse since his illness. 'Will you allow me to play you this?' he asked. 'Then I must return to my lodgings.' He held up a folder.

'But of course, of course. How remiss of me. Dreadfully selfish.' The Archduke crossed to the tall windows and closed them.

The sudden silence enveloped Ludwig and he hoped the other man would not speak. Now he wanted only to hear music. Silently he walked over to the piano, his feet sinking into the thick Chinese carpet, and sat at it. He felt the presence of the Archduke at his shoulder. He pointed to the word he had written at the top of a page which was otherwise in the neat hand of the copyist Wenzel Schlemmer. *Das Wiedersehen*. The Return. Underneath it, *Vivacissimamente*.

He played a *forte* chord of E flat in both hands. He held it longer than the sharp quaver on the page, allowing the sound to enter his head, to flood his brain and banish all others.

Lowering his head slowly he allowed the fingers of both hands to run up the keyboard in the series of unbroken semiquavers, then right hand only, another huge chord, and suddenly the music slowed, a gentle, swaying theme. Ludwig allowed his head to sway with the notes, first in the right hand, then the left, more driving semiquavers, before an extraordinary sequence of *sforzando* staccato crotchets, their sounds blurring into each other by the pedal being held down, a key change, and then off with flying semiquavers again.

The Archduke turned the page, but it was not necessary. Ludwig knew the notes as intimately as other people knew the words of a language; and as others did in speech or writing, he varied what he had said, embellished it, took it in a different direction. He smiled as the Archduke hesitated, not knowing whether to turn the page, unable any longer to follow because the notes he was playing were not on the page. Ludwig sang as he played, allowing his fingers to roam where they wished. So many ideas to explore, he thought. A feeling of exhilaration and even relaxation flowed through his body. The notes did not jar or clash with each other. Each was in its rightful place and he heard it clearly. He began to experiment. Lifting his hands from the keys, the music continued in his head. He was hearing music although he was not playing. And when he played again, he heard not only the music in his head but the music he was making too. Perfectly they blended. Not a single harsh sound. A perfect language.

A small pause, a raise of the head. Enough, he thought. No more to say for the moment. Two chords of E flat, the home key, and he stopped. As he had learned to do in company, he kept his hands on the keys, head bowed, to allow the sounds to revolve in his mind until finally they died away to nothing. Then he placed his palms on his thighs, slowly raised his head and sat for a moment. Finally he reached forward, took the manuscript papers, made a neat pile of them, inserted them in the folder and stood up, supporting himself on the piano.

Archduke Rudolph knew better than to talk. Instead he reached forward, clasped Ludwig's hands in his and directed him gently towards the door.

Ludwig nodded his thanks, at the last moment handing him the manuscript. He descended the Amalienhof staircase and went out into the Ballhausplatz, covering his ears as he walked until the sound of church bells faded.

'It must be the air in Vienna,' Zmeskall said, as he, Gleichenstein and Ludwig walked round the statue to the Danube river in the Neuer Markt and into the Schwan, where the sour smell of spilled wine seeped up from the stained sawdust that coated the floor. As Ludwig passed the counter he threw down a few coins and lifted a filled pipe from the rack.

He went straight to the round table at the back of the room where the Rhinelanders and their friends usually sat, waiting for the other two to bring wine and glasses. He struck the long taper, which stood upright on a small metal stand on the side of the box, touched it to the tobacco, and inhaled deeply. The smoke caught in his chest, making him cough and bringing tears to his eyes. The pain quickly subsided, he sat back, and took the glass of wine Zmeskall handed him.

He saw that his two friends were talking. He could not hear what they said but knew that sooner or later they would bring him into the conversation. He was not filled with trepidation at the thought: they knew his ears had worsened and how to speak to him so that he could hear. He was among friends, drinking wine and enjoying a pipe.

Zmeskall sat forward. 'I was saying to Ignaz, it must be the effect of all these church bells. Marriage is in the air. I have only just heard from Franz Brunsvik that his sister Josephine has married. Do you remember, I mentioned it to you some time ago?'

Ludwig drew on the pipe. He felt no hurt, and remembered his futile visits to the house on the Rothenturmgasse with some small amusement. How could Josephine compare with . . . ?

Gleichenstein was speaking now. 'Herr Beethoven, sir. Would you allow me to introduce you to the Malfatti family? You remember Doktor Malfatti, who tended you when you were sick? He is the cousin of Herr Malfatti, a merchant. I believe I have already mentioned him to you. They are a delightful family.'

Zmeskall threw back his head with a bellow of laughter. 'Hah! I shall tell you more, Ludwig. I shall tell you what Ignaz is keeping from you.' His eyes were twinkling behind the thick spectacles. 'A certain Fräulein Malfatti has rather taken his fancy. Is that not so, Ignaz? Anna, if I am not mistaken.'

Ludwig saw the colour rise in Gleichenstein's cheeks. 'Enough, Nikola. You are embarrassing me. But would you allow me to introduce you, sir? Herr Malfatti's other daughter Therese is an accomplished pianist. She frequently entertains the family to an evening of music. She sings beautifully too. I know she would like to meet you.'

Bettina Brentano bustled about the room, tidying cushions and clearing a place on the table for the tray and cups. She had a lively, vivacious face. Her hair was pulled tightly back and bundled into a knot with a net round it, which made her look older than she was. Ludwig wondered if he could ask for coffee – strong Turkish coffee in a small cup – instead of tea, but decided against it.

'Toni told me to make you tea, Herr Beethoven. She will return very soon with the children. She is so happy to be reunited with them. Mind you, she is exhausted with the effort, poor darling. I will help her while I am here, and we are employing a guardian to look after them, but it is still a strain for her. She is not strong, you know. It will be easier when Franz arrives.'

The room was heavily furnished, with a thick carpet on the floor and heavy curtains hanging alongside the windows, and Bettina's voice, which was naturally strong and rather high-pitched, floated easily to Ludwig. It was obvious, too, that Antonie had told her about his hearing: she looked directly at him when she spoke and took extra care with her enunciation. So be it, he thought. The days when he had felt ill at ease when people did this had long since passed.

'When is Herr Brentano coming?'

'I am not sure. It depends on his business. He is such a busy man. He always has been. I remember when I was a child, he was already a grown man. He is twenty years older than I. He is my half-brother, I don't know if you knew that. I have always looked up to him. So impressive, so important. Father took him into his business, and after he died, poor Papa, Franz took it over. He has expanded it, not just spices and dyes but banking now too. I think,' she said, 'that is why he is considering expanding the business to Vienna. So many banking opportunities. Of course, dear Toni is thrilled.'

'She is happy here?'

'Oh, so happy.' Bettina clasped her hands. 'I can see it so clearly. She is not really happy in Frankfurt. She pretends, to keep Franz happy, but it is a large house, rather cold. And of course, this is her city, where she was born. Franz understands that.'

Suddenly the door opened and a small girl bounded in. She stood in front of Ludwig, looking straight into his eyes. 'Hello. My name is Maximiliane. Maximiliane Euphrosyne Kunigunde Brentano. You may call me Maxi. I am seven. You are a musician, aren't you? My mummy told me to speak loudly to you, so I am.'

Ludwig could not prevent the smile that spread across his face, but before he could speak Antonie hurried over and swept her daughter out of the way. 'I am so sorry, Ludwig. You must forgive her. She is so high-spirited.' She pulled a chair close to him, saying as she sat down, 'Run along, Maxi. To the playroom – find the others. Leave us undisturbed for now.'

The child hurried off, clearly pleased to be ordered to leave the adults.

'So you have met my dear sister-in-law Bettina. I am so sorry to have made you wait. I was delayed. Maxi insisted on dragging me into yet one more shop on the Kohlmarkt.'

'Poor Herr Beethoven,' said Bettina, 'I have been bombarding him with information. He has been exceedingly patient.'

Ludwig smiled but said nothing.

'Well, Ludwig,' said Antonie, 'I shall spare you my other offspring. Maxi is quite enough for now. Tina, have you told Ludwig of your distinguished friend?'

'I am afraid I did not get round to that. But, Herr Beethoven, I must tell you. Herr Goethe is a great friend of my family. My father knew him well.'

At first Ludwig was not sure that he had heard her properly. 'Goethe?'

'Yes. The great poet and playwright. I believe you are acquainted with his works.'

'I am,' said Ludwig. 'I have set several of his poems to music, and I am working on accompanying music for his play *Egmont*, which is to be put on at the Burg.'

Bettina's hands flew to her mouth. 'Oh, how marvellous! When you have finished, you must send the music to Herr Goethe. I know he will be delighted to receive it. Will you do that?'

'I . . . Maybe, yes.'

'Oh, but you must meet him. He takes the waters in Bohemia most summers. Why do you not go there and meet him?'

Ludwig had never considered contacting Goethe before, let alone meeting him, but before he could give any further thought to the matter, Antonie said, 'We, too, sadly, must shortly go to Bohemia, Franz and I. With our precious little Fanny. She is only four, and she suffers dreadfully with her lungs. The doctors have recommended the Bohemian spas.'

'Have you been to Bohemia, Herr Beethoven?' Bettina asked.

'No. To Prague, but not to Bohemia.'

'Oh, it is so beautiful. You really must go one day.'

'Bettina is right, Ludwig. It *is* beautiful.' Antonie picked up the teapot and moved towards him.

He put out his hand to stop her. 'Thank you, but I must return to my apartment and continue working. It has been a pleasure.'

'For us too,' she said. 'I will let you know when Franz arrives. I am so looking forward to you meeting him. Now, I must go to little Fanny.'

Ludwig stood up, bowed formally to the two women and left.

Chapter 4

Ludwig accompanied Gleichenstein with some reluctance to the wide-fronted house on the busy Kärntnerstrasse. Only Gleichenstein's assurances that the Malfattis were a truly delightful family had persuaded him to come.

As Doktor Malfatti had predicted his deafness had not improved but, perhaps perversely, now that a doctor had confirmed what Ludwig had always known, he had the confidence to accept it – and admit to it. He had already found that the words 'My doctor has advised me' carried so much more weight than his own prediction, which had always been dismissed by his friends as unnecessarily pessimistic. And that Doktor Malfatti would certainly have informed the family of his famous patient's disability made it less difficult for Ludwig to yield to Gleichenstein's urgings to accompany him to meet Anna, her sister Therese and their parents.

A sharp, irregular rasping sound bewildered Ludwig when he and Gleichenstein entered the Malfattis' drawing room until he saw Gleichenstein drop nearly to the floor, his arms stretched out. The dog – a spaniel with floppy ears and a shiny black nose – stopped barking and advanced towards him tail wagging.

A large woman in a voluminous dress swept towards them. 'Gigons!' she ordered. 'Stop now! Come! Sit! Ignaz, how good of you to come to see us.'

'Madame.' Gleichenstein took her hand and bent his head over it. 'This is Herr Beethoven, of whom I have spoken to you. Sir, Madame Malfatti.'

Ludwig bowed but did not take her hand.

'Sir, such an honour to meet you. But how impolite of Gigons to give you such a noisy welcome. Now, come through to the salon and meet my husband and daughters.'

The drawing room was not large, but hung with sumptuous curtains and with a thick carpet on the floor that felt luxuriously soft under Ludwig's feet. He followed Gleichenstein's lead and bowed to the portly man with black wavy hair, who Ludwig estimated was about his own age and who stood with hands clasped behind him under his tailcoat.

'Herr Malfatti, sir. May I present the renowned musician Herr Beethoven, whom I am honoured to call my friend?'

'Delighted, sir,' said Malfatti. 'Great honour indeed. No musician myself, but I've heard, sir, I've heard. Daughters are great admirers.' He nodded to his wife who in turn nodded towards an open door.

Two young women entered, one a pace in front of the other. Ludwig caught his breath at the effect. Rustling dresses, delicate hands holding them a little above the floor so that small pointed shoes peeped out, and the scent of sweet perfume that floated across the room.

'Gigons!' The first young woman bent low and began to caress the dog, which wagged its tail so hard that the rest of its body moved in time to it.

'Therese!' said Malfatti sharply. 'You will allow me to introduce you.'

'So sorry, Papa,' she said, standing upright and casting a look towards Ludwig that almost caused his heart to stop.

'My daughters, sir. Therese and Anna, whom we call Netty. Girls, this is Vienna's distinguished musician, Herr van Beethoven. No need to introduce you to young Gleichenstein. You know him well enough.'

Ludwig watched Gleichenstein approach Anna, and knew immediately from the young man's smile that Zmeskall had spoken the truth. It was as clear as daylight that they were in love.

'Herr Beethoven,' said Therese, holding her hand towards him. He took it and bowed his head.

'Mademoiselle,' he said, 'I am honoured.' He felt movement at his feet, looked down and saw the little dog brushing against his ankle.

'Do you see, sir?' said Therese, with a delightful lilt in her voice. 'Gigons has taken to you straight away. He is a most musical dog. He loves it when Netty and I play.'

'Oh, girls, you must play for Herr Beethoven. Sir, my daughters are such accomplished musicians.'

'Mama,' said Netty, quietly. 'Please do not –'

'Yes, we will, we will, won't we, Netty?' said Therese exuberantly.

'Enough, girls!' said Malfatti. 'Therese, you sound like a chattering bird. Now, come, sit down everybody. I will ask Werner to bring in a bottle of wine. Girls, you will have tea.'

Ludwig sat down, sinking back into the soft chair. He immediately pulled himself a little further forward – its padded wings would prevent voices reaching his ears. He was rather uncomfortable, and had to grasp the sides of the chair to stop himself slipping back.

Therese was chattering. He could hear her voice clearly but was paying no attention to what she was saying, beyond registering that it was to do with a shopping trip she and her sister had made. He was trying to judge the welcome she had given him. She had come straight over and made a point of saying how the dog had taken to him. It must be, he thought, that she was trying to tell him how she herself had taken to him, but could not be quite that bold.

He looked at her lively face, so animated. She was young, with all the vivaciousness of her age. She could not be more than eighteen – he was over forty. How could she possibly . . . ?

Frau Malfatti was talking to him. '. . . need your advice, Herr Beethoven. We are purchasing a new pianoforte. Ours is a little old now and scarcely up to the demands we impose on it. I have been to Schanz's pianoforte shop on the Wallnerstrasse. Close to the Kohlmarkt. Do you know it?'

Ludwig nodded. 'Mine are made –'

'Herr Schanz is so delightful. He helped me choose a very nice instrument and he said he would lower the price to below five hundred gulden. Is that not a very good price?'

Ludwig coughed into his hand to clear his throat. 'I have heard his pianofortes are excellent. I am sure you will be pleased.'

'Papa, Mama! Netty and I will play for Herr Beethoven. You will let us, won't you?'

'Would you like to hear my daughters play, Herr Beethoven?' asked Frau Malfatti.

Ludwig glanced at Malfatti and saw that he could no longer restrain both his wife and his daughters. 'Of course. I would be delighted.' He knew that after they had played he would be asked to play and, of course, he did not want to. But how could he refuse?

With some interest he saw Netty reach behind a sofa and bring out a mandolin. She went to the piano where her sister was already sitting and striking an A for Netty to tune the strings.

Therese turned to him and said, 'I believe you will recognise this, Herr Beethoven. Though I confess to making some of the passages simpler. I hope you will not mind.'

Ludwig sat back; the wings of the chair now channelled the music directly towards his ears. He smiled at the piece for mandolin and piano he had composed years earlier for old Krumpholz, the mandolin player.

It was gentle, lyrical. Netty was plucking the strings with a delicate touch, too delicate to allow the instrument to sing with its natural voice, and Therese had reduced the piano part to little more than simple chords with an occasional flourish. The sisters were playing it as though it was a funeral march, he thought, but what did it matter? It was bringing them pleasure. At least they knew the piece and that he had composed it.

When it ended he joined the others in applauding. He saw the radiant smile on Gleichenstein's face as he looked at Netty. Therese's cheeks were flushed and she was breathing heavily, her bosom rising and falling. She was looking straight at him.

'Did we play it well, Herr Beethoven? Oh, I do hope you think so.' She hurried back to her chair and fixed her eyes on him.

He sat forward in his chair and glanced round the room. Everyone was awaiting his judgement.

'I . . . Yes, it was delightfully played. You are – both – very talented musicians.'

Therese let out a small squeal, her cheeks colouring even more. 'There, Papa, I told you he would like it. Imagine! Playing a piece of music in front of the very person who composed it and being complimented by him. Oh, Herr Beethoven –' She stopped suddenly. 'Your name is Ludwig, isn't it? May I call you Ludwig?'

'You may not, young lady,' said her father sternly. 'You are addressing a most distinguished man who is frequently received at the Hofburg by the highest in the land. You shall refer to him with proper respect.'

'Herr Beethoven,' she said, excitement filling her voice, 'would you do me the great honour of composing a piece of music for me? That I can play on the piano. Not too difficult, of course. I would be so much obliged to you.'

'Therese,' said her mother, 'sometimes I am shocked at your boldness. Herr Beethoven, you must forgive my impetuous daughter. But perhaps you would not mind if I asked you a much simpler favour. Maybe you would entertain us on the piano instead. We would enjoy that greatly.'

'Madame,' Ludwig said, 'you will forgive me, I am sure. Gleichenstein will tell you that only recently I was in poor health. And my hearing causes me problems. But I would gladly fulfil your daughter's request. I will compose a short piece for you, Therese.'

Two days later Ludwig accompanied Frau Malfatti to Schanz's pianoforte shop in the Wallnerstrasse. Schanz fussed around him, clearly aware of who he was, and invited him to play on the piano he had selected for Frau Malfatti. Ludwig sat at it and played a few chords. It rocked under his heavy touch. How flimsy it was compared to Streicher's pianos, Ludwig thought, and the keys did not play as smoothly either – there seemed to be a slight resistance to them. He played a run. One of the keys stayed depressed.

Schanz said, 'It's nothing. Just a touch of oil where the string . . .' He hurried over to a table and returned holding a dirty can with a long thin spout, curved at the end. He leaned over the piano with it, pulling some strings. Ludwig watched several keys move, as if pressed by invisible fingers. 'There. Because it's new, you see. Play it now, Herr von Bethofen.'

Ludwig played a simple theme. It had been in his head and he allowed his fingers to wander where they wished.

Slowly a tune emerged, a revolving, turning phrase in the right hand, answered by a rising response in the left. He played it several times, refining it each time, finally ending with a chord.

'Oh, so delightful,' said Frau Malfatti. 'May I ask what it is?'

Ludwig kept his eyes closed until the chord had died away. 'Just a *rondo*. Nothing more. A fine piano, Frau Malfatti. I can recommend it.'

Schanz rubbed his hands together. 'Sir, Herr von Bethofen, what an honour. May I say that you recommend my pianos? I know –'

'No, Schanz. Ask Hummel. He will be pleased to recommend them, I am sure.'

As Ludwig walked Frau Malfatti towards her carriage, she said to him, 'You are so kind, Herr Beethoven. You know, my daughter has become exceedingly fond of you.'

Ludwig was startled. Could it be that his first suspicions

were correct? The way Therese had greeted him, looked at
him . . .

'We are having a soirée in a week's time. Other friends are
coming. Would you honour us with your presence? Ignaz will,
of course, be coming for Netty. We would be so pleased. I
know how happy it would make Therese.'

Ludwig thanked her, bowed and helped her on to the
carriage step.

In his apartment Ludwig again played the simple *rondo* theme
that had grown under his fingers in Schanz's. He took a piece
of manuscript paper and scribbled it down, a turning phrase in
the right hand, descending, answered by the left ascending. The
middle section was insistent chords, but not difficult to play,
before the main theme resumed. The whole thing lasted no
more than two or three minutes.

He smiled when he finished, shaking his head. The piece was
not worthy of him, but who knew where it might lead? If it
achieved its objective, it would have been worth it. No one of
importance, no musicians certainly, would ever hear it. It would
disappear, forgotten, in a matter of weeks or even days. He took
clean manuscript paper and began to copy it out. There was no
point in sending it to Schlemmer; he could do it himself in an
hour. And he would certainly never offer it for publication.

That evening, the wine relaxing him after composing the
piece, he decided to write some letters, first to his old friend
Franz Wegeler in Koblenz. He began with the usual courtesies
and then came to the purpose of the letter.

> I know that you will not refuse a friend's request when I ask
> you to obtain for me *my certificate of baptism*. But take note of
> the fact that I had a brother *born before me*, who was also called
> Ludwig, but with the additional name of 'Maria', and who died.
> The sooner you send the certificate of baptism, the greater will
> be my gratitude . . . Embrace and kiss your beloved wife and
> your children and all whom you are fond of – on behalf of
>
> >   Your friend
> >   BEETHOVEN

When he had finished, he walked into the bedroom and over to
the washstand. A mirror stood on it, behind the porcelain bowl.
He picked it up and clucked in disgust. A crack ran diagonally
across it, and he moved it this way and that, amused at the

disfigurement it caused to his face. He ran one hand through his hair, pulling at it with his fingers. The comb that lay on the marble top was missing several teeth. He went to the chest of drawers that stood by the wardrobe. In the top drawer lay his linen. He pulled it out and sorted it into piles on the bed. Four shirts, one with a tear, and only two neckcloths, neither pure white.

He returned to the table and wrote a note to Gleichenstein.

Dear kind Gleichenstein
  I am sending you herewith 300 florins and please, since I understand nothing whatever about such matters but also such things are distasteful to me, do please buy for me some linen or Bengal cotton for shirts and at least half a dozen neckcloths, and have the tailor Lind make them up for me at the earliest opportunity and without delay –

An idea came to him. He pushed the piece of paper to one side and pulled across a clean one. How could he ask this of his old friend without in consequence being made to suffer mercilessly? He poured more wine, and picked up the quill his friend had given him.

Cursed tipsy Zmeskallovich – not Count of Music, but Count of gluttony – Count of breakfast, lunch and supper and Count of wine at all times – Do please send me for a short time your looking-glass which I know hangs beside your window so that you can admire yourself and judge how your sight slowly weakens and your white hair swiftly whitens. Mine is broken, tired of the arduous daily duty I submit it to. If you would also be so kind as to buy a new one for me today, you would thereby do me a great favour.

He put down the quill and picked up the glass. He stared into the wine: tiny bubbles formed in the centre, expiring at the next moment. He thought of Doktor Schmidt and shook his head. What would he say? 'Drink less', 'eat regularly', 'sleep more'? And where was he now? Dead at fifty.

He closed his eyes and heard in his head the peal of bells that for so many days had dominated the city. A joyous sound. The sound of a wedding. He remembered how Gleichenstein had looked at Netty and how she had returned his gaze. Mutual happiness. And Stephan's face when he had spoken of Julie's sudden death.

Could happiness never be unconfined? Did it always carry within it the risk that it would die, leaving behind only pain? If so, he thought, why do we seek it all the time, as if it is the purpose of our lives?

Because we hope. We aspire. We yearn for something that we know is always just beyond our reach. And we are prepared to risk the heartache that failure will bring.

Chapter 5

Ludwig caught the unmistakable apprehension on Gleichenstein's face. 'What is it, Gleichenstein, Gleichenberg, Gleichenholz?' He laughed at his pun on Gleichenstein's name. 'Here, share a glass with me. It will give you strength and confidence.'

'No, sir, thank you. If you will forgive me.'

'Forgive you? For all the mistakes of your life? Am I God? Yes, maybe I am. You are forgiven, Gleichenfels. See? Not *stein* but *fels*. Not a stone but a rock. Far stronger.'

Gleichenstein smiled. 'I am pleased to see you in good spirits, sir.'

'Good spirits? Yes, damnable good spirits, particularly when I consider how you have tried to make me as uncomfortable as possible.' He put two fingers behind his neckcloth and loosened it slightly. 'Bengal cotton? This feels more like sackcloth. You kept the money I gave you and stole it from a mason's yard.'

Gleichenstein looked shocked.

'Don't worry, my friend,' said Ludwig. 'I am making a joke.' He put a hand on the younger man's shoulder. 'You are right. I am in good spirits. Hartl has his *Egmont*. I have begun a new piano trio which the Archduke shall have. He requested it and I cannot ignore a royal command. And this evening I shall spend in the company of two delightful young ladies, one of whom,' he squeezed Gleichenstein's shoulder, 'I do believe, has stolen not sackcloth but the heart of my noble and loyal friend from Freiburg.' He was gratified to see the colour rise in Gleichenstein's cheeks. 'Now, come, shall we not join the ladies?'

'Sir, I am looking forward to the evening as much as you. But I just wanted to say that others will be there, other guests. Other friends of . . . of Therese and, of course, Anna.'

'So much the better. The Musikus will no doubt be called on to play for them, and for once I will do as I am asked. And

I will present them with this.' He snatched up a folder from the table. 'A simple little *rondo*, Gleichenstein. Nothing more. That a child could play. A gift. From me to a lady. In response to her request. Ah, Gleichenstein, I shall make her so happy with it. And then . . . then . . .'

They walked round St Stephansdom and turned down the broad Kärntnerstrasse.

'As I said, sir, there will be quite a large company this evening. I will ensure, as far as I can, that you are looked after, that you are not . . . put at a disadvantage, that you –'

'You will be my ears, Gleichenstein. Is that what you are trying to say?'

'Yes, sir. Forgive my tactlessness.'

'I will have your ears, but a certain young lady will have your eyes. Is that not right?'

They entered the wide building and walked up to the double doors that led towards the Malfattis' salon. They were open and a servant stood by them. He bowed. Ludwig saw Gleichenstein speak quietly to him. The servant, bewigged and wearing a gold braid tailcoat, led them in to the salon. 'Their Excellencies Herr Gleichenstein and Herr Bettoffen.'

Ludwig's chest tightened as he glanced round the room. Perhaps fifteen or twenty people, all conversing easily. He saw eyes flick towards him.

He felt something at his feet. Gigons was welcoming him. He smiled and lifted his foot gently, easing the little dog away. He saw a swirl of satin. Anna – Netty – was advancing towards Gleichenstein, her hands outstretched. He took them both in his and raised them to his lips.

'My sister bids me to welcome you on her behalf,' she said, turning to Ludwig. 'She is temporarily absent, but will return in a moment.'

Ludwig found her voice difficult to hear but he understood the message. A servant with a silver tray approached him. 'Punch, sir.'

Ludwig took a a dimpled crimson wine glass with a thicker than usual stem. The liquid it contained was an even deeper ruby. A piece of lemon rind floated in it. He raised it to his nose and sniffed, then tasted it. It had a rich, thick flavour, and at first the sweetness was cloying, but he took a second sip and the flavour pleased him. Within moments he felt a deep, warming sensation in his stomach.

'Herr Beethoven, delighted to see you.' Herr Malfatti held out his hand. He stood with his back as straight as a linden tree, his other hand held behind him. He was dressed in an immaculate black velvet suit, which made his crisp white shirt appear even whiter. The neckcloth was perfectly tied, the neat knot secured with a pearl-topped pin.

Ludwig coughed uneasily into his hand, conscious of the roughness of his shirt against his skin. He wanted to loosen the neckcloth, which seemed to have trapped a layer of heat against his neck. He shook Malfatti's hand and withdrew his own as quickly as he could.

Malfatti was leaning towards him. 'Be much obliged if you would step into the library for a moment. Shan't detain you. But a few words. If you don't mind.'

Ludwig followed him out of a side door, glad to leave the heat of the salon. The book-lined room calmed him.

'Thought I should tell you in advance. Fine young man here this evening. Name of Drosdick. Baron Drosdick. Inherited the title after his father died. Large estate in Styria.' He nodded at Ludwig, as if expecting a response.

Ludwig raised his glass to his lips and emptied it.

'Make sure it's refilled. In a moment. This Drosdick, Baron, as I said, has asked for my daughter's hand. Therese. Of course I gave my consent. Make a fine husband. Now, come on. I'll get that glass refilled. Like it, eh? Fine punch.'

Ludwig followed him back into the salon, trying to digest the words he had just heard. Therese was to marry another man. A baron. A damn fool baron.

As he entered the salon he saw Therese immediately.

She turned to him, smiled, turned away, said a few words to the young man she was talking to – obviously the Baron – and came over. 'Herr Beethoven. I do hope you have brought me the composition you promised. Is that it in the folder you have under your arm?' She spoke with force and clarity.

'I . . . Yes. Just a *rondo*.'

'Oh, I do hope I can play it. Will you play it for everyone tonight? Then I can learn it and say it is my very own piece of music.'

Ludwig said, 'Your father tells me . . .' He saw that Malfatti was standing nearby, as if to ensure that he heard what was said.

'Yes,' said Malfatti, 'I have told our distinguished guest the good news. We must all drink to your health, Therese. Yours and your fiancé's.'

Before Ludwig could say another word, Malfatti called for silence. 'Ladies and gentlemen, distinguished guests. May I welcome you all to our humble home and thank you for giving us the opportunity to enjoy your company. You have made my dear wife and me most happy. Shortly I shall ask our most distinguished guest the Musikus, here to entertain us with his formidable talent. But first may I ask you all to raise your glasses and toast our beloved daughter Therese and her fiancé Wilhelm, Baron Drosdick.'

A murmur of assent flowed around the room and glasses were raised to lips. Ludwig lifted his, finding that it had been refilled. 'Our guest will entertain us.' Had Malfatti really said that? Did he not understand how insulting it was?

He saw Therese talking again to Drosdick, her arm through his. They were smiling at each other, she looking up at him. Ludwig felt sad. How happy they looked. How perfect! He shook his head at the memory of his own desires. How absurd they were. He, a man of over forty, she not yet twenty. How had he ever imagined she could be in love with him?

The heat was beginning to affect him and he pulled at his neckcloth to loosen it. The punch had made him light-headed which seemed to shut out the pain of the last few minutes. He drank some more, relishing the almost syrupy sweetness.

Through the clamour of voices, he heard one close to his ear. It was deep and mournful, perfectly matched to the doleful face from which it came. 'You recovered well, Herr Beethoven.'

'Doktor Malfatti,' Ludwig said. 'Have you just come from the mortuary?' His eyes twinkled at the effect of his words: Malfatti's had opened wide in shock and his lips pulled down at the corners.

'Mortuary? No, I –'

'Because your face resembles a gravestone. Forgive my impertinence. No "entertainer", no "Musikus" should speak so to such a distinguished man. But you will forgive me, will you not?' Ludwig thought he detected the faint stirring of a smile on the doctor's face. He took another mouthful of punch. 'Good medicine, Doktor. Did you prescribe it? Cures my ills more effectively than any other of the quack remedies I have been given over the years. Poor Schmidt. Maybe he is watching and shaking his finger disapprovingly. And still bald. Hah!'

He saw Gleichenstein – the anxiety in his eyes. 'Ah, Gleichenstein,' he said, in a low voice. 'Most fortunate of men. Do not fret for me. I have my own *amour*. My own fiancée, my own wife. It is the gift I was born with and which will never leave me. Which will be constant to me. Faithful and true.'

'Sir, would you not like to sit for a while, and –'

'Sit? Yes, at the piano, where I belong. Where I must be to "entertain" the assembled company.'

He drained his glass and handed it to Gleichenstein. 'Have it refilled, faithful servant, and bring it to me, for now I must fulfil the duty which has brought me here, which has gained me entry into the highest salons in the land. Not just a house in Kärntnerstrasse, but palaces and even the Hofburg itself.'

'Sir,' said Gleichenstein urgently, 'I entreat you, lower your voice and do not say anything that will upset or offend. Forgive me for saying such things, but I implore you.'

Ludwig turned to Malfatti. He saw the same disquiet on the doctor's face.

'Herr Beethoven, if I may give you a little advice. Doctor's advice. You should sit, allow a servant to bring you some cold chicken, and drink no more than a single glass of punch to accompany it.'

Ludwig looked round the room and a giddiness came over him. Everyone talking so animatedly, smiling faces, heads thrown back in laughter. Young men, backs straight, one leg slightly out with bent knee affecting nonchalance, one hand holding a crimson glass, the other in the pocket of tight breeches, black tailcoat and shiny black boots; the young women in flowing dresses, hair piled high and tumbling ringlets, faces turned up to the men in admiring expectation . . .

And I have something none of them has, Ludwig thought, that will compel the men to gaze in envy and the women in wonder. But when my fingers have left the keyboard, and after they have praised me and congratulated me, they will turn away – and I will be left alone.

He emptied his glass and put it down. He heard Gleichenstein's voice. 'Sir, shall I . . . ?'

Ludwig stumbled across to the piano, supporting himself on the backs of chairs. He saw Herr Malfatti hurrying over. 'My dear Beethoven, too soon, too soon. But if you insist . . . May I say a few words?' He did not wait for a response but went on, 'Ladies and gentlemen, my dear friends. I said our friend the Musikus would entertain us. And he will now do so. I believe he has composed a piece especially for our dear Therese, as an engagement present, no doubt. Is that what you will play for us, sir?'

For a split second Ludwig wanted to slam the palms of both hands flat on the keys. Instead he frowned and nodded wearily. Malfatti continued, 'Herr Beethoven, as you all know, is the finest pianist in all Vienna. I have heard it said that he can perform tricks with the piano that will make you gasp as much as if you were watching an acrobat at the circus.'

An acrobat at the circus! A performer!

'Will you now demonstrate to us, sir, your magical skills?' Malfatti continued, leading a round of applause and bidding everyone to be seated.

Ludwig opened the folder on the music stand. There they were, his notes. Such simple notes. An elementary, unadorned – modest, almost – *rondo*. He had written it like that so that Therese would be able to play it. Now he would play it for them – all of them – and they would be disappointed. Disappointed, because any one of them, probably, could sit at the piano and play it. They wanted a performance, magical tricks, feats of daring. He reached his hands forward and began the turning sequence in the right hand alone, descending, and met by the left ascending. Repeat. He was playing it swiftly, but allowing it at the same time to sing. The central section of insistent chords he played lightly. No drama required. This was a different kind of piece. And return to the main theme. No variations. Just straight, to the end.

He finished and turned to the audience. They sat in silence, clearly not knowing what to make of it. Was it a prelude, an introduction to something? Was the real performance now about to begin?

Ludwig stood up, supporting himself on the piano frame. His head felt light and the sounds were dying slowly away. He felt the heaviness descend, but no throbbing, no pain.

Someone clapped. Herr Malfatti. It cut into his head. Instinctively he raised his hand and immediately realised his mistake. Faces looked expectant, eyebrows up, eyes wide. Clearly, they thought the 'performance' was about to begin. He took a deep breath, turned back to the piano and sat down again. He heard more applause, but it did not matter now. He would play. He would play for them. He would fill his head with his music. Only his music.

The opening turning phrase of the *rondo*. But not answered this time from the bass, but played again, as a series of trills, followed by explosive arpeggios, first in the right hand then the left. The piano shook under his fingers as he brought them down in a crashing sequence of chords. Furiously his hands flew up and down the keyboard in a torrent of sound. But underneath it, deep inside it, hidden almost, the insistent turning phrase of the *rondo*.

My language. Are you listening to what I am saying to you? This is how I talk to you. All of you. The only language in which I can truly express myself.

Key change. Sudden. Octaves played alternately, his hands almost a blur in front of his eyes as they rose and fell in swift chopping movements. Slower now, quieter. And still the insistent theme, pure and simple as it has been all along amid the turbulence and turmoil. He wanted to stop now. He had spoken enough to them. He played a series of chords, through a succession of key changes, ending in the key in which he had started. He held his hands high above the keyboard.

The applause cut into his head. He shook his head. 'No! Stop! Do you not know what you are doing to me?' He played more chords, louder now, to drown the applause. He played on to stop them clapping. He turned his head as he played. 'Fools! Do you think you understand me? My language?' he shouted.

He allowed his fingers to roam over the keyboard. He looked at the faces, whispering behind hands, laughing. Mocking me! 'No! Don't talk. Listen! Listen to what I am saying!' He bent his head low over the keys, his fingers working furiously, as if he could not say enough, a torrent of words pouring out of him. Yes, yes, this is what I want to say to you. But you cannot talk back and that is why my ears are deaf to you. Because they do not want to hear your language, and you cannot speak mine. I speak the most powerful and beautiful language in the world and no one can speak it with me. 'Hah!' He laughed as he played.

'Hah! Enough!' He allowed his fingers to slow almost to a halt, wait, wait, not yet, hold the chord, make them stop breathing, wonder what . . . and an explosive sequence of chords to end. Finally.

Now I understand, he thought. Now I know why I am deaf.

He turned to the audience and laughed. But they were no longer smiling.

I have offended them. No matter.

He played the simple opening of the *rondo* again. 'There!' he called out. 'Your language. You understand that. Now we can all speak together.' He played the piece right through, listening intently to the notes. *So pure, so simple. Yet as much my music as the great symphonies and concertos. Just as in language. This is a poem, a gentle poem, destined to be ignored and forgotten. What does it matter?*

He brought it to its delicate conclusion and turned again to the audience. They had not been listening. They were talking to each other. *It did not matter.*

He stood up, and was grateful for Gleichenstein's strong grip on his arm.

'Come and sit down, sir.'

Ludwig allowed Gleichenstein to lead him to a chair. 'Get me more punch, Gleichenstein.'

'I am afraid there is none, sir. It is finished. And everyone will shortly be leaving.'

'I should not have called them fools. I know that. I should not have shouted at them.' He let out a long breath.

'There is no offence, sir. Most of your words were hidden by the music. In any case they know they have witnessed a masterly performance. I am not sure about the *rondo*. But what you played in between . . .'

Ludwig was conscious of a lump in his throat as Therese came towards him. Her young man – he could not remember his name – was close behind. He saw that she was carrying the folder with the *rondo* inside it.

'Is this really for me, Herr Beethoven? Really?'

'A fine honour for my fiancé, Herr Bettoffen,' said the young man. 'Damn fine show. Don't know what you were saying while you played, sir. But damn fine all the same.'

Ludwig felt very tired. He did not want to talk. He did not want to hear voices.

'Herr Beethoven, if this is really for me, will you write on the top of it? So everyone will believe me?'

Ludwig thought he detected a spark of jealousy on the face of Therese's fiancé. Perversely it pleased him. *Let him be jealous: he will have Therese for the rest of his life.*

The young man passed him a pencil. He took the folder,

opened it and looked at the first page. Rondo, he had written at the top. Just a simple little piece, he thought. Why not let Therese have it? As a reminder. It serves no other purpose.

Alongside the word Rondo, he wrote his name, the final 'n' descending in an unsteady line. Even more unsteadily he wrote 'Für Therese.' For Therese. He closed the folder and handed it back to her.

She opened it. A look of petulance crossed her face. 'But – but – it doesn't look like Therese. It doesn't look like my name. The way you've written it. It looks like . . . like Elise. People will think you have given it to someone called Elise. You must change it.'

'You must change it,' Ludwig repeated to himself quietly. 'You must change it. You must play this. You must play that.' He looked up at her. 'No more music tonight, Therese. No more words. No more writing.'

Chapter 6

Ludwig did not attend the performance of Goethe's *Count Egmont* in the Burgtheater. He could not listen to a play – he would not be able to hear the words. Nor did he attend a concert a few days later in which works by Mozart and Haydn were played, as well as his own symphony in C minor, the fifth.

He was anxious to leave the city, to get away from the noise and bustle and breathe the clean air of the countryside, and he was pleased when Zmeskall told him he had taken rooms on his behalf in the Sauerhof, the large, run-down bath-house where Ries and young Czerny had come to see him some years before. Zmeskall told him it had been rebuilt and modernised and was now the finest bath-house in Baden.

The Sauerhof had a piano, he remembered that, but he had no intention of using it. He did not need it to compose. What a startling and wonderful revelation that was! His ears might be practically useless, but by closing his eyes and listening he could hear the music – his music – as surely as if his ears were perfect.

The piano trio for the Archduke occupied his time. A large work, larger than any trio he had written before. Almost a symphony for three instruments. He did not know why he had decided on that – maybe a reaction to the drama of the *Egmont* music or, more likely, to the drama in his life.

He had not seen Therese Malfatti since the fateful soirée. Gleichenstein had told him the family was planning to spend the summer at their estate near Krems on the banks of the Danube. After that Therese would probably go with her fiancé to visit his family in Styria. Ludwig asked Gleichenstein if he had offended them. The young man smiled benevolently, but it was enough to indicate to Ludwig that he had at least upset them. Gleichenstein told him they had decided to give no more soirées until the autumn at least, which Ludwig correctly interpreted as a way of informing him he would no longer be invited to the house on the Kärntnerstrasse. So what? He had pursued a young lady and she had rejected him. Not really 'reject'. She had probably intended to become engaged to Drosdick even before he had first met her. In fact she had been cruel not to tell him of her interest elsewhere. Gleichenstein, too, for that matter. Well, he thought, she has her wedding present from me.

The sulphurous waters of the Sauerhof began to relax him. He lay back, his head resting on the tiled edge of the small pool, the waters bubbling around his ears, warm and comforting. The smell, so strong, nauseated him for a few seconds before he grew accustomed to it.

His room was comfortable, with a small kitchen where he could boil water to make coffee. Fresh bread and sweet cakes were brought to him every day, and he had given instructions that the carafe of wine was never to stand empty.

After several days, when he could feel the strength in his limbs, he strode out along the banks of the Schwechat towards the Helenenthal valley, the walk he had often taken during his last stay in Baden. He went through the flat pasture that ran alongside the river, where cows grazed, until the tall pine trees began to take over, coming ever closer to the water's edge, and turned up through dense undergrowth, ignoring the winding path and climbing up, up, to the ruined castle of Rauhenstein. Breathlessly he stood among the old, jagged stone, relishing its cool damp feel on his hot hands. He was high above the valley, looking down on the Schwechat as it ran past, descending from the western edge of the Vienna Woods to the Danube. No Rhine this, he thought. He looked up at the ruin. No Drachenfels.

The castle was larger than the Drachenfels, and its remains traced the shapes of rooms and its high towers. But it seemed not to exude the power, the menace, of the Dragon Rock. Perhaps because it has no dragon, he thought wryly. No legends here. No maidens crying for help and no Siegfried to save them.

Ludwig beamed in delight when he saw that his visitor was none other that Nikolaus Zmeskall. 'So, Nikola! You have come to the wilds of the countryside to improve your health.'

'I need to, Ludwig. You forget, I give you more than ten years. I am over fifty now. My sixth decade. Hard to believe. And my poor old body is not what it was.'

'You abuse it too much. You have only yourself to blame.'

'I do not deny it. How is your health?'

Ludwig sat next to his friend by a bow window that gave out on to a gentle slope running down to the Schwechat. 'Better for being here. That is undeniable. I hear you. There is still a dullness in my head but no throbbing and no pain. And no noises. Though they could return at any moment. But look there. The river. No carriages come thundering past me, no shouting street-sellers, and no one begging the Musikus to play for them.'

Zmeskall laughed. 'Yes, I heard. Still, it seems no one took too much offence. By the way, I have news of Steffen.'

'Steffen? I haven't seen him since . . . How is he?'

'He took Julie's death badly, as you know. He loved her deeply. He regrets that they did not have a child for him to remember her by. He went away to get over it. To Teplitz in Bohemia. He said it restored his sanity and lessened his grief. He is now much like the old Steffen. But his face bears more lines.'

'I keep hearing about Bohemia. Maybe I should go there too.'

'Now, Ludwig, I will tell why I have come to see you.' Zmeskall pulled a newspaper from his case. 'See here. The *Allgemeine Musikalische Zeitung*.'

'Aaargh!' Ludwig exclaimed. 'No. Not the *Musikalische Zeitung*. It criticises everything I do. It criticised the Eroica. It criticised *Leonore*.'

'Then I won't read you what their critic Herr Hoffmann has to say about your symphony in C minor. Da–da–da–*daaa*!' sang Zmeskall dramatically.

'Enough! Who is this Hoffmann?'

Zmeskall shrugged his shoulders. 'Not come across the name before. But I have a feeling we will be coming across it again. He feels your symphony is not at all bad. Allow me to quote from him. "This reviewer has before him one of the most important works of the master whose position in the first rank of composers of instrumental music can now be denied by no one."'

Ludwig sat forward. 'He has written that about me? Nikola, do not tease me.'

'I am not, Ludwig. He has written that about you. Since I now have your attention, I shall read you more. "So imbued is he with the subject at hand" – that's Hoffmann, not you – "that he hopes no one will take it amiss if he oversteps the boundaries of ordinary reviewing in an attempt to put into words the profound feelings which this composition has stirred within him."'

Ludwig sat back. He was used to Zmeskall's voice now and could hear him without strain.

'He talks a bit about the art of music, then Mozart and Haydn – I won't read that – then –'

'No, no. Read it.'

'"When one considers music as an independent art, one should always mean instrumental music which, with nothing else to assist it, no interference from any of the other arts, exclusively expresses its own individual artistic essence."'

'Yes, yes,' said Ludwig enthusiastically. 'He's right. Think of my *Leonore*.'

'"It is the most romantic of all the arts – in fact, one might almost say the only purely romantic one. Haydn and Mozart, the creators of the newer instrumental music, first revealed this art to us in the fullness of its glory. He who looked upon it and who penetrated its innermost substance is – Beethoven."'

Ludwig face had lit up. 'Someone else once said something similar. Wrote it, rather. Count Waldstein. Someone I knew in Bonn. He gave me a little album when I left. He wrote in it that I would receive Mozart's spirit through Haydn's hands. Go on. Read more.'

'"Although the instrumental compositions of all three masters –"'

'All three masters! He calls us all masters. Mozart, Haydn and me. In the same breath!'

'Ludwig, will you let me read it? It's long, and if I want to have any voice left at the end of it, you must stop interrupting. Unless you read it. Why don't you read it? Here.'

He held out the paper but Ludwig refused it. 'No. I am sorry. It would hurt my eyes. Go on.'

'Not as much as it's hurting mine, I assure you.' Zmeskall pushed the thick spectacles on to the bridge of his nose, squinted, and read on. '"Although the instrumental compositions of all three masters breathe the same romantic spirit which lies precisely in the same intimate ability to comprehend the individual essence of this art, the nature of their compositions differs markedly." Now he describes the differences between your music. Do you want me to read it?'

'Yes, yes,' said Ludwig impatiently.

Zmeskall carried on. '"In Haydn's compositions the expression of a youthful, light-hearted spirit is dominant. His symphonies lead us into an infinite green grove, in a cheerful, gaily-coloured throng of merry people. Mozart leads us into the depths of the spiritual world. Fear grips us, but without torment; it is more a foreboding of the eternal –"'

'Yes,' said Ludwig, 'that is right. It is because of the subject matter of his operas. Too . . . too trivial to allow torment.'

'"Beethoven's instrumental music also opens up to us the world of the immense and the infinite. Glowing rays of light blaze through the dark night of this world and we are made conscious of gigantic shadows which surge up and down, gradually closing in on us more and more, and annihilating everything within us, except the torment of endless longing."'

This man, Ludwig thought, was seeing everything. At last, someone who could comprehend what he was striving to achieve. 'Go on. Go on.'

'"Beethoven is a pure romantic and because of this a truly musical composer. That may be the reason why he is less successful in vocal music and his instrumental music rarely appeals to the crowd."'

'He is right! Again.'

'"Beethoven bears deep within his nature the romantic spirit of music, which he proclaims in his works with great genius and presence of mind." He talks about your symphony now. "Your reviewer has never felt this so clearly as in this particular symphony which, more than any other of his works, unfolds Beethoven's romantic spirit in a climax rising straight to the end and carries the listener away irresistibly into the wondrous spirit world of the infinite."'

'Wondrous spirit world of the infinite,' Ludwig marvelled.

'"Beethoven has retained the usual sequence of movements in this symphony; in their form they appear to be linked one to the other. The whole work storms past some people like an ingenious rhapsody. But the soul of every sensitive listener will surely be deeply and intimately seized right up to the final chord by an enduring feeling which is exactly that inexpressible prophetic longing." I don't know what he means by that. Anyway, he goes on. "Indeed, for a while after the final chord he will not be able to step out of that wonderful realm of the spirit where the torment and joy, expressed in sound, embrace him. Apart from the construction and instrumentation, it is especially the inner relationship of the individual themes to one another which produces a unity that preserves the listener's mood. In Haydn's and Mozart's music this unity prevails everywhere. But a deeper relationship often speaks only from the spirit to the spirit."'

Ludwig held up his hands. 'Nikola, he is right. He has seen what I am trying to do. He has seen it better than me. From the spirit to the spirit. From my spirit to the spirit of the listener. That is why my music will endure. Long after I am gone. Because my spirit will be there in my music for ever.'

Zmeskall pulled out a handkerchief and blew his nose vigorously. 'Almost at the end now, I am pleased to say. "And it is this relationship –" I suppose he means of the spirit to the spirit, whatever that means. I am glad you understand it. "– which dominates the two Allegro movements and the Minuet –'

'Minuet? No, there is no minuet.'

'Hah! Our Herr Hoffmann has got something wrong, then. However, I doubt you will disagree with this final bit. "– and gloriously proclaims the master's thoughtful genius. This reviewer believes he can express the verdict on this glorious artistic creation of the master in a few words by saying that it is conceived with genius, carried out with profound thoughtfulness, and expresses in the highest degree the romantic spirit in music."' With a sigh of relief Zmeskall threw down the paper.

Ludwig sat quietly, nodding slowly. '"Conceived with genius",' he said under his breath. 'Conceived with genius. Gottlob Neefe said I had genius but my father disagreed. That is why it took so long for me to come to Vienna – he wouldn't let me come.'

'Well, Ludwig, you can be proud of what Herr Hoffmann has to say about you. In the *Musikalische Zeitung*, too.'

'Are they talking about it in Vienna?'

'Most certainly. Schuppanzigh was the first to see it because he takes the paper regularly. He told Steffen and me. And he said Count Razumovsky had seen it too, and other important people.'

'Razumovsky?'

Zmeskall blinked behind his spectacles. 'He was recalled to Moscow after the French invaded, but now he's back and the palace is almost finished.'

'In the Landstrasse. I remember now. That was why I composed the quartets for him.'

'I think you might be hearing from him soon. He is keen to have you perform at the new palace.'

Ludwig rubbed his jaw. 'I don't know how much longer I will be able to perform, Nikola. My hearing will make it more and more difficult. Even when I play the piano now, I hear it more in my head.'

'You mustn't worry, my old friend. Your hearing will never become that bad, I am sure of it.'

'You are sure of it?' asked Ludwig, an edge to his voice. Then, apologetically, 'I am sorry. I didn't mean to . . . but everyone always tells me not to worry about it.'

'Well, Ludwig, there are worse fates. I do not wish to sound callous. But I have something to tell you that I fear will come as something of a shock, that will take your mind off your own problem, maybe.'

Ludwig's heart sank. He did not want to hear bad news, particularly after the euphoria of the *Musikalische Zeitung* review. Maybe that was why Zmeskall had read him the review first: to prepare him for bad news. What could it be? Somehow it had to involve Hartl and the imperial theatres. *Egmont* was unsatisfactory; he wanted it rewritten. Or no further works would be commissioned. Or . . .

'It is your brother. Carl. He is unwell. He is coughing and the doctors fear he has consumption, that he will slowly get worse and that . . . there will be no hope for him.'

Ludwig tried to absorb Zmeskall's words. 'Carl? That is impossible. He is younger than I.'

'There is consumption in your family. Your mother . . . isn't that right?'

Ludwig exhaled and ground his teeth. 'But . . . how long?'

Zmeskall shrugged. 'They don't know. But it won't be quick. They say it's not a steady deterioration. You can recover to such an extent that you think it is gone for ever. Then it takes hold again. Once you have contracted it you can never truly shake it off.'

'I cannot believe it. Carl. Impossible. More likely that wretched wife of his. Evil woman. She's probably –'

'Ludwig, no. Stop. You shouldn't say that. Johanna is doing her best, and she will need help. Particularly with the child.'

Ludwig slapped his thigh. 'He should never have married her. I curse the day he ever met her.'

BOOK ELEVEN

Chapter 1

The people of Vienna were in a state of shock. Some said they had warned of this, but no one would listen. Others said it was the only solution but that the Hofburg would never dare. Most had simply ignored all the signs and carried on regardless. Once it became known that it was inevitable, the same name was on all lips, but whispered only with the utmost caution: Metternich.

On 15 March 1811, the government devalued the currency to a fifth of its value. Tradesmen were ordered to reduce their prices by four-fifths, but almost as soon as they did so they began to raise them again, slowly but inexorably.

For the aristocracy, whose wealth largely vanished overnight, it meant a severe adjustment in their lifestyle. Servants found themselves without employment; carriages were sold; paintings and silver were auctioned. The ordinary people of Vienna could barely afford a daily loaf of bread. There was a sudden dearth of strollers taking the evening air on the Bastion promenade, or in the Augarten or Prater public parks. Street-sellers became scarce; those who remained offered chestnuts or sweet cakes for practically nothing.

Among the worst affected was Prince Lichnowsky. His finances were already depleted and he now found his situation dire. Once one of the wealthiest aristocrats in the city, he had given large amounts of money to the government to allow them to wage war against the French, always on the written undertaking that he would be repaid with interest. But when the government had found that contributions from the Prince and other aristocrats were not enough, it had resorted to the simple expedient of printing more banknotes. Inevitably the value of money had declined as more and more came on to the streets, until the realisation dawned at the Hofburg that the government was insolvent.

There was no alternative but to take the action they had, and barely a person in the city – whatever their social status – was unaffected.

Ludwig walked down the Kohlmarkt, usually the busiest street in Vienna, along with the Kärntnerstrasse, towards Michaelerplatz. He glanced in shop windows as he walked. How they had changed! Gone were the luxury items that had made this the favoured shopping street of the nobility. The latest fashions from Paris had been replaced by workaday clothes in green and grey wool. The confectionery shops no longer offered elaborately baked almond and chocolate cakes; in their place were loaves of bread. He glanced in the window of the publisher Artaria. The framed prints and portraits were nowhere to be seen: instead Bibles and housekeeping manuals were stacked unappealingly in piles.

A lone news vendor stood on the corner of Michaelerplatz, saving his vocal cords by allowing the single sheet proclaiming the latest news to do his work for him. Faces glanced in its direction, unmoved by the joyous message it proclaimed. Ludwig looked at it.

OUR PRINCESS GIVES THE FRENCH EMPEROR THE SON HE LONGED FOR!

Napoleon Bonaparte. When would the man curtail his ambition? Sooner or later, surely, he would take a step too far. And then what? Would the people of Vienna finally be rid of this tyrant, who had twice invaded their city, breaching the mighty Bastion – that had withstood the Turks – as if it were no more than a garden wall? Would they be allowed to resume their lives without the fear of further attack? And would they be able to spend their hard-earned income as they wished, without seeing it depleted by the expensive business of war?

He walked across Michaelerplatz and under the massive arch into the palace courtyard, turning towards the Amalienhof, the wing occupied by Archduke Rudolph. He carried a folder under his arm, but there was no music in it: he knew what the Archduke wanted to discuss.

Ludwig had hoped that Gleichenstein would come in his place, but he had seen little of him since his engagement to Netty Malfatti. Also he had heard from Stephan that after their marriage the young couple would leave for Freiburg; Ludwig knew that he had therefore to take control of his affairs.

He climbed the stairs, to be greeted at the top by the Archduke himself. 'My dear Herr Beethoven, so good of you to come. Their Excellencies are in the salon.'

Ludwig followed him into the ornate room, with its tapestries and curtains. All three men with whom he was about to engage in conversation were fully aware of his disability. He had no reason to feel anxious.

He held up his hands to try to prevent Prince Lobkowitz getting up and limping across to greet him. He was immediately struck by the Prince's haggard face. His eyes were dull; his hair, always unkempt, had thinned and lost its lustre. And it seemed to Ludwig that his limp was more pronounced, his reliance on the crutch greater than before.

'Bad times, eh, Beethoven?' he said, thrusting his hand forward. Ludwig took it. 'Need your youth at times like this. Need your energy. Envy these two youngsters, eh?' He smiled thinly.

Ludwig turned to greet Prince Kinsky, who had risen too. Ludwig estimated that he was around thirty, a good ten years younger than Lobkowitz and at least half a dozen years older than the Archduke. Lobkowitz was right. He and Ludwig, both past their fortieth birthdays, were middle-aged men.

Kinsky's appearance belied his age. Always corpulent, he was now rotund, his flesh straining against his uniform, but he clicked his heels smartly and, left hand holding the pommel of his sword, he bowed as deeply as his bulk would allow.

Ludwig noticed quickly – and with relief – that the Archduke had grouped a cluster of chairs close to each other. He should have no trouble in following the conversation, which he knew would be complicated and probably grim. A servant girl was placing a tray of freshly made coffee and cakes on a table. She curtsied and left.

'Hah! So the strict economies have done you one favour at least, Your Highness,' said Lobkowitz, sitting down heavily and laying his crutch on the floor alongside the chair.

'My servants have all been deployed elsewhere in the Hofburg,' said the Archduke, colour rising in his cheeks. 'Marie works in the laundry. Her mother is a seamstress there. Everyone is now filling more than one position. Many had to leave, after years of faithful service to the Habsburg family.

The Empress had no choice. She has to set an example to the people.'

'Damn bad business,' said Lobkowitz. 'Damn bad.'

'Wonder why we fought them at all,' said Kinsky. 'The French, I mean. We fought them to a standstill on the Marchfeld. Lost thousands of men. Saw them dying around me. Damn man goes and marries into the family. Your niece, sir. No disrespect. Now he has an heir, half-French half-Austrian. In Paris the people cheer. In Vienna they scrounge for crumbs. Damn bad, as you say, sir. Damn bad.'

Coffee cups were passed round. Ludwig took his carefully, unable to fit his forefinger through the tiny handle.

The Archduke sat down, picked up a folder that lay on the table next to his chair and opened it. 'Herr Beethoven, I know how busy you are, how much work you always have, and these two gentlemen also have pressing engagements, so I will come straight to the point. Are you happy for me to proceed?'

Ludwig nodded, and tried to fasten his mind on what he was about to hear. He, too, opened his folder and took a pencil from his pocket, touching his tongue to the lead.

'It concerns your annuity, to which we three have signed and pledged ourselves. We are all painfully aware of the unfortunate events of the last week. The government, I regret, had no choice –'

'Printed too much damn money,' said Lobkowitz. 'Damn fools.'

'I am not going to sit judgement on anyone's behaviour,' said the Archduke. 'It is not for me – for any of us, if I might say so – to criticise. But the currency has been devalued. And it has its effect.' He looked at Lobkowitz, giving him the floor to spell out his own position.

The Prince did not delay in coming straight to the point. 'Situation somewhat sticky, Beethoven. Find myself in strait-ened circumstances. Here in Vienna, that is. Not in Bohemia, of course. But unfortunately my assets there are all tied up. Castle at Hradcany and estate at Eisenberg. Costly. Here, though, there's a problem. Find myself embarrassed.' He massaged the knee of his lame right leg. 'Might have to return to Prague before the summer's out. Will have to suspend my payments to you.'

'Suspend?'

'Just suspend, of course. Temporary situation only. But con-sider how much I have done for you in the past. Finest concert

room in Vienna, mmh? Remember the first performance of
your new symphony there? You named it Eroica and gave
me the dedication. Most proud, most proud. As I say, just
temporary. Karolina and I will go to Bohemia, probably – give
us a chance to sort things out.'

'The Prince is not alone in his difficulties,' said the Archduke
in a mollifying voice. 'Everyone is suffering to some degree
or other.'

'I too, Herr Beethoven,' said Kinsky, 'though not . . . I
must say . . . the situation is retrievable.' He gestured towards
Lobkowitz. 'I have to go to Prague too, where my business
affairs are handled. I'll make arrangements with them. Have to
obey the Finanz-Patent. Cut my amount to a fifth.' He pulled
a piece of paper from his pocket. 'Three hundred and sixty.
From eighteen hundred. But, as my distinguished friend says,
only temporary.'

Ludwig wrote in the folder, 'Lobwtz, nil. Kinsky, 360.' Why
had he not realised it would be this bad? The contract into which
Countess Erdödy and Gleichenstein had talked him had been
flawed from the start. At the mercy of the men who signed
it. He turned to the Archduke. With his payment reduced to
a fifth, three hundred, he would be left with barely enough to
live on.

The young man smiled reassuringly. 'I at least am in a position
where I can do something of benefit to you, Herr Beethoven.
I have given the necessary instructions in writing and will
maintain my payments at the agreed level of fifteen hundred.
Thus your situation is more favourable than it might have been,
given the constrictions on us all.'

Ludwig wrote, 'Rdlph, 1500. Total 1860. One fourth quarterly.' He calculated quickly, scribbling on the paper. Less than
half of what he had become accustomed to.

'The figure is actually somewhat higher than you are calcu-
lating,' said the Archduke. 'The government has decreed that all
contracts signed prior to the Finanz-Patent will benefit from an
adjustment according to the fall in value of the currency. They
will shortly issue a table. There will be a back payment from
myself and His Excellency Prince Kinsky.'

'Yes, yes,' said Kinsky. 'Back payment. Certainly. I will
arrange it in Prague. Not thinking of coming to Prague,
eh, sir?'

Ludwig said that he was not.

'I'll be there for some months,' Kinsky went on. 'Let me know if you come and I will arrange the payment there and then.'

Archduke Rudolph smiled. 'So you see, Herr Beethoven, it is not as bad as it might have been, which befits a musician of your distinction. And I, like my good friends, am convinced that this desperate situation will not last.'

Zmeskall had been correct: Stephan Breuning's face had aged since Julie's untimely death. There were even the beginnings of grey flecks above his ears, although he was not yet forty. Ludwig said, 'Thank you for coming with me, Steffen. You are a good friend.'

'I am anxious about Carl too. Remember, I have known all you Beethoven brothers since you were boys. My mother was fond of you all.'

'Is she well? Have you heard from her?'

'Yes,' Stephan said. 'Mama is keeping well. But tell me, Ludwig, what is it you don't like about Johanna? I am right, aren't I? You do not like her.'

Ludwig's head began to pound – the effect of the walk across the Glacis and through the city, he knew, but it had been the mention of his sister-in-law's name that had made him aware of it. After a time, he answered slowly, 'She has a dark side to her character. Sinful. Corrupt. I –'

'You must not say that, Ludwig,' said Stephan, stopping dead and looking at him. 'You have no right.'

A bolt of anger ran through him, but he kept it under control and his voice low. 'No right? I am related to her now, thanks to Carl. I am the uncle of their child. A Beethoven. I have the right. More than anyone, I have the right.'

'Then what is your evidence? You cannot make accusations without –'

'You know as well as I do, Steffen. She was . . . she was already –'

Stephan sighed. 'And that is entirely her fault, Ludwig? Could not your brother take some of the blame?'

'He is a Beethoven. Do not forget that.' Ludwig began to walk again. He did not want to have to explain his feelings towards Johanna – in fact, he felt that Stephan did not have the right to ask. He was aware that there was an element of irrationality in his attitude, but he could not help it, nor control it. It was instinctive. He was convinced she was not to be trusted.

Johanna opened the door to them and stepped back. She held her head high, her chin pointed defiantly. She was dressed in a shapeless shift that had grown threadbare where her elbows pressed against it, and the print of small flowers had long since faded. But her eyes flashed, again as if she were defying anyone to blame her for what had happened to her husband.

Stephan took her hand and raised it to his lips. Ludwig bowed curtly and walked into the room. It was darker than he remembered. The curtains were drawn across the windows, but did not quite meet, allowing shafts of light into the room, which gave it a certain eeriness. He saw a movement off to one side. It was Carl, entering from the bedroom.

'Why is it so dark in here?' Carl demanded in an agitated tone. 'Always so dark in here. Open the curtains, woman, for God's sake.'

'The doctor said not to put a strain on your eyes. You know that.'

Carl clicked his tongue in irritation and walked over to the windows, pulling aside the curtains.

Ludwig was dazzled momentarily as the light filled the room although it was not bright.

He looked at his brother. He could see no difference. Still the pale lustreless hair, the darting head that came forward when he walked. He may have lost a little weight, his cheeks not quite so full, but he bore none of the signs of incipient illness.

Carl coughed, lightly at first, then with a hacking bark he could not control. Swiftly he pulled a handkerchief from his sleeve and held it to his mouth, wiping it dry when the spasm at last subsided. 'Come to a funeral, have you?' he said, a sly smile on his face. 'Well, you're too early. Long time to go yet. It'll take more than this to get rid of me. Get into the kitchen, woman, and bring some coffee.'

Johanna sighed. 'Sit down, Carl, and stop agitating yourself. You know what the doctor said.'

'Doctor! Doctor! Everything the doctor says is sacrosanct. Every word is inscribed on stone. Now go and get some coffee. Where's Karl?'

'He's in his room. I'll bring him in when I've made the coffee. Sit down, all of you.'

Ludwig watched as Carl sagged into a large easy chair. It was a ponderous movement that culminated in a deep sigh. He was tired, clearly, and he had a cough. No worse than I have felt on many an occasion, Ludwig thought. He pulled out a chair from the table and sat on it. Stephan did the same.

They were awkwardly silent for a few minutes until Ludwig said, 'How are you, Carl? I must say, you do not look ill. A little tired, maybe.'

'Just a cough, nothing more,' his brother replied. 'Everyone fusses around unnecessarily.'

Ludwig shifted in his chair. 'Do not listen to doctors. They know nothing. No doctor has ever told me anything that has turned out to be true. They are charlatans.'

Carl laughed, then cursed at the cough it induced. 'At last there is something upon which we agree, my brother!'

'Are you able to work?' Stephan asked.

'Of course. Anyway I can't afford not to, with a child in the house. Also my wife is a woman with expensive tastes. I have to satisfy her needs.'

'What do you mean?' asked Ludwig, a note of hostility in his voice.

'She wants the latest fashions from Paris. If a pair of shoes –'

'Now, Carl, stop talking like that,' said Stephan. 'She is a fine woman and you are maligning her.'

'God, Steffen. Always defending the defenceless,' said Ludwig. 'Always on the side of the victim. Sometimes I think you are so saintly you should have taken holy orders.'

Stephan looked hurt and Ludwig's conscience pricked him.

Johanna returned with the coffee and put it on the table. Ludwig took the cup she offered him, and a piece of cake, which he laid on the saucer.

Carl was speaking again. 'I had a letter from Johann a day or two ago. A long one telling me the whole history of his famous apothecary shop. Did you know we have a wealthy brother, Ludwig? One of us, at least, has made his way in the world.'

'What do you mean?'

'You remember how little money he had when he left here for Linz?'

Ludwig nodded.

'The situation was apparently more grave than any of us realised. When he left Vienna he had only three hundred florins to his name and a commitment to repay a loan of twenty-five thousand – the cost of the shop – as well as interest.'

'I didn't know it was so bad,' said Stephan, shaking his head. 'If I had known –'

'Hah! It's worse even than that.' Carl began to laugh, which led to a renewed attack of coughing. Finally, he was able to continue. 'Within a matter of months he had exhausted his savings and he was not making enough money to meet the loan. So he sawed off the iron gratings that covered the windows and sold them. That covered two months' payments. Then he faced disaster again.'

Ludwig was now listening avidly to Carl's story. Johann, he had always known, was less stupid than he appeared. He was vain, certainly, and immoral – he recalled that strumpet of a girl Johann had once brought to Stephan's apartment – but lurking somewhere deep within him, Ludwig believed, was a stratum of intelligence.

'Someone came into the shop one day and just happened to comment on the jars and pots lining the shelves with the medicines and powders in. He asked to see one and told Johann that they were made of solid English tin and very valuable. All the more so because Napoleon had banned trade in any English goods. So our clever brother sold them all, for a very handsome profit, substituting them with earthenware pots. That gave him enough money to meet his payments for a year.'

Stephan chuckled and shook his head. 'Well, what good fortune!'

'And then,' Carl continued, his voice rising in excitement, 'another stroke of luck. The French army invaded Austria once again and established their commissariat at Linz. And their main field hospital. All the seriously wounded from the battlefield were brought there. And who do you think won the contract to supply the medicines and bandages?'

'But that will not have made him popular,' Stephan said, worriedly.

'Correct,' said Carl. 'In fact, in his letter he says he is one of the wealthiest men in Linz and one of the most detested. But which would you rather have, he puts at the end, riches or popularity?'

'It is a lonely life if you are disliked,' said Johanna.

'Quiet, wife. I do not require your opinion on my brother. Where's the boy? Go and get him. I have something to say and I do not want you in the room.'

Johanna made a *moue* of disgust and left the room.

Carl leaned towards Stephan and Ludwig. 'Johann is indeed the most fortunate of men. He has a housekeeper who does more than keep house.'

'No. Stop!' said Ludwig, unable to contain himself. 'Do not talk like that. It is immoral. A Beethoven would not consort with a housekeeper.'

'Oh, yes,' said Carl. 'Johann van Beethoven, no less, consorts very regularly with a housekeeper.'

'I will not allow it,' said Ludwig. 'I will write to him. He will stop.'

Carl laughed again and coughed, holding the handkerchief to his mouth. The cough was even more prolonged this time, brought on by so much talking.

Ludwig thought of his younger brother with revulsion. What Carl had said was typical of Johann and nothing would ever change him. Why could he not realise how inviolable the name of Beethoven must be, and that he should do nothing to besmirch it?

The door opened with a crash and Ludwig watched his nephew – now almost five – run towards Stephan and hug him round the knees.

'Hello, young man,' said Stephan, kindly. 'Go and bid your father good day.'

The child ran to Carl, planted a cursory kiss on his cheek and returned to his mother's side.

'And your uncle,' said Johanna.

Ludwig looked at the little boy. A Beethoven. The next generation. And surely destined to be a musician, to carry the name forward.

Karl clung to his mother's dress. She urged him again to go to Ludwig, but he would not move.

Chapter 2

Ludwig's heart skipped a beat when he read the note. It was from Antonie Brentano and she invited him to come to the house on the Erdbeergasse for dinner to meet her husband Franz. He went immediately to the wardrobe to check that he had enough clean clothes – otherwise it would mean a trip to see Nanette – and was pleased to note that he had. He smiled inwardly: he had never before carried out such a check.

As the hour approached he became nervous. He had not seen Antonie for some time but her image had not left him, nor the gentle timbre of her voice – the only voice that cut through the fog in his head. When he thought of her, when he saw in his mind's eye her deep-set eyes and tumbling curls, other women seemed ordinary, coarse. Take Josephine Deym – Stackelberg now. That look almost of desperation in her eyes, a cry for help. He shuddered at the thought that he had once seriously considered marriage to her. Zmeskall had been undoubtedly right. She was unstable. Or Therese Malfatti, even. He had hardly given her a thought since the débâcle at the soirée with Gleichenstein, but when he did he found himself almost repulsed by her. She was everything that Antonie was not. She wore her character on her sleeve. Her primary concern, in whatever she said or did, was for herself. 'Do this for me, Herr Beethoven, do that. Play this for me, Herr Beethoven, play that. Compose something for me, Herr Beethoven . . .'

And what had Antonie done? He remembered her words as clearly as if it she had just spoken then. 'You expected me to ask you to play the piano for me. Instead I am going to play for you.'

He was surprised but not displeased when the servant said a lady was asking to be admitted, a Fräulein Bettina Brentano. He greeted her warmly, raising her hand to within an inch of his lips.

'Oh, Herr Beethoven, how elegant you look. I do declare I have never before seen you so elegant.' Hastily she pressed her fingers over her lips. 'Oh, you must forgive me. I did not mean to suggest . . .'

But Ludwig had not forgotten Bettina's liveliness, her ceaseless chatter, and he was amused.

'Franz asked me to come for you. We told him you knew the way, but he is concerned for your welfare. Before we leave, I must tell you I have heard from my good friend. Do you remember I told you?'

Ludwig held up his hands to calm the torrent of words. 'You must speak more slowly – and a little more clearly, young lady – if you want me to understand what you are saying.'

'Of course, you must forgive me. Franz is always saying the same. Apparently I was just like it as a child. My mother said I could talk before I could walk! Herr Goethe, that is who I am talking about. A friend of mine – my family. Do you remember I said I would send him a copy of your *Egmont* music? Will you allow me? Oh, do say you will.'

Ludwig nodded at Bettina's reminder of what she had said the last time they met.

'Oh good, good,' she cried. 'Have you a copy?'

'Wait, wait. I did not give you an answer. I doubt he would want to see it. Does he know about music?'

'Oh, he is such a clever man. I sometimes think he knows everything about everything. He would certainly understand music.'

'I am not sure. I think –'

'Do you remember that I told you he goes to Bohemia? You must meet him there. I know he would be thrilled. Toni and Franz are going to Bohemia. Did you know? With poor little Fanny. But I'll let them tell you about that. Do you have a copy?'

Ludwig smiled a little wearily. 'Go and see Schlemmer. Wenzel Schlemmer. He is my copyist. Tell him I told you to ask for a copy. It has not been published yet. Here, I will write you a note.'

He went to the table and scribbled a few words authorising Schlemmer to make her a copy. 'Send it to Herr Goethe. With my greatest compliments.'

'Oh, yes, wonderful, wonderful!' she exclaimed. 'Now we will leave. I have a carriage outside.'

Ludwig took his coat from behind the door and put it on.

'But you cannot wear that coat, Herr Beethoven. Look.' She turned the sleeve to show him where it had frayed.

He laughed. 'Do you think I have only old clothes? I have several good coats. Come and see.' He led her into the bedroom and opened his wardrobe.

'Will you permit me?' Without waiting for an answer she took another coat off a hanger and handed it to him. He threw the old one on the bed and put on the one she had selected.

Together they left the apartment and went down the four flights to the street. Ludwig was in buoyant mood. He was going to see Antonie – Toni – and he felt as if he had drunk a glass of the finest French wine.

The air was chilly. 'Ah, wait!' he said. 'Get into the carriage. I will return immediately.' He hurried back up the stairs.

A few minutes later he reappeared at the carriage door, breathing heavily with the exertion, and smiling broadly. 'See? The latest fashion from Paris.'

'Herr Beethoven,' she said, sternly, 'I insist. You must not wear that coat. Will you return and get the other one?'

He laughed and disappeared again. Why, he wondered as he ran down the stairs yet again, with the better coat on once more, was he behaving like this? Excitement at seeing Toni? There was no other explanation.

Mercifully Bettina did not speak during the ride to the Landstrasse suburb. Ludwig wondered what Franz Brentano would be like. He remembered the sadness in Toni's eyes the first time he had met her, but that was probably because she was having to leave Vienna for a strange city. And hadn't Bettina said Franz was considering opening a branch of his business here in Vienna? Then he remembered the joy in Toni's voice when she had told him Franz would soon be coming to join her here.

He allowed Bettina to lead him through the entrance hall. He noticed as he walked past the curios and antiques that each now had a label attached to it. What a thankless task faced Toni, disposing of her father's collection.

When he saw her, he gasped. She looked unwell, tired and strained. It showed clearly in her face. There were dark circles round her eyes and her cheeks were thin. Her hair, piled high on her head, was not securely fastened so that strands tumbled down over her forehead and ears. It made her look vulnerable, as if an adverse word would be enough to crush her.

She walked towards him, her hands outstretched. 'Dear Ludwig,' she said, as he raised them to his lips.

'You are cold. Are you well?'

'I have been ill, but I am a little better now. The strain of all I have to do. And poor Fanny. But tell me about yourself. How is your health?'

'I have been working. Composing. That is all that matters.'

'I am glad. Has Bettina taken good care of you? Franz insisted on sending her to fetch you.' She glanced round but Bettina was not there. 'I hope she did not tire you out.'

'I enjoyed talking to her. I played a little trick on her with my coat. She will tell you about it. I am pleased to see you, Toni. It always makes me feel . . . Your voice soothes me.'

Suddenly Toni took away her hands and looked over her shoulder. 'Franz. Ah, good, there you are. At last I am able to introduce you to my good friend, Herr Beethoven.'

Ludwig was surprised at Franz Brentano's appearance. He was shorter than he had imagined, about his own height but without the stockiness; in fact his build was slight. His face was different too. He had expected that a woman of Antonie's grace and beauty would have a husband with imposing good looks, a strong face and firm jaw. Franz's face was angular, his long nose and jaw sloping forward to give the impression that his head had been set at an angle on his neck. His hair was a mass of tight dark curls, but his most immediately striking feature was his eyes. They were more prominent than was normal, as if they had been set not quite fully into his head. They glistened noticeably and beneath them were heavy dark folds of flesh.

Ludwig could not immediately discern whether Franz's health was poor or whether he was overworked and showing signs of strain. Either way his appearance was a revelation. Could this really be the man for whom Antonie had left her beloved Vienna?

'Herr Beethoven.' Franz bowed. 'What an enormous privilege. Had my wife not spoken endlessly to me about you, I would still have known of you. In Frankfurt your music is regularly heard and your name frequently spoken. You are, after all, almost a native son.'

Franz's appearance had led Ludwig to anticipate a doleful man, but this was not so. He had smiled, which transformed his face, and his voice was deep and mellifluous.

'Thank you, sir.' Ludwig returned the bow.

'Come now,' said Franz, 'let us dispense with this Viennese formality. We are almost cousins, you from Bonn, me from Frankfurt, barely a day's carriage-ride apart. Will you call me Franz, and allow me to call you Ludwig?'

Ludwig smiled and nodded. Franz was not, strictly speaking, a Rhinelander, but he already felt at ease in his company. And the man's approach pleased him: it was good to leave aside the etiquette and decorum that would have accompanied a first meeting with a Viennese businessman of high standing.

The usual heaviness and ringing were in Ludwig's ears, but he knew already that they would not trouble him unduly. Franz's voice was not only strong, but the way in which he spoke reminded Ludwig of home. He took the glass of wine Franz passed to him and sipped it.

'Toni has given me great pleasure by playing your music to me,' Franz said. 'I wish, though, she would learn more than one piece. I do believe I know every note of it. It has an Italian name, she tells me.'

'Andante Grazioso,' Ludwig said. 'Though I have renamed it Andante Favori.'

'I only wish I could do it justice,' Antonie said. 'Such a lovely piece.'

Again Ludwig was struck by how tired she looked, her shoulders seemingly weighed down.

Franz must have caught the concern on his face. 'Toni is indeed very tired, Ludwig. She has so much work to do here, dealing with her father's collection. It is sad for you, too, isn't it, my dear? So many memories.'

Antonie was evidently fighting tears. At last, she said, 'And poor Fanny. She is no better. Still such trouble breathing.'

Bettina swirled into the room. 'I have just been with Fanny and she is in very good spirits. Much better this evening. I have read her a story and she is insisting on more. Will you go ahead with dinner? I'll leave you three to talk, and, Toni, you need not worry about her.'

Antonie's face lightened. She stood up. 'I will come and say goodnight to her. Will you excuse me for just a minute? I will tell the cook to begin serving dinner.'

After she had gone Franz led Ludwig through to the dining room. 'I am concerned about Toni, you know,' he said, as they sat at the table. 'She is pushing herself too hard. All this work with the collection and the strain of the children. But,' he smiled, shaking his head, 'she is in Vienna, which she loves dearly. She has never really taken to Frankfurt, you know.'

Ludwig said, 'She told me so. She returns here whenever she can.'

Franz leaned a little across the table. 'I think this business of auctioning her father's collection might take her a little longer than it need. But I will not complain. If she is happy here, she can stay. In fact I think the trip to Bohemia will do her as much good as Fanny.'

'Bettina mentioned that. When are you going?'

Franz shrugged his shoulders. 'Not until the summer, when we can be sure of the weather. I may not go. It depends on my business. In fact, I have to return to Frankfurt in a day or two but I hope to be back here. I think the break would do me good too.'

'Your children are here?'

'All four. They love Vienna as much as Toni does. They find the house exciting – it is like a museum which they have all to themselves.'

'And when you go to Bohemia?'

'Bettina will take the three eldest back to Frankfurt. She is so good with them. Toni won't need to worry.'

'I met one. Maxi, I think.'

Franz laughed. 'Ah yes, Fräulein Maximiliane. Very high-spirited young lady. In fact, she is rather a devoted admirer of your music. She plagues her mother to teach her to play, so much so that we have allowed her to begin lessons. She is making progress – though less progress than she believes she is making!'

'Are you talking about Maxi?' said Antonie, coming into the room and sitting at the table.

'Yes, my dear. How is Fanny?'

'Breathing more easily, I am pleased to say. Now what have you been talking about?'

'I was telling Ludwig we are going to Bohemia with Fanny. I am sure the waters will cure her. All that fresh air in her lungs. That's what she needs. Bohemia is so beautiful, Ludwig. You must go there, you really must.'

'Maybe one day. I like taking the waters – I find it helps my hearing, though it's more likely because I am away from the city and all the noise.'

They ate quietly for a few moments. Then Franz spoke. 'It's very gloomy here in Vienna. I have never seen so many grim faces. The Finanz-Patent has really taken its toll.'

'Oh, it's so sad,' said Antonie, distress on her face. 'The poor people can barely afford to buy bread – beggars on street corners, and most of them husbands and fathers who have lost everything and cannot feed their children.'

'War is not cheap,' said Franz. 'The statesmen and diplomats never consider that before they start.'

'And crippled people too,' said Antonie. 'I have never seen so many. They stand against a wall on their crutches and the sign at their feet always says the same thing. "Wounded in the struggle of the Fatherland against the French tyrant." But no one can afford to give them money.'

Ludwig clenched a fist. 'It will have to end soon. He cannot go on trying to conquer Europe. Sooner or later he will be defeated.'

'I rather fear,' said Franz, mopping his plate with a piece of bread, 'that soon he will no longer need to go to battle. He is defeating the enemy by other means.'

'What do you mean?' asked Ludwig.

'He is conquering his opponents by bankrupting them. Take Vienna. Take my own plans. I have, I am pleased to say, a prosperous business in Frankfurt. I have expanded my father's firm. We are bankers now as well as merchants. I intended to open a branch here in Vienna. It made sound financial sense. But now, with the Finanz-Patent, it is impossible. One cannot do business with people who have no money.'

Ludwig glanced at Antonie. A look of ineffable sadness had settled on her face. She turned her eyes up to Ludwig. 'It means I will soon no longer have any excuse to return to Vienna,' she said.

'The situation will change,' said Ludwig.

'I doubt it,' said Franz. 'It will take a long time for this city to return to prosperity. Napoleon Bonaparte has defeated it as surely as if he had soldiers here at every turn.'

Bettina came into the room. 'Dear little Fanny wants to sleep now. At last!' she said, feigning exhaustion. 'She is asking you to come and say goodnight again, Toni.'

Antonie jumped to her feet and left the room.

Immediately Franz's attention was on Ludwig. 'As I said, Ludwig, I have to return to Frankfurt in a day or two. I am worried about Toni. She is not well, I know that. Will you keep an eye on her? She is so fond of you, you know.'

Chapter 3

Ludwig strolled on the green slope, Schuppanzigh at his side.

'I had heard it was a splendid building, but I had no idea. Seems inappropriate with people unable to afford a loaf of bread.'

'Ambassadors are not like the rest of us,' said Schuppanzigh. 'But even the Count had his problems. He was recalled to Moscow to explain the expense, but it seems he got what he wanted. The most magnificent building in Vienna, I heard someone say.'

They walked towards the columned portico. 'How have rehearsals gone?' Ludwig asked.

'Well. Young Czerny is a remarkable pianist, you know. Technically perfect. He seems incapable of playing a wrong note.'

'Is he inspired? Is there emotion in his playing?'

'It will come. He is still young. Not much more than twenty. He has total command.'

'I remember. I taught him for a while. Scales, arpeggios, broken chords. He preferred playing those to pieces by Mozart.'

'And he can play the opening sequence. The only pianist I know who can. Why did you write that, Ludwig? Were you in a particularly bad mood?'

Ludwig smiled. 'I heard that Clementi in London has given it a name. The Emperor Concerto. Which emperor? Totally inappropriate.'

'It is certainly grand enough for such a name.'

'And the quartets? How have they gone?'

'Again, well. Count Razumovsky is insisting on playing second violin. Mind you, he is better than I thought. And I can assure you Linke will play the opening of the second movement of number one without protest!'

Razumovsky saw them enter the grand salon and came over to greet them. 'Ah, gentlemen! Fellow musicians. What a wonderful soirée we will have. Ludwig, such an honour for me to have your music performed in my new palace, and for me to participate in the quartets. Will you allow me to present you as my guest of honour?'

The chatter in the room hurt Ludwig's ears and the air was oppressive. He said, 'No. If you will forgive me, Count. I would rather just sit and listen. I am rather tired.'

'Of course, of course. I am so sorry. Are you not well? Would you like –?'

'No,' said Ludwig, sharply, and walked to the back of the room. Several heads turned to him in expectation and he bowed this way and that. At last he found a chair and placed it near the double doors that led out on to the grass. He crossed his legs and folded his arms, leaned his head against the wall and closed his eyes. He felt as if he had no strength in his body, and he did not know why. Should he call Doktor Malfatti? Maybe. He would think about it tomorrow.

Antonie's face came into his mind. Not so long ago it had been fresh and vivacious but now she was suffering in the same way as he was. But she at least had the trip to Bohemia to look forward to. Her beauty had matured, her pain giving it an added fragility.

The stirring chord that opened the concerto flooded into his head and Czerny's fingers flew up the keyboard in the massive virtuosic opening Ludwig had written.

Suddenly the notes jarred in Ludwig's head. Jangling, discordant sounds, so real that he wondered for a moment if the musicians were deliberately playing wrong notes. Slowly, though, the tones returned to normal, but it was as if he was hearing his music through a thick pane of glass. The musicians were playing furiously, and he could see Czerny's thick black curls bobbing up and down, occasionally a hand raised high. They were playing his music, but the sounds were distorted again.

Ludwig stood up, stepped quietly out on to the grass and drank in the fresh evening air. How good and soothing it felt. He longed for the calm and peace of the countryside. He walked a few paces and leaned against a tree. He could hear his music again, but in the distance now, and it was quietly overlaid by a strange noise.

Applause. Czerny must have done well. He was pleased. He heard a jumble of voices, and young Czerny, accompanied by Razumovsky and Schuppanzigh, was walking towards him.

Czerny's expectant face looked up at him and he extended his hand. Czerny took it, his face flushed.

'You play well, young man. As well as any in Vienna. Hummel must be envious.'

'I am happy if I have pleased you, sir. Such fine music.'

'Excellent reception, Ludwig,' said Razumovsky. 'Greatly admired.'

'I believe Clementi may not have erred when he named it the Emperor, Ludwig,' said Schuppanzigh. 'It is worthy of it. Will you come and hear the quartets next?'

But Ludwig's head was throbbing and his ears hurt. 'You must forgive me. All of you. Count. But my head . . . You will have to tell me of the reception.'

'Better than in Moscow, I promise you. They are such ignorant imbeciles, although they are my own people,' averred Razumovsky. 'They claim to appreciate art. But what do they know? Nothing. The cellist refused to play the opening of the second movement of the first because it was on a single note. On a single note! As if somehow it was strange music. And yet it is not strange music, it is divine. Divine! Joseph Linke has no such problems. If he did, he would not be paid.'

'That is the best way to treat musicians,' Ludwig said, with a faint smile. 'Threaten to withhold their pay and they will play anything you ask of them. Now, gentlemen, please return to your guests. Good luck with the quartets. And, Czerny, again, I am proud of you.'

He received a note from Bettina, telling him that Antonie had taken to her bed. The doctor had ordered her to stay in her room with the curtains drawn. Her head ached so badly that the smallest ray of light was unbearable.

We are sharing the pain, Ludwig thought. He should write to her, tell her he understood, tell her to be brave.

He looked at the table, strewn with papers, and sighed, then moved across to the sideboard and poured a glass of wine. He glanced at the table again, walked to it and swept away the papers so that they fell to the floor like autumn leaves. They were letters to Johann, attempts to dissuade him from marrying his housekeeper. Marry his housekeeper! A Beethoven! It was unthinkable. One brother married to an immoral woman – whatever Steffen said, that was what she was – another contemplating marriage to a housekeeper.

With a weariness that seemed to push down on his shoulders he turned and looked up at the wall. Are you proud of us,

Grandfather? The mess we have made of our lives? You never knew Carl and Johann. You were spared that. But me? I have made my way as a musician but ... but ...

He went to the piano and picked up a sheet of manuscript paper, which he had filled with notes. 'An die Geliebte', he had written at the top. To the Beloved.

He looked across at his grandfather again. But, Grandfather, what I desire above all things can never be mine. Never.

He read the words under the notes. A poem he had found by someone whose name meant nothing to him, but which when he had read it had illuminated his mind.

> Oh, that I should never cause
> The tears to flow from your sweet eye,
> And if they do, that I should pause
> To dry them ere your love should die.
> But see, they linger on your cheek
> As if to prove our love's divine.
> So let me kiss you as I seek
> To make the pain I caused you mine.

To make the pain I caused you mine. The pain, Toni, the pain we share. He picked up the sheet, and several more that stood behind it, shoved them under his arm and left the apartment.

At the house on the Erdbeergasse the housekeeper admitted him with a small smile of recognition. He walked through the entrance hall, which still resembled a museum, and down the corridor to Antonie's rooms. Quietly he let himself into the anteroom that contained the piano. He glanced across to the door that led to her bedroom. It was closed.

He sat at the piano. Gently, he said to himself. Gently. He placed his hands on the keys and, barely stroking them, played the lilting opening bars of the Andante Favori, the piece she had played for him, the piece that would tell her who was playing for her now.

Legato, legato. His body swayed and he smiled to himself at how different the piece felt played in this way. He had always been fond of it – it was just the ham-fisted way in which the amateur pianists of the city had handled it, in their delight at being able to play a piece by Beethoven, that had made him disdain it.

Even the furious passage near the end he played with a

smoothness that made it seem to grow naturally from what had gone before.

Slowly the music calmed him. Is it doing that for you, Toni? he wanted to ask her. Is it?

He stroked the two *piano* chords that, so surprisingly, ended the piece and laid his hands on his thighs. His breathing was steady now.

He placed the song on the stand. 'An die Geliebte'.

He played the delicate opening bars, the unexpected but still mild discord in the third bar. The voice comes in then, but Ludwig played its part with his right hand, accompanying it with the left. He brought the first verse to a quiet end and began the second, similar to the first but more embellished. And the chords which ended it on the word 'mine'.

Mine. Mine. 'To make the pain I caused you mine.' He paused, then played again from the beginning, still softly so that the notes seemed to float in the air. There, Toni, he thought. Have I taken the pain away from you? Still moving carefully to avoid any noise he left the room and went out of the house.

With a feeling of overwhelming sadness, which he tried, he knew unsuccessfully, to keep from his face, he shook Gleichenstein's hand. 'And you too, young lady,' he said, turning to Netty. 'I wish you both good fortune.'

'It is a long journey to Freiburg,' said Gleichenstein, 'but, ah, just to see the Rhine again and to show it to Netty. And my parents are so looking forward to meeting her.'

'Sir,' said Netty, her face wide-eyed with nervousness, 'my sister Therese asks me to remember her to you. She is in Venice with her fiancé. She says I should thank you again for the piece you composed for her.'

But Ludwig seemed not to have heard her. 'I am grateful to you, Gleichenstein. You were a great help to me.'

'We will be returning to Vienna, sir. Frequently I expect, so that Netty can see her family. Will you permit us to call on you?'

'Of course. I wish you both well.'

He accompanied them to the door and watched them go down the stairs, Gleichenstein holding Netty's arm protectively. He wished, oh, how he wished, he could experience a hundredth part of what Gleichenstein was feeling now. But it was something, he knew, that would always be denied him.

Chapter 4

Ludwig went several more times to the house on the Erdbeergasse, always playing softly for Antonie and gazing at the closed door behind which he knew she was listening. How he wished to see her; how he ached to hear her say that his music was helping her.

One day the servant brought him a note that made his heart soar.

> Dear, Dear Ludwig
> More than any medicine ever can, your sweet music banishes all pain. My heart goes out to you in gratitude. I am much recovered and will soon venture out. Will you come and play for me one more time?
>
> In Hope
> Toni B'tano

He had barely time to digest the contents of the note, to relish the words that brought him such joy, before he received an unexpected visit, which drove any thoughts of happiness from his mind.

It was Carl whom the servant ushered in. He was breathing heavily and collapsed into a chair. His cheeks were sunken and crimson yet with an almost deathly quality. As soon as he sat down he began to cough rackingly until he almost retched into a handkerchief, which he then folded and put into a pocket.

'Calm yourself, Carl,' said Ludwig. 'Will you drink wine?'

Carl shook his head. 'No. No. Ludwig, I must talk to you.'

What could have happened? Ludwig thought. Was the child hurt?

'It's Johanna,' said Carl, strength returning slowly to his voice.

'What has she done? She has not . . . she has not . . .' Ludwig's face was a mask of horror. Had she dared be unfaithful to her husband and violated the name of Beethoven?

'No, no. Not that. If it was that I might even forgive her, sick as I am. It is worse. Immoral and indefensible.'

'What could be worse?'

'Ludwig, she has stolen money from me. She knew where I kept it, and it has gone. My savings.'

'*Stolen money?*'

'Like a common thief. For days she denied it. But in the end she confessed. My own wife. She is an evil woman, Ludwig. Evil.'

'I have always known that, Carl. Where is the money?'

'Gone. She has spent it. I don't know what on. She said something about clothes for the boy, but I don't believe her. How can I ever believe her?'

Fury rose in Ludwig, partly against Carl for having married such an obviously wicked woman. 'She must be punished,' he said. 'You must punish her.'

'I have.' He began to cough again.

Ludwig hurried out and returned with a carafe of water. He poured his brother a glass, but Carl waved it away. 'What have you done?'

'I have reported her to the police. They have questioned her and this morning they told me they are going to bring charges and she will have to answer in court.'

Ludwig gasped. Johanna van Beethoven in court! He was still trying to assimilate the news when the servant came in and said that Herr von Breuning was demanding to be admitted. Before Ludwig could reply Stephan marched into the room. 'Here you are, Carl. Now, will you explain what you have done?'

Carl coughed again, but more dryly this time. He held his hand out for the water and sipped it. 'So you have heard, Steffen. You might as well know. The police agree with me. She is wicked. She has stolen from me, and that is a crime.'

'Can you really believe that, Carl?'

'She confessed to me.'

'Because you attacked her with a knife. You did, didn't you?'

Carl drew breath. 'I had the knife in my hand. I was at the end of my tether. I stuck it into the table in anger. I did not mean to hit her hand. She put it in the way.'

Stephan cast up his eyes and sighed. 'I have spoken to her, Carl. Yes, she did take the money – but she took it to pay the rent.'

'She took it without my consent. That is stealing. She should have asked me. And I know she spent it on other things too, for herself.'

'If she did, Carl, it was only trivial. And, of course, she should have asked you. But you are unwell. She did not want to cause you concern.'

'Hah! Steffen, you are interfering in matters that do not concern you. I know the woman. She is wicked. Ludwig said so right at the start. I should never . . . I should never . . . If she hadn't been . . . Well, this time she has broken the law. She took money without asking me. The police say she broke the law and she must appear in court.'

'For God's sake, Carl, stop this before it is too late. You will ruin her reputation if you do this.'

Ludwig understood the shame and anger that consumed his brother. Why was Stephan always acting as peacemaker, always giving people the benefit of the doubt? Could he not see the simple difference between right and wrong? 'Reputation?' he said, his voice rising. 'She never had a reputation. I knew that right from the beginning. I said so.'

'Ludwig is right. Do you know what else I found out? This is not the first time. When she was a girl she accused her parents' maid of stealing money. In the end she admitted she had stolen it herself and she appeared before the police court. They acquitted her because she was only a girl.'

Stephan threw up his arms in despair. 'You Beethoven brothers! You can be harsh men. Do you understand? Harsh.' He turned on his heel and left them.

Carl sat still for a moment, breathing rapidly. 'I should not have married her,' he said finally. 'You were right, Ludwig. It was a mistake. Except for one thing. I have a son. Ludwig, I am worried about what will happen to him when I die. I am going to die, Ludwig. I don't how long I have got. A year. Maybe two or three. But I will not see my fortieth birthday.'

Tears filled his eyes and Ludwig felt the emotion well up in him too. The Beethoven brothers. He had never thought of it like that. Stephan's words had affected him. He put his hand on Carl's shoulder. 'Do not worry. He will grow up to be a fine man. A fine Beethoven. I will make sure of it.'

In the days that followed Ludwig had hardly been able to stop thinking of Carl and Johanna. And when he wasn't thinking of them, his mind turned to Johann and the housekeeper. And in the dead of night, lying awake and hearing the silence that enveloped him, he wondered how different he was from his brothers. Different in that he had not made a ghastly mistake as Carl had, and was not about to as Johann appeared to be. But was he *really* different?

He thought of his parents. What is marriage but a chain of sorrows? How many times had he heard his mother say that? Looking back to his childhood he could not remember a single moment of affection between them. He saw again the uncomprehending look in his mother's eyes, and the vacant, confused, alcohol-deadened gaze of his father.

But his mother's image faded from his mind and in its place was the beautiful vulnerable face of Antonie. Yes, he thought, I am different from my brothers. Unlike them I have found the perfect woman, the one with whom I want to spend the rest of my life. And I cannot have her.

How fated we Beethoven brothers are. Fated to lives of misery.

His heart was heavy as he took the carriage once more to the Erdbeergasse. He walked into the large musty-smelling house, acknowledged the housekeeper without looking at her, and went through to Antonie's rooms.

He propped the music on the stand, sat down and began to play. Gently, softly. *Oh, that I should never cause the tears to flow from your sweet eye.* On he played, wishing that his life had been different. *To make the pain I caused you mine. Mine. Mine.*

He sat back, looking at the tops of his hands. He glanced at Antonie's door and his heart stood still.

It was open. It had never been open before. He felt his heart race and his mouth felt dry but he did not want water. He was aware of a delicious feeling of warmth spreading through his legs and up into his chest.

He reached forward again. His hands were unsteady; an almost imperceptible trembling that no onlooker would have noticed. He had intended playing the simple opening phrase of the

Andante Favori. Instead he spread out his fingers for the massive C minor chord that opened the Pathétique sonata. No, no, no, he thought. Calm. Restful. No need to impress her. Watching the door, he played the graceful, almost simplistic, opening of the little Rondo he had written for Therese Malfatti.

On he played, never more than *mezzo-forte*, slowing slightly towards the end. He nodded. A good piece, wasted on Therese, who would pound the keys. So would other pianists, who would say that since it was by Beethoven it needed to be played with drama and fire. But it must flow, like water. Forward, back, ceaseless movement. He played it again, allowing himself to sway as the melody alternated between his hands.

The dryness came back into his mouth, and with it a delectable feeling of anticipation. Why should he not walk to the door, open it further and step inside? Why should he not want to know how Antonie was?

He crossed the room, feeling the weight in his legs, put out his hand and eased the door further open. He stepped inside, and his eyes swept round an empty room.

He almost laughed as he walked back to the piano. He had barely sat down before he sounded the opening chord of the Pathétique. His fingers played the chords that followed and then flew across the notes. Hoffmeister the publisher had given it its name. Nothing so full of tragic passion had ever been composed for the piano before, he had said. So let the tragic passion sound, Ludwig thought, as his hands flew furiously over the keys. Barely a pause in the right hand as quavers became crotchets then quavers again. And the massive chords return. Oh, yes, they will always find the drama and the passion and the pain in my music. But will they find the humour?

He lightened his fingers and suddenly the character of the music changed. Did I not write *piano*? And will not every pianist play the chords *forte*? And does the *piano* not lead to *pianissimo*? Before the final sequence, still *piano*, but now . . . yes . . . now . . . allow your fingers their freedom. *Fortissimo* chords to end. And wait. Wait. A full bar's rest to allow the last C minor chord to die slowly away.

He looked across at the open door of Antonie's bedroom and stood up. He picked up the folder, which contained his setting of 'An die Geliebte', walked to the door and out into the short corridor.

In the sudden dimness, he caught a rushing sound then felt himself almost knocked over.

'Maxi!' he heard a voice call, and he knew immediately whose it was. 'Maxi, be careful! Oh, Ludwig, and to think I nearly missed you.' Without hesitating Antonie stood on tiptoe and kissed his cheek lightly – a fleeting movement, so swift he was barely aware that it had happened. 'Do come back in, just for a moment. Will you? Maxi is so excited you're here.'

That voice! Then a sudden discord hit his ears.

'No, Maxi! Now stop, will you? After such beautiful playing, we do not need to hear you splashing about.'

Splashing about. It was what his father had said to him when he was a child. *Stop your splashing about and play what is written, or I will box your ears.*

'No, let her. I don't mind.'

'Sit down, Ludwig. Let me tell the housekeeper to bring some tea.'

'I thought you were in your room,' Ludwig said. 'I am glad you are recovered.'

'Oh, yes, much better, thank you. And, Ludwig,' she came over to him and took his hands in hers, 'how can I ever thank you? You will never know what your wonderful music did for me. How it helped me.'

'Mama! Listen, Mama! Listen to what I can play.'

Ludwig smiled at the sounds of Mozart's Minuet in G, written when he was himself just a child and beloved of children ever since. So simple, so direct. He saw Antonie leave the room and found himself counting the moments until she returned. He watched the effort Maxi was putting into her playing, her arms spread out wide from her little body. Her fingers, arched, struck the notes like tiny hammers.

He stood up and crossed to the piano. Standing to the side of Maxi, he played a variation in the treble. She laughed. His ornamentation – trills, triplets – accompanied her perfectly. As she brought the piece to an end, he played an arpeggio chord high in the treble, like bells pealing.

Antonie laughed and clapped. 'Wonderful, wonderful! There, Maxi. Are you not proud? You have played with Vienna's most famous pianist.'

'Will you compose something for me, Herr Bettoffen? Will you?'

He looked over the child's head at her mother.

'No, Maxi, of course he will not. He is far too important for that.'

'I will, Maxi. I shall compose a short piece and dedicate it to you.'

'Young lady, you do not know how privileged you are. Now, you must run along. Are you not meeting your friend Lotti?'

Maxi nodded firmly. 'First, play something for us, Herr Bettoffen. Something loud.'

'Enough, Maxi!' said Antonie. She turned to the housekeeper, who was putting a tray on the table. 'Thank you, Frau Schneider. You may leave now. I will look after this. I shall see you tomorrow?'

The housekeeper curtsied and left the room.

'Please, Herr Bettoffen. Will you?'

Her mother gave an exasperated sigh and looked despairingly at Ludwig.

'So, Maxi. For you. Just for you. I will play what I was playing before you came in.'

She let out a delighted squeal. He sat at the piano and played the C minor chord. Yes, now is the moment for drama, he thought. He watched the tendons in his hand stand out as his fingers came down on the keys. He threw back his head. *Allegro, crescendo . . . allegro, crescendo.* He was playing the Pathétique faster and more furiously now than he had ever done. This is for Toni, he thought. For you, Toni. I am playing it – my music – as no one else can.

Someone screamed. Water cascaded down his hair on to his face and hands. What? His hands arrested on the keys. Water dripped off his nose and chin. He turned, eyebrows raised uncomprehendingly. Maxi stood by him, an empty jug in her hand, her face frozen in horror. Ludwig looked at her. Had she *really* emptied a jug of water over his head? He saw her lips begin to move.

'I – I thought you needed it. I – I thought you were going to catch fire.'

Slowly Ludwig's face dissolved into a grin and he began to laugh. He could not stop. Drops of water fell off his hair as he bellowed. Finally he calmed down. He put out his arms. 'Come here, Maxi.'

She shot a look at her mother, then moved cautiously towards him.

He put his hands on her shoulders. 'You were right. If you

had not done that, I might have caught fire.' He laughed again and Maxi laughed with him.

Antonie hurried over. 'Go on, Maxi. Leave now. Go and see your friend. Hurry. Go on.'

Maxi, relief all over her face, ran from the room and Antonie hastened into her bedroom. Ludwig heard the front door slam in the distance as the little girl left the house.

Antonie emerged with a towel. 'Oh, Ludwig, I am so, so sorry. Come into my room. Let me dry you. The naughty, naughty girl.'

He followed her into the bedroom, wiping the water from his eyes.

'Here. Sit on the bed.' Vigorously she rubbed his hair with the towel. He closed his eyes and felt her wipe gently round his face, over his eyelids and down his nose. 'Now, stand up, Ludwig. Oh dear, you poor, poor man. You are wet through. I will – such a little minx, that girl. Here, let me.'

She tossed the towel on the bed and slid his jacket off his shoulders. She untied the string that held his shirt closed, then dried his chest with the towel.

He was not aware of how it started, but his lips were against hers. His arms were round her shoulders, pulling her against him. Her head was thrown back, her eyes closed and her lips parted as Ludwig kissed her again and again. He put one hand on the back of her head to bring her ever more closely against him.

After the first moments, he began to savour the taste of her, the sweetness of her lips and mouth, her scent.

He felt her press herself against him, against his hardening groin. He was aware that her hands were moving. She was pulling her chemise out of her skirt and opening it. The soft shiny silkiness of her shift felt slippery against his skin. 'Ludwig,' she murmured, 'Ludwig, at last. Make love to me. Will you?'

She pulled him down on to the bed and her hands were fumbling with the cord that ran round his waist. He gasped as he felt her grip him. He buried his face in her neck, breathing in the scent of her skin.

'Toni, Toni. Stop. No.' He heard his own words and could scarcely believe he was uttering them. 'Toni. Stop.'

She loosened her grip. 'Ludwig, what is it? Do you not love me?'

His throat was tight and he nodded, his hair brushing against her neck. 'But we must not. We must not.'

Her hand pushed his head deeper into the hollow where her neck met her shoulder and he tasted the saltiness that ran down her neck to his lips. She began to tremble with small sobs she fought to control.

They lay together, silent but for Antonie's tiny chokes.

He kissed her neck and pushed himself up on his arm. He picked up the corner of the towel and wiped under her eyes and down her cheeks. Then he sat on the edge of the bed, looking down at the floor. His breathing, fast at first, slowly calmed.

He felt her sit up, get off the bed and walk round to him. She sat next to him and put her hand on his thigh. 'You are a good man, Ludwig. I love you, you know.' She looked up at him.

The words, soothing and quiet . . . The words he had dreamed of hearing one day, soft and calm . . . Now he had to brace himself against them. 'Do not say it, Toni. It will only bring pain.'

'Do you love me, Ludwig? Do you?'

He turned to her. Her face, so elegant, so serene, so vulnerable. The face that was ever in his mind. And now she was offering herself to him, *giving* herself to him. He wanted to say the words, the words she needed to hear. But what would that bring but more pain? He nodded briefly. 'But it cannot be, Toni.'

She squared her shoulders and took a deep breath. 'You are right, Ludwig,' she said, in a stronger voice. 'Fate has decreed it. It cannot be.'

She got up and walked unsteadily to the dressing table. There she tied her chemise and tucked it into her skirt. She brushed her long hair. Ludwig watched the ringlets bounce. Then she wiped her face with a small cloth, and dusted it with a fine powder. Finally she turned to him, with a smile. 'So. Come.' She took his hand and led him back into the anteroom where she poured him some tea. 'It will be cold, but you are probably thirsty. Drink it. It will refresh you. Ludwig, we leave for Bohemia soon. After Franz has returned. Then we return to Frankfurt.'

'But do you not have work to do here?'

'It is done. I cannot delay it any longer. Papa's collection is to be auctioned in a week and the house will be sold. Everything will be done by the time we leave for Bohemia.'

'Where are you going?'

'Prague first. Then Karlsbad – for Fanny to take the waters.'

'And you will not return here?'

'Only to settle the paperwork on the house. Franz will deal with it. And it will be farewell to my native city.'

There was a lump in Ludwig's throat. 'It will be difficult to imagine this city – this *damned* city,' he added, vehemently, 'without you.'

Chapter 5

Reflecting coolly on his situation, Ludwig could not escape the conclusion that he was enduring one of the most difficult periods of his life. The strain of family affairs, combined with the burden of his own misfortunes, seemed almost more than he could bear.

His health was poor. He had considered a hundred times calling in Doktor Malfatti, always at the last moment resisting the urge to do so, knowing that nothing could be done. His hearing was stable, but the noises were ever present and the heaviness that accompanied them made ordinary conversation near impossible. His friends spoke loudly and clearly, but it was a constant and debilitating effort for Ludwig to listen to them. His stomach and bowels hurt, sometimes dully, sometimes with a sharpness that made him gasp. Heavy red wine – thank God – suppressed the pain.

As for his brothers, he pushed them to the back of his mind. What else could he do? Stephan Breuning, it seemed, had given up on the Beethovens. Once Carl had determined to press the case against his wife, Stephan, in disgust, had told him it would be a long time before he could associate with them again.

There had been no word from Johann. Had he come to his senses? Ludwig doubted it. He knew of his brother's weakness when it came to women. If this housekeeper had set out to ensnare Johann, he would have been easy prey.

And what of his own ill luck with women? He had fallen in love with someone and she with him. Was it possible? Yes, he thought wryly. Possible and impossible.

For days he sat alone in his room, staring at the portrait of his grandfather and looking longingly at the piano. He did not play but in his head he heard music, whirling music. It built up in him, taking shape. He jotted notes on the manuscript paper that lay on the table beside him, but it was not until he knew exactly the form the music would take that he crossed to the piano and played a huge chord of A major. A major!

He smiled at the incongruity of it. Not the C minor of the Pathétique, doom-laden and full of foreboding but A major, the brightest of keys, full of hope and optimism. And what, in his life, was there to feel optimistic about?

In a matter of days he had set down the broad shape of a new symphony, his seventh. And hardly had he done that than he took a clean sheet of paper and, after a few preliminary sketches, came up with a perfectly formed three-bar phrase. F major! Bright and cheerful. He had the opening for the eighth.

And with all this music filling his head, bursting to be released on to paper, he put it to one side. There was time enough, and its freshness would not diminish. Did ordinary people forget language and words? How could he forget his own language?

Instead he went to the piano with a clean sheet of manuscript paper and played a theme that formed under his fingers even as he played. A simple, childlike theme, almost hymnlike. Oh, what he could do with this theme! He could vary it almost infinitely, turn it into a fugue, give it drama, weight, pathos; examine it, explore it . . . But no. Just the theme and the second subject that derived from it and complemented it. He jotted down the notes. B flat major was the key. Warm and reassuring.

He played the theme over and over again until he was satisfied with it. A little embellishment here and there, a short *forte* passage to lift it but not difficult to play, a trill in the treble like a bird hovering over a field . . . and two swift chords to end it. Piano, violin, cello. He wrote the three words at the top of the page. A trio. Perfect.

Alongside the words he wrote,

For my little friend Maxi Brentano, to encourage her in pianoforte playing.

The burst of creativity left Ludwig's strength depleted. His limbs were weak, his head rang to the sounds of his music, but gradually, inexorably, as the music faded the dreadful noises returned. Finally, he gave in and sent a note to Doktor Malfatti, asking him to visit.

'Not difficult to give a diagnosis,' said Malfatti, looking round the room. 'You're working too hard.'

'Pfft!' exclaimed Ludwig dismissively. 'Hard work is not a disease!'

'Depends how you treat it. Look.' He pointed at the papers strewn around the room. 'Does your servant not tidy up for you?'

'I will not let him.'

'Then you are causing yourself more strain than you need.'

'I cannot alter how I work. I cannot choose when I work.'

Malfatti pulled up a chair and sat opposite his patient. 'Herr Beethoven, let me speak candidly to you. I do not need to examine you to establish that you are unwell. I can see the symptoms with my own eyes. I do not need to hold tuning forks to your ears to see if you can hear. I know you have a deafness which is not going to improve. Whether it will worsen I cannot tell you, since it is impossible to say what caused it in the first place.'

'It will worsen, Malfatti.'

'You may be right. But it is not connected to your general ill health. When your health recovers, I fear your hearing will not.'

'My hearing will be worse. What *causes* it, Malfatti?'

'I only wish I knew. If we could look inside your ears we could probably tell you. But you do not need me to tell you that we cannot do it while you are living.'

'Hah! You will do it when I am dead, though, won't you, Malfatti? Cut open my head and show it to your students. This is why Beethoven could hardly hear voices, except his own, which rang in his head so loud that it hurt him. You will enjoy that.'

'Enjoy is hardly the appropriate word.' Malfatti's face seemed to become longer, his expression even more morose. 'Let us return to the question of your general health. You are unwell, and as I have told you before there's no name for your illness.'

'But I am ill.'

'You are exhausted, Herr Beethoven. You are working too hard. And you have family problems. I am aware of that. I know about your brother Carl. One of my colleagues is treating him. Doktor Bertolini.'

Ludwig sighed. 'He believes he is going to die.'

'It may be so, Herr Beethoven. It may be so. I am not going to tell you he won't. But he has improved somewhat lately. That business with his wife seems to have given him strength. But once consumption takes hold . . .' His voice trailed away.

'Then if you have nothing more to tell me, Malfatti –'

'There is something more I can tell you, but I am tempted to save myself the effort because I know you will not heed my advice. You are not a good patient, Herr Beethoven.'

Ludwig smiled at Malfatti. He could not help liking the man. The long lugubrious face, which seemed incapable of transmuting into a smile, the heavy-lidded eyes with the ponderous folds of skin underneath, made Ludwig think he would be perfectly suited to the role of undertaker, dealing with people after death rather than trying to cure them to avoid that sad event.

'If you tell me to stop work, stop drinking wine, stop eating my meals at odd hours . . .'

'What I have to tell you would be – if you will forgive the rather apt choice of words – music to most people's ears.' The ends of his lips turned up in the faintest hint of pleasure at his cleverness.

Ludwig sat back and folded his arms.

'Take a holiday. An extended holiday. Go to Bohemia – the spa towns – and take the waters. Enjoy the countryside. Summer in Bohemia. What could be better? Rest your body and rest your ears.'

Ludwig ignored the beggars sitting in the shadow of the Bastion and turned into the Mölkerbastei. His hands were thrust deep into his pockets. He had come from the court building in the Hofplatz where he had witnessed the humiliation of his brother, Carl.

It was clear that the magistrate felt the case should never have been brought. He asked the police officer in charge of it why he had not effected an amicable settlement of the matter, since this was a domestic dispute. The officer explained that the plaintiff had insisted on bringing a charge of embezzlement, and since the defendant had admitted taking money he had had no choice but to file a prosecution.

After questioning both Carl and Johanna, the magistrate said that, given the circumstances as outlined by the police officer, he would have to punish Johanna and that the normal sentence for such an offence was a month in a prison cell.

Ludwig was at the back of the court and saw victory written on Carl's face. Johanna's, in comparison, was deathly pale.

'But I have no intention, in this case,' said the magistrate gravely, 'of sending the defendant to prison. Instead I sentence her to one month's house arrest. By which I mean she will spend all reasonable time – when she has no other pressing engagement – at her home in the . . .' he looked down at some papers '. . . Rauhensteingasse. Except, of course, when needs dictate that she must go out, to purchase food and so on. There shall be no police surveillance of her.' He stared at Carl over the top of his spectacles. 'Maybe the plaintiff will deduce from the sentence that this court believes it should not be called in to settle domestic disputes.'

Now it was Carl's face that had turned pale. Johanna, Ludwig noticed, did not turn to her husband to savour the moment, but rushed out of the court.

Ludwig climbed the final set of stairs and paused at the top to catch his breath.

'A lady and her daughter in the anteroom to see you,' said the servant.

Ludwig felt a twist in his stomach. 'Wait two minutes, then send them in.' He went into his bedroom and tried to smooth his hair with a wide-toothed comb.

When he came out into the main room Antonie and Maxi were already standing there. Antonie was wearing a hat that covered the top part of her forehead, making her deep-set eyes appear even deeper as they looked up from beneath the rim. What should he say? What should he do?

But before he could decide he heard her soft but insistent voice. 'May I sit down, Ludwig?' She smiled. 'I have brought one extremely mischievous young lady to apologise to you.'

Maxi bounded over to him, the same upturned look on her face as her mother. He could see in her that she would be beautiful, too, one day. She curtsied, frowned, then said studiedly, 'I am very sorry, Herr Bettoffen, for what I did. It is my profound hope that you will forgive me.'

Ludwig walked to the piano. He picked up the manuscript of the piano trio. 'Here, Maxi. For you. To help with your practice.'

'Oh, thank you, sir. Thank you. Will you play it for me?'

'No, not now. Take it home and study it. And maybe in a few weeks . . .'

'Ludwig, we have also come to say goodbye,' said Antonie. 'I leave soon for Prague. Franz has returned. We are going with Fanny to Bohemia. To take the waters. Maxi and the other children are returning to Frankfurt with Bettina.'

Ludwig's jaw fell. 'I . . . Malfatti has recommended I should go to Bohemia too. For the waters.'

He saw her catch her breath. 'You are going too?'

'I . . . I hadn't decided. I –'

'Oh, yes, Ludwig. You must, if the doctor has recommended it. You must.'

'Yes, Herr Bettoffen,' said Maxi. 'You must. Then you can keep my mama company.'

BOOK TWELVE

Chapter 1

'Dear Ludwig,' said Nanette Streicher, 'I am so glad you took Doktor Malfatti's advice. The rest will do you so much good. You look worn out.'

Ludwig took the cup of coffee she handed him.

'I will come to your apartment and make sure you have all the clean clothes you need. When do you leave?'

Ludwig looked up at Nanette's kind face. 'Monday morning.'

'Oh, that gives me time. Put all the clothes that need cleaning in a pile and I'll deal with them.'

'You don't need to. The servant can do it.'

Nanette waved away his words and sat close to him. 'Andreas will be in from the workshop in a moment. There is something he wants to ask you – that we both want to ask you, but I will leave it to him. Now, tell me, where are you going and what are you going to do?'

'Prague first. I have to see Prince Kinsky. He owes me money from my contract. Then to Teplitz to meet Goethe.'

'Goethe?' Nanette squeaked. 'You are going to meet *Goethe*?'

'Bettina Brentano arranged it. She . . . Do you know her?'

'I know the family name. Stephan has spoken to me about them. From Frankfurt, aren't they? But the name Bettina doesn't . . .' She frowned. 'I thought it was . . . I can't remember.'

Ludwig looked down at the black liquid and swirled it round the cup, watching the little bubbles form and disappear. 'She is Franz Brentano's sister. Half-sister. Her family knows Goethe. They are friends. Apparently he wants to meet me.'

'He wants to meet you! Ludwig, how wonderful. He is such a great poet.'

'She sent him my *Egmont* music. I don't know if he understands music, but I would be pleased if he approved of it.'

'He will. And how long will you be in Teplitz?'

'I don't know exactly. Two or three weeks. Then I go to Karlsbad to meet the Brentanos.'

'Not Bettina?'

'No.' He emptied his cup, and held it out to Nanette. She filled it while he spoke. 'Franz and his wife Antonie. Toni, she is called. I am going to stay with them in Karlsbad.'

'Oh, that's nice. It'll stop you being lonely, to have friends to stay with. Do they have children?'

'Their youngest is with them. Fanny. She has asthma. That's why they're going to Bohemia, for her to take the waters.'

Andreas walked in, untying his leather apron and tossing it over the back of a chair. He took a handkerchief out of his pocket and wiped his hands, then his forehead. 'Ah, Ludwig. Good to see you. I smelled coffee and knew you must be here. Have you heard the news from Paris? Client was in an hour ago and he told me. Extraordinary. Absolutely extraordinary. Napoleon Bonaparte has crossed the river Niemen on the Polish-Russia border with an army of more than five hundred thousand men, and has invaded Russia.'

'Invaded *Russia*?' repeated Ludwig. 'You can't invade Russia. What is he trying to do?'

'Defeat the Russian army and depose the Tsar. He is hoping, so my client told me, to engage the Russians as soon as possible and crush them. He will keep going east until they stand and fight.'

'Maybe he has at last made a fatal mistake,' Ludwig mused.

'Maybe,' said Andreas. 'But I have heard that said about the man before, and he has always emerged triumphant. But enough of that. I hear you're going away.'

'To Bohemia. For the waters.' Ludwig did not want to go through it again so he changed the subject. 'And the piano business?' he asked. 'Are the people of Vienna, who claim such artistic interests, keeping you occupied?'

Andreas pulled up a chair and sat down, his hands locked between his knees. 'I have more work than I can handle. People complain about the price of a loaf of bread, but those same people still want a new piano.'

'That is because you offer very lenient terms, Andreas,' put in his wife.

'Well, my dear, the alternative is no orders. And I would rather work, even if payment is somewhat deferred. Has Nanette told you about our new music room, Ludwig?'

Ludwig was finding that now when he was in company his eyes flitted between people's eyes and their lips. With those he knew well he was content to watch their lips more than their eyes and in turn they were careful with their enunciation.

'We are building a new music room on the back of the building. It's for people to try our pianos – we've never had anywhere for them to compare them. I'll keep all our models in there and people can try them one after the other. That way they'll be able to judge them properly. Maybe, occasionally, we'll have a soirée. We might invite certain of our musical friends to come and play. Young Czerny, say, or Wölffl. Maybe even Hummel.'

Ludwig smiled. 'If I am not too busy, Andreas!'

'Excellent, Ludwig. But there is something you could do for us that would take up very little of your time.' He glanced at Nanette who shook her head to signify that she had not already mentioned it. 'Have you heard of a sculptor called Franz Klein? Friend of Willi Mähler. Good artist. Known as the Head Lopper.'

Ludwig looked puzzled.

'He specialises in head-and-shoulders busts. Only interested in people from the shoulders up. Hence the nickname.'

'I am not giving him piano lessons. Him or anybody else.'

'No, no, of course not. But would you let him sculpt you?'

'By lopping my head off?'

Both Streichers laughed heartily, more out of relief at Ludwig's display of humour than at the joke itself.

'All that is required is that you sit still for ten minutes. No more. He will take a life mask and work from that.'

'Why does he want a bust of me?'

'*He* doesn't, Ludwig,' said Nanette. 'We do, don't we, Andreas?'

'To put in pride of place in our new music room. To look over our pianos. Will you let me arrange an appointment?'

A small smile stole across Ludwig's face. 'If it will make the Streichers happy.'

Andreas and Nanette beamed at each other and, Nanette said, 'Now, Ludwig, has Stephan told you his news?'

Ludwig's stomach lurched. 'I haven't seen Steffen for a while.'

'You haven't? Oh, you must go and see him. He is such a happy man. And no one deserves to be happy more than he. He has become engaged. And to such a nice young lady. Constanze is her name.'

Ludwig's heart sank. First Gleichenstein, now Stephan Breuning. Such happiness in store for them.

'I hope he will be happy. I am sure he will. I will send him a note.'

'Go to see him, Ludwig,' implored Nanette. 'He would be so pleased to see you.'

'If I have time,' he answered curtly. 'Now, I must return to my apartment. Thank you for the coffee, Nanette.'

He thought of his old friend as the carriage rumbled across the cobbles, past St Stephansdom and into the Graben. He was jealous. Stephan had suffered when Julie had died, but there was something about him, some quality, that always seemed to ensure that in the end things turned out right for him. Maybe that accounted for his occasional smugness, his air of piety. Ludwig decided he would not visit his friend before he left for Bohemia.

He alighted in the Freyung and climbed the stairs to his apartment. When the servant told him that a gentleman was waiting to see him, he thought, Typical Stephan! Just when I have decided . . .

But it was Nikolaus Zmeskall. 'Come, Ludwig. To the Schwan. Some wine, yes? I have something to tell you.'

Ludwig allowed himself to be led out again. Zmeskall wanted to take a carriage, but Ludwig said he needed to walk, and the two men strode back through the Freyung and into the Graben. Ludwig kept a pace ahead of Zmeskall so that conversation was not possible, turned down the Spiegelgasse and into the Neuer Markt, round the fountain and into the Schwan. 'Here.' He handed Zmeskall some coins. 'And bring me a pipe as well.' He went to the back of the room and sat at a small round table.

The Schwan was not as full as in the days before the Finanz-Patent, but there were more drinkers now than there had been immediately after it had been enacted. Slowly the Viennese were coming to terms with the sudden diminution in their worth and adapting accordingly.

Ludwig breathed in the smell of stale alcohol and sawdust, enjoying its sourness. The carriage-ride first and then the walk had left him with a thirst. At the first taste of the rough red wine he sighed with satisfaction and with his sleeve wiped away the tears that it brought to his eyes.

'You leave on Monday, I hear,' said Zmeskall.

'For the peace and calm of Bohemia. To sit in hot bubbling water and let the sun shine on my face. Walk across fields and sit by streams. Soak up the warmth of summer.'

Zmeskall smiled. 'I envy you, Ludwig. Those of us who have to sit behind our desks every day of the week can enjoy no such luxury.' He drank a mouthful of wine and grimaced. 'The wine in this wretched place does not improve.'

'It is wine, Nikola. The best medicine known to man. Already I feel the effects in my head. Soon the fog will clear and, who knows? Maybe I will even be able to hear everything you say.'

'Only if you want to, I suspect. You know, I've often wondered how much you really cannot hear and how much you choose not to hear.'

Ludwig remonstrated, 'No, Nikola. You do not know the pain of it. It is different when I sit here with you. I am relaxed. The wine is having its effect. The noise of talking is far enough away. But sometimes . . . sometimes I cannot even hear the notes I play, and if someone tries to talk to me their voice cuts into my head like a knife. Either that or it is muffled, as if the words are wrapped in a blanket. The only voice I always hear is my own. Here, in my head.'

'You are right. You need the calm of the countryside. The sounds of nature.' He leaned forward. 'And the touch of the soft flesh of a woman. A Bohemian peasant girl who –'

Ludwig put his glass down firmly. 'Enough, Nikola. I do not want to –'

'Not in love, are you, Ludwig? Surely I don't detect –'

'Stop, Nikola. No more of that – that word. Do not use it lightly. It is too – too precious.'

Zmeskall sat back and folded his arms. 'Well, I'm not sure I know what has caused this sudden philosophising. I will not ask questions. But, Ludwig, on the subject of women, there is something I should tell you. Rather sad news, actually. Remember Josephine Deym? Stackelberg, as she now is? Poor woman is slowly losing her mind. At least that's what her brother Franz thinks. Stackelberg has been cruel to her beyond measure. In every way possible.'

'What has he done?'

'First of all he has spent all her money. Ruined her. He bought an expensive estate in Moravia. Josephine gave him all the money Deym had left her. But he was unable to keep up payments on the place and there was a lawsuit against him and he lost everything. He blamed Josephine.'

'Blamed Josephine?'

'Yes. I don't know the details. But he wanted her to give him more money, from the Brunsvik estate in Martonvasar. He said that would enable him to clear the debt, then he would be able to make money. She refused. She had to. Her mother would never have allowed it.'

Ludwig was appalled. 'He is obviously a scoundrel. She should —'

'It's even worse than that.' Zmeskall lowered his eyes, and his voice. 'He left her. Moved into a small apartment somewhere in the city. But one night, drunk, he came to the house and . . . you can imagine. Now she is expecting another child. Another mouth to feed. I don't know how she'll manage.'

'He should be arrested.'

'What for? They are married. He is legally entitled to. Ludwig, I don't want to put any burden on your shoulders, but she is asking to see you. She says she regrets the way she behaved and she wants to see you.'

Ludwig exhaled sharply. 'No. I don't . . . She . . . If I go to see her, she will want me to go again. And again. It's better . . .' He looked up at Zmeskall.

Zmeskall nodded. 'I think you're right — in fact I told her you would not come. Actually, I said I thought you had already left for Bohemia. But I thought I should put it to you.'

Ludwig poured more wine. 'You did the right thing. There are enough problems over marriage in my own family. Carl and his thieving wife —'

'Ludwig, I —'

'And Johann in Linz. Have you heard about him?'

Zmeskall had. 'Better to remain a bachelor, like me.'

There was a sudden commotion at the front of the room, near the door. Unnoticed by Ludwig and Nikola, the Schwan had filled considerably while they had been talking. Twenty or thirty men stood at the circular bar or sat at tables, drinking wine or beer and smoking pipes. Now they all looked up, the surprised expressions on their faces changing in an instant to delighted laughter.

Four men dashed into the bar. Three were dressed in the unmistakable uniform of Cossack soldiers, baggy trousers, tight blue jackets and tall black hats. The fourth was smaller than the others. He wore a black tailcoat with a white sash across his chest to which a bunch of red grapes was tied. His hair was combed forward over his forehead. He held one hand under the grapes. The other he swung imperiously as he strode in small circles, his stomach jutting out over his trousers. No words were spoken as the small man waved his free arm and the three Cossacks tumbled to the ground, their faces masks of agony. Each time they rose he made to smite them and they fell to the floor again. But each time they rose they beckoned him with their arms, like sirens luring their prey. They moved slowly across the room, drawing the small man inexorably with them.

There was laughter from the drinkers, accompanied by rhythmic clapping. Ludwig noticed that one man was standing by the door, keeping watch on the market place outside.

Finally the three Cossacks surrounded the small man, crouching now and no longer falling to the ground. He looked nervously around him and tried to break free, but he had no escape. The Cossacks, their arms open wide, danced on their haunches, their arms folded and their legs kicking out. The small man's face expressed bewilderment, as if to ask how only three Cossacks could so effectively bar his path. But they whirled round him, whooping, kicking in time to the drinkers' clapping.

The little man seemed to shrink, as he realised he was trapped.

The Cossacks remained crouched but stopped kicking. The clapping ceased and there was silence. Imperceptibly the Cossacks moved slightly to the side, then a little more.

The small man saw the gap and gradually, looking around him nervously, moved towards it. The Cossacks did not stop him. Lightly he trod away from them. They stood and watched as his paces shortened and he walked in circles again. He held both arms across his chest and began to shiver, his teeth chattering.

Suddenly a Cossack darted up to him and squeezed a grape. The deep red juice ran down his white shirt to a burst of guffaws.

He took a few more short paces and another Cossack sprang at him, burst another grape. Seconds later the third Cossack did the same.

The small man's chest ran with rivulets of the dark red juice. One by one the cossacks darted up to him and burst more grapes. Soon his chest was no more than a mess of juice.

On his knees the small man crawled towards the bar, defeated and broken, all the pride gone out of him. His head swung in time to the sobbing that convulsed his shoulders. Finally the three Cossacks stood around him again, each with a boot on his bent shoulders. Cheering erupted in the room, accompanied by applause.

Suddenly the man at the door hissed. In an instant the small man rose to his feet, all four bowed quickly, ran to the door and were gone.

Ludwig looked at Nikola. 'I once thought he was one of the people, an ordinary man like them. But he is nothing more than a tyrant. And he will fall, like all tyrants.'

Nikola nodded. 'This time his ambition has gone too far. If he really is marching all the way to Moscow, he will soon find he is further away from home than he thought. And what will his soldiers say when they run out of wine and there is no more to be had?'

Chapter 2

Nanette Streicher busied herself in Ludwig's apartment. On his bed she had made neat piles of clothes, which she was beginning to transfer to the large leather bag that stood open on the floor.

Ludwig sat at the piano, playing tuneless phrases and scribbling notes on a sheet of manuscript paper. He was continuing work on the symphony in F and intended taking it with him to Bohemia. So deeply involved was he that he started when Nanette laid a hand on his shoulder. 'We should go now. Professor Klein will be expecting us.'

He muttered in frustration, but put the sheet in a folder and tied the string round it. 'This must go in the bag. With quills.' He handed it to Nanette. 'We must not be long.'

They took a carriage to St Stephansdom and walked down the Kärntnerstrasse, which was slowly resuming its role as the busiest street in the city, with more shops and cafés than even the Graben. Two-thirds of the way down, with the Bastion and the Kärntnertor Gate visible ahead of them, they turned left into the narrow Annagasse, which ran to the eastern section of the wall.

'I like this street,' said Nanette, 'maybe because it has three churches in it. It gives it a rather spiritual feel.'

'If you are going to ask me to pray, I shall return to my lodgings right away,' said Ludwig, with a grin.

They entered a narrow courtyard and climbed a small dark circular staircase.

'His rooms overlook the Ursuline convent,' she said. 'He likes the quiet. The only sound he hears is the chanting of the nuns.'

On the top floor the door swung open as they reached it. 'I heard your footsteps,' said the little man. 'Please do come in. Frau Streicher.' He bowed and turned to Ludwig.

'And Herr Beethoven. Such an honour. Franz Klein, at your service.'

At first Ludwig was dazzled by the brightness of the room. Everything was brilliant white – the walls, the curtains, the sheets that hung over easels and sculptures. The sun streamed in through two wide windows, which made the room almost too warm.

In the middle stood a chair, the seat and arms covered in shiny black leather, a head-rest protruding from the back. It looked like the ones that stood in the barbers' shops between Petersplatz and the Hoher Markt. Klein gestured towards it. 'If you would be so good, sir, we will begin right away. I have prepared the gypsum. We are ready.' He had a long thin face that matched his body. His eyebrows were broad and wiry and almost met above his nose. He wore small round spectacles and from his chin hung a straggly beard. He looked every bit the artist, Ludwig thought, but in a rather contrived way. Ludwig sat in the chair and gripped the arms as it tilted back under his weight.

Before he could move Klein had spread a white sheet over him and was tucking it into his collar. 'Now, sir, allow me to explain. First I will cover your eyes, so there will be no danger to them. I will then spread wet gypsum over your face. With my fingers I will work the gypsum into every crevice of your face. It is essential, my good sir, absolutely essential, that while I do this you do not move. If you do, the cast will not take. Do you understand?'

Klein's face was close to Ludwig's, and his beard tickled his cheek. On the other man's breath was the stale odour of sausage. His voice was severe and humourless and Ludwig felt the first twinge of disquiet.

Klein told him to close his eyes, then placed heavy damp cotton pads over them. Next Ludwig felt Klein's hand smearing a thick wet substance over his face. It was cold and it made his cheeks twitch. Klein's hand stopped moving. 'No, sir. Still. Totally still. Not a muscle or a nerve must move.'

Klein's hand continued to daub and the substance hardened almost as soon it touched Ludwig's face. It became heavy and dragged his cheeks and lips down. He wanted to speak, to tell Klein that it was hurting his face, but he could not move – there was too much weight on his face.

He felt Klein's fingers smear the gypsum on his nose and

under his nostrils, then the man's little finger at the entrance to his nostrils. 'There. I make two small holes so you can breathe.'

Ludwig tried to open his mouth but could not. He drew in a sharp breath. Several fragments of wet gypsum entered his nose, blocking his nostrils. He breathed in again, drawing the pieces further up his nose.

Panic overcame him and he leaped from the chair, almost overbalancing as it tilted forward with him. With his fingers he clawed at his face, tearing away the gypsum. He pulled the cotton pads off his eyes, throwing them to the ground. He coughed and spluttered, trying to breathe but he still could not. A violent sneeze shook his frame and he saw, through half-closed eyes, dozens of tiny shards of gypsum fly off his face.

He tore again at his mouth until he could open it, and gulped in huge draughts of air. His nostrils were clear now too. He could breathe again.

He felt Nanette's hand on his arm, propelling him gently towards an easy chair. 'Dear oh dear. Poor Ludwig. Sit and rest a few moments. What happened, Professor Klein?'

The Professor, irritably sweeping the bits of hardening gypsum into a pile, shrugged his shoulders. 'He believed he couldn't breathe so he panicked. It's not the first time.'

Ludwig gazed at the small, rather ridiculous figure of Klein. 'You tried to suffocate me, you imbecile. No one can breathe through that stuff.'

'I assure you, Herr Beethoven, I know my art, just as you know yours. However, if you wish I shall make the holes a little bigger next time. But they cannot be too big otherwise I will not get a faithful cast. You must learn to breathe more gently. Just for the time it takes for the gypsum to set.'

Ludwig considered leaving there and then, but he knew how much Nanette and Andreas wanted a bust of him for their new music room.

'So, I am ready, sir,' said Klein, indicating the chair.

Ludwig did not move. Klein clucked in annoyance and turned to a table standing near the window, where he went through the motions of arranging papers, scribbling a few words on one, making a small sketch on another. Finally he turned to Ludwig. 'I need to mix more gypsum, sir. I take it you will have resumed your place in the chair when I return?'

Ludwig nodded, and Klein left the room. He turned to

Nanette. 'Pompous ass,' he said. 'I enjoyed watching him clear up the mess I made.'

'You will let him do it this time, won't you, Ludwig?' Nanette asked, carefully.

In response Ludwig walked to the chair. He sat in it more gently this time, easing himself slowly back and reclining his head on the padded rest. He closed his eyes and a sensation of peace filled him. Soon, he thought, soon I shall be on the road to Prague and then to Bohemia. Away from the city. Away from pressures. And I will see Antonie. Her soft voice will soothe my ears. The sun will soothe my body and the waters will cleanse my soul.

He did not flinch as Klein once more placed the wet pads over his eyes and began to work the gypsum into the contours of his face. Its weight again dragged down his cheeks. He wanted to tell Klein that the cast would not be true, because his face would be pulled down in a way that it was not naturally. But the process was going ahead and there was nothing he could do to stop it, short of jumping out of the chair again.

He felt Klein probe under his nostrils making the holes for him to breathe. Slowly, tentatively at first, he drew air into his nose. It was clear. He could breathe.

'Now, still, sir. Very still.'

Ludwig breathed slowly but steadily, wanting to rid his face of the heavy plaster but resisting the temptation. He heard muffled voices, Nanette and Klein talking to each other, but he made no attempt to listen.

At last Klein said in his ear. 'Right. Do not move now, sir. Not even the slightest twitch. The most crucial moment has arrived. I shall remove the gypsum and we shall know if it has succeeded.'

He felt Klein's fingers scratching at the top of his forehead, immediately under his hair. They worked their way round and down the sides of his face. Suddenly he felt a blast of cold air against his skin. The ache in his muscles dissipated. Klein peeled the wet pads from his eyes. 'There. I am finished with you.'

Ludwig opened his eyes. He saw Klein pick up a jug and pour water into the mask. He swirled it round, then tipped it into a bucket. Carefully he turned the mask the right way up and laid it on a cloth on his workbench. He stood back, hands on hips. 'There. A masterpiece!' he said. 'Your face, sir. Perfectly re-created. Better than any painter can do.'

Ludwig climbed out of the chair, straightening his legs painfully. He took the towel Klein was holding out and wiped his face. Then he walked to the bench and looked down. It was his face! The same expression, nose and lips, staring sightlessly up at the ceiling. 'My lips are pulled down because of the weight of that stuff. You have made me look angry.'

'You *were* angry, sir!'

Ludwig looked at Klein, then at Nanette, whose face was wreathed in a smile. He looked again at the mask. There was no doubting it. It was his face. Klein was right. Using this he would be able to create a bust that really would look like him. Not some fanciful representation as Mähler had made.

'There. You have what you want. Now I must go.'

He bowed to Klein, took Nanette's hand, bent his head over it, and left.

A letter was waiting for him at his apartment. Recognising the handwriting instantly, he tore open the seal and read it.

Dear, dear Ludwig

God speed on your journey. Franz and I leave with little Fanny the day after you. We arrive Thursday in Prague. Franz insists you join us for dinner at our hotel, the Rothes Haus. It is only a short walk from the Charles Bridge.

Need I tell you how happy it will make me to see you again?

In anticipation
A.B.

Chapter 3

The rain had begun as the carriage crossed the border into southern Bohemia and Ludwig's clothes were wet and cold against his back. The police building at Drosendorf, the last town on the Austrian side of the border, was set back from the road, so that he and the other passengers had had to walk through the pouring rain to present their documents to the bored official behind the desk.

Now he could barely see the countryside through the rivulets of water that cascaded down the windows of the coach, but he was aware that the sky seemed darker, the trees a deeper green, the roads, judging by the irregular motion of the carriage, less firm. He paid scant attention to his fellow passengers who, to his relief, made no attempt to engage him in conversation. He clutched the leather bag on his lap, resting his head on it to sleep.

In the early evening of the first day he took out the small paper bag Nanette had put in an outside pocket and extricated the sausages and ham slices she had wrapped. He chose not to take a room, or to share one, at the coach station at Teltsch, preferring to lie on a bench, his head again resting on the leather bag. His clothes had dried and a heater burned all night, and he slept more comfortably than he had expected.

The second day two men opposite him, the only passengers still on the coach who had boarded in Vienna, began to talk, exchanging reasons for their journey, predicting the consequences of Napoleon's invasion of Russia, and bemoaning the ceaseless clatter of the rain on the carriage roof. Ludwig knew it was only a matter of time before they attempted to draw him in to their conversation, and when finally one of them did, he reacted in a way he had never expected to do: he pointed to his ears and shrugged his shoulders. The men smiled weakly and did not speak to him again.

He sat alone to take lunch at the coach station at Pilgrams, ordering an extra beer to help him sleep in the afternoon, and at Vlaschim he again chose to sleep in the main hall. There was no fire this time, but the effect of the Bohemian beer ensured that he managed a few hours' sleep. But the insistent sound of the rain on the low roof woke him in the early hours of the morning and he was unable to sleep again.

On the third day he found the jolting of the carriage painful. More than anything it upset his stomach. When the coach stopped he ate, and an hour later he wished he had not. He wished now he had taken a bed on the overnight stops.

His stomach was still hurting and his head throbbed when at last he dismounted from the coach in the Old Town Square in Prague. He climbed the incline to the Charles Bridge and walked along it. The air coming off the Vltava was cold: people had scarves round their necks, their coats buttoned up and belted. Strangers exchanged bewildered looks, as if to express mutual amazement that it could be so damp and chilly at the beginning of July.

Ludwig barely glanced at the medieval statues touched with gilt that he had first seen in the company of Prince Lichnowsky more than a decade and a half ago. He remembered it had been raining then, but it was early in the year, January or February. Did the sun ever shine in Prague? he wondered.

He walked down the steps at the end of the bridge and across the cobbles to the hotel Zum Schwarzen Ross, the Black Horse Inn, lying almost in the shadow of the tower that stood at the entrance to the Lesser Town. Inside a fire roared in the grate and a wave of heat flowed over him. He signed the register, took a key from the clerk and climbed the stairs to the first floor.

To his surprise the clerk had given him a small suite. An outer room had chairs and a round table, and a fire had been laid, piled high with small pieces of wood and charcoal. Through a door was the bedroom, which contained a large bed, wardrobe and washstand. Ludwig put down the leather bag on the floor. He decided he would have a short rest, then ask the chambermaid to light the fire. He kicked off his boots, but the moment he lay down on the bed he fell into a deep sleep and did not wake until the early hours of the next morning.

He breakfasted well, returned to his room and dragged a comb through his hair. Before leaving he pulled a piece of paper from his pocket and went down to the desk in the entrance hall.

'Under the bridge, sir, on to Kampa island. Past the mill wheel, and it'll be the second or third building.'

'And the Rothes Haus hotel. It is near here, isn't it?'

'Other direction, sir.' The clerk pointed over his shoulder. 'That way. A hundred metres or so.'

Ludwig murmured his thanks and walked out. The air was still cool and damp but the rain was holding off.

He walked under the arch of the Charles Bridge to the path that ran along the narrow branch of the Vltava, creating the island that, Ludwig remembered being told on his last visit, was a haven of tranquillity and favoured by the city's artists. Why it should also be where Prince Kinsky had his office was not a question on which he wasted any thought, but he was grateful for its convenience.

The Prince lumbered towards him, seeming even larger than he was when Ludwig had last seen him at the Hofburg. 'Glad you came, Beethoven. Sit down.'

Kinsky's voice, given force by the size of his body, carried through the heaviness that hung in Ludwig's ears. There was less formality about him, now that he was in his own office in Prague. He did not click his heels, but extended his hand. Nor was he dressed in military uniform, the multi-coloured ribbons on his left breast the only indication of his commission. He spoke, as Ludwig remembered from their last meeting, in short bursts, which gave even more power to his voice. Ludwig felt his nervousness evaporate. Kinsky went round his desk and sat down. 'Damn bad business, this Finanz-Patent, eh?'

'You said I would receive a back payment. His Imperial Highness said that would be the case,' said Ludwig, deciding to come straight to the point and feeling that to bring Archduke Rudolph into the conversation would not harm his cause.

'Yes. I remember,' Kinsky agreed. 'Won't be a problem, I can assure you. I'll speak to my bankers here. They'll make a transfer to Vienna.'

'Can you tell me the amount?'

'Complicated. Needs to be worked out in accordance with the court decree and the table it issued. It'll be substantial. No doubt about that.'

Ludwig waited a moment. 'I was hoping . . . You said if I came to Prague –'

'Didn't expect you, though. Took me by surprise. But don't be alarmed.' With an effort Kinsky heaved himself out of the chair and crossed the room. He opened a drawer, reached into it and took out a large key. He then went to the wall at the back of the room and lifted down on oil painting to reveal a safe, which he unlocked. He withdrew a pile of banknotes, locked the safe again and replaced the picture. 'To prove to you I am a man of my word.' He returned to his chair behind the desk and counted the notes. 'Sixty ducats. Six hundred florins – sounds better, hah! Here, as a token of my commitment.'

Ludwig took the notes and pushed them deep into a pocket inside his jacket.

'You know, Beethoven, I've been an admirer of your music since I first heard it. Father took me. Burgtheater, wasn't it? Met you there for the first time. My father told me, "Watch out for this musician." He'd be pleased I'm doing this. Great patron of the arts. Aim to be the same.' He was panting with the effort of his little speech, and his face was flushed. 'Dinner tonight, eh? Allow me. Great honour for me to take you to the regimental club here.'

Ludwig's mind raced. 'No. I'm sorry. I . . . I have an engagement. Friends from Vienna. I am having dinner with them.'

'Damn shame. Tomorrow, then. Still here tomorrow? Mmh?'

The prospect of an evening with Prince Kinsky dulled Ludwig's spirits, but he knew he was in no position to refuse, particularly with the comforting feel of the bundle in his inside pocket.

'Good. That's settled then. Eight o'clock. I'll come and collect you. Schwarzen Ross, mmh?'

That afternoon the rain began again. Ludwig lay on his bed, wondering how to quell his apprehension. Finally he went to his bag, which he had not unpacked, and pulled a clean shirt from it. He went downstairs and told the clerk he wanted a pitcher of hot water brought to his room.

He was going to see Toni again. The thought sent a quiver of anticipation through him. She would be with Franz. He had liked Franz when he had met him at dinner in the house on the Erdbeergasse. Ludwig remembered how worried he had been about his wife's well-being. Then he thought of the last time he had seen Toni, and a wave of heat flooded over him. But he knew he would be able to look Franz in the eye and feel no guilt. Ah, how he envied Franz for having married Toni. What must it be like to live with a wife like that? A calm, kind person whose voice was like a soothing balm, whose face was an image of beauty, soft and gentle and vulnerable.

The heat stayed in his body, warming his skin even before he splashed the steaming water over his arms and chest. My friends the Brentanos, he thought. Franz and Antonie Brentano.

Then he said the names aloud. 'Franz and Antonie Brentano.' No, not Antonie. Toni. Was ever a name more appropriate? Short and charming, like a child's nickname. He said it aloud. 'Toni.'

He sat on the edge of the bed and buried his face in the towel. He did not expect the tears to come or the sobs that racked his body. Toni. Yes, he thought. I love her.

He dried quickly and dressed, annoyed that he had allowed his feelings to get the better of him. 'My friends the Brentanos,' he said again. There is no other way of thinking of it. No other way. I am fond of them both and I value their friendship.

He ran down the single flight of stairs and at the door he took one of the cluster of umbrellas that stood in a holder to the side. He stepped outside and the heat that still flowed through his body kept the chill away. He put a hand to his forehead – it was hot.

A light drizzle fell, making the cobbles shiny and slippery, and he walked away from the bridge, in the direction the clerk had indicated. The road began to slope down. On the left was a high wall. Through a gate set in it he saw gardens. For a moment he stood and looked at them. They were informally laid out, so different from the Augarten. Paths were set haphazardly into them, trees and flowers grew where they had taken root, the grass was in need of scything. A handful of strollers, no hats or umbrellas, were gesticulating and arguing, oblivious of the rain. Opposite stood the Rothes Haus hotel, a plaque set into the wall showing the turrets of a castle painted red. He crossed to it, feeling the thump of his heart as he walked. The ringing in his ears intensified, but he knew he would relax once he was in the company of his friends.

When he went in he walked to the desk. 'Herr and Frau Brentano, from Vienna. They are staying here with their child. They arrived today.'

The clerk looked down at the register. 'No, sir. I'm sorry, sir, they haven't arrived.'

Had he miscalculated? Was today not the right day?

The clerk, seeing his expression, said, 'They were due, sir, we were expecting them, but they were not on the stage, apparently – we checked. They must have been delayed in Vienna. We are keeping their room for them. Maybe they will arrive tomorrow.'

Chapter 4

The next day the sun came through the cloud and Ludwig walked as fast and vigorously as he could. He wanted to feel the exertion in the muscles of his legs. He strode up the steep hill to Hradcany, pushing on his thighs with the flat of his hands. The cobbles were hard and irregular beneath his feet. If he closed his eyes he could imagine he was climbing the Drachenfels, could feel the undergrowth scratching at his face, breathe in the air of the Siebengebirge, smell the water of the Rhine . . .

He walked through the gates of Prague castle and past St Vitus's cathedral – smaller, more intimate than St Stephansdom – down the sloping narrow street until he stood outside the building he sought. It hardly looked like a palace, more just a grander house than those on either side of it. He rang the large bell to the side of the double doors. 'I am a friend of Prince Lobkowitz,' he said to the servant, who wore a black jacket and no wig.

'His Excellency is not here. He's at his estate in Eisenberg.'

Ludwig almost ran back down to the Lesser Quarter, stopping briefly to look at the Golden Unicorn Hotel in Lazenska Street where he had stayed with Prince Lichnowsky. He strode across the Charles Bridge, hands plunged deep into his pockets, not looking up until he stood before the giant statues of Hercules on either side of the entrance to the Clam-Gallas palace. *Moriro. Moriro.* How Josefa Duschek had held the word. What drama she had brought to the aria he had composed for her. And what a disaster young Josephine Killitzky's performance of it had been at the Theater an der Wien! He shook his head at the memory, striding on until he stood before the diminutive Nostitz theatre, within whose walls the sounds of *Don Giovanni* and *La Clemenza di Tito* had first been heard.

Wolfgang Amadeus Mozart! He slapped his forehead and

walked on, he did not know where. Mozart, dead at thirty-five. How many symphonies, how many operas, how many concertos? Around a hundred in all, and every one a work of genius that will endure. And what am I? Over forty and only a fraction composed. Not yet eight symphonies, and a single failed opera. So much more work to do. So much.

He paused on the Charles Bridge and looked down into the fast-moving water of the Vltava. The water, greyish green, flowed almost in a straight line, rapidly and firmly, as if it had a definite goal and nothing was going to prevent it reaching it. He glanced up at the pitying face of the saint staring down at him, St Adalbert, his mitre high on his head, bishop's crook in his left hand, his right raised in benediction.

He was almost out of breath when he reached the Schwarzen Ross and at first did not see the clerk raise his hand to attract his attention. 'Sir, a lady called. She left you this note.'

Ludwig's head was throbbing from the exertion of the walk. He slumped into a chair, and tried to steady his breathing, willing the pain not to come. So much to think of. So much work to do. Slowly, through the ringing, he heard the sounds of his music. A jumble at first, then more clearly. He did not know what piece it was, just that it was the glorious sounds of instruments playing in harmony.

After a while his breathing became more regular and the pain he so dreaded did not come. Almost cursorily he unfolded the note he was holding and read it.

Dear Ludwig
A delay put our departure from Vienna back by a day. We have now arrived. Will you come to the Rothes Haus at seven and we will all go out to dinner? Franz and I so want to see you.

Antnie Brntno

Ludwig felt curiously calm as he made his way up to his room.

Ludwig saw Antonie almost as soon as he entered the Rothes Haus. She still looked tired, he thought, as he observed her unseen. He walked towards her and Franz. Franz smiled at him – worriedly, it seemed to Ludwig.

'Hello, Herr Beethoven,' he said, bowing. 'At last.'

Ludwig returned the courtesy, then took Antonie's hand, inclining his head over it.

'I am so sorry we let you down yesterday,' Antonie said.

Her voice, as calm and measured as ever, flowed over him, banishing all unwanted noises from his head. But he detected an anxious tone. 'We were delayed. Franz was delayed. We could not leave.'

'My fault entirely. I had a meeting I had to attend. Meant a bit of a rush, or we'd have missed you. Toni insisted.'

'I thought that was what happened. I'm glad to see you. And your daughter?'

'Poor little Fanny,' said Antonie. 'She's exhausted. Such a tiring journey. She didn't sleep properly at all. At least she will sleep well tonight. The hotel has arranged a nurse to sit with her. I should really stay here with her.' She looked at Franz rather reprovingly.

'No, no, my dear. Absolutely unnecessary. Fanny will sleep soundly.' He turned to Ludwig. 'I have upset poor Toni's plans yet again. First we leave Vienna behind schedule because of me. Now I cannot accompany you to dinner.'

Ludwig saw rather than heard Antonie's sigh of exasperation. 'Business, again. Always meetings. Franz, can you never get away from them?'

'In Bohemia, my dear. In Karlsbad. There will be nothing to distract me there.' He turned back to Ludwig. 'You will come and stay with us there, won't you? You are going to Teplitz, isn't that right?'

Ludwig nodded.

'Karlsbad is a half day's carriage-ride. Less. That's all. You will come. You would like that, wouldn't you, Toni? We're on the Wiese, at the Aug' Gottes. Now, say you will come and my wife will forgive me for everything. Won't you, Toni?'

Ludwig was aware that she was looking at him. He caught the unmistakable pleading in her eyes. 'Yes. But I'm not sure when. After I have seen Goethe.'

'Good. That's settled then. Now you must take my wife to dinner. It's all arranged. At the Zwei Adler. Just across the bridge. Everything is taken care of. If you will excuse me.' He kissed Antonie on both cheeks, bowed again to Ludwig and left.

Ludwig watched him go, then turned to Antonie. 'I brought an umbrella,' he said, 'from the hotel.'

A smile transformed her face. 'Good. Then I won't need one. I . . . I'm pleased to see you, Ludwig. Wait here. I will kiss Fanny goodnight, then we will go.'

As naturally as if they were husband and wife, Antonie slipped her arm through Ludwig's as they crossed the bridge. The sun was setting to their left, its rays a watery yellow where they tried to break through the grey streaks of cloud. The twin spires of St Vitus's cathedral stood starkly against the sky. All the roofs on both banks of the river shone from the rain that had fallen and the air was damp.

At dinner they said little. The red wine, like velvet on Ludwig's tongue, warmed his blood and his spirit. Antonie outlined to him the rigours of the journey, Ludwig listening more to the timbre of her voice than to her words. He interjected occasionally, telling her of how he had slept on benches.

As Antonie drank the wine Ludwig saw her begin to relax and the colour return to her cheeks.

They finished eating and sat finally with their wine.

'Poor Franz. I am unkind to him,' Antonie said, looking up at Ludwig. 'He works so hard. But sometimes –'

'It is difficult. After the Finanz-Patent. Everyone is having to work harder.'

'I know. But sometimes I do not see him for days on end. Even in Frankfurt. At *home*,' she emphasised the word, as if to question its meaning, 'he works seven days a week, from dawn until night. Sometimes I think I might as well be a widow.'

'No. Do not say that. He is a kind man. A good father.'

'Yes, when he is there. You know, Ludwig, I have never said this to anyone before.' Ludwig saw moisture glisten in her eyes. 'I did not fall in love with Franz. I did not marry him because I . . . It was my father's wish. Promise you will never tell anyone this.'

'No. Of course not.'

'I met Franz in Vienna one summer. We became friends, nothing more than that. The next summer he sent his sister – not Bettina – and stepmother to Vienna to meet my father and question him about me. They were deciding if I would make a suitable wife for Franz. My father, my dear father . . . I cannot blame him. My mother was dead. He needed to find me a suitable husband. But at first he was reluctant. He said he would not allow me to go to Frankfurt because the French army had occupied the Rhineland.'

'I know. It affected everybody.'

'But, Ludwig, this is the extraordinary thing.' She leaned

even further across the table. 'Franz, who was supposed to be in love with me, instead of coming to Vienna to make me his bride, wrote to my father. He wrote to him more than twenty times. Letters. I read them. They were like letters you write to a business partner. I was – I was being treated like a – a – chattel.'

Tears stood in her eyes and Ludwig put his hand on hers, patting it gently.

'He wrote to my father. He never once came to Vienna to see me. Then, one day, my father announced to me that I was engaged. To Franz Brentano. And would go to live in Frankfurt.'

She paused, took out her handkerchief and dabbed her eyes. 'But I should not complain. He is a kind man. You are right. And a good father. He works hard to give us all a good life.'

At that moment, the head waiter appeared and confirmed that everything had been settled in advance by Herr Brentano. 'I will have a receipt and the change due to him ready for collection tomorrow, Monsieur, Madame. I wish you good evening.'

They were not half-way across the bridge when the rain began, softly at first, but within seconds it was pouring steadily. Ludwig fumbled with the umbrella, finally managing to open it, while Antonie stood, hopping from one foot to the other, laughing at his ineptness. Then she came under it and Ludwig pulled her closer, his arm around her waist. He felt hers around his. As they walked their hips touched. The rain hammered on the umbrella, making conversation impossible. But Ludwig heard her laughter, sweet and pure. She was pushing up against him as they walked, a natural movement to avoid the rain, and he held her tightly to make sure the umbrella covered her.

They walked quickly, almost breaking into a run. The water bounced off the cobbles, splashing their feet and legs. At the end of the bridge they hurried down the steps. 'Quick!' Antonie said. She ran ahead of Ludwig towards the arch of the Charles bridge. Ludwig saw the rain cascade over her as she went.

He struggled to lower the umbrella, then caught her up under the arch. For a moment they stood there, watching the rain fall like a curtain of glass beads at both its entrances.

Antonie threw back her head, laughing still and pulling her hair clear of her face. He saw drips of rain run down her neck and on to her dress, where they were instantly absorbed. 'Oh, it makes me feel so free,' she said, her eyes sparkling. 'Look. Watch me!'

She ran to the entrance of the arch, looked back at him and stepped out into the pouring rain. She lifted up her face, threw out her arms and spun round, allowing the water to drench her. Then she ran back in, her arms close to her sides. 'Put your arms round me. Hold me, Ludwig. Warm me.'

He clasped her to him and the umbrella fell to the ground. She turned up her face to his and without thinking about it, without considering the consequences, he kissed her lips.

They were chilly and moist and they tasted to him like honey and wine, sweeter than anything he had ever tasted. He felt her tongue against his and her face was so wet he did not know if he was kissing her tongue, her lips or her cheeks.

She moved her face under his so that he was kissing all of her, the wetness of the rain mingling with the wetness of her mouth. He felt her body against his and his hardness against her yielding flesh.

He knew she was breathing in gasps, short hot gasps of increasing intensity. She was pulling him with her to the entrance of the arch. He did not resist.

They stepped outside and the rain drummed down on them, through their hair and over their faces, round their lips and down inside their clothes to their skin.

'Ludwig,' she said. 'Ludwig. At last. You understand, don't you? It has to be.'

She pulled him under the arch again, kissed his cheek and stepped back. 'Now look at me,' she said. 'So dreadfully wet up on that nasty bridge. Just when we were crossing it. I cannot stay like this. I will catch a chill, then fever, then . . . Can you not help me, kind sir?'

He picked up the umbrella. 'Come. Quickly.'

Together, arms around each other, they skipped across the cobbles and into the warmth of the Schwarzen Ross. 'Send hot water to my room immediately,' Ludwig said to the clerk. 'And tell the chambermaid to bring a clothes stand and light the fire.'

He led the way to his room. As soon as they entered Antonie ran to the washstand in the bedroom and snatched the two towels from the rail. She handed one to Ludwig and buried her face in the other. Then she took down her hair, pulled it forward so that it fell in front of her and dried it.

Ludwig took off his sodden jacket and hung it over the back of a chair.

There was a knock at the door. Antonie ran back into the bedroom. The chambermaid came in, carrying a clothes stand. Without speaking she knelt by the fire and lit a taper, blew on the flame until it caught, then fanned it with a small piece of board that was lying by the side of the grate. Soon the fire was roaring. 'I shall come with water in a few moments, sir,' she said, hurrying from the room.

Antonie said, 'Sit down, Ludwig. Here.' She pulled out a chair from the table. Ludwig sat. She began to rub his hair and he closed his eyes, enjoying the feel of her fingers against his scalp. Her hip brushed against his shoulder, sending waves of warmth through his body.

Another knock on the door and Antonie again ran to the bedroom. The chambermaid carried in a large pitcher of steaming water. 'There, by the fire,' said Ludwig pointing. 'To keep it warm.'

The maid set it down, hurried back to the door and brought in a second pitcher. 'Will there be anything else, sir?'

Ludwig told her there would not, closed the door behind her and locked it.

He carried one pitcher to the bedroom and poured the water into the basin. He turned round to see Toni with her dress off her shoulders. He felt a constriction in his chest, a tightness in his breathing.

She seemed to dissolve into his arms, kissing him hungrily now, running her hands through his hair, biting his lips. She took his hand and massaged her breast with it. He pushed against her, drawing his hands down to her waist, feeling her shape.

He felt her untie his cravat, pull open his shirt, and rub the hair on his chest. He brought his hands round to her breasts. Now she had untied her dress to the waist and he slipped his hands inside and round to her naked back. She slipped the dress down her waist and stepped out of it. She was pulling him with her, moving back, until they both almost fell on to the bed. He tore off his shirt, untied his waistband and kicked off his trousers.

He was on top of her and he felt her writhe underneath him, her eyes half open. She took hold of him and guided him into her. He heard her breathe his name over and over again. She began to move with him, rhythmically. She pulled his head down to her, devouring his lips.

He felt the softness of her breasts moving against him, the points of her nipples. She was breathing with him, small gasps. He felt himself harden and the fire grow in him. His other hand went round her back, so that he was pulling her whole body up to his.

He heard the sound in his throat, quietly at first, then building. Her gasps matched it, tiny sounds that floated in the air.

When it seemed they both could breathe no more, he released himself into her and she arched her back to receive him.

They lay there panting, her hand at the back of his head, pushing it against her neck. He breathed the scent of her skin, her hair curling around his nose and lips. His mouth was open, his tongue pressed against her skin.

Slowly his breathing steadied. He tasted salt. He knew it was her tears, running down the side of her face and her neck.

They sat behind the clothes stand, wrapped in towels, watching their clothes dry. He looked at her face, now forlorn and wretched. She turned to him, her lips parted.

Ludwig shook his head. 'No, Toni. Do not say anything. It will only cause us pain. Both of us.'

'Ludwig. I wish . . . How I wish I could come to live with you in Vienna.'

'No,' he said, almost before her words were out. 'No. Toni, you know it cannot be. It cannot.' He reached across and took her hand. 'Understand that, my love. My angel. My all. We have our love and we have loved. More than that can never be.'

'Why, Ludwig? Why?' More tears were in her eyes.

He reached forward and flicked them away. 'Unless we can live as one, you for me and I for you, it can never be. And we cannot. You know that, Toni.'

She sniffed and wiped her eyes with the corner of the towel. She looked at him and a determination had come into her face. 'I will not stop loving you, Ludwig.'

He smiled. 'Come. Get dressed. I will take you back to your hotel.'

'You are right. Franz will be back soon. He might even be back already.' She smiled at him mischievously.

They dressed quickly, Antonie exclaiming at the warmth of her dress against her skin. 'You will come to Karlsbad, won't you? Franz would find it strange if you did not.'

'If you want me to.'

'I want you to, Ludwig.' She kissed his cheek lightly. 'You must write to me!' she said suddenly. 'Write to me at Karlsbad. Do you promise?'

'I am not good at writing letters, Toni.'

'Here.' She opened the bag she had been carrying, pulled out a sheet of paper and tore off a strip. 'Here's the address. Aug' Gottes, three hundred and eleven auf der Wiese, Karlsbad. Put this somewhere safe.' Ludwig folded it and put it in his pocket. 'And take this pencil. My pencil. It will remind you to write.' He put the pencil in his pocket too.

He glanced round the room, put his arm round her and led her down the stairs and out of the hotel. The rain had stopped. She took his arm and they walked quickly away from the bridge and down the narrow hill to the Rothes Haus.

Outside the hotel she turned to him and kissed him briefly. 'You do promise, don't you? You will come to Karlsbad?'

'Yes. I'll come,' he said, and walked back up the slope, each step seeming a monumental effort as if his shoes were made of lead.

She sent him a note the next morning.

> My dear, dear Ludwig
> Such joy and now such sorrow. I have never known such sorrow. Tell me fate will grant our wish and that one day we will be together. One day. Give me hope. Only hope, that one day we will live our lives together. I ask no more than that. Just give me hope. Or else this sorrow will never go.
>
> Yr Toni

He folded the note carefully and put it in his pocket. He felt a lump in his throat and tears behind his eyes.

Oh Toni, he thought, it cannot be. How can I make you understand?

Postscript

The single greatest mystery in Beethoven's life is the identity of the Eternally Beloved, as he referred to her in the second postscript of the famous letter he was to write on his arrival in Teplitz (and, like Emily Anderson, editor of the Letters, I prefer the more appropriately romantic, if strictly less literal, translation of the original, *Unsterbliche Geliebte*, to the more widely used Immortal Beloved).

By not doing us the service of either naming the woman he is writing to, nor – other than the initial K. – telling us where she is, Beethoven set in motion a detective hunt that continues to this day. Thayer/Forbes, in Appendix F, lists the various conclusions of scholars up to 1954, which amount to four different names and four cases of Unknown – also five different years in which the letter was written, including two in which 6 July did not fall on a Monday! (*Life of Beethoven*, Wheelock Thayer, revised and edited by Elliot Forbes, Princeton University Press, 1967.) This, despite the fact that he writes at the top of the first postscript 'Monday evening on 6 July'.

The American Beethoven scholar Maynard Solomon, in his book *Beethoven* (Schirmer Books, 1977), devoted a chapter to the problem, the fruit of the most comprehensive research anyone had undertaken. In his words, 'what was required was to test every woman of Beethoven's acquaintance who might be the Immortal Beloved against the requirements of the evidence'. And he concludes, 'It is not presumptuous to conclude that the riddle of Beethoven's Immortal Beloved has now been solved.'

His nominee was a woman who had not previously featured in research: Antonie Brentano. I will not detail his research, other than to say that he is able to prove that Antonie – given the internal evidence of the letter itself – was in the right place at the right time, i.e. Prague between 1 and 4 July 1812 and Karlsbad thereafter. Some other candidates – and Josephine Deym is the only serious contender – *could* have been in the right place at the right time. But, again in Solomon's words, 'the arguments by [Josephine's] advocates . . . are necessarily attempts to prove a hypothesis by the assertion that no evidence exists to the contrary.' (*Beethoven Essays*, Harvard University Press, 1988.)

But the argument is not over. Josephine's candidature is still advocated by the Freiburg-based musicologist Marie-Elisabeth Tellenbach. And as recently as 1996 an attempt by Gail Altman to establish Countess Erdödy as the Eternally Beloved was refuted by the British Beethoven scholar Barry Cooper (in the *Beethoven Journal* of the American Beethoven Society, Fall 1996).

Further possibilities remain. Beethoven was notoriously careless of the day and date in his letter writing. It is possible that 6 July in the year he wrote the letter did not fall on a Monday, or that he wrote it on a Monday that was not 6 July (although given that he wrote 7 July on the second postscript that is unlikely). It is possible – as Antony Hopkins argues (*The Nine Symphonies of Beethoven*, Heinemann, 1981) – that the letter was 'a way of acting out a fantasy . . . a few hours of make-believe alone in a strange hostelry'. If that was so, would Beethoven have detailed his frightful journey so poignantly, or his problems in finding a room, or the mailcoach timetable? I doubt it. But thank goodness he did, for only in those passages are the clues contained.

In 1949 thirteen hitherto unknown letters from Beethoven to Josephine Deym came to light – all but one undated! – forcing a reassessment of his relationship with her. Who knows what epistolary evidence relating to the Eternally Beloved might be hidden in some private collection somewhere in the world?

Finally on the subject, having read practically everything that has been written about the Eternally Beloved, I believe she is either Antonie Brentano or a woman unknown to history. And writing a novel, therefore detailing Beethoven's life in a more intimate way than a musicologist or biographer would, my initial reluctance to accept Antonie on the basis that she was a wife and mother melted away as the relationship between them seemed to develop its own momentum.

The apartment on the Mölkerbastei where Beethoven lived –

unusually for him – for so many years, is today a Beethoven museum, containing such artifacts as the door to the apartment where he died, a music-stand used by him, a lock of his hair, a sugar bowl he used, a salt and pepper set, and many pictures and portraits, including the painting by Willibrord Mähler and the bust by Franz Klein sculpted from the life mask. There is also a piano from the Streichers' workshop.

Climbing the four flights to the apartment today, one can sympathise with Schuppanzigh's complaints! The view, sadly, is no longer of the Vienna Woods but the university on the other side of the Ringstrasse.

The vinegar maker's house in Döbling where Beethoven composed the *Eroica* is also a museum, albeit rebuilt in the middle of the last century and renovated thirty years ago. The rooms are mostly empty, save for numerous prints, paintings and busts. Looking out on to the rather drab suburban street gives one little or no idea of what it must have been like in the tranquil rural setting Beethoven knew.

The Theater an der Wien stands where it stood in Beethoven's day, the original entrance with Schikaneder's statuettes above it still in place, albeit now on a side street. The new main entrance is now on the busy Linke Wienzeile. The theatre maintains the popular image – the 'people's theatre', almost – it had in Beethoven's day, specialising today in musicals and operetta. Opposite it the busy market still exists, although the Wien river is now largely underground.

The Walfischgasse is still a relatively narrow street running parallel to the Ringstrasse, showing no signs of the particular need it fulfilled nearly two hundred years ago.

Baden is the largest and most important spa town in the vicinity of Vienna, maintaining something of the old imperial feel about it. The Sauerhof, completely renovated in 1978, is now a luxury 'Beauty Farm'. The Helenenthal valley and Rauhenstein ruins – destined to play such a fateful role in Beethoven's life – remain largely unchanged. More on them in Volume Three.

In the woods outside Heiligenstadt, where Beethoven sat planning the Pastoral Symphony, there is now a bust on a tall pedestal, erected in 1863; and in Heiligenstadt Park a full-size 'walking' statue of Beethoven, his frock-coat blown open in the wind, unveiled in 1902. The Viennese sculptor Robert Weigl captures perfectly the short stocky figure with the large leonine head. Looking at it one can almost feel the power emanating from it, as Beethoven's friends remarked it emanated from the man himself.

The house in Heiligenstadt where Beethoven stayed in the summer of 1808, at the same time as the Grillparzers, mother and son, still stands and is now in private hands.

The sketchbook for the Pastoral Symphony, on the first page of which Beethoven famously wrote his intentions for the work, is in the British Museum in London (Add. Ms. 31766).

The appalling weather Beethoven experienced in Prague in July 1812 – and which continued for the whole of his stay in Bohemia – is documented.

By coincidence, although my wife Bonnie and I visited the city slightly earlier in the year, it rained continuously while we were there and temperatures came close to a record low. Prague – I have been told – is a city whose roofs sparkle in the sunlight. I have not seen it. When the sun does not shine, the dark stone of the buildings seems even darker, becoming all the more so as the rain seeps in. Although it made for an uncomfortable visit, the unseasonal weather at least allowed me to see the city much as Beethoven must have seen it.

The unfortunate George Bridgetower did not return to Vienna after his contretemps with Beethoven. He remained in London until about 1820, living abroad after that, mostly in Rome and Paris. He may have been in Vienna briefly in 1845.

He died in a back street at Peckham, south London in 1860 at the age of seventy-eight. The witness of his death, Ann Chapman, signed the death certificate with a cross, showing she was illiterate – suggesting that Bridgetower died in penury and poor surroundings.

He is buried in Kensal Green Cemetery, west London, his name forgotten.

Finally I am most grateful to two of Britain's most distinguished musicians, the conductor Sir Colin Davis, who recently recorded Beethoven's symphonies, and the concert pianist John Lill OBE, who has twice recorded the piano sonatas, for the interest they have taken and their kind comments about *The Last Master*.

Chronology

1803   Beethoven appointed composer at the Theater an der Wien, moving into lodgings there with his brother Carl.

      Beethoven composes oratorio *Christus am Ölberge*.

      29 March, Beethoven's first patron in Vienna, Baron van Swieten, dies.

      5 April, Beethoven's benefit concert in the Theater an der Wien.

      24 May, Beethoven gives first performance of Violin Sonata op. 47, with George Bridgetower as soloist.

      Summer, Beethoven composes *Eroica* Symphony in Döbling.

      Beethoven composes 'Waldstein' Sonata, with Andante Grazioso as second movement.

1804   Baron von Braun buys the Theater an der Wien and terminates Beethoven's contract.

      Beethoven is commissioned to compose an opera, with Sonnleithner as librettist.

      20 May, Napoleon proclaimed Emperor. Beethoven tears up the title page of the *Eroica* bearing the dedication to Napoleon.

      Beethoven moves into Stephan von Breuning's apartment, but the arrangement lasts only a short time.

      Beethoven's *Eroica* Symphony performed at Prince Lobkowitz's palace.

      Beethoven becomes acquainted with Josephine Deym, recently widowed, and begins giving her piano lessons.

      He composes the song *An die Hoffnung* for her.

1805   Beethoven composes the Piano Sonata op. 57.

      Beethoven completes composition of his opera *Leonore*, but the censor bans its projected performance at the Theater an der Wien.

September, Ries leaves Vienna for Bonn to be conscripted into the French army.

Andante Grazioso published separately as WoO 57.

5 October, the censor lifts the ban on *Leonore*.

November, the French army occupies Vienna and Napoleon establishes his headquarters at Schönbrunn Palace.

20 November, first performance of *Leonore*.

2 December, Napoleon defeats the combined Austrian and Russian armies at the Battle of Austerlitz.

1806 Beethoven revises *Leonore*, with an altered text by Stephan von Breuning.

29 March, revised version of *Leonore* performed at the Theater an der Wien.

Beethoven withdraws *Leonore*, accusing Braun of cheating him of receipts.

25 May, Carl van Beethoven marries Johanna Reiss.

Beethoven works on the Razumovsky Quartets and the Fourth Symphony.

17 July, Napoleon creates the Confederation of the Rhine. Autumn, Beethoven travels with Prince Lichnowsky to his country estate at Grätz, near Troppau, Silesia.

4 September, Beethoven's nephew Karl is born.

Count Oppersdorff, a near neighbour of Lichnowsky in Silesia, buys the Fourth Symphony.

Beethoven begins work on the Fifth Symphony.

1807 Piano Sonata op. 57 published as the 'Appassionata' Sonata.

Beethoven completes work on the Fifth Symphony.

Muzio Clementi in London secures rights to publish several works in Great Britain for the sum of £200.

1808 March, Johann van Beethoven buys an apothecary shop in Linz.

27 March, performance of Haydn's *Creation* in honour of the composer's seventy-sixth birthday.

April, Stephan von Breuning marries Julie Vering.

Summer, Beethoven composes the *Pastoral* Symphony while staying in Heiligenstadt.

27 August, Ferdinand Ries arrives back in Vienna.

Autumn, Beethoven is offered the post of *Kapellmeister* to King Jerome of Westphalia in Kassel, at a salary of 600 ducats.

22 December, Beethoven gives his much-postponed and long-awaited benefit concert at the Theater an der Wien, which sees the first performances of the Fifth and *Pastoral* Symphonies.

1809 January, Beethoven accepts the offer of *Kapellmeister* at Kassel. His friends begin drawing up an alternative contract to persuade him to stay in Vienna.

Beethoven begins work on the Fifth Piano Concerto, the 'Emperor'.

9 April, Austria declares war on France.

4 May, Archduke Rudolph and other members of the Imperial family flee from Vienna in the face of the advancing French army. Beethoven composes the beginning of the Piano Sonata op. 81a, 'Les Adieux', for the Archduke.

10 May, French army surrounds Vienna.

11–12 May, French bombard and capture Vienna.

31 May, Haydn dies aged seventy-seven.

Antonie Brentano returns to Vienna.

Beethoven is commissioned by Joseph von Hartl, Director of the Imperial Court Theatres, to compose music for Goethe's *Egmont*.

1810 30 January, Archduke Rudolph returns to Vienna.

13 February, Josephine Deym marries Baron von Stackelberg, her children's tutor.

1 April, Napoleon marries Marie Louise, daughter of Emperor Franz.

Beethoven becomes acquainted with the Malfatti family. He composes the Bagatelle WoO 59 for Therese Malfatti.

Dr Giovanni Malfatti becomes Beethoven's doctor.

July, the critic E.T.A. Hoffmann's famous review of Beethoven's Fifth Symphony is published in the *Allgemeine Musikalische Zeitung*.

1811 15 March, Austria's currency is devalued fivefold under a *Finanz-Patent*, drastically reducing the amount Beethoven receives under his annuity.

Beethoven completes the 'Archduke' Trio.

28 May, Gleichenstein marries Anna Malfatti and they leave Vienna soon after for Freiburg.

Beethoven begins the Seventh Symphony.

During a long period of illness, Antonie Brentano is regularly visited by Beethoven, who plays the piano

for her. He sets the poem *An die Geliebte* to music
for her.

1812   Beethoven begins the Eighth Symphony.

24 June, Napoleon embarks on his invasion of Russia.

Beethoven composes the Piano Trio WoO 39 for
Maximiliane Brentano.

29 June, Beethoven leaves Vienna for Prague on his
way to Teplitz in northern Bohemia.

1 July, Beethoven arrives in Prague.

2 July, Beethoven sees Prince Kinsky concerning his
annuity.

3 July, Franz and Antonie Brentano and their daughter
Fanny arrive in Prague on their way to Karslbad in
northern Bohemia.